Gregory Hawthorne

C0-CEX-390

CIVIL LIBERTIES AND CIVIL RIGHTS DEBATED

HERBERT M. LEVINE *and* JEAN EDWARD SMITH

PRENTICE HALL, Englewood Cliffs, New Jersey 07632

Library of Congress Cataloging-in-Publication Data

Levine, Herbert M.
   Civil liberties and civil rights debated.

   Bibliography
   1. Civil rights—United States.   I. Smith, Jean
Edward.   II. Title.
KF4749.L46   1988   342.73'085   87-7308
ISBN 0-13-134966-X   347.30285

Editorial/production supervision and
   interior design: Serena Hoffman
Cover design: Ben Santora
Manufacturing buyer: Margaret Rizzi

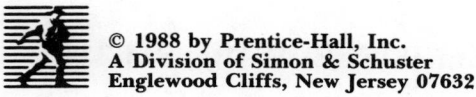 © 1988 by Prentice-Hall, Inc.
A Division of Simon & Schuster
Englewood Cliffs, New Jersey 07632

*All rights reserved. No part of this book may be
reproduced, in any form or by any means,
without permission in writing from the publisher.*

Printed in the United States of America

10 9 8 7 6 5 4 3 2

ISBN 0-13-134966-X   01

PRENTICE-HALL INTERNATIONAL (UK) LIMITED, *London*
PRENTICE-HALL OF AUSTRALIA PTY. LIMITED, *Sydney*
PRENTICE-HALL CANADA INC., *Toronto*
PRENTICE-HALL HISPANOAMERICANA, S.A., *Mexico*
PRENTICE-HALL OF INDIA PRIVATE LIMITED, *New Delhi*
PRENTICE-HALL OF JAPAN, INC., *Tokyo*
SIMON & SCHUSTER ASIA PTE. LTD., *Singapore*
EDITORA PRENTICE-HALL DO BRASIL, LTDA., *Rio de Janeiro*

CONTENTS

CHAPTER II: CIVIL LIBERTIES   69

CHAPTER IV: FREEDOM IN CRIMINAL PROCEEDINGS 225

PREFACE

Civil liberties and civil rights provide the most contentious battleground in United States politics. Issues such as abortion, school prayer, and affirmative action divide Americans more sharply than most other public questions do. The nationalization of the Bill of Rights, the application of federal standards of criminal procedure to the states, the exclusionary rule, and the death penalty are issues of continuing controversy.

In all of these matters the role of the Supreme Court is pivotal. And the authority of the Court—the source of its power and obligation to the original intent of the Constitution—offers one of the most fundamental questions facing the people of the United States. It is an area that has witnessed the unusual spectacle of the nation's attorney general taking direct issue with the most senior associate justice of the Supreme Court in public debate.

The purpose of the book is to provide the student with a deeper insight into the pros and cons of these various issues. Each subject is treated in a debate context. That format permits the alternative arguments to be presented in the traditional adversarial approach that underlines our entire judicial system. Indeed, it is a fundamental precept of the common law that issues can be clarified only when the opposing sides are given equal opportunity to present their arguments to the court. Thus this text differs from traditional casebooks on constitutional law, which generally present only the holdings of the Supreme Court and the reasoning of the Court in reaching decisions.

The book is divided into four major chapters: the role of the Supreme Court, the civil liberties that stem from the First Amendment, civil rights, and the criminal procedure guarantees of the Bill of Rights. The chapter introductions provide a general discussion of the issues involved and highlight the previous judicial decisions that bear on the topics. They also include a section on each of the debates that follow, putting the question in context and providing specific background information. Questions for discussion and a brief list of recommended readings follow each debate.

The student should be aware that the advantages of the adversarial process are also its disadvantages. First, it leaves no issue resolved. While this lack of resolution encourages critical thinking, it can also be a source of confusion. Second, the debate approach suggests that there are only *two* sides to a given issue; shades of gray are eliminated. Third, the relative skill of the advocate sometimes determines the issue. In assembling a book of this nature, it is not always possible—regardless of the effort—to find two advocates of equal ability on each question. If the editors have failed, it has not been for want of trying.

Finally, this book betrays no ideological or substantive bias. Our concern has been to raise contentious issues, often in the most challenging manner possible. Our purpose is to stimulate the student to address some of the questions that confront contemporary society and to recognize that there are *at least* two points of view on each.

We wish to express our appreciation to the following reviewers, whose comments and evaluations contributed to the writing of the book: Philip Jerry Hannon, Texas Technical University; Larry Elowitz, Georgia College; Walter Giles, Georgetown University; and Heinz Hink, Arizona State College. In addition, we are grateful for the cooperation and assistance of the people at Prentice Hall: Karen Horton, our acquisitions editor; Ann Grogg, our copy editor; and Serena Hoffman, our production editor.

Herbert M. Levine
Jean Edward Smith

CONTRIBUTORS

Moise Berger served as county attorney of Maricopa County, Arizona, and was a member of the Legislative Criminal Code Revision Commission.

Hugo L. Black was Associate Justice of the Supreme Court from 1937 to 1971. He was a U.S. Senator from Alabama from 1927 to 1937.

William Brennan, Jr. has been Associate Justice of the Supreme Court since 1956. Earlier he served as a judge in the Supreme Court of New Jersey.

John V.R. Bull is Assistant to the Executive Editor, *The Philadelphia Inquirer.*

Center for Constitutional Rights is an organization concerned with civil liberties issues.

Thomas W. Church, Jr. is Associate Professor of Political Science and Director of the Court Systems Management Program at the State University of New York at Albany.

Rhoda Copelon is Associate Professor of Law at the City University Law School of Queens College. She is a board member of the Center for Constitutional Rights.

Talbot D'Alemberte is Dean of the Florida State University School of Law. He is a former president of the American Judicature Society.

Eletha Duffy is a student at the University of Pennsylvania School of Law. She was a University Scholar at New York University, where she graduated magna cum laude in 1985.

Hope Eastman is an attorney in private practice in Bethesda, Maryland. She served as Assistant Director of the Washington office of the American Civil Liberties Union for eight years.

Felix Frankfurter was an Associate Justice of the Supreme Court from 1939 to 1962. He was an advisor to President Franklin D. Roosevelt in the early days of the New Deal.

Leon Friedman is Professor of Law at Hofstra University. He is an author with Norman Dorsen of *Disorder in the Courts.*

Judy Goldsmith served as President of the National Organization for women from 1982 to 1985.

Lino A. Graglia is Rex G. Baker and Edna Heflin Baker Professor of Constitutional Law at the University of Texas Law School. He is the author of *Disaster by Decree: The Supreme Court Decisions on Race and the Schools.*

Joy Anne Grune served as the Executive Director of the National Committee on Pay Equity.

John Marshall Harlan was Associate Justice of the Supreme Court from 1955 to 1972. He was a judge of the U.S. Court of Appeals for the Second Circuit, 1954–1955.

Joel Hirschhorn is an attorney in Miami, Florida. He is Chairman Emeritus of the First Amendment Lawyers Association.

Lewis H. Lapham is editor of *Harper's Magazine.*

Barry W. Lynn is Legislative Counsel for the American Civil Liberties Union.

Thurgood Marshall has been Associate Justice of the Supreme Court since 1967. Earlier he was chief counsel of the National Association for the Advancement of Colored People.

Michael P. McDonald is general counsel to the American Legal Foundation.

Edwin Meese III is Attorney General of the United States. He was counsellor to President Ronald Reagan from 1981 to 1985.

John T. Noonan, Jr. is a judge in the U.S. Court of Appeals for the 9th Circuit in San Francisco. He was a Professor of Law at the University of Notre Dame and the University of California at Berkeley.

Sister Renée Oliver is Executive Director of Citizens for Educational Freedom, a private group concerned with educational matters.

June O'Neill is Assistant Staff director, Program and Policy, U.S. Commission on Civil Rights. She served as Director of the Program of Policy Research on Women and Families of the Urban Institute.

R. G. Puckett is the former Executive Director of Americans United for Separation of Church and State. He is editor of the *Biblical Recorder* in North Carolina.

Norman Redlich is Dean and Professor of Law at the New York University School of Law. He is coauthor with Bernard Schwartz of *Constitutional Law: Cases and Materials*.

Grover Rees III is Assistant Professor of Law at the University of Texas in Austin. He has served as a special counsel in the Department of Justice.

Eugene V. Rostow is Professor Emeritus at Yale Law School, where he served as Dean and Sterling Professor of Law and Public Affairs. He was director of the Arms Control and Disarmament Agency from 1981 to 1983.

Sidney Schanberg is a columnist for *Newsday*.

Steven R. Schlesinger is Director of the Bureau of Justice Statistics at the Department of Justice. He taught at the Catholic University of America. He is the author of *Exclusionary Injustice: The Problem of Illegally Obtained Evidence*.

Potter Stewart was Associate Justice of the Supreme Court from 1958 to 1981. He was a judge on the U.S. Court of Appeals for the Sixth Circuit from 1954 to 1958.

Fred Wertheimer is President of Common Cause, a public interest organization. Earlier he served as counsel to the House Small Business Committee.

J. Skelly Wright is a senior U.S. Circuit Federal Judge. He was Chief Judge, U.S. Court of Appeals, D.C. Circuit, from 1978 to 1981.

Howard Zinn is Professor of Government at Boston University. He is the author of *A People's History of the United States*.

EDITORS

Herbert M. Levine is a writer based in Chevy Chase, Maryland. He taught political science at the University of Southwestern Louisiana for twenty years and is author and editor of several political science textbooks, including *Political Issues Debated* and *Public Administration Debated*.

Jean Edward Smith is Professor of Political Science at the University of Toronto and Visiting Professor of Government and Foreign Affairs at the University of Virginia. He is the author of *The Defense of Berlin, Germany Beyond the Wall*, and *The Constitution and Foreign Affairs*.

I RIGHTS, THE SUPREME COURT, AND THE CONSTITUTION

The ringing words of the Declaration of Independence that "all men . . . are endowed by their Creator with certain unalienable Rights" represented a novel and revolutionary idea in 1776. It rejected the traditional view of politics that the individual existed merely to serve the state. It asserted instead that each person was a unique human being who possessed certain fundamental rights that even the government could not violate. And the most important of these rights, as they were expressed by Thomas Jefferson, were "Life, Liberty and the pursuit of Happiness."

The idea of inherent or unalienable rights traces back to older concepts of *natural law*, to the idea that human relations are governed by a fixed set of laws, similar to those of physics, based on knowledge and reason. According to this view the individual possessed rights originally in a state of nature and then created government to help protect those rights. This view contrasted sharply with the more prevalent one that rights and privileges (used interchangeably here) were created by the state and that the individual enjoyed only such rights as the government might grant.

The American view that the individual possesses certain rights and privileges which even the state cannot violate is not widely held throughout the world, even today. But that belief has given a special quality to life in the United States. It has meant that each person enjoys the freedom to choose his or her own goals and the means of pursuing them. Those who framed the Declaration of Independence (and later the Constitution) believed that freedom and individual liberty were the key to social and economic progress. The greater the people's freedom, the greater the opportunity for everyone to enjoy a better life.

But it is the idea that the individual enjoys certain basic rights which the government (even a democratically elected government) cannot violate that is most typically American. Many of these rights are specified in the original Bill of

1

Rights, which was proposed by the first Congress in 1789 and went into effect in 1791. These first ten amendments to the Constitution place important restrictions on government in its dealings with individual citizens. They specify which rights cannot be violated. Some of these rights are political, such as the right of free speech and a free press. Others are personal, such as freedom of religion, the right to keep or bear arms, and the right to own private property, free from confiscation by government. Still others pertain to procedural guarantees, such as the protection against unreasonable searches and seizures and against self-incrimination, and the right to trial by jury and to be represented at trial by a lawyer. It is important to note, however, that the Bill of Rights regulates and restricts governmental action. It does not regulate individual or group behavior, except to the extent that the underlying ideas of these guarantees have become ingrained in American life.

The guarantees of the Bill of Rights are often referred to as *civil liberties*. These are the constitutional protections of persons, opinions, and property from the arbitrary interference of government officials. They are essential to a free society. *Civil rights*, as distinguished from civil liberties, are generally understood to refer to positive policies of government to protect individuals from arbitrary or discriminatory treatment both by government and by other individuals. *Civil rights* must also be distinguished from *political rights*, which generally refer to participation in the political process. Thus the right to vote, to peaceable assembly, to free speech, and to a free press are generally considered political rights.

For much of American history the rights guaranteed by the Constitution were defined as *freedom from* and were designed primarily to protect the individual from a potentially oppressive federal government. This perspective was especially true of the economic rights contained in the document: the protection of private property, the sanctity of private contractual obligations, and the guarantee against governmental confiscation without just and fair compensation. The word *liberty* was interpreted by successive Supreme Courts to mean economic liberty, and these interpretations greatly facilitated the development of American capitalism, free from governmental regulation or restraint.

Under the impact of the Great Depression of the 1930s, however, Americans began to rethink the economic definition of *liberty*. The question was not simply liberating people from government, but how to use government for positive economic and social purposes. Gradually the meaning of liberty has shifted from its earlier economic connotation to a more personal definition involving the protection of individual dignity from governmental abuse. This meaning involves more rigorous application of the procedural rules of law enforcement, the application of those rules to the states as well as to the national government (some refer to this as the *nationalization* of the Bill of Rights), and a more stringent enforcement of the separation between church and state.

These are controversial issues. Liberty, regardless of how it is defined, does not exist in a vacuum. The absolute freedom of any one person may result in serious harm being done to others. Freedom for the individual may interfere seriously with what is good for society as a whole. The urgent need for the

United States to defend itself may place serious restrictions on an individual's personal liberty, but those restrictions are essential if the nation is to survive. The task of democratic government is to reconcile the rights of the individual, on the one hand, with those of society, on the other. And for Americans, a written Constitution that clearly establishes the basic rights of the individual, an independent judicial branch of government that is capable of enforcing those rights, and an informed electorate that is capable of choosing between alternative candidates have been the means by which that accommodation has been achieved.

The line between liberty and order is difficult to draw. To some extent it is a continuing test of trial and error. The boundaries sometimes shift to accommodate new concerns. The transition from the protection of economic liberty to the defense of individual civil liberty is one such example. The current struggle between the authority of the state to regulate abortion and a woman's right of choice represents another. But over the years the American legal system—with its emphasis on a pragmatic, case-by-case approach to such issues—has proven extraordinarily resilient in fashioning new solutions to such issues as they have arisen. More important, the adversarial approach of the American legal system, in which both sides of an argument are presented fairly and equally to the court, has provided abundant opportunity for the airing of antagonistic positions involving liberty and order.

Some of these controversies, particularly those involving the rules of criminal procedure, often appear to pit the interests of society against those who would destroy it. But it has been a cardinal principle of American jurisprudence that the rights of the accused must not be sacrificed to the momentary need to obtain a conviction. As U.S. Supreme Court Justice Felix Frankfurter once noted: "It is a fair summary of history to say that the safeguards of liberty have been forged in controversies involving not very nice people."[1]

THE CONSTITUTION AND DEMOCRACY

It is not clear whether the Constitution created, or was even intended to create, a democratic government. Certainly the Framers did not intend to create a *pure democracy*, in which the people would rule directly. Instead they created a *republic*, in which the representatives of the people would rule. But the Framers recognized that even an elected government can become oppressive and that popular majorities are no guarantee that the rights of the minority will be protected. Therefore they divided political power, first, between the states and the national government (this was a revolutionary innovation at the time); then, within the national government itself, they further fragmented power along functional lines. The power to legislate was vested in Congress; the power to execute the laws was given to a president (who was independent of Congress); and the power to settle legal cases and controversies was given to a third branch, the judiciary. This division of power within the national government also represented a novel experiment and, according to James Madison, represented a republican remedy for a republican disease: the unchecked will of the majority.

The Framers were not content merely to separate power; they also established an elaborate system of *checks and balances* by which each branch participates in the affairs of the others. Thus, while primary responsibility to pass laws rests with Congress, the president possesses a veto power by which he or she may reject legislation, and the Supreme Court can reject measures passed by Congress as unconstitutional. Similarly Congress possesses the power to impeach—that is, to remove from office—both the president and the justices of the Supreme Court, and it enjoys the sole right to raise money and provide for its expenditure.

But the essence of American constitutionalism was to limit legislative power. This is another way of saying that the United States (unlike parliamentary systems elsewhere) does not give complete authority to the elected representatives of the people. Instead that power must be shared both with the states and with the two other branches of the national government. That arrangement sometimes makes timely response difficult, but, more important, it ensures that the rights of a particular minority will not be trampled underfoot in the name of majority rule.

Of course the most important check on majority rule is the Constitution itself, which not only limits the power of government but specifies for what purposes it can be employed. Is this "democratic"? Critics have argued that the elected representatives of the people (the president and Congress) should be free to act as they deem necessary because they are, after all, the representatives of the people. That is the way parliamentary government operates. But the contrary argument is perhaps even more compelling: namely, that it is the Constitution that represents the will of the people, and the temporary, elected officials (who serve for limited terms) must conduct their business within the limits that the people themselves established.

The idea that the Constitution arose directly from the people, sometimes known as the *federalist view of the Union,* is contrasted with the so-called *compact theory,* which held that the national government was created by the states and was therefore less powerful and essentially a creature of the states. There is documentary evidence within the Constitution itself to support both points of view. Indeed the Constitution represented a compromise between these antagonistic viewpoints, allowing for the coexistence of both. Until 1860 much of the constitutional litigation in the United States revolved around the question of which view was correct. The argument was settled conclusively by the victory of the Union in the Civil War, and since 1865 the view that the Constitution emanated from the people, not the states, has been generally accepted.

Because the Constitution came directly from the people, it enjoys what judges and legal scholars refer to as a *higher law* status. That means that the Constitution is superior to mere laws passed by Congress or the states (statutory law) and that such laws, if in conflict with the Constitution, are *unconstitutional* and cannot be enforced. Since the Bill of Rights is part of the Constitution, it also enjoys a *higher law* status, and neither Congress nor the president can transgress it. (Whether the Bill of Rights applies directly to the states remains a contentious issue, but it is relatively clear that values contained in the first ten amendments are applicable to all governments, whether they are federal, state, or local.) Thus the guarantees of the Bill of Rights provide additional limits to governmental power. It makes no difference that the government may be freely elected and may clearly represent majority sentiment at the moment. This arrangement is deliberate. The very purpose of the Bill of Rights, as expressed by Justice Robert Jackson,

> was to withdraw certain subjects from the vicissitudes of political controversy . . . and establish them as legal principles to be applied by the Courts. One's right to life, liberty and property, to free speech, a free press, freedom of worship and assembly, and other fundamental rights may not be submitted to vote; they depend on the outcome of no election.[2]

THE ROLE OF THE SUPREME COURT

The Constitution left unclear who would adjudicate conflicts between the individual and society. In countries with a parliamentary form of government, that responsibility rests with parliament. And a strong argument can be made that since the Constitution is basically a political document, the responsibility for interpreting it should belong to the *political* branches of government—the president and Congress. That was the view taken by Presidents Thomas Jefferson[3] and Andrew Jackson,[4] and in his inaugural address in 1861, President Abraham Lincoln argued strongly that matters of public policy arising out of the Constitution should be left to those whom the people had elected, not the Supreme Court.[5]

But the fact is that in the early years of the Republic it was the Supreme Court that asserted its responsibility to interpret the Constitution and ultimately established its final authority. The Constitution itself is vague as to where ultimate authority resides. It makes no mention of the authority of the Supreme Court to declare acts of Congress or the president unconstitutional. Proposals to grant such power to the Court had been considered by the Constitutional Convention and explicitly rejected, the majority of the Convention fearing that such a check on the popular will would be unwarranted. It remained for the Supreme Court itself to establish its authority.

At first the Court was not considered a serious rival for power. With a few limited exceptions its jurisdiction rested on congressional determination, and the tradition of colonial jurisprudence made the courts subordinate to legislative authority. In fact John Rutledge, the second chief justice, resigned in 1793 to become South Carolina's chief judicial officer.

But in 1801, with the appointment of John Marshall as chief justice, the Supreme Court embarked on a course that saw it challenge the authority of Congress and the president and eventually establish its final authority to definitively interpret the Constitution: that is, to exercise *judicial review.* The idea of judicial review is another distinctly American contribution to political science. It involves the authority of the Supreme Court to declare acts of Congress, the executive, and the states unconstitutional. It is a power that the Supreme Court established for itself, and the confirming effect of precedent and tradition has been so great that the power is no longer seriously challenged.

The basis for the Court's authority traces to Marshall's landmark decision in *Marbury v. Madison* in 1803. It rests on three premises. First, the Constitution is a higher law than mere statutory law because it was framed by the people themselves as the basis for their government. Subsequent laws enacted by that government must conform to the original decision of the people as manifested in the Constitution or be held void: that is, the lesser power of the government must yield before the greater power of the people, as expressed in the Constitution.

Second, and perhaps most controversial, Marshall argued that the Constitution was "law," and therefore could be utilized by the Court in arriving at its decision. (An alternative view, which at the time was perhaps more commonly held, was that the Constitution was a "political" document and therefore should be interpreted by the political officials of government—the president and Congress.)

Third, having established that the Constitution was law and therefore properly interpretable by the courts, Marshall said that the opinion of the Supreme Court on matters of law was final. That much was clear, because the Constitution did indeed entrust final legal authority to the Supreme Court.

For many years Marshall's decision for the court in *Marbury v. Madison* remained a dead issue. The Supreme Court did not declare another act of Congress unconstitutional until 1857, when in the *Dred Scott* case it struck down the Missouri Compromise of 1820.[6] But with the victory of the Union in the Civil War and the authority of the national government reestablished, the Supreme Court began increasingly to assert its authority to exercise judicial review, striking down (as unconstitutional) a wide variety of acts of Congress and of the individual states.

In this context it may be important to note that in *Marbury v. Madison,* Chief Justice Marshall did not assert that the authority to interpret the Constitution rested *exclusively* with the Supreme Court. Marshall acknowledged (at least implicitly) the equal authority of the president and Congress to interpret that document and simply maintained that *as a matter of law* the decision of the Supreme Court was final as to the case that was then before it and to similar cases that might arise in the future. But Marshall carefully avoided making any claim as to the *ultimate* authority of the Supreme Court to interpret the Constitution.

It was not until 1958 in *Cooper v. Aaron,* a civil rights case arising in Little Rock, Arkansas, that the Supreme Court suggested that its constitutional decisions were the "supreme law of the land" and therefore binding on all government officials, both state and national.[7] Four years later the Supreme Court for the first time referred to itself as the "ultimate interpretation of the Constitution," superior to the president, the Congress, and the states.[8] Any doubt as to the Supreme Court's authority over the other branches was surely set to rest when it ruled successfully against President Richard Nixon in the case of the Watergate tapes.[9]

Nevertheless the precise role of the Supreme Court remains a contentious issue, particularly when it comes to the adjudication of individual rights. The four debates in Chapter I address the fundamental parameters of the role of the Supreme Court in a democratic society and focus on the Bill of Rights. The first debate examines whether a written Bill of Rights is necessary to protect individual freedom. The second looks at whether freedom of speech, as guaranteed by the First Amendment to the Constitution, is absolute or subject to reasonable limits. The third debate considers whether the Bill of Rights is applicable to the states. The Bill of Rights was originally written to apply only to the national government, and it is a part of the national Constitution. Did later amendments (particularly the Fourteenth) have the effect of making it applicable to the states as well? Finally, we look at the contemporary debate on whether the Supreme Court, in interpreting the Constitution, should be limited by the original intent of the Framers. Or do the words stand on their own, to be applied freely by the Court to contemporary circumstance? This issue appears to divide the judiciary and the legal profession and has prompted the attorney general of the United States, Edwin Meese III, to take the unusual step of criticizing the Supreme Court directly.

Is the Bill of Rights Necessary to Protect Individual Freedom?

The Constitution as originally drafted did not contain a Bill of Rights. It specified the powers of the national government, denied certain other powers to the states (such as the authority to make war or issue currency), and divided the national government into legislative, executive, and judicial branches. But when the Constitution was submitted to the various state conventions for ratification, concern grew that the rights of the people were not sufficiently protected against the proposed new government. Thomas Jefferson, then serving in Paris as United States ambassador, was particularly troubled by the omission and wrote to James Madison that "a bill of rights is what the people are entitled to against every government on earth . . . and no just government should refuse [to provide one]."[10]

The more conservative of the Framers—Alexander Hamilton and James Wilson—thought a bill of rights was unnecessary. Wilson believed such a proposal would dangerously limit the powers of government, while Hamilton argued that such a proposal "would sound much better in a treatise on ethics than in a constitution of government."[11]

Jefferson's view prevailed. Many state conventions made their ratification of the Constitution contingent upon the addition of a Bill of Rights, and when the first Congress convened in 1789, Madison introduced a series of amendments that were quickly adopted. Jefferson had argued that a written Bill of

Rights would give an important legal weapon to the courts. In presenting his amendments Madison noted that the courts would "consider themselves the guardians of those rights" and oppose any usurpation by the legislative or executive branches.[12] To be sure fundamental rights such as free speech and a free press gain no greater moral status by being written into the Constitution. But as Jefferson and Madison observed, individuals henceforth could look to the courts for their protection.

The role of the Supreme Court in protecting the privileges guaranteed in the Bill of Rights remains controversial. Indeed the very question of whether a Bill of Rights is necessary—the dispute between Jefferson and Hamilton—can be answered in different ways. In Great Britain, for example, there is no written constitution, and Parliament reigns supreme. There is no Bill of Rights to bar the way, should Parliament decide to suppress civil liberties, abolish trial by jury, invoke press censorship, or confiscate private property. And British courts are powerless to invalidate an act of Parliament. (The last suggestion of judicial power to overrule an act of Parliament was by Sir John Holt, lord chief justice of England, in 1694, and his comments were merely *dicta* and thus not binding.)[13] Yet Great Britain is generally regarded as one of the most democratic of countries, and in it the rights of the individual, though not written down and certified, have survived remarkably well.

The example of Britain suggests that the preservation of individual rights involves far more than a written document. The traditions a country has evolved, as well as the expectations of a people about their government, may be equally important. The preservation of individual rights may also depend upon the way in which a written guarantee is interpreted. A written Bill of Rights would be of little solace if the will to enforce it was lacking. For example, in 1798 the United States was bitterly divided between the conservative followers of President John Adams (known as Federalists) and the more radical supporters of Jefferson. The Federalists controlled Congress as well as the presidency and, in a misguided attempt to stifle Jefferson's supporters, passed a series of laws known as the Alien and Sedition Acts making it, among others, a crime to "write, print, utter, or publish . . . any false, scandalous, and malicious writing . . . against the government of the United States."[14] President Adams applied the act vigorously against Jefferson's supporters, and the Supreme Court never considered whether the law violated the rights of free speech and free press guaranteed under the First Amendment to the Constitution.

In fact for the first one hundred years of United States history the Supreme Court rarely, if ever, used the Bill of Rights to protect individual liberty against governmental encroachment. When it began to do so in the 1890s, the action was usually to defend private property and the individual's right to utilize his or her property free from governmental restraint. In other words the "liberty" guaranteed by the Bill of Rights was interpreted almost exclusively as "economic liberty." But as times changed, the Supreme Court gradually widened its enforcement of the other liberties guaranteed by the Bill of Rights.

The following brief catalog of dates indicates when these rights became judicially enforceable. It also emphasizes that written guarantees, unless they are enforced, may be meaningless.

Freedom of speech—1927[15]
Freedom of the press—1931[16]
Right to counsel—1932[17]
Freedom of assembly—1937[18]
Guarantee against self-incrimination—1965[19]

In the debate on this topic, Judge J. Skelly Wright of the U.S. Court of Appeals looks at the respective experience of Great Britain and the United States in protecting individual liberty. Judge Wright argues forcefully that without a written Bill of Rights the courts would be powerless to enforce such protections as freedom of speech and freedom of religion against the power of a tyrannical government, especially if that government enjoyed majority support. Judge Wright speaks from personal experience. As a U.S. District Court judge in Louisiana in the 1950s, he presided over some of the earliest desegregation cases. His efforts to enforce the Constitution met stormy public resistance. His house was fire-bombed, and Wright himself was subjected to intense pressure and intimidation. Yet it was the written Constitution that allowed the court to prevail.

It may be noteworthy that Judge Wright's article derives from a speech that he was invited to give at Tulane Law School in New Orleans some twenty-five years after his sharp confrontation with racist sentiment in Louisiana. It was both a personal vindication and a moving testament to how deeply the rule of law is accepted in the United States.

By contrast, Professor Lino A. Graglia of the University of Texas Law School raises some disturbing questions about the way the written Constitution has been interpreted by the Supreme Court. Graglia restates in forceful terms the traditional argument that the unelected Court has exceeded its authority and now sits as an all-powerful censor over popularly elected officials at both state and national levels. According to Graglia, the Court itself has become the greatest threat to American liberty because its justices interpret the Bill of Rights to meet their personal predilections.

The changing complexion of the Supreme Court is important. As justices leave and are replaced by new justices with differing views, the meaning of the Constitution sometimes changes. Although this may illustrate that the Constitution is a living document capable of changing with the times, it also means that the Constitution can become dependent on the whims of a majority of the justices.

Is Freedom of Speech Absolute?

The First Amendment to the Constitution provides that "Congress shall make no law . . . abridging the freedom of speech, or of the press; or the right of the people peaceably to assemble, and to petition the government for a redress of grievances." Are the words "Congress shall make no law" to be taken literally? Do they mean that the government cannot regulate speech or the press even in the national interest? Or do they mean that Congress shall make no *unreasonable* law curtailing the freedom of expression?

For example the Supreme Court has frequently held that freedom of speech does not protect libel or slander. Similarly speech that incites others to commit illegal acts is not protected. A third category of speech that is not protected by the First Amendment involves what the courts have called "fighting words," words considered so threatening and offensive that the person to whom they are addressed has the immediate right to fight back. It is also not clear whether advertising and commercial speech are fully protected. And in time of war or national emergency the courts have recognized that the government may have a compelling need to restrict or censor free speech and free press. But these are temporary exceptions designed to ensure that the nation survives, and the government bears a heavy burden to justify such action—a burden it was not able to meet in the so-called Pentagon papers case during the Vietnam War.[20]

Over the years the Supreme Court has developed a variety of tests by which to measure government regulation of speech. Perhaps the best known of these is the *clear and present danger* test devised by Justice Oliver Wendell Holmes, Jr., in *Schenck v. United States.* According to Holmes: "The question in every case is whether the words are used in such circumstances and are of such a nature as to create a clear and present danger that they will bring about the substantive evils that Congress has a right to prevent."[21]

A somewhat more restrictive test that no longer enjoys Supreme Court support is known as the *bad tendency doctrine.*[22] Adherents of this view hold that the legislative branch, not the courts, has the primary responsibility to determine when speech should be outlawed. And it may do so when speech *has a tendency* to lead to illegal action.[23] This view, of course, narrows considerably the protection of the First Amendment.

A third constitutional test, known as the *preferred position doctrine,* derives from the idea that the rights guaranteed by the First Amendment (speech, press, assembly) enjoy the highest priority in our scheme of values.[24] According to this view free speech and free press are fundamental to the political process and all the liberties we cherish. As a result judges have a special duty to protect these freedoms from governmental encroachment. Those who adhere to the preferred position doctrine, such as the late Justice Hugo L. Black, come close to the view that freedom of expression may *never* be curtailed. By contrast, those who accept the clear and present danger test, as it has evolved, agree that free speech is essential to democratic processes but not *absolute;* that is, the high value of free speech must be *balanced* against other competing interests of government.

In the debate on this subject, Justice Black, in the first James Madison Lecture delivered at the New York University School of Law, sets forth the literalist interpretation of the Bill of Rights. According to Black, the Framers of the document did all of the balancing that was required, and when they said that

Congress should make *no law* abridging free speech and free press, they meant exactly that.

But Justice Black's literalist view has never been endorsed by the Supreme Court. Justice Holmes, speaking for the Court in *Gompers v. United States,* in 1914 restated the more commonly accepted doctrine when he observed:

> the provisions of the Constitution are not mathematical formulas having their essence in their form; they are organic living institutions transplanted from English soil. Their significance is vital, not formal; it is to be gathered not simply by taking the words and a dictionary, but by considering their origin and the line of their growth.[25]

A classic confrontation between the literalist or absolutist view of the First Amendment and those who believe its injunctions require the "balancing" of competing interests occurred in the leading case of *Konigsberg v. State Bar of California* in 1961.[26] At issue was whether California could deny bar admission to an applicant who had refused to answer questions about Communist party membership. Speaking for the Supreme Court, Justice John Marshall Harlan abruptly rejected Black's thesis. Those portions of Harlan's decision dealing with the question of *absolutes* vs. *balancing* are reproduced in the debate. The upshot of the case was to uphold California's action, and it is Harlan's position as articulated in *Konigsberg,* not Black's, that has continued to enjoy the Supreme Court's approval.

Is the Bill of Rights Applicable to the States?

When the Bill of Rights was added to the Constitution in 1789, it was the clear intent of the Framers that its protections applied only to the national government. Many states already had their own bills of rights in their constitutions, and it was the power of the new central government that people feared. (It was, in fact, the Virginia Bill of Rights that served as one of Madison's models when he proposed the federal version.)

Perhaps because the United States Bill of Rights was more inclusive, or perhaps because not all states provided similar guarantees, it was inevitable that the issue of the Bill of Rights' applicability to the states would come before the Supreme Court. And in 1833, in his last great constitutional decision, Chief Justice John Marshall held on behalf of a unanimous Court that the Bill of Rights applied only to the national government. The case was *Barron v. Baltimore,* and the question involved the last phrase of the Fifth Amendment, that private property shall not be "taken for public use, without just compensation." According to Marshall:

> The question . . . presented is . . . of great importance, but not of much difficulty. The Constitution was ordained and established by the people of the United States for themselves, for their own government, and not for the government of the individual states.[27]

The decision in *Barron v. Baltimore* has never been overruled by the Supreme Court. But the adoption of the Fourteenth Amendment in 1868—which *does* apply to the states—has made the situation somewhat ambiguous. Specifically the Fourteenth Amendment—which was designed to ensure equality for the newly freed slaves—provides that:

> No State shall make or enforce any law which shall abridge the privileges and immunities of citizens of the United States; *nor shall any State deprive any person of life, liberty, or property, without due process of law;* nor deny to any person within its jurisdiction the equal protection of the laws. [Italics added.]

Does the Fourteenth Amendment incorporate the Bill of Rights and make it applicable to the states? Virtually from the time of its adoption, some lawyers have tried to persuade the Supreme Court that the Due Process Clause of the amendment (italicized above) means that whatever the Bill of Rights forbids the national government to do, the states are also forbidden to do. In effect this understanding would repeal the holding of *Barron v. Baltimore* and make the entire Bill of Rights applicable to the states.

The historical evidence as to the meaning of the amendment is murky.[28] Even the Supreme Court has been sharply divided. By and large the majority of the Court have declined to interpret the Due Process Clause of the Fourteenth Amendment as "shorthand" for the Bill of Rights. But gradually, over the years, the Court has extended the Fourteenth Amendment on a case-by-case basis to include virtually all of the guarantees contained in the Bill of Rights.[29] The first such example was in *Gitlow v. New York* in 1925, when the Court announced:

> For present purposes we may and do assume that freedom of speech and of press—which are protected by the First Amendment from abridgment by Congress—are among the fundamental personal rights and "liberties" protected by the due process clause of the Fourteenth Amendment from impairment by the States.[30]

What was crucial for the Court was that free speech and a free press were so *fundamental* that "liberty" could not survive without them. This reasoning, known as *selective incorporation,* has allowed the Supreme Court to expand the protection of the Fourteenth Amendment as our concept of personal liberty has expanded. It differs, in legal terms, from the doctrine of *total incorporation,* which argues that the entire Bill of Rights has been incorporated into the Fourteenth Amendment and thus made automatically applicable to the states.

On the Supreme Court itself, the issue of *total* versus *selective* incorporation was joined most forcefully in the case of *Adamson v. California.*[31] Adamson claimed that his murder conviction violated the Due Process Clause of the Fourteenth Amendment because the state prosecutor had commented to the jury on his failure to take the witness stand and testify. The Supreme Court, speaking through Justice Stanley F. Reed, conceded that in a federal court the prosecution's statement would have violated the Bill of Rights' guarantee against self-incrimination contained in the Fifth Amendment. But the Court held that not all of the Bill of Rights' guarantees were protected against state action by the Fourteenth Amendment, and in the view of the Court in 1947 the privilege of the Fifth Amendment against self-incrimination was one of those not protected.[32]

In a stinging dissent Justice Hugo L. Black wrote what is considered the classic argument for *total* incorporation of the Bill of Rights. The concurring opinion of Justice Felix Frankfurter, which attacks Black's position head on, is the equally classic rebuttal.

The student should note Black's reliance on the original intent of the Fourteenth Amendment, as well as his overriding concern that anything short of total incorporation leaves the final decision to the judges—whom he fears can be capricious. Justice Frankfurter refutes Black's history and argues that it has always been the judgment of the courts that provides the best assurance that liberty will be secure.

Should the Supreme Court Be Limited by the Framers' Intent?

The role of the Supreme Court in contemporary society always provides a valuable topic for debate. Today that issue frequently turns on the question of whether the Court should be limited by the intent of the Framers of the Constitution, or whether it should try to adapt the broad language of the document to the issues of the present—as those issues are perceived by the justices of the Court.

Attorney General Edwin Meese III has taken a leading position in contending that the Supreme Court should return to the intent of the Framers. Meese argues that unless the text of the Constitution is taken seriously, it tends to become "an empty vessel into which each generation may pour its passion and prejudice." The attorney general condemns recent judicial activism as lacking in "demonstrable textual or historical support." Instead of a jurisprudence of original intent, Meese suggests that the Court too often bases its decisions on social theory, moral philosophy, and personal notions of human dignity. Such decisions, to paraphrase Dean John Hart Ely of Stanford Law School, are not merely bad constitutional law; they are not constitutional law at all.

Meese has made a number of telling points in the current dialogue. His first salvo was fired in an address to the American Bar Association in London, England, on July 17, 1985. That was followed by a speech given to the Federalist Society and by an article drawn from that speech published in *Policy Review* in 1986. It is the latter article in which Meese's position is most cogently developed, and it is reprinted in the debate.

The contrary position is argued by Justice William J. Brennan, Jr. In a highly unusual departure from the tradition of silence that the justices of the

Supreme Court maintain on public issues, Brennan responded to Meese's criticism in a speech at Georgetown University. In Brennan's words:

> We current Justices read the Constitution in the only way we can: as Twentieth Century Americans. . . . For the genius of the Constitution rests not in any static meaning it might have had in a world that is dead and gone, but in the adaptability of its great principles to cope with current problems and current needs.

The confrontation between the two views expressed in this exchange is all the more notable because it pits the attorney general of the United States against the senior associate justice of the Supreme Court in a public dispute that goes to the heart of the role of the judiciary in American society.

NOTES

1. *United States v. Rabinowitz*, 339 U.S. 56, 69 (1950).
2. *West Virginia State Board of Education v. Barnette*, 319 U.S. 624 (1943).
3. Thomas Jefferson to Abigail Adams, Sept. 11, 1804, in *The Writings of Thomas Jefferson*, ed. Paul L. Ford (New York: Putnam's, 1897), vol. 8, p. 310.
4. Andrew Jackson, Veto Message on the Bill to Recharter the Bank of the United States, July 10, 1832, in *Messages and Papers of the Presidents*, ed. James D. Richardson (Washington, D.C.: Government Printing Office, 1896–1899) vol. 2, pp. 576–83.
5. Abraham Lincoln, First Inaugural Address, Mar. 4, 1861, in *Messages and Papers*, vol. 6, pp. 5–10.
6. *Dred Scott v. Sandford*, 19 How. 393 (1857).
7. 358 U.S. 1 (1958).
8. *Baker v. Carr*, 369 U.S. 186 (1962).
9. *United States v. Nixon*, 418 U.S. 683 (1974). Also see *Powell v. McCormack*, 395 U.S. 486, 549 (1969).
10. Thomas Jefferson to James Madison, Dec. 20, 1787.
11. *The Federalist* No. 84. Alexander Hamilton, James Madison, and John Jay, *The Federalist*, Modern Library Edition (New York: Random House, n. d.), p. 559.
12. *Annals of Congress*, 424 (Gales and Seaton, eds.) 1789.
13. See Theodore F.T. Plucknett, *A Concise History of the Common Law*, 5th ed. (Boston: Little, Brown, 1956), pp. 245–47, 337.
14. Act of July 14, 1798, 1 Stat. 596.
15. *Fiske v. Kansas*, 274 U.S. 380 (1927).
16. *Near v. Minnesota*, 283 U.S. 697 (1931).
17. *Powell v. Alabama*, 287 U.S. 45 (1932).
18. *De Jonge v. Oregon*, 299 U.S. 353 (1937).
19. *Griffin v. California*, 380 U.S. 609 (1965).
20. *New York Times v. United States*, 403 U.S. 713 (1971).
21. 249 U.S. 47 (1919).
22. In 1982, in *Brown v. Hartlage*, 456 U.S. 45, the Supreme Court reversed a decision of the Kentucky Court of Appeals based on the bad tendency doctrine.
23. *Gitlow v. New York*, 268 U.S. 652 (1925).
24. *United States v. Carolene Products Co.*, 304 U.S. 144 (1938).

25. 233 U.S. 604, 610 (1914).

26. 366 U.S. 36 (1961).

27. 7 Peters 243 (1833).

28. Compare, for example, the argument of Professor Charles Fairman that the Fourteenth Amendment does not incorporate the Bill of Rights (*Does the Fourteenth Amendment Incorporate the Bill of Rights? The Original Understanding*, 2 STAN. L. REV. 5 [1949]) with that of Professor Robert Crosskey that it does (*Charles Fairman, 'Legislative History', and the Constitutional Limitation on the States*, 22 U. CHI. L. REV. 1 [1954]).

29. For a useful summary, see Henry J. Abraham, *Freedom and the Court: Civil Rights and Civil Liberties in the United States* 4th ed. (New York: Oxford University Press, 1982), pp. 29–91.

30. 268 U.S. 652 (1925).

31. 322 U.S. 46 (1947).

32. The holding of *Adamson v. California* was subsequently overruled in *Griffin v. California*, 380 U.S. 609 (1965).

1 *Is the Bill of Rights necessary to protect individual freedom?*

YES THE BILL OF RIGHTS IN BRITAIN AND AMERICA: NOT QUITE A FULL CIRCLE

J. Skelly Wright

. . . Is it the lesson of history that even an entrenched Bill of Rights is no safeguard of liberty; that, in the end, even judges will yield before strong rulers, willful legislatures, powerful vested interests, or popular clamor? The historical record shatters any illusion that a piece of parchment will assure our freedoms. It has been rightly said that "the price of liberty is eternal vigilance." I do not assert that an enforceable Bill of Rights will always be enforced. I do contend that *without it,* we have little hope of securing civil liberties against the evil winds that blow all too often even in this blessed land.

The inordinate delay in the practical implementation of the Bill of Rights is, no doubt, largely a matter of different preoccupations for most of our relatively short history. We were devoting our energies to the enormous problems of a new nation, which was creating itself out of disunited parts; establishing its government; maintaining itself against foreign and domestic enemies; expanding territorially, economically, and socially; tearing itself apart in a civil war and its aftermath; healing itself and, once again, growing, internally and externally, with abnormal appetite. Only recently has the country settled down to

Excerpted from J. Skelly Wright, "The Bill of Rights in Britain and America: A Not Quite Full Circle," *Tulane Law Review*, 55 (Feb. 1981), pp. 312–15.

self-examination, finally noticing the injustices done to its own citizens.

It is true that, in many contexts, the standards and procedures announced in the Bill of Rights are today read more generously in favor of the citizen and against government, so that what once was deemed no violation is now seen as offending constitutional guarantees. In law, as in much else, we are more fastidious than we were, except where property rights are concerned. Indeed, the apparent judicial indifference to liberty for so many decades may, in some measure, be attributed to this preoccupation with the weighty issues of the pocketbook.

The fault is not entirely with the judges. The focus of the courts—so far as they were concerned at all with public law and not private disputes—was concentrated on the claims of property rather than liberty because that was the meat of the lawyers, and the familiar diet of those lawyers who became judges. Even so, the eventual vindication of civil liberties in this country is also the work of lawyers and judges. Much credit belongs to organizations like the ACLU and its local branches, including the Louisiana chapter. Particular tribute is due to those who toiled in the difficult days of the '30's, 40's, and 50's—among them George Dreyfous—long before civil rights and civil liberties had become respectable causes. Nor should we forget the judges.

Occasionally, we had a patrician speaking out: the first Justice Harlan or, much later, Oliver Wendell Holmes (albeit with great lapses).[93] It is no accident that the rights of ordinary people were recognized when judges with more humble backgrounds ascended the Supreme Court bench. To mention only those who have gone, I notice Hugo Black, William Douglas, Tom Murphy, and Earl Warren.

Yet the most dedicated lawyers and the most liberal judges could not have prevailed without the Bill of Rights and the post Civil War amendments. I have some reason to know how difficult it has been, at times, to enforce the rights of a few against the "massive resistance" of officials supported by a prevailing majority. No court could have succeeded by simply invoking the "natural rights of man" as it conceived them. It was essential to have a written text —however imprecise—embodying commands of unquestionable authority and concededly binding on all officials. It was equally essential to have a tradition, established so long ago, as to have unimpeachable credentials, to the effect that "[i]t is emphatically the province and duty of the judicial department to say what the law is,"[94] and the corollary, that once the judges have construed the Constitution, their ruling controls the President, the Congress, the governors, the state legislatures, and all lesser officers of both federal and state governments.

No doubt, in a democracy like ours, some liberties would survive without a constitutional text and judges to enforce it. There are presumably some things with which no legislature or official would dare interfere, either because the ingrained habits of too many people are involved or because everyone agrees that the law has no business controlling freedom of choice about very personal matters. I have some difficulty giving examples, however, because, in fact, government has long sought to control the most private activities (including contraception) and the most trivial (including hair length). Perhaps no liberty is secure against the occasional excesses of democracy. What is clear is that popular governments in our country have not hesitated to trample the rights of minorities, especially the weak, the outcast, the original, and the unpopular. As Judge Wyzanski put it, a little bluntly, in a previous lecture in this series: "Is it not perfectly clear that the majority of the representatives like the majority of the people of the United States don't give a hoot about the first ten amendments except when their own ox is gored?"[95]

Of course, judges could intervene when the act was contrary to law in the ordinary sense, such as a violation of a statute. But what if the statute itself discriminates or infringes fundamental liberties? Then, courts must invoke a higher law. In theory, they could claim to be applying "natural law," superior to the law of legislatures. That will not wash in a democracy like ours. Judges are not recognized as having a special "pipeline to God." Moreover, God is not supposed to be mentioned by lay judges. Only a constitutional text adopted by the sovereign people themselves authorizes courts to override regularly enacted, but oppressive, legislation.

There are, of course, problems in translating to the needs of the present a Bill of Rights written two centuries ago, or even the provisions of the century-old fourteenth amendment.[96] My argument does

---

[93] *See, e.g.,* Debs v. United States, 249 U.S. 211 (1919); Giles v. Harris, 189 U.S. 475 (1903). [*Note from editors:* Footnote numbering from original source is retained here and elsewhere in this book.]

[94] Marbury v. Madison, 5 U.S. (1 Cranch) 137, 177 (1803).

[95] Wyzanski, *Equal Justice through Law,* 47 Tul. L. Rev. 951, 958 (1973).

[96] All else aside, the first eight amendments do not address substantive rights, except those mentioned in

not depend on the precision with which our fundamental rights are stated. Some might prefer a generalized bill of rights reduced to a single provision declaring simply that the freedom of the individual shall not be infringed by government except as compellingly necessary in the general interest and pursuant to fair procedures, previously established by law, equally applicable to all persons, and that the courts are empowered to enjoin and redress any disregard of this rule. I would like more specifics to be included, though it is not my task to rewrite our constitu-

tional guarantees. I simply assert that the experience of this and other nations teaches the value of a written, constitutional, and enforceable declaration, however brief and subject to varying interpretations. No bill of rights, even with independent judges, will assure respect for civil liberties. Our own history proves this much. But history also teaches that an enforceable bill of rights is a useful and necessary mechanism for protecting the citizen against his government. I suggest the great majority of the American people agree with this statement.

Footnote 96 (cont.)
the first amendment. Suppose Congress, following proper procedures, were to enact a law requiring every person—men and women alike—to wear a hat in public. What pretext would the judges have to intervene? Some, like Mr. Justice Black, would say "none." *See* H. Black, A Constitutional Faith 8–14, 23–31 (1968). That was, in a more important context, the issue the Court faced in the birth control and abortion cases. Rightly, in my view, a majority of the Justices struck down the illiberal laws. But they had to

go beyond the text. Perhaps, here, the ninth amendment comes into play: if the people "retain" rights not specifically enumerated, it must follow that government may not take them away. It must fall to the courts to identify such unspecified liberties when occasion arises. This is dangerously open-ended and judges must be reluctant to discover new rights. Yet, in a sufficiently clear case, I would argue that there is constitutional authority for a judicial vindication of rights too obvious to be declared.

NO HOW THE CONSTITUTION DISAPPEARED

Lino A. Graglia

Attorney General Edwin Meese's recent statement in a speech to the American Bar Association that judges should interpret the Constitution to mean what it was originally intended to mean probably did not strike most people as controversial. Nevertheless it brought forth immediate denunciation by a sitting Supreme Court Justice as "doctrinaire," "arrogant," and

the product of "facile historicism." "It is a view," Justice William J. Brennan, Jr. said in a speech at Georgetown University,* "that feigns self-effacing deference to the specific judgments of those who forged our original social compact," but that "in truth . . . is little more than arrogance cloaked as humility" because it is not possible to "gauge accurately the intent of the

Lino A. Graglia, "How the Constitution Disappeared," *Commentary,* 81 (Feb. 1986), pp. 19–27. Reprinted by permission; all rights reserved.

* "The Constitution of the United States: Contemporary Ratification," delivered at a "Text and Teaching Symposium," October 12, 1985.

Framers on application of principle to specific, contemporary questions." The view is not only mistaken, but misguided, Justice Brennan continued, because it would require judges to "turn a blind eye to social progress and eschew adaptation of overarching principles to changes of social circumstance."

To state that judges should interpret the Constitution as intended by those who wrote and ratified it ("the Framers") is only to state the basic premise of our political-legal system that the function of judges is to apply, not to make, the law. Indeed, it would be difficult to say what interpretation of a law means if not to determine the intent of the lawmaker. Justice Brennan's angry attack on the obvious as if it were disreputable, soon joined by the attacks of his colleague Justice John Paul Stevens and a legion of media commentators, makes evident that much is at stake in this debate on a seemingly esoteric matter of constitutional interpretation. What is at stake is nothing less than the question of how the country should be governed in regard to basic issues of social policy: whether such issues should be decided by elected representatives of the people, largely on a state-by-state basis, or, as has been the case for the last three decades, primarily by a majority of the nine Justices of the United States Supreme Court for the nation as a whole.

The modern era of constitutional law began with the Supreme Court's 1954 decision in *Brown* v. *Board of Education,* holding compulsory school racial segregation and, it soon appeared, all racial discrimination by government, unconstitutional. The undeniable rightness of the decision as a matter of social policy, in effect ending legally-imposed second-class citizenship for blacks, and its eventual acceptance by the public and ratification by Congress and the President in the 1964 Civil Rights Act, gained for the Court a status and prestige unprecedented in our history. The moral superiority of decision-making by judges to decision-making by mere "politicians" seemed evident. The result was to enable the Court to move from its historic role as a brake on social change to a very different role as the primary engine of such change.

In the years since *Brown,* nearly every fundamental change in domestic social policy has been brought about not by the decentralized democratic (or, more accurately, republican) process contemplated by the Constitution, but simply by the Court's decree. The Court has decided, on a national basis and often in opposition to the wishes of a majority of the American people, issues literally of life and death, as in its decisions invalidating virtually all restrictions on abortion and severely restricting the use of capital punishment. It has decided issues of public security and order, as in its decisions greatly expanding the protection of the criminally accused and limiting state power to control street demonstrations and vagrancy, and issues of public morality, as in the decisions disallowing most state controls of pornography, obscenity, and nudity. The Court has both prohibited the states from making provision for prayer in the schools and disallowed most forms of aid, state or federal, to religious schools. It has required that children be excluded from their neighborhood public schools and bused to more distant schools in order to increase school racial integration; ordered the reapportionment of state and federal legislatures on a "one-man-one-vote" basis; invalidated most of the law of libel and slander; and disallowed nearly all legal distinctions on the basis of sex, illegitimacy, and alienage. The list could easily be extended, but it should be clear that in terms of the issues that determine the nature and quality of life in a society, the Supreme Court has become our most important institution of government.

Since his appointment to the Court by

President Eisenhower in 1956, Justice Brennan has participated in all of the Court's major constitutional decisions, has consistently voted in favor of Court intervention in the political process, and often was a leader on the Court in reaching the decision to intervene. Indeed, he has ordinarily differed with the Court only in that he would often go even farther in disallowing political control of some issues; he would, for example, go farther than the Court has in disallowing state regulation of the distribution of pornographic material and he would prohibit capital punishment in all cases. If the Court has been our most important institution of government for the past three decades, Justice Brennan—although his name is probably unknown to the great majority of his fellow citizens—has surely been our most important government official. To argue that the Supreme Court should confine itself or be confined to interpreting the Constitution as written is to undermine the basis of this status and challenge the legitimacy of his life's work.

Constitutional law is as a practical matter the product of the exercise of the power of judicial review, the power of judges, and ultimately of Supreme Court Justices, to invalidate legislation and other acts of other officials and institutions of government as inconsistent with the Constitution. The central question presented by constitutional law—the only question the great variety of matters dealt with under that rubric have in common—is how, if at all, can such a power in the hands of national officials who are unelected and effectively hold office for life be justified in a system of government supposedly republican in form and federalist in organization? The power is not explicitly provided for in the Constitution and had no precedent in English law—where Parliament, not a court, is said to be supreme—which could well be taken as

reason enough to assume that no such power had been granted. Alexander Hamilton argued for the power in *Federalist 78,* however, and Chief Justice John Marshall established it in *Marbury* v. *Madison* in 1803 on the ground that it is inherent in a written constitution that declares itself to be supreme law. The argument is hardly unanswerable—other nations have written constitutions without judicial review—but judicial review limited to interpretation of the Constitution in accordance with the Framers' intent does obviate the problem of policy-making by judges.

Constitutional limitations on popular government are undoubtedly undemocratic, even if they were themselves democratically adopted by a super-majority, but the only function of judges in exercising judicial review on the basis of a written constitution with determinate meaning would be the entirely judicial one of enforcing the Constitution as they would any other law. The judges, Hamilton assured the ratifying states, would have neither "force nor will"; able to "take no active resolution whatever" in enforcing the Constitution, their power would be "next to nothing." "Judicial power," Marshall reiterated, "has no existence. Courts are mere instruments of the law, and can will nothing." The notion that a court has "power to overrule or control the action of the people's representatives," Justice Owen Roberts confirmed during the New Deal constitutional crisis, "is a misconception"; the Court's only function in a constitutional case is "to lay the article of the Constitution which is invoked beside the statute which is challenged and to decide whether the latter squares with the former."

Even Justice Brennan purports to recognize what, as he notes, Alexander Bickel called "the counter-majoritarian difficulty" presented by judicial review. "Our commitment to self-governance in a representative democracy must be reconciled,"

Justice Brennan concedes, "with vesting in electorally unaccountable Justices the power to invalidate the expressed desires of representative bodies on the ground of inconsistency with higher law." Supreme Court Justices, he acknowledges at the beginning of his speech, echoing Judge Learned Hand, "are not platonic guardians appointed to wield authority according to their personal moral predilections." At several points he even seems to offer the standard justification for judicial review, that the judges merely interpret the written Constitution. He states, for example, that the duty of the judge is to "draw meaning from the text" and "remain faithful to the content" of the Constitution and that "the debate is really a debate about how to read the text, about constraints on what is legitimate interpretation." These statements are consistent with the remainder of his speech, however, only if reading or interpreting a document is considered indistinguishable from composing or rewriting it.

Unfortunately, however, the debate is not about how judges should read or interpret the text of the Constitution, but about whether that is what they should in fact confine themselves to doing in deciding constitutional cases. The view that the duty of judges is to read and interpret the Constitution—to attempt to determine what the Framers intended to say—is precisely the view that Justice Brennan seeks to rebut and derides as uninformed and misguided. The whole point of his speech is that judges should not be confined to that task, for so to confine them would be to give them much too limited a role in our system of government and leave us insufficiently protected from the dangers of majority rule.

Justice Brennan is far from alone today in his view of the proper role of judges in exercising judicial review and of the essential irrelevance of the Constitution to constitutional law. It is, indeed, the view taken by most contemporary constitutional-law scholars, who share the political ideology of the modern-era Supreme Court and see it as their professional duty to legitimize the fruits of that ideology. Because it has become increasingly difficult—in fact, impossible—to justify the Court's controversial decisions as the result of constitutional interpretation, the bulk of modern constitutional-law scholarship consists of the invention and elaboration of "noninterpretivist" or "non-originalist" theories of judicial review—justifications for a judicial review that is not confined to constitutional interpretation in any sense that would effectively restrain judicial choice. Because the product of this review is nonetheless always called "constitutional law" and attributed in some way to the Constitution, the result is the paradox of noninterpretivist constitutional interpretation, constitutional law without the Constitution.

That more and more constitutional scholars, and now a Supreme Court Justice, should come to recognize and acknowledge that the Supreme Court's constitutional decisions of recent decades cannot be justified on any other basis—that they are not in fact based on the Constitution—can be taken as a hopeful sign. Although the effort today in an increasing flood of books, articles, and speeches is to justify those decisions nonetheless, the inevitable failure of such efforts must, it would seem, eventually cause the enterprise to be abandoned and the fact that they cannot be justified in a system of self-government to be also generally recognized and acknowledged. Justice Brennan has performed a public service by bringing this extremely important and little understood issue to greater public attention, conveniently summarizing the standard arguments for "non-interpretivist" or "non-originalist" review—i.e., what is popularly referred to as "judicial activism"—and stating his own position with unusual, even if not total, clarity and candor.

Defenders of judicial activism face the dilemma that, on the one hand, judicial policy-making cannot be defended as such in our system—the Justices, even Justice Brennan must concede, are not authorized to enact their "personal moral predilections" into law and must therefore claim that their decisions derive somehow from the Constitution. On the other hand, it happens that the Constitution is most ill-suited as a basis for substantial judicial policy-making by frequent judicial intervention in the political process in the name of protecting individual rights from majority rule. The central difficulty is that although the Constitution does create some individual rights, they are actually rather few, fairly well-defined, and rarely violated. The first task of the defender of judicial activism, therefore, is to dispose of the Constitution as unhelpful, inadequate, or irrelevant to contemporary needs. Reasons must be found why the Constitution cannot be taken to mean what it rather clearly is known to mean—especially when read, as all writings must be, in historical context—or, even better, to have any determinate meaning at all.

After disposing of the Constitution by depriving it of its historic meaning, the next task of defenders of judicial activism is to imagine a much more expansive, elevated, and abstract constitution that, having no specific meaning, can be made to mean anything and serve therefore as simply a mandate for judges to enact their versions of the public good. In response to the objection that the very thinly veiled system of government by judges thus achieved is obviously inconsistent with democracy, the argument is made that the value of democracy is easily overrated and its dangers many. The "very purpose of a Constitution," as Justice Brennan states the standard argument, is to limit democracy by declaring "certain values transcendent, beyond the reach of temporary political majorities." In any event, no real inconsistency with democracy is involved, the

argument concludes, because the judges, though unrestrained by the actual text of the Constitution, will continue to be restrained by its principles, the adaptation of which to changing circumstances is the true and indispensable function of judges. Justice Brennan's speech can serve as a textbook illustration of each of these moves.

Justice Brennan's attack on the notion of a constitution with a determinable historic meaning could hardly be more thorough. First of all, he finds that the Court's "sources of potential enlightenment" as to the intended meaning are often "sparse or ambiguous." Even more serious, the search for meaning is likely to be futile in any event because even the Framers, he believes, usually did not know what they meant: "Typically, all that can be gleaned is that the Framers themselves did not agree about the application or meaning of particular constitutional provisions, and hid their differences in cloaks of generality." Then there is the question of "whose intention is relevant—that of the drafters, the congressional disputants, or the ratifiers in the states?" Indeed, there is the most basic question of all, whether the very notion of intent makes sense, "whether the idea of an original intention is a coherent way of thinking about a jointly drafted document drawing its authority from a general assent of the states." It is almost as if the Constitution and its various provisions might have been drafted and adopted with no purpose at all. Finally, there is the problem that "our distance of two centuries cannot but work as a prism refracting all we perceive." For all these reasons, the idea that judicial review is legitimate only if faithful to the intent of the Framers can be held only by "persons who have no familiarity with the historical record."

Justice Brennan has still another, although it would seem unnecessary, nail to put in the coffin of the now demolished Constitution. Should any shred of constitutional meaning somehow survive the many obstacles he sees to finding it, he would accord it little or no value. The world of the Framers is "dead and gone," and it would not do, he believes, to hold the Constitution captive to the "anachronistic views of long-gone generations." "[A]ny static meaning" the Constitution "might have had" in that dead world must, therefore, be of dubious relevance today. In any event, "the genius of the Constitution rests," in his view, not in any such meaning but in "the adaptability of its great principles to cope with current problems and current needs," strange as it may seem that a writing can be great apart from its meaning and solely by reason of its supposed ability to mean anything.

Most of Justice Brennan's objections regarding the difficulties of constitutional interpretation have some basis, but they could also be made in regard to interpretation of almost any law. For example, one can almost always wish for a clearer or more detailed legislative history, and it is always true that legislators cannot foresee and agree on every possible application of a law. If these difficulties made the effort to determine legislative intent futile, a system of written law would hardly be possible. In any event, from the premise of an unknowable or irrelevant Constitution, the conclusion should follow that judges have no basis or justification for declaring laws unconstitutional, not that they are therefore free to invalidate laws on some other basis and still claim to be interpreting the Constitution.

Most important, whatever the difficulties of legal interpretation, they have little or no relevance to actual constitutional decision-making by the Supreme Court because no issue of interpretation, no real dispute about the intended meaning of the Constitution, is ordinarily involved. For example, the Constitution contains no provision mentioning or apparently in any way referring to the authority of the states to regulate the practice of abortion.

However one might undertake to defend the Court's abortion decisions, it does not seem possible to argue that they are the result of constitutional interpretation in any non-fanciful sense. As another example, although the Constitution does mention religion, no process that could be called interpretation permits one to go from the Constitution's protection of religious freedom from federal interference to the proposition that the states may not provide for prayer in the schools.

A constitution so devoid of ascertainable meaning or contemporary relevance would seem quite useless as a guide to the solution of any contemporary problem and certainly as a written law enforceable by judges. The judges might as well be told to enforce a document written in an unknown language or, more in keeping with Justice Brennan's view, in disappearing ink. Having effectively eliminated the actual Constitution, however, Justice Brennan proceeds to remedy the loss—judicial activism cannot proceed with no constitution at all—by imagining and substituting a much more impressive, inspiring, and usefully uncertain one.

The constitution of Justice Brennan's vision is undoubtedly a wonderful thing, one of "great" and "overarching" principles and "majestic generalities and ennobling pronouncements [that] are both luminous and obscure." It is nothing less grand than the embodiment of "the aspiration to social justice, brotherhood, and human dignity that brought this nation into being," "a sublime oration on the dignity of man," and "a sparkling vision of the supremacy of the human dignity of every individual." Justice Brennan accurately reflects current constitutional-law scholarship, here as throughout his speech, by seeing the Constitution as simply "the lodestar for our aspirations." It is a source of constant wonderment that scholars and judges of otherwise the most secular and rationalist turn of mind can grow mystical when discussing the Constitution.

The temptation is strong, of course, to dismiss Justice Brennan's rapturous statements as mere flights of poetic fancy or utopian ecstasy, obviously not meant as serious descriptions or explanations of the Constitution. The fact remains, however, that this view of the Constitution is the only justification offered by him, or other contemporary defenders of judicial activism, for the Court's assumption and exercise of enormous government power. Fanciful as it may seem, a constitution that is simply the embodiment of "our," or at least his, aspirations accurately describes the constitution he has been enforcing for nearly three decades to override the will of the people of this country on issue after issue. It cannot be too strongly emphasized, therefore, that the Constitution we actually have bears almost no relation to, and is often clearly irreconcilable with, the constitution of Justice Brennan's vision. No more is necessary to rebut all contemporary defenses of judicial activism than that a copy of the Constitution be kept close at hand to demonstrate that the defenders of judicial activism are invariably relying on something else.

Although it may come as something of a disappointment to some, an "aspiration for social justice, brotherhood, and human dignity" happens not to have been what brought this nation, or at least the government founded on the Constitution, into being. The convention to revise the Articles of Confederation was called and the Constitution was drafted and ratified not to provide additional protections for human rights—on the contrary, the stronger national government created by the Constitution was correctly seen as a potential danger to human rights—but almost entirely for commercial purposes. The primary motivating force for the creation of a stronger national government was the felt need of a central authority to remove state-imposed obstacles to inter-state trade. How little the Constitution had to do with aspirations for brotherhood or human dignity is perhaps most clearly seen in its several provisions regarding slavery. It provides, for example, that a slave was to be counted as three-fifths of a free person for purposes of representation and that slaves escaping to free states were nonetheless to be returned to their masters. It is not, as Justice Brennan would explain this, that part of the "egalitarianism in America has been more pretension than realized fact," but that there was at the time the Constitution was adopted very little pretension to egalitarianism, as is illustrated by, for example, the widespread use of property qualifications for voting.

Given the original Constitution's limited and mundane purposes, it is not surprising that it provides judges with little to work with for the purpose of advancing their personal notions of social justice. The Constitution is, first of all, a very short document—easily printed, with all twenty-six Amendments and repealed matter, on fewer than twenty pages—and apparently quite simple and straightforward, not at all like a recondite tome in which many things may be found with sufficient study. The original Constitution is almost entirely devoted to outlining the structure of the national government and setting forth the sometimes complicated methods of selection, and the responsibilities, of members of the House of Representatives, Senators, the President, and Supreme Court Justices. It contains few provisions protecting individual rights from the national government—federalism, i.e., limited national power and a high degree of local autonomy, was considered the principal protection—and even fewer restrictions on the exercise of state power. As to the national government, criminal trials are to be by jury, treason is narrowly defined, the writ of habeas corpus is protected, and bills of attainder and ex-post-facto laws are prohibited. The prohibition of bills of attainder and ex-post-facto laws is repeated as to the states, which are also prohibited from discriminating against citizens of other states. Finally and by far the most important in terms of actual challenges to state laws, the Framers, nicely illustrating their lack of egalitarian pretension, undertook to protect creditors from debtor-relief legislation by prohibiting the states from impairing contract rights.

The first eight of the first ten Amendments to the Constitution, the Bill of Rights adopted in 1791, provide additional protections of individual rights, but only against the federal government, not the states, and these, too, are fewer than seems to be generally imagined and certainly fewer than is typical of later declarations of rights, such as in the United Nations Charter. In terms of substantive rights, the First Amendment prohibits Congress from establishing or restricting the free exercise of religion—the main purpose of which was to leave matters of religion to the states—and from abridging the freedom of speech, press, or assembly. In addition, a clause of the Fifth Amendment prohibits the taking of private property without just compensation; the Second Amendment, rarely mentioned by rights enthusiasts, grants a right to bear arms; and the Third Amendment, of little apparent contemporary significance, protects against the forced quartering of troops in private homes. The Seventh Amendment, requiring jury trials in civil cases involving more than twenty dollars, is hard to see today as other than an unnecessary inconvenience. The remaining provisions (search and seizure, grand-jury indictment, double jeopardy, privilege against self-incrimination, due process, jury trial, right to counsel and to confront adverse witnesses, and cruel and unusual punishment) are related to criminal procedure.

Additional protections of individual rights are provided by the post–Civil War Amendments. The Thirteenth Amendment prohibits slavery and the Fifteenth

prohibits denial of the right to vote on grounds of race. The great bulk of constitutional litigation concerns state law and nearly all of that litigation purports to be based on a single sentence of the Fourteenth Amendment and, indeed, on one or the other of two pairs of words, "due process" and "equal protection." If the Constitution is the embodiment of our aspirations, it must have become so very largely because of those four words. The clear historic purpose of the Fourteenth Amendment, however, was to provide federal protection against certain state discriminations on the basis of race, historically our uniquely intractable problem, but not otherwise to change fundamentally the constitutional scheme. Finally, the Nineteenth Amendment protects the right to vote from denial on grounds of sex, and the Twenty-sixth from denial on grounds of age for persons over eighteen.

The Constitution's protections of individual rights are not only few but also, when read in historical context, fairly clear and definite. State and federal legislators, all of whom are American citizens living in America and generally at least as devoted as judges to American values, have, therefore, little occasion or desire to violate the Constitution. The result is that the enactment of a clearly unconstitutional law is an extremely rare occurrence; the clearest example in our history perhaps is a 1933 Minnesota debtor-relief statute plainly prohibited by the contract clause, although, as it happens, the Supreme Court upheld it by a five-to-four decision. If judicial review were actually confined to enforcing the Constitution as written, it would be a much less potent force than the judicial review argued for and practiced by Justice Brennan.

The Constitution is undoubtedly a great document, the foundation of one of the freest and most prosperous nations in history. It does not detract from that greatness to point out that it is not, however, what Justice Brennan would make of it, a compendium of majestic generalities and ennobling pronouncements luminous and obscure; indeed, its greatness and durability surely derive in large part from the fact that the Framers' aims were much more specific and limited. Far from intending to compose an oration to human dignity, the Framers would have considered that they had failed in their effort to specify and limit the power of the national government if the effect of the Constitution should be to transfer the focus of human-rights concerns from the state to the national level. The Framers' solution to the problem of protecting human freedom and dignity was to preserve as much as possible, consistent with national commerce and defense requirements, a system of decentralized democratic decision-making, with the regulation of social conditions and personal relations left to the states. Justice Brennan's solution, virtually unlimited Supreme Court power to decide basic social issues for the nation as a whole, effectively disenfranchising the people of each state as to those issues, is directly contrary to the constitutional scheme.

Judicial review on the basis of a constitution divorced from historical meaning and viewed, instead, as simply "the lode-star for our aspirations" is obviously a prescription for policy-making by judges. It should therefore be defended, if at all, as such, free of obfuscating references to "interpretation" of the Constitution. The only real question it presents is, why should the American people prefer to have important social-policy issues decided for the whole nation by the Supreme Court—a committee of nine lawyers unelected to and essentially unremovable from office—rather than by the decentralized democratic process? Justice Brennan's answer to this question is, in essence, why not? The argument that judicial interpretation of the Constitution in accordance with the Framers' intent is essential for "depoliticization of the judiciary," he points out, has its own "political

underpinnings"; it "in effect establishes a presumption of resolving textual ambiguities against the claim of constitutional right," which involves "a choice no less political than any other."

Justice Brennan is certainly correct that the presumption of constitutionality accorded to challenged acts of government officials has a political basis, but it is surprising that he should find "far from clear what justifies such a presumption." What justifies it is the basic premise of democratic government that public-policy issues are ordinarily to be decided through the electoral process, not by unelected judges; that constitutional restrictions on representative government—even if, unlike judge-made restrictions, they were once democratically adopted—are the exception, not the rule. To refuse to assume the validity of the acts of the electorally responsible officials and institutions of government is to refuse to assume the validity of representative self-government. It has, therefore, from the beginning been considered the bedrock of constitutional litigation that one who would have a court invalidate an act of the political branches must assume the burden of showing its inconsistency with the Constitution, ordinarily a most difficult task. By reversing the presumption of constitutionality, Justice Brennan would simply reject political decision-making as the norm and require elected representatives to justify their policy choices to the satisfaction of Supreme Court Justices, presumably by showing that those choices contribute to the Justices' notion of social progress.

Justice Brennan would justify the judicial supremacy he favors on the not entirely consistent grounds that, on the one hand, the Justices are the true voice of the people and, on the other, that the people are in any event not always to be trusted. "When Justices interpret the Constitution," Justice Brennan assures us, "they speak for their community, not for themselves alone" and "with full consciousness that it is, in a very real sense, the community's interpretation that is sought." Apart from the fact that no question of constitutional interpretation is in fact involved in most "constitutional" cases— the judges do not really decide cases by studying the words "due process" or "equal protection"—the community is, of course, fully capable of speaking for itself through the representatives it elects and maintains in office for that purpose. Justice Brennan does not explain why he thinks the community needs or wants unelected judges to speak for it instead or why the judges can be expected better to reflect or express the community's views.

The actual effect of most judicial rulings of unconstitutionality is, of course, not to implement, but to frustrate the community's views. For example, Justice Brennan would disallow capital punishment as constitutionally prohibited despite not only the fact that it is repeatedly provided for in the Constitution, but also the fact that it is favored by a large majority of the American people. In some cases, however, he explains, a Justice may perceive the community's "interpretation of the text to have departed so far from its essential meaning" that he "is bound, by a larger constitutional duty to the community, to expose the departure and point toward a different path." On capital punishment, Justice Brennan hopes to "embody a community striving for human dignity for all, although perhaps not yet arrived." Interpreting an aspirational constitution apparently requires prescience as well as a high degree of self-confidence.

The foundation of all defenses of judicial activism, however, is not any fanciful notion that the judges are the true voice of the people, but on the contrary, the conviction that the people, and their elected representatives, should not be permitted to have the last word. Rarely has this conviction, common among our intellectual elite, been expressed with more certainty than in Justice Brennan's speech. Judicial acceptance of the "predominant contemporary authority of the elected branches of government" must be rejected, he argues, for the same reason he rejects judicial acceptance of the "transcendent historical authority of the Framers." That reason, it now appears, is not so much that original intent is unknowable or irrelevant as that its acceptance as authoritative would be inconsistent with his notion of "proper judicial interpretation" of the Constitution because it would leave judges with too little to do. "Faith in the majoritarian process," like fidelity to original intent, is objectionable, he is frank to admit, simply because it "counsels restraint." It would, he points out, lead the Court generally to "stay its hand" where "invalidation of a legislature's substantive policy choice" is involved. Justice Brennan's confidence that his university audience shared his suspicion of democracy and distrust of his fellow citizens was such as to put beyond need of argument the unacceptability of a counsel of restraint by Supreme Court Justices in deciding basic issues of social policy.

Legislative supremacy in policy-making is derided by Justice Brennan as the "unabashed enshrinement of majority will." "Faith in democracy is one thing," he warns, but "blind faith quite another." "The view that all matters of substantive policy should be resolved through the majoritarian process has appeal," he concedes, but only "under some circumstances," and even as so qualified "it ultimately will not do." It will not do because the majority is simply not to be trusted: to accept the mere approval of "a majority of the legislative body, fairly elected," as dispositive of public-policy issues would be to "permit the imposition of a social-caste system or wholesale confiscation of property," a situation "our Constitution could not abide." How a people so bereft of good sense, toleration, and foresight as to adopt such policies could have adopted the Constitution in the first place is not explained. Justice Brennan seems to forget that if the Constitution prohibits such things—indeed, if it is an oration to human dignity, as he maintains—it must be because the American people have made it so and therefore, it would seem, can be trusted. It cannot be Justice Brennan's position that political wisdom died with the Framers and that we are therefore fortunate to have their policy judgments to restrain us; he rejects those judgments as unknowable or irrelevant. Like other defenders of judicial activism, however, he seems to view the Constitution not as an actual document produced by actual people but as a metaphysical entity from an extraterrestrial source of greater authority than the mere wishes of a majority of the American people, which source, fortunately, is in effective communication with Supreme Court Justices.

The social-caste system feared by Justice Brennan would probably be prohibited by the post-Civil War Amendments, without undue stretching, and confiscation of property by the national government—though not by the states—would be prohibited by the just-compensation clause of the Fifth Amendment. (These constitutional provisions, it may be noted in passing, would operate as impediments to such policies, providing grounds for opposing arguments, even if they were not judicially enforceable.) The real protection against such fears, however—and columnist Anthony Lewis's similar fear that without activist judicial review Oregon might establish the Reverend Sun Myung Moon's Unification Church as the official state religion—is simply the good sense of the American people. No extraordinary degree of confidence in that good sense is necessary in order to believe that these and similarly outrageous policies that are invariably offered as providing an unanswerable justification for judicial activism are so unlikely to be adopted as

not to be a matter of serious concern. If they should be a matter of concern nonetheless—if, for example, it is truly feared that the people of some state might establish a church and believed that no state should be free to do so—the appropriate response would be the adoption of a constitutional amendment further limiting self-government in the relevant respects. To grant judges an unlimited power to rewrite the Constitution, Justice Brennan's recommended response, would be to avoid largely imaginary dangers of democratic misgovernment by creating a certainty of judicial misgovernment.

Judicial activism is not necessary to protect us from state-established churches, favored by almost no one, but it does operate to deprive the people of each state of the right to decide for themselves such real issues as whether provision should be made for prayer in the public schools. In any event, the issue presented by contemporary judicial activism is not whether majority rule is entirely trustworthy—all government power is obviously dangerous—or even whether certain specific constitutional limitations on majority rule might not be justifiable; the issue is whether freewheeling policy-making by Supreme Court Justices, totally centralized and undemocratic, is more trustworthy than majority rule.

Defenders of judicial activism invariably match their skepticism about democratic policy-making with a firm belief in the possibility and desirability of policy-making on the basis of principle. To free judicial review from the constraint of a constitution with a determinate meaning is not to permit unrestrained judicial policy-making in constitutional cases, it is argued, for the judges will continue to be constrained by the Constitution's principles, which, like the smile of the Cheshire cat, somehow survive the disappearance of the Constitution's text. According to this argument, judicial activism amounts to nothing more than the adaptation and application of these basic principles to changing circumstances, a necessary task if the Constitution is to remain a "living document" and a contributor rather than an obstacle to the national welfare. Thus, judicial activism is necessary in Justice Brennan's view, as already noted, if we are not to "turn a blind eye to social progress and eschew adaptation of overarching principles to changes of social circumstance" and because the genius of the Constitution rests not in what, if anything, the Framers actually intended to provide, but in the "adaptability of its great principles to cope with current problems and current needs."

The argument that judges are constrained by constitutional principles, even though not by the constitutional text, bears no relation to reality. In the first place, it is not possible to formulate useful constitutional principles apart from or beyond the Constitution's actual provisions. The Constitution protects certain interests to a certain extent, from which fact the only principle to be derived is that the Constitution does just that. An even more basic fallacy is the argument's assumption that the solution of social problems lies in the discovery, adaptation, and application of pre-existing principles to new situations. Difficult problems of social choice arise, however, not because of some failure to discern or adapt an applicable principle, but only because we have many principles, many interests we regard as legitimate, and they inevitably come into conflict. Some interests have to be sacrificed or compromised if other interests are to be protected—for example, public demonstrations will have to be regulated at some point in the interest of maintaining public order—and there is no authoritatively established principle, rule, or generality that resolves the conflict. If there were

such a principle, the conflict would not present a serious problem, but would be a matter that has already been decided or that anyone can decide who can read and reason. Value judgments have to be made to solve real policy issues, and the meaning of self-government is that they are to be made in accordance with the collective judgment of those who will have to live with the results.

There is also very little basis for Justice Brennan's apparent belief that judicial review confined to the Constitution as written would somehow be incompatible with social progress—unless social progress is simply defined as the enactment of his views. The Constitution does contain several provisions that we would probably be better off without, for example, the Seventh Amendment's requirement of a jury trial in federal civil cases involving more than twenty dollars and the Twenty-second Amendment's limitation of Presidents to two terms. Apart from the fact, however, that the Constitution, of course, provides procedures for its amendment—it can be updated if necessary without the Court's help—judicial activism has not generally served to alleviate the undesirable effects of such provisions. In any event, the Constitution's restrictions on self-government are, as already noted, relatively few and rarely such as a legislature might seek to avoid. Rarely if ever will adaptation of the Constitution's overarching principles, if any, be necessary in order to permit a legislature to implement its views of social progress.

Indeed, on the basis of our actual constitutional history—which includes the Supreme Court's disastrous decision that Congress could not prohibit the extension of slavery and, after the Civil War that decision helped bring on, the decision that Congress could not prohibit racial segregation in public places—it is possible to believe that social progress might go more smoothly without the Court's supposed adaptations of principles. If the Constitution can be said to have an overarching principle, the principle of federalism, of decision-making on most social-policy issues at the state level, is surely the best candidate, and that principle is not adapted or updated but violated by the Court's assertion of power to decide such issues. Far from keeping the Constitution a "living document," judicial activism threatens its demise.

Whatever merit Justice Brennan's justifications for judicial activism might have in theory, they do not seem relevant to the judicial activism actually practiced by the Supreme Court for the past three decades. It would be very difficult to justify the Court's major constitutional decisions during this period, and particularly its most controversial decisions, on any of the grounds Justice Brennan suggests. It would not seem possible to argue, for example, that the Justices spoke for the community, not for themselves, in reaching their decisions on abortion, busing, criminal procedure, and prayer in the schools. Nor does it seem that any of those decisions can be justified as providing a needed protection from a possible excess of democracy, as merely delaying effectuation of the aberrational enthusiasms of "temporary political majorities" until they could return to their senses. Judicial review may, as Chief Justice Harlan Fiske Stone put this standard rationalization, provide the people with an opportunity for a "sober second thought," but no amount of thought or experience is likely to change the view of the vast majority of the American people that, for example, their children should not be excluded from their neighborhood public schools because of their race or that no new protections of the criminally accused should be invented with the effect of preventing the conviction and punishment of the clearly guilty.

Finally, the contribution of most of the Court's constitutional decisions of recent decades to social progress—for example, its decision that California may not prohibit the parading of vulgarity in its courthouses or that Oklahoma may not impose a higher minimum drinking age on men than on women—is at best debatable. Very few of these decisions, it seems, could be used to illustrate the adaptation of overarching constitutional principles or transcendent constitutional values to changing circumstances. They could probably more easily be used to illustrate that, rather than helping us to cope with current problems and current needs, the Court's constitutional decisions have often been the cause of those problems and needs.

Whatever the merits of the Supreme Court's constitutional decisions of the past three decades, they have as to the issues decided deprived us of perhaps the most essential element of the human dignity Justice Brennan is concerned to protect, the right of self-government, which necessarily includes the right to make what others might consider mistakes. It is not the critics of judicial activism but the activist judges who can more properly be charged with being doctrinaire and arrogant, for it is they who presume to know the answers to difficult questions of social policy and to believe that they provide a needed protection from government by the misguided or ignorant. An opponent of judicial activism need not claim to know the answer to so difficult a question of social policy as, say, the extent, if any, to which abortion should be restricted to know that it is shameful in a supposedly democratic country that such a question should be answered for all of us by unelected and unaccountable government officials who have no special competence to do so.

QUESTIONS FOR DISCUSSION

1. A written Bill of Rights imposes limits on what the elected representatives of the people can do. Is this democratic?
2. How does a written Bill of Rights enable the judiciary to protect the basic values of American society?
3. Is the Bill of Rights too vague?
4. Who is the more reliable defender of freedom—the Congress or the Supreme Court? Why?
5. Can the people (i.e., the *majority*) always be trusted to protect individual freedom?
6. Are there certain rights that are so fundamental that democracy could not exist without them?

RECOMMENDED READINGS

ABRAHAM, HENRY J. *Freedom and the Court: Civil Rights and Liberties in the United States.* 4th ed. New York: Oxford University Press, 1982.

BARKER, LUCIUS J., and TWILEY W. BARKER. *Civil Liberties and the Constitution: Cases and Commentaries.* 5th ed. Englewood Cliffs, N.J.: Prentice-Hall, 1986.

BRANT, IRVING. *The Bill of Rights.* Indianapolis: Bobbs-Merrill, 1965.

CORWIN, EDWARD S. *The Constitution and What It Means Today.* 14th ed. Revised by Harold W. Chase and Craig R. Ducat. Princeton: Princeton University Press, 1978.

ELY, JOHN HART. *Democracy and Distrust: A Theory of Judicial Review.* Cambridge: Harvard University Press, 1980.

GOLDWIN, ROBERT A., and WILLIAM A. SCHAMBRA, eds. *How Does the Constitution Secure Rights?* Washington, D.C.: American Enterprise Institute, 1985.

HALPERN, STEPHEN C., ed. *The Future of Our Liberties: Perspectives on the Bill of Rights.* Westport, Conn.: Greenwood Press, 1982.

HAND, LEARNED. *The Bill of Rights.* Cambridge: Harvard University Press, 1958.

PRITCHETT, C. HERMAN. *Constitutional Civil Liberties.* Englewood Cliffs, N.J.: Prentice-Hall, 1984.

RUTLAND, ROBERT A. *The Birth of the Bill of Rights, 1776–91.* New York: Collier, 1962.

SCHWARTZ, BERNARD. *The Great Rights of Mankind: A History of the American Bill of Rights.* New York: Oxford University Press, 1977.

2 *Is freedom of speech absolute?*

YES THE BILL OF RIGHTS

Justice Hugo L. Black

I am honored to be the first speaker in your new annual series of James Madison lectures.* The title of the series suggested the title of my talk: The Bill of Rights. Madison lived in the stirring times between 1750 and 1836, during which the Colonies declared, fought for, and won their independence from England. They then set up a new national government dedicated to Liberty and Justice. Madison's role in creating that government was such a major one that he has since been generally referred to as the Father of our Constitution. He was a most influential member of the Philadelphia Convention that submitted the Constitution to the people of the states; he alone kept a comprehensive report of the daily proceedings of the Convention; he was an active member of the Virginia Convention that adopted the Constitution after a bitter fight; finally, as a member of the First Congress, he offered and sponsored through that body proposals that became the first ten amendments, generally thought of as our Bill of Rights. For these and many other reasons, Madison's words are an authentic source to help us understand the Constitution and its Bill of Rights. In the course of my discussion I shall have occasion to refer to some of the many things Madison said about the meaning of the Constitution and the first ten amendments. In doing so, I shall refer to statements made by him dur-

ing the Bill of Rights debates as reported in the *Annals of Congress*. There has been doubt cast upon the accuracy of the reports of Congressional debates and transactions in the *Annals*. I am assured by Mr. Irving Brant, the eminent biographer of Madison, that Madison's discussions of the Bill of Rights as reported in the *Annals* are shown to be correct by Madison's own manuscripts on file in the Library of Congress.[1]

What is a bill of rights? In the popular sense it is any document setting forth the liberties of the people. I prefer to think of our Bill of Rights as including all provisions of the original Constitution and Amendments that protect individual liberty by barring government from acting in a particular area or from acting except under certain prescribed procedures. I have in mind such clauses in the body of the Constitution itself as those which safeguard the right of habeas corpus, forbid bills of attainder and ex post facto laws, guarantee trial by jury, and strictly define treason and limit the way it can be tried and punished. I would certainly add to this list the last constitutional prohibition in Article Six that "no religious Test shall ever be required as a Qualification to any Office or public Trust under the United States."

I shall speak to you about the Bill of Rights only as it bears on powers of the Federal Government. Originally, the first ten amendments were not intended to apply to the states but, as the Supreme

Justice Hugo L. Black, "The Bill of Rights," *New York University Law Review* 3 (Apr. 1960), pp. 865–81.

* This article was delivered as the first James Madison Lecture at the New York University School of Law on February 17, 1960.

[1] See also Brant, The Madison Heritage, 35 N.Y.U.L. Rev. 882 (1960).

Court held in 1833 in *Barron v. Baltimore*,[2] were adopted to quiet fears extensively entertained that the powers of the big new national government "might be exercised in a manner dangerous to liberty." I believe that by virtue of the Fourteenth Amendment, the first ten amendments are now applicable to the states, a view I stated in *Adamson v. California*.[3] I adhere to that view. In this talk, however, I want to discuss only the extent to which the Bill of Rights limits the Federal Government.

In applying the Bill of Rights to the Federal Government there is today a sharp difference of views as to how far its provisions should be held to limit the lawmaking power of Congress. How this difference is finally resolved will, in my judgment, have far-reaching consequences upon our liberties. I shall first summarize what those different views are.

Some people regard the prohibitions of the Constitution, even its most unequivocal commands, as mere admonitions which Congress need not always observe. This viewpoint finds many different verbal expressions. For example, it is sometimes said that Congress may abridge a constitutional right if there is a clear and present danger that the free exercise of the right will bring about a substantive evil that Congress has authority to prevent. Or it is said that a right may be abridged where its exercise would cause so much injury to the public that this injury would outweigh the injury to the individual who is deprived of the right. Again, it is sometimes said that the Bill of Rights' guarantees must "compete" for survival against general powers expressly granted to Congress and that the individual's right must, if outweighed by the public interest, be subordinated to the Government's competing interest in denying the right. All of these formulations, and more with which you are doubtless familiar, rest, at least in part, on the premise that there are no "absolute" prohibi-

tions in the Constitution, and that all constitutional problems are questions of reasonableness, proximity, and degree. This view comes close to the English doctrine of legislative omnipotence, qualified only by the possibility of a judicial veto if the Supreme Court finds that a congressional choice between "competing" policies has no reasonable basis.

I cannot accept this approach to the Bill of Rights. It is my belief that there *are* "absolutes" in our Bill of Rights, and that they were put there on purpose by men who knew what words meant, and meant their prohibitions to be "absolutes." The whole history and background of the Constitution and Bill of Rights, as I understand, belies the assumption or conclusion that our ultimate constitutional freedoms are no more than our English ancestors had when they came to this new land to get new freedoms. The historical and practical purposes of a Bill of Rights, the very use of a written constitution, indigenous to America, the language the Framers used, the kind of three-department government they took pains to set up, all point to the creation of a government which was denied all power to do some things under any and all circumstances, and all power to do other things except precisely in the manner prescribed. In this talk I will state some of the reasons why I hold this view. In doing so, however, I shall not attempt to discuss the wholly different and complex problem of the marginal scope of each individual amendment as applied to the particular facts of particular cases. For example, there is a question as to whether the First Amendment was intended to protect speech that courts find "obscene." I shall not stress this or similar differences of construction, nor shall I add anything to the views I expressed in the recent case of *Smith v. California*.[4] I am primarily discussing here whether liberties *admittedly* covered by the Bill of Rights can nevertheless be abridged on the ground that a superior

---

[2] 32 U.S. (7 Pet.) 242, 249 (1833).

[3] 332 U.S. 46, 71–72 (1947) (dissenting opinion).

[4] 361 U.S. 147, 155 (1959) (concurring opinion).

public interest justifies the abridgment. I think the Bill of Rights made its safeguards superior.

Today most Americans seem to have forgotten the ancient evils which forced their ancestors to flee to this new country and to form a government stripped of old powers used to oppress them. But the Americans who supported the Revolution and the adoption of our Constitution knew firsthand the dangers of tyrannical governments. They were familiar with the long existing practice of English persecutions of people wholly because of their religious or political beliefs. They knew that many accused of such offenses had stood, helpless to defend themselves, before biased legislators and judges.

John Lilburne, a Puritan dissenter, is a conspicuous example.[5] He found out the hard way that a citizen of England could not get a court and jury trial under English law if Parliament wanted to try and punish him in some kind of summary and unfair method of its own. Time and time again, when his religious or political activities resulted in criminal charges against him, he had demanded jury trials under the "law of the land" but had been refused. Due to "trials" either by Parliament, its legislative committees, or courts subservient to the King or to Parliament, against all of which he vigorously protested as contrary to "due process" or "the law of the land," Lilburne had been whipped, put in the pillory, sent to prison, heavily fined and banished from England, all its islands and dominions, under penalty of death should he return. This last sentence was imposed by a simple Act of Parliament without any semblance of a trial. Upon his defiant return he was arrested and subjected to an unfair trial for his life. His chief defense was that the Parliamentary conviction was a nullity, as a denial of "due process of law," which he claimed was guaranteed under Magna Charta, the 1628 Petition of Right, and statutes passed to carry them out. He also challenged the power of Parliament to enact bills of attainder on the same grounds—due process of law. Lilburne repeatedly and vehemently contended that he was entitled to notice, an indictment, and court trial by jury under the known laws of England; that he had a right to be represented by counsel; that he had a right to have witnesses summoned in his behalf and be confronted by the witnesses against him; that he could not be compelled to testify against himself. When Lilburne finally secured a jury, it courageously acquitted him, after which the jury itself was severely punished by the court.

Prompted largely by the desire to save Englishmen from such legislative mockeries of fair trials, Lilburne and others strongly advocated adoption of an "Agreement of the People" which contained most of the provisions of our present Bill of Rights. That Agreement would have done away with Parliamentary omnipotence. Lilburne pointed out that the basic defect of Magna Charta and statutes complementing it was that they were not binding on Parliament since "that which is done by one Parliament, as a Parliament, may be undone by the next Parliament: but an Agreement of the People begun and ended amongst the People can never come justly within the Parliament's cognizance to destroy."[6] The proposed "Agreement of the People," Lilburne argued, could be changed only by the people and would bind Parliament as the supreme "law of the land." This same idea was picked up before the adoption of our Federal Constitution by Massachusetts and New Hampshire, which adopted their constitutions only after popular referendums. Our Federal Constitution is largely attributable to the same current of thinking.

Unfortunately, our own colonial history also provided ample reasons for people to be afraid to vest too much power in the

---

[5] See The Trial of John Lilburne and John Wharton (Star Chamber 1637) in 3 How. St. Tr. 1315 (1816).

[6] Leveller Manifestoes of the Puritan Revolution 423 (Wolfe ed. 1944).

national government. There had been bills of attainder here; women had been convicted and sentenced to death as "witches"; Quakers, Baptists and various Protestant sects had been persecuted from time to time. Roger Williams left Massachusetts to breathe the free air of new Rhode Island. Catholics were barred from holding office in many places. Test oaths were required in some of the colonies to bar any but Christians from holding office. In New England Quakers suffered death for their faith. Baptists were sent to jail in Virginia for preaching, which caused Madison, while a very young man, to deplore what he called that "diabolical hell-conceived principle of persecution."[7]

In the light of history, therefore, it is not surprising that when our Constitution was adopted without specific provisions to safeguard cherished individual rights from invasion by the legislative, as well as the executive and judicial departments of the National Government, a loud and irresistible clamor went up throughout the country. These protests were so strong that the Constitution was ratified by the very narrowest of votes in some of the states. It has been said, and I think correctly, that had there been no general agreement that a supplementary Bill of Rights would be adopted as soon as possible after Congress met, the Constitution would not have been ratified. It seems clear that this widespread demand for a Bill of Rights was due to a common fear of political and religious persecution should the national legislative power be left unrestrained as it was in England.

The form of government which was ordained and established in 1789 contains certain unique features which reflected the Framers' fear of arbitrary government and which clearly indicate an intention absolutely to limit what Congress could do. The first of these features is that our Constitution is written in a single document. Such constitutions are familiar today and it is not always remembered that our country was the first to have one. Certainly one purpose of a written constitution is to define and therefore more specifically limit government powers. An all-powerful government that can act as it pleases wants no such constitution—unless to fool the people. England had no written constitution and this once proved a source of tyranny, as our ancestors well knew. Jefferson said about this departure from the English type of government: "Our peculiar security is in the possession of a written Constitution. Let us not make it a blank paper by construction."[8]

A second unique feature of our Government is a Constitution supreme over the legislature. In England, statutes, Magna Charta and later declarations of rights had for centuries limited the power of the King, but they did not limit the power of Parliament. Although commonly referred to as a constitution, they were never the "supreme law of the land" in the way in which our Constitution is, much to the regret of statesmen like Pitt the elder. Parliament could change this English "Constitution"; Congress cannot change ours. Ours can only be changed by amendments ratified by three-fourths of the states. It was one of the great achievements of our Constitution that it ended legislative omnipotence here and placed all departments and agencies of government under one supreme law.

A third feature of our Government expressly designed to limit its powers was the division of authority into three coordinate branches, none of which was to have supremacy over the others. This separation of powers with the checks and balances which each branch was given over the others was designed to prevent any branch, including the legislative, from infringing individual liberties safeguarded by the Constitution.

Finally, our Constitution was the first to

---

[7] 1 Rives, History of the Life and Times of James Madison 44 (1859).

[8] 4 Jefferson, Writings 506 (Washington ed. 1859).

provide a really independent judiciary. Moreover, as the Supreme Court held in *Marbury v. Madison*,[9] correctly I believe, this judiciary has the power to hold legislative enactments void that are repugnant to the Constitution and the Bill of Rights. In this country the judiciary was made independent because it has, I believe, the primary responsibility and duty of giving force and effect to constitutional liberties and limitations upon the executive and legislative branches. Judges in England were not always independent and they could not hold Parliamentary acts void. Consequently, English courts could not be counted on to protect the liberties of the people against invasion by the Parliament, as many unfortunate Englishmen found out, such as Sir Walter Raleigh, who was executed as the result of an unfair trial, and a lawyer named William Prynne, whose ears were first cut off by court order and who subsequently, by another court order, had his remaining ear stumps gouged out while he was on a pillory. Prynne's offenses were writing books and pamphlets.

All of the unique features of our Constitution show an underlying purpose to create a new kind of limited government. Central to all of the Framers of the Bill of Rights was the idea that since government, particularly the national government newly created, is a powerful institution, its officials—all of them—must be compelled to exercise their powers within strictly defined boundaries. As Madison told Congress, the Bill of Rights' limitations point "sometimes against the abuse of the Executive power, sometimes against the Legislative, and in some cases against the community itself; or, in other words, against the majority in favor of the minority."[10] Madison also explained that his proposed amendments were intended "to limit and qualify the powers of Government, by excepting out of the grant of power those cases in which the Government ought not to act, or to act only in a particular mode."[11] In the light of this purpose let us now turn to the language of the first ten amendments to consider whether their provisions were written as mere admonitions to Congress or as absolute commands, proceeding for convenience from the last to the first.

The last two Amendments, the Ninth and Tenth, are general in character, but both emphasize the limited nature of the Federal Government. Number Ten restricts federal power to what the Constitution delegates to the central government, reserving all other powers to the states or to the people. Number Nine attempts to make certain that enumeration of some rights must "not be construed to deny or disparage others retained by the people." The use of the words, "the people," in both these Amendments strongly emphasizes the desire of the Framers to protect individual liberty.

The Seventh Amendment states that "In Suits at common law, where the value in controversy shall exceed twenty dollars, the right of trial by jury shall be preserved. . . . " This language clearly requires that jury trials must be afforded in the type of cases the Amendment describes. The Amendment goes on in equally unequivocal words to command that "no fact tried by a jury, shall be otherwise re-examined in any Court of the United States, than according to the rules of the common law."

Amendments Five, Six, and Eight relate chiefly to the procedures that government must follow when bringing its powers to bear against any person with a view to depriving him of his life, liberty, or property.

The Eighth Amendment forbids "excessive bail," "excessive fines," or the infliction of "cruel or unusual punishments." This is

---

[9] 5 U.S. (1 Cranch) 137 (1803).
[10] 1 Annals of Cong. 437 (1789).
[11] Ibid.

one of the less precise provisions. The courts are required to determine the meaning of such general terms as "excessive" and "unusual." But surely that does not mean that admittedly "excessive bail," "excessive fines," or "cruel punishments" could be justified on the ground of a "competing" public interest in carrying out some generally granted power like that given Congress to regulate commerce.

Amendment Six provides that in a criminal prosecution an accused shall have a "speedy and public trial, by an impartial jury of the State and district wherein the crime shall have been committed, which district shall have been previously ascertained by law, and to be informed of the nature and cause of the accusation; to be confronted with the witnesses against him; to have compulsory process for obtaining witnesses in his favor, and have the Assistance of Counsel for his defence." All of these requirements are cast in terms both definite and absolute. Trial by jury was also guaranteed in the original Constitution. The additions here, doubtless prompted by English trials of Americans away from their homes, are that a trial must be "speedy and public," "by an impartial jury," and in a district which "shall have been previously ascertained by law." If there is any one thing that is certain it is that the Framers intended both in the original Constitution and in the Sixth Amendment that persons charged with crime by the Federal Government have a right to be tried by jury. Suppose juries began acquitting people Congress thought should be convicted. Could Congress then provide some other form of trial, say by an administrative agency, or the military, where convictions could be more readily and certainly obtained, if it thought the safety of the nation so required? How about secret trials? By *partial* juries? Can it be that these are not absolute prohibitions?

The Sixth Amendment requires notice of the cause of an accusation, confrontation by witnesses, compulsory process and

assistance of counsel. The experience of centuries has demonstrated the value of these procedures to one on trial for crime. And this Amendment purports to guarantee them by clear language. But if there are no absolutes in the Bill of Rights, these guarantees too can be taken away by Congress on findings that a competing public interest requires that defendants be tried without notice, without witnesses, without confrontation, and without counsel.

The Fifth Amendment provides:

> No person shall be held to answer for a capital, or otherwise infamous crime, unless on a presentment or indictment of a Grand Jury, except in cases arising in the land or naval forces, or in the Militia, when in actual service in time of War or public danger; nor shall any person be subject for the same offence to be twice put in jeopardy of life or limb; nor shall be compelled in any criminal case to be a witness against himself, nor be deprived of life, liberty, or property, without due process of law; nor shall private property be taken for public use, without just compensation.

Most of these Fifth Amendment prohibitions are both definite and unequivocal. There has been much controversy about the meaning of "due process of law." Whatever its meaning, however, there can be no doubt that it must be granted. Moreover, few doubt that it has an historical meaning which denies Government the right to take away life, liberty, or property without trials properly conducted according to the Constitution and laws validly made in accordance with it. This, at least, was the meaning of "due process of law" when used in Magna Charta and other old English Statutes where it was referred to as "the law of the land."

The Fourth Amendment provides:

> The right of the people to be secure in their persons, houses, papers, and effects, against unreasonable searches and seizures,

shall not be violated, and no Warrants shall issue, but upon probable cause, supported by Oath or affirmation, and particularly describing the place to be searched, and the persons or things to be seized.

The use of the word "unreasonable" in this Amendment means, of course, that not *all* searches and seizures are prohibited. Only those which are *unreasonable* are unlawful. There may be much difference of opinion about whether a particular search or seizure is unreasonable and therefore forbidden by this Amendment. But if it *is* unreasonable, it is absolutely prohibited.

Likewise, the provision which forbids warrants for arrest, search or seizure without "probable cause" is itself an absolute prohibition.

The Third Amendment provides that:

> No Soldier shall, in time of peace be quartered in any house, without the consent of the Owner, nor in time of war, but in a manner to be prescribed by law.

Americans had recently suffered from the quartering of British troops in their homes, and so this Amendment is written in language that apparently no one has ever thought could be violated on the basis of an overweighing public interest.

Amendment Two provides that:

> A well regulated Militia, being necessary to the security of a free State, the right of the people to keep and bear Arms, shall not be infringed.

Although the Supreme Court has held this Amendment to include only arms necessary to a well-regulated militia, as so construed, its prohibition is absolute.

This brings us to the First Amendment. It reads:

> Congress shall make no law respecting an establishment of religion, or prohibiting the free exercise thereof; or abridging the free-

dom of speech, or of the press; or the right of the people peaceably to assemble, and to petition the Government for a redress of grievances.

The phrase "Congress shall make no law" is composed of plain words, easily understood. The Framers knew this. The language used by Madison in his proposal was different, but no less emphatic and unequivocal. That proposal is worth reading:

> The civil rights of none shall be abridged on account of religious belief or worship, nor shall any national religion be established, nor shall the full and equal rights of conscience be in any manner, or on any pretext, infringed.
>
> The people shall not be deprived or abridged of their right to speak, to write, or to publish their sentiments; and the freedom of the press, as one of the great bulwarks of liberty, shall be inviolable.
>
> The people shall not be restrained from peaceably assembling and consulting for their common good; nor from applying to the Legislature by petitions, or remonstrances, for redress of their grievances.[12]

Neither as offered nor as adopted is the language of this Amendment anything less than absolute. Madison was emphatic about this. He told the Congress that under it "The right of freedom of speech is secured; the liberty of the press is **expressly declared to be** *beyond the reach of this Government. . . .*"[13] (Emphasis added in all quotations.) Some years later Madison wrote that "it would seem scarcely possible to doubt that *no power whatever* over the press was supposed to be delegated by the Constitution, as it originally stood, and that the amendment was intended as a *positive and absolute reservation of it.*"[14] With reference to the positive nature of the First

[12] 1 Annals of Cong. 434 (1789).

[13] 1 Annals of Cong. 738 (1789).

[14] 6 Madison, Writings 391 (Hunt ed. 1906).

Amendment's command against infringement of religious liberty, Madison later said that "there is not a shadow of right in the general government to intermeddle with religion,"[15] and that "this subject is, for the honor of America, perfectly free and unshackled. The *government has no jurisdiction over it.*"[16]

To my way of thinking, at least, the history and language of the Constitution and the Bill of Rights, which I have discussed with you, make it plain that one of the primary purposes of the Constitution with its amendments was to withdraw from the Government all power to act in certain areas—whatever the scope of those areas may be. If I am right in this then there is, at least in those areas, no justification whatever for "balancing" a particular right against some expressly granted power of Congress. If the Constitution withdraws from Government all power over subject matter in an area, such as religion, speech, press, assembly, and petition, there is nothing over which authority may be exerted.

The Framers were well aware that the individual rights they sought to protect might be easily nullified if subordinated to the general powers granted to Congress. One of the reasons for adoption of the Bill of Rights was to prevent just that. Specifically the people feared that the "necessary and proper" clause could be used to project the generally granted Congressional powers into the protected areas of individual rights. One need only read the debates in the various states to find out that this is true. But if these debates leave any doubt, Mr. Madison's words to Congress should remove it. In speaking of the "necessary and proper" clause and its possible effect on freedom of religion he said, as reported in the *Annals of Congress:*

> Whether the words are necessary or not, he did not mean to say, but they had been required by some of the State Conventions, who seemed to entertain an opinion that under the clause of the Constitution, which gave power to Congress to make all laws *necessary and proper* to carry into execution the Constitution, and the laws made under it, enabled them to make laws of such a nature as might infringe the rights of conscience, and establish a national religion; to prevent these effects he presumed the amendment was intended, and he thought it as well expressed as the nature of the language would admit.[17]

It seems obvious to me that Congress, in exercising its general powers, is expressly forbidden to use means prohibited by the Bill of Rights. Whatever else the phrase "necessary and proper" may mean, it must be that Congress may only adopt such means to carry out its powers as are "proper," that is, not specifically prohibited.

It has also been argued that since freedom of speech, press, and religion in England were narrow freedoms at best, and since there were many English laws infringing those freedoms, our First Amendment should not be thought to bar similar infringements by Congress. Again one needs only to look to the debates in Congress over the First Amendment to find that the First Amendment cannot be treated as a mere codification of English law. Mr. Madison made a clear explanation to Congress that it was the purpose of the First Amendment to grant greater protection than England afforded its citizens. He said:

> In the declaration of rights which that country has established, the truth is, they have gone no farther than to raise a barrier against the power of the Crown; the power of the Legislature is left altogether indefinite. Although I know whenever the great rights, the trial by jury, freedom of the press, or liberty of conscience, come in question in that body, the invasion of them is resisted by

[15] 5 Madison, Writings 176 (Hunt ed. 1904).

[16] Id. at 132.

[17] 1 Annals of Cong. 730 (1789). (Emphasis added.)

able advocates, yet their Magna Charta does not contain any one provision for the security of those rights, respecting which the people of America are most alarmed. The freedom of the press and rights of conscience, those choicest privileges of the people, are unguarded in the British Constitution.

But although the case may be widely different, and it may not be thought necessary to provide limits for the legislative power in that country, yet a different opinion prevails in the United States.[18]

It was the desire to give the people of America greater protection against the powerful Federal Government than the English had had against their government that caused the Framers to put these freedoms of expression, again in the words of Madison, "beyond the reach of this Government."

When closely analyzed the idea that there can be no "absolute" constitutional guarantees in the Bill of Rights is frightening to contemplate even as to individual safeguards in the original Constitution. Take, for instance, the last clause in Article Six that "no religious Test shall ever be required" for a person to hold office in the United States. Suppose Congress should find that some religious sect was dangerous because of its foreign affiliations. Such was the belief on which English test oaths rested for a long time and some of the states had test oaths on that assumption at the time, and after, our Constitution was adopted in 1789. Could Congress, or the Supreme Court, or both, put this precious privilege to be free from test oaths on scales, find it outweighed by some other public interest, and therefore make United States officials and employees swear they did not and never had belonged to or associated with a particular religious group suspected of disloyalty? Can Congress, in the name of overbalancing necessity, suspend habeas corpus in

peacetime? Are there circumstances under which Congress could, after nothing more than a legislative bill of attainder, take away a man's life, liberty, or property? Hostility of the Framers toward bills of attainder was so great that they took the unusual step of barring such legislative punishments by the States as well as the Federal Government. They wanted to remove any possibility of such proceedings anywhere in this country. This is not strange in view of the fact that they were much closer than we are to the great Act of Attainder by the Irish Parliament, in 1688, which condemned between two and three thousand men, women, and children to exile or death without anything that even resembled a trial.[19]

Perhaps I can show you the consequences of the balancing approach to the Bill of Rights liberties by a practical demonstration of how it might work. The last clause of the Fifth Amendment is: "nor shall private property be taken for public use, without just compensation." On its face this command looks absolute, but if one believes that it should be weighed against the powers granted to Congress, there might be some circumstances in which this right would have to give way, just as there are some circumstances in which it is said the right of freedom of religion, speech, press, assembly and petition can be balanced away. Let us see how the balancing concept would apply to the just compensation provision of the Bill of Rights in the following wholly imaginary judicial opinion of Judge X:

"This case presents an important question of constitutional law. The United States is engaged in a stupendous national defense undertaking which requires the acquisition of much valuable land throughout the country. The plaintiff here owns 500 acres of land. The location of the land gives it a pecu-

[18] 1 Annals of Cong. 436 (1789).

[19] See Joint Anti-Fascist Refugee Comm. v. McGrath, 341 U.S. 123, 146–49 (1951) (appendix to concurring opinion of Black, J.).

liarly strategic value for carrying out the defense program. Due to the great national emergency that exists, Congress concluded that the United States could not afford at this time to pay compensation for the lands which it needed to acquire. For this reason an act was passed authorizing seizure without compensation of all the lands required for the defense establishment.

"In reaching a judgment on this case, I cannot shut my eyes to the fact that the United States is in a desperate condition at this time. Nor can I, under established canons of constitutional construction, invalidate a Congressional enactment if there are any rational grounds upon which Congress could have passed it. I think there are such grounds here. Highly important among the powers granted Congress by the Constitution are the powers to declare war, maintain a navy, and raise and support armies. This, of course, means the power to conduct war successfully. To make sure that Congress is not unduly restricted in the exercise of these constitutional powers, the Constitution also gives Congress power to make all laws 'necessary and proper to carry into execution the foregoing powers. . . .' This 'necessary and proper' clause applies to the powers to make war and support armies as it does to all the other granted powers.

"Plaintiff contends, however, that the Fifth Amendment's provision about compensation is so absolute a command that Congress is wholly without authority to violate it, however great this nation's emergency and peril may be. I must reject this contention. We must never forget that it is a constitution we are expounding. And a constitution, unlike ordinary statutes, must endure for ages; it must be adapted to changing conditions and the needs of changing communities. Without such capacity for change, our Constitution would soon be outmoded and become a dead letter. Therefore its words must never be read as rigid absolutes. The Bill of Rights' commands, no more than any others, can stay the hands of Congress from doing that which the general welfare imperatively demands. When two great constitutional provisions like these conflict—as here the power to make war conflicts with the requirements for just compensation—it becomes the duty of courts to weigh the constitutional right of an individual to compensation against the power of Congress to wage a successful war.

"While the question is not without doubt, I have no hesitation in finding the challenged Congressional act valid. Driven by the absolute necessity to protect the nation from foreign aggression, the national debt has risen to billions of dollars. The Government's credit is such that interest rates have soared. Under these circumstances, Congress was rationally entitled to find that if it paid for all the lands it needs it might bankrupt the nation and render it helpless in its hour of greatest need. Weighing as I must the loss the individual will suffer because he has to surrender his land to the nation without compensation against the great public interest in conducting war, I hold the act valid. A decree will be entered accordingly."

Of course, I would not decide this case this way nor do I think any other judge would so decide it today. My reason for refusing this approach would be that I think the Fifth Amendment's command is absolute and not to be overcome without constitutional amendment even in times of grave emergency. But I think this wholly fictitious opinion fairly illustrates the possibilities of the balancing approach, not only as to the just compensation clause, but as to other provisions of the Bill of Rights as well. The great danger of the judiciary balancing process is that in times of emergency and stress it gives Government the power to do what it thinks necessary to protect itself, regardless of the rights of individuals. If the need is great, the right of Government can always be said to outweigh the rights of the individual. If "balancing" is accepted as the test, it would be hard for any conscientious judge to hold otherwise in times of dire need. And laws adopted in times of dire need are often very hasty and oppressive laws, especially when, as often happens, they are carried over and accepted as normal. Furthermore, the balancing approach to basic individual liberties assumes to legislators and judges more power than either the Framers or I myself believe should be entrusted, without limitation, to any man or any group of men.

It seems to me that the "balancing" approach also disregards all of the unique features of our Constitution which I described earlier. In reality this approach returns us to the state of legislative supremacy which existed in England and which the Framers were so determined to change once and for all. On the one hand, it denies the judiciary its constitutional power to measure acts of Congress by the standards set down in the Bill of Rights. On the other hand, though apparently reducing judicial powers by saying that acts of Congress may be held unconstitutional only when they are found to have no rational legislative basis, this approach really gives the Court, along with Congress, a greater power, that of overriding the plain commands of the Bill of Rights on a finding of weighty public interest. In effect, it changes the direction of our form of government from a government of limited powers to a government in which Congress may do anything that Courts believe to be "reasonable."

Of course the decision to provide a constitutional safeguard for a particular right, such as the fair trial requirements of the Fifth and Sixth Amendments and the right of free speech protection of the First, involves a balancing of conflicting interests. Strict procedures may release guilty men; protecting speech and press may involve dangers to a particular government. I believe, however, that the Framers themselves did this balancing when they wrote the Constitution and the Bill of Rights. They appreciated the risks involved and they decided that certain rights should be guaranteed regardless of these risks. Courts have neither the right nor the power to review this original decision of the Framers and to attempt to make a different evaluation of the importance of the rights granted in the Constitu-

tion. Where conflicting values exist in the field of individual liberties protected by the Constitution, that document settles the conflict, and its policy should not be changed without constitutional amendments by the people in the manner provided by the people.

Misuse of government power, particularly in times of stress, has brought suffering to humanity in all ages about which we have authentic history. Some of the world's noblest and finest men have suffered ignominy and death for no crime— unless unorthodoxy is a crime. Even enlightened Athens had its victims such as Socrates. Because of the same kind of bigotry, Jesus, the great Dissenter, was put to death on a wooden cross. The flames of inquisitions all over the world have warned that men endowed with unlimited government power, even earnest men, consecrated to a cause, are dangerous.

For my own part, I believe that our Constitution, with its absolute guarantees of individual rights, is the best hope for the aspirations of freedom which men share everywhere. I cannot agree with those who think of the Bill of Rights as an 18th Century straitjacket, unsuited for this age. It is old but not all old things are bad. The evils it guards against are not only old, they are with us now, they exist today. Almost any morning you open your daily paper you can see where some person somewhere in the world is on trial or has just been convicted of supposed disloyalty to a new group controlling the government which has set out to purge its suspected enemies and all those who had dared to be against its successful march to power. Nearly always you see that these political heretics are being tried by military tribunals or some other summary and sure method for disposition of the accused. Now and then we even see the convicted victims as they march to their execution.

Experience all over the world has demonstrated, I fear, that the distance between stable, orderly government and one that has been taken over by force is not so great as we have assumed. Our own free system to live and progress has to have intelligent citizens, citizens who cannot only think and speak and write to influence people, but citizens who are free to do that without fear of governmental censorship or reprisal.

The provisions of the Bill of Rights that safeguard fair legal procedures came about largely to protect the weak and the oppressed from punishment by the strong and the powerful who wanted to stifle the voices of discontent raised in protest against oppression and injustice in public affairs. Nothing that I have read in the Congressional debates on the Bill of Rights indicates that there was any belief that the First Amendment contained any qualifications. The only arguments that tended to look in this direction at all were those that said "that all paper barriers against the power of the community are too weak to be worthy of attention."[20] Suggestions were also made in and out of Congress that a Bill of Rights would be a futile gesture since there would be no way to enforce the safeguards for freedom it provided. Mr. Madison answered this argument in these words:

> If they [the Bill of Rights amendments] are incorporated into the Constitution, independent tribunals of justice will consider themselves in a peculiar manner the guardians of those rights; they will be an impenetrable bulwark against any assumption of power in the Legislative or Executive; they will be naturally led to resist every encroachment upon rights expressly stipulated for in the Constitution by the declaration of rights.[21]

I fail to see how courts can escape this sacred trust.

Since the earliest days philosophers have dreamed of a country where the mind and spirit of man would be free; where there would be no limits to inquiry; where men would be free to explore the unknown and to challenge the most deeply rooted beliefs and principles. Our First Amendment was a bold effort to adopt this principle—to establish a country with no legal restrictions of any kind upon the subjects people could investigate, discuss and deny. The Framers knew, better perhaps than we do today, the risks they were taking. They knew that free speech might be the friend of change and revolution. But they also knew that it is always the deadliest enemy of tyranny. With this knowledge they still believed that the ultimate happiness and security of a nation lies in its ability to explore, to change, to grow and ceaselessly to adapt itself to new knowledge born of inquiry free from any kind of governmental control over the mind and spirit of man. Loyalty comes from love of good government, not fear of a bad one.

The First Amendment is truly the heart of the Bill of Rights. The Framers balanced its freedoms of religion, speech, press, assembly and petition against the needs of a powerful central government, and decided that in those freedoms lies this nation's only true security. They were not afraid for men to be free. We should not be. We should be as confident as Jefferson was when he said in his First Inaugural Address:

> If there be any among us who would wish to dissolve this Union or to change its republican form, let them stand undisturbed as monuments of the safety with which error of opinion may be tolerated where reason is left free to combat it.[22]

---

[20] 1 Annals of Cong. 437 (1789).
[21] 1 Annals of Cong. 439 (1789).

[22] 8 Jefferson, Writings 2–3 (Washington ed. 1859).

NO DECISION: *KONIGSBERG V. STATE BAR OF CALIFORNIA*

Justice John Marshall Harlan

. . . We reject the view that freedom of speech and association, . . . as protected by the First and Fourteenth Amendments, are "absolutes," not only in the undoubted sense that where the constitutional protection exists it must prevail, but also in the sense that the scope of that protection must be gathered solely from a literal reading of the First Amendment.[10] Throughout its history this Court has consistently recognized at least two ways in which constitutionally protected freedom of speech is narrower than an unlimited license to talk. On the one hand, certain forms of speech, or speech in certain contexts, has been considered outside the scope of constitutional protection.[11] . . . On the other hand, general regulatory statutes, not intended to control the content of speech but incidentally limiting its unfettered exercise, have not been regarded as the type of law the First or Fourteenth Amendment forbade Congress or the States to pass, when they have been found justified by subordinating valid governmental interests, a prerequisite to constitutionality which has necessarily involved a weighing of the governmental interest involved. . . . Whenever, in such a context, these constitutional protections are asserted against the exercise of valid governmental powers a reconciliation must be effected, and that perforce requires an appropriate weighing of the respective interests involved. . . . With more particular reference to the present context of a state decision as to character qualifications, it is difficult, indeed, to imagine a view of the constitutional protections of speech and association which would automatically and without consideration of the extent of the deterrence of speech and association and of the importance of the state function, exclude all reference to prior speech or association on such issues as character, purpose, credibility, or intent. On the basis of these considerations we now judge petitioner's contentions in the present case.

Petitioner does not challenge the constitutionality of §6064.1 of the California Business and Professions Code forbidding certification for admission to practice of those advocating the violent overthrow of government. It would indeed be difficult to argue that a belief, firm enough to be carried over into advocacy, in the use of illegal means to change the form of the

Excerpted from *Konigsberg v. State Bar of California*, 366 U.S. 36 (1961).

[10] That view, which of course cannot be reconciled with the law relating to libel, slander, misrepresentation, obscenity, perjury, false advertising, solicitation of crime, complicity by encouragement, conspiracy, and the like, is said to be compelled by the fact that the commands of the First Amendment are stated in unqualified terms: "Congress shall make no law . . . abridging the freedom of speech, or of the press; or the right of the people peaceably to assemble. . . ."

[11] That the First Amendment immunity for speech, press and assembly has to be reconciled with valid but conflicting governmental interests was clear to Holmes, J. ("I do not doubt for a moment that by the same reasoning that would justify punishing persuasion to murder, the United States constitutionally may punish speech that produces or is intended to produce a clear and imminent danger that it will bring about forthwith certain substantive evils that the United States constitutionally may seek to prevent." *Abrams* v. *United States,* 250 U.S. 616, 627); to Brandeis, J. ("But, although the rights of free speech and assembly are fundamental, they are not in their nature absolute." *Whitney* v. *California,* 274 U.S. 357, 373); and to Hughes, C.J. ("[T]he protection [of free speech] even as to previous restraint is not absolutely unlimited." *Near* v. *Minnesota,* 283 U.S. 697, 716.)

State or Federal Government is an unimportant consideration in determining the fitness of applicants for membership in a profession in whose hands so largely lies the safekeeping of this country's legal and political institutions. . . . Nor is the state interest in this respect insubstantially related to the right which California claims to inquire about Communist Party membership. This Court has long since recognized the legitimacy of a statutory finding that membership in the Communist Party is not unrelated to the danger of use for such illegal ends of powers given for limited purposes. . . .

As regards the questioning of public employees relative to Communist Party membership it has already been held that the interest in not subjecting speech and association to the deterrence of subsequent disclosure is outweighed by the State's interest in ascertaining the fitness of the employee for the post he holds, and hence that such questioning does not infringe constitutional protections. . . . With respect to this same question of Communist Party membership, we regard the State's interest in having lawyers who are devoted to the law in its broadest sense, including not only its substantive provisions, but also its procedures for orderly change, as clearly sufficient to outweigh the minimal effect upon free association occasioned by compulsory disclosure in the circumstances here presented. . . .

QUESTIONS FOR DISCUSSION

1. Does Justice Black really mean that freedom of speech is absolute?
2. Is advertising (commercial speech) protected by the First Amendment?
3. Why is freedom of speech considered to be *fundamental*?
4. Should freedom of speech be limited in wartime?
5. Why do public officials not have the same protection from libel and slander as private citizens?

RECOMMENDED READINGS

BERNS, WALTER. *The First Amendment and the Future of American Democracy.* New York: Basic Books, 1976.

CHAFEE, ZECHARIAH, JR. *Free Speech in the United States.* Cambridge: Harvard University Press, 1941.

EMERSON, THOMAS. *The System of Freedom of Expression.* New York: Random House, 1970.

HAIMAN, FRANKLYN S. *Speech and Law in a Free Society.* Chicago: University of Chicago Press, 1981.

HENTOFF, NAT. *The First Freedom.* New York: Delacorte Press, 1980.

LEVY, LEONARD. *Legacy of Suppression: Freedom of Speech and Press in Early American History.* Cambridge: Harvard University Press, 1960.

MEIKELJOHN, ALEXANDER. "The First Amendment Is an Absolute." 1961 *Supreme Court Review* 245.

O'BRIEN, DAVID M. *The Public's Right to Know: The Supreme Court and the First Amendment.* New York: Praeger, 1981.

TUSSMAN, JOSEPH. *Government and the Mind.* New York: Oxford University Press, 1977.

3 Is the Bill of Rights applicable to the states?

YES DISSENTING OPINION: *ADAMSON V. CALIFORNIA*

Justice Hugo L. Black

... This decision reasserts a constitutional theory ... that this Court is endowed by the Constitution with boundless power under "natural law" periodically to expand and contract constitutional standards to conform to the Court's conception of what at a particular time constitutes "civilized decency" and "fundamental liberty and justice." Invoking this ... rule, the Court concludes that although comment upon testimony in a federal court would violate the Fifth Amendment, identical comment in a state court does not violate today's fashion in civilized decency and fundamentals and is therefore not prohibited by the Federal Constitution as amended. ...

The first ten amendments were proposed and adopted largely because of fear that Government might unduly interfere with prized individual liberties. The people wanted and demanded a Bill of Rights written into their Constitution. The amendments embodying the Bill of Rights were intended to curb all branches of the Federal Government in the fields touched by the amendments—Legislative, Executive, and Judicial. The Fifth, Sixth, and Eighth Amendments were pointedly aimed at confining exercise of power by courts and judges within precise boundaries, particularly in the procedure used

Excerpted from *Adamson v. California*, 332 U.S. 46 (1947).

for the trial of criminal cases. Past history provided strong reasons for the apprehensions which brought these procedural amendments into being and attest the wisdom of their adoption. For the fears of arbitrary court action sprang largely from the past use of courts in the imposition of criminal punishments to suppress speech, press, and religion. Hence the constitutional limitations of courts' powers were, in the view of the Founders, essential supplements to the First Amendment, which was itself designed to protect the widest scope for all people to believe and to express the most divergent political, religious, and other views.

But these limitations were not expressly imposed upon state court action. In 1833, *Barron v. Baltimore* ... was decided by this Court. It specifically held inapplicable to the states that provision of the Fifth Amendment which declares: "nor shall private property be taken for public use, without just compensation." In deciding the particular point raised, the Court there said that it could not hold that the first eight amendments applied to the states. This was the controlling constitutional rule when the Fourteenth Amendment was proposed in 1866.

My study of the historical events that culminated in the Fourteenth Amendment, and the expressions of those who sponsored and favored, as well as those who opposed its submission and passage, persuades me that one of the chief objects that the provisions of the Amendment's first section, separately, and as a whole, were intended to accomplish was to make the Bill of Rights, applicable to the states. With full knowledge of the import of the *Barron* decision, the framers and backers of the Fourteenth Amendment proclaimed its purpose to be to overturn the constitutional rule that case had announced. This historical purpose has never received full consideration or exposition in any opinion of this Court interpreting the Amendment. . . .

For this reason, I am attaching to this dissent an appendix which contains a résumé, by no means complete, of the Amendment's history. In my judgment that history conclusively demonstrates that the language of the first section of the Fourteenth Amendment, taken as a whole, was thought by those responsible for its submission to the people, and by those who opposed its submission, sufficiently explicit to guarantee that thereafter no state could deprive its citizens of the privileges and protections of the Bill of Rights. Whether this Court ever will, or whether it now should, in the light of past decisions, give full effect to what the Amendment was intended to accomplish is not necessarily essential to a decision here. However that may be, our prior decisions, . . . do not prevent our carrying out that purpose, at least to the extent of making applicable to the states, not a mere part, as the Court has, but the full protection of the Fifth Amendment's provision against compelling evidence from an accused to convict him of crime. And I further contend that the "natural law" formula which the Court uses to reach its conclusion in this case should be abandoned as an incongruous excrescence on our Constitution. I believe that formula to be itself a violation of our Constitution, in that it subtly conveys to courts, at the expense of legislatures, ultimate power over public policies in fields where no specific provision of the Consti-

tution limits legislative power. And my belief seems to be in accord with the views expressed by this Court, at least for the first two decades after the Fourteenth Amendment was adopted. . . .

I cannot consider the Bill of Rights to be an outworn 18th Century "strait jacket". . . . Its provisions may be thought outdated abstractions by some. And it is true that they were designed to meet ancient evils. But they are the same kind of human evils that have emerged from century to century wherever excessive power is sought by the few at the expense of the many. In my judgment the people of no nation can lose their liberty so long as a Bill of Rights like ours survives and its basic purposes are conscientiously interpreted, enforced and respected so as to afford continuous protection against old, as well as new, devices and practices which might thwart those purposes. I fear to see the consequences of the Court's practice of substituting its own concepts of decency and fundamental justice for the language of the Bill of Rights as its point of departure in interpreting and enforcing that Bill of Rights. If the choice must be between the selective process of . . . applying some of the Bill of Rights to the States, or the . . . rule applying none of them, I would choose the [former] selective process. But rather than accept either of these choices, I would follow what I believe was the original purpose of the Fourteenth Amendment—to extend to all the people of the nation the complete protection of the Bill of Rights. To hold that this Court can determine what, if any, provisions of the Bill of Rights will be enforced, and if so to what degree, is to frustrate the great design of a written Constitution.

Conceding the possibility that this Court is now wise enough to improve on the Bill of Rights by substituting natural law concepts for the Bill of Rights, I think the possibility is entirely too speculative to agree to take that course. I would therefore hold in this case that the full protection of the

Fifth Amendment's proscription against compelled testimony must be afforded by California. This I would do because of reliance upon the original purpose of the Fourteenth Amendment.

It is an illusory apprehension that literal application of some or all of the provisions of the Bill of Rights to the States would unwisely increase the sum total of the powers of this Court to invalidate state legislation. The Federal Government has not been harmfully burdened by the requirement that enforcement of federal laws affecting civil liberty conform literally to the Bill of Rights. Who would advocate its repeal? It must be conceded, of course, that the natural-law-due-process formula, which the Court today reaffirms, has been interpreted to limit substantially this Court's power to prevent state violations of the individual civil liberties guaranteed by the Bill of Rights. But this formula also has been used in the past, and can be used in the future, to license this Court, in considering regulatory legislation, to roam at large in the broad expanses of policy and morals and to trespass, all too freely, on the legislative domain of the States as well as the Federal Government.

Since *Marbury* v. *Madison* . . . was decided, the practice has been firmly established, for better or worse, that courts can strike down legislative enactments which violate the Constitution. This process, of course, involves interpretation, and since words can have many meanings, interpretation obviously may result in contraction or extension of the original purpose of a constitutional provision, thereby affecting policy. But to pass upon the constitutionality of statutes by looking to the particular standards enumerated in the Bill of Rights and other parts of the Constitution is one thing; to invalidate statutes because of application of "natural law" deemed to be above and undefined by the Constitution is another. "In the one instance, courts proceeding within clearly marked constitutional boundaries seek to execute policies written into the Constitution; in the other, they roam at will in the limitless area of their own beliefs as to reasonableness and actually select policies, a responsibility which the Constitution entrusts to the legislative representatives of the people." . . .

NO CONCURRING OPINION: *ADAMSON V. CALIFORNIA*

Justice Felix Frankfurter

. . . Between the incorporation of the Fourteenth Amendment into the Constitution and the beginning of the present membership of the Court—a period of seventy years—the scope of that Amendment was passed upon by forty-three judges. Of all these judges, only one [John

Excerpted from *Adamson v. California*, **332 U.S. 46 (1947).**

Marshall Harlan], who may respectfully be called an eccentric exception, ever indicated the belief that the Fourteenth Amendment was a shorthand summary of the first eight Amendments therefore limiting only the Federal Government, and that due process incorporated those eight Amendments as restrictions upon the powers of the States. Among these judges were not only those who would have to be included among the greatest in the history of the Court, but—it is especially relevant to note—they included those whose services in the cause of human rights and the spirit of freedom are the most conspicuous in our history. It is not invidious to single out Miller, Davis, Bradley, Waite, Matthews, Gray, Fuller, Holmes, Brandeis, Stone and Cardozo (to speak only of the dead) as judges who were alert in safeguarding and promoting the interests of liberty and human dignity through law. But they were also judges mindful of the relation of our federal system to a progressively democratic society and therefore duly regardful of the scope of authority that was left to the States even after the Civil War. And so they did not find that the Fourteenth Amendment, concerned as it was with matters fundamental to the pursuit of justice, fastened upon the States procedural arrangements which, in the language of Mr. Justice Cardozo, only those who are "narrow or provincial" would deem essential to "a fair and enlightened system of justice." . . . To suggest that it is inconsistent with a truly free society to begin prosecutions without an indictment, to try petty civil cases without the paraphernalia of a common law jury, to take into consideration that one who has full opportunity to make a defense remains silent is, in de Tocqueville's phrase, to confound the familiar with the necessary.

The short answer to the suggestion that the provision of the Fourteenth Amendment, which ordains "nor shall any State deprive any person of life, liberty, or property, without due process of law," was a way of saying that every State must thereafter initiate prosecutions through indictment by a grand jury, must have a trial by a jury of twelve in criminal cases, and must have trial by such a jury in common law suits where the amount in controversy exceeds twenty dollars, is that it is a strange way of saying it. It would be extraor-

dinarily strange for a Constitution to convey such specific commands in such a roundabout and inexplicit way. . . . Those reading the English language with the meaning which it ordinarily conveys, those conversant with the political and legal history of the concept of due process, those sensitive to the relations of the States to the central government as well as the relation of some of the provisions of the Bill of Rights to the process of justice, would hardly recognize the Fourteenth Amendment as a cover for the various explicit provisions of the first eight Amendments. Some of these are enduring reflections of experience with human nature, while some express the restricted views of Eighteenth-Century England regarding the best methods for the ascertainment of facts. The notion that the Fourteenth Amendment was a covert way of imposing upon the States all the rules which it seemed important to Eighteenth Century statesmen to write into the Federal Amendments, was rejected by judges who were themselves witnesses of the process by which the Fourteenth Amendment became part of the Constitution. Arguments that may now be adduced to prove that the first eight Amendments were concealed within the historic phrasing of the Fourteenth Amendment were not unknown at the time of its adoption. A surer estimate of their bearing was possible for judges at the time than distorting distance is likely to vouchsafe. Any evidence of design or purpose not contemporaneously known could hardly have influenced those who ratified the Amendment. Remarks of a particular proponent of the Amendment, no matter how influential, are not to be deemed part of the Amendment. What was submitted for ratification was his proposal, not his speech. Thus, at the time of the ratification of the Fourteenth Amendment the constitutions of nearly half of the ratifying States did not have the rigorous requirements of the Fifth Amendment for instituting criminal proceedings through a grand jury. It could hardly have occurred to these States that by ratifying the Amendment they uprooted their established methods for prosecuting crime and fastened upon themselves a new prosecutorial system.

Indeed, the suggestion that the Fourteenth Amendment incorporates the first eight Amendments as such is not unambiguously urged. Even the boldest innovator would shrink from suggesting to more than half the States that they may no longer initiate prosecutions without indictment by grand jury, or that thereafter all the States of the Union must furnish a jury of twelve for every case involving a claim above twenty dollars. There is suggested merely a selective incorporation of the first eight Amendments into the Fourteenth Amendment. Some are in and some are out, but we are left in the dark as to which are in and which are out. Nor are we given the calculus for determining which go in and which stay out. If the basis of selection is merely that those provisions of the first eight Amendments are incorporated which commend themselves to individual justices as indispensable to the dignity and happiness of a free man, we are thrown back to a merely subjective test. The protection against unreasonable search and seizure might have primacy for one judge, while trial by a jury of twelve for every claim above twenty dollars might appear to another as an ultimate need in a free society. In the history of thought "natural law" has a much longer and much better founded meaning and justification than such subjective selection of the first eight Amendments for incorporation into the Fourteenth. If all that is meant is that due process contains within itself certain minimal standards which are "of the very essence of a scheme of ordered liberty," . . . putting upon this Court the duty of applying these standards from time to time, then we have merely arrived at the

insight which our predecessors long ago expressed. . . .

It may not be amiss to restate the pervasive function of the Fourteenth Amendment in exacting from the States observance of basic liberties. . . . The Amendment neither comprehends the specific provisions by which the founders deemed it appropriate to restrict the federal government nor is it confined to them. The Due Process Clause of the Fourteenth Amendment has an independent potency, precisely as does the Due Process Clause of the Fifth Amendment in relation to the Federal Government. It ought not to require argument to reject the notion that due process of law meant one thing in the Fifth Amendment and another in the Fourteenth. The Fifth Amendment specifically prohibits prosecution of an "infamous crime" except upon indictment; it forbids double jeopardy; it bars compelling a person to be a witness against himself in any criminal case; it precludes deprivation of "life, liberty, or property, without due process of law. . . . " Are Madison and his contemporaries in the framing of the Bill of Rights to be charged with writing into it a meaningless clause? To consider "due process of law" as merely a shorthand statement of other specific clauses in the same amendment is to attribute to the authors and proponents of this Amendment ignorance of, or indifference to, a historic conception which was one of the great instruments in the arsenal of constitutional freedom which the Bill of Rights was to protect and strengthen.

A construction which gives to due process no independent function but turns it into a summary of the specific provisions of the Bill of Rights would, as has been noted, tear up by the roots much of the fabric of law in the several States, and would deprive the States of opportunity for reforms in legal process designed for extending the area of freedom. It would assume that no other abuses would reveal themselves in the course of time than those which had become manifest in 1791. Such a view not only disregards the historic meaning of "due process." It leads inevitably to a warped construction of specific provisions of the Bill of Rights to bring within their scope conduct clearly condemned by due process but not easily fitting into the pigeon-holes of the specific provisions. It seems pretty late in the day to suggest that a phrase so laden with historic meaning should be given an improvised content consisting of some but not all of the provisions of the first eight Amendments, selected on an undefined basis, with improvisation of content for the provisions so selected.

And so, when, as in a case like the present, a conviction in a State court is here for review under a claim that a right protected by the Due Process Clause of the Fourteenth Amendment has been denied, the issue is not whether an infraction of one of the specific provisions of the first eight Amendments is disclosed by the record. The relevant question is whether the criminal proceedings which resulted in conviction deprived the accused of the due process of law to which the United States Constitution entitled him. Judicial review of that guaranty of the Fourteenth Amendment inescapably imposes upon this Court an exercise of judgment upon the whole course of the proceedings in order to ascertain whether they offend those canons of decency and fairness which express the notions of justice of English-speaking peoples even toward those charged with the most heinous offenses. These standards of justice are not authoritatively formulated anywhere as though they were prescriptions in a pharmacopoeia. But neither does the application of the Due Process Clause imply that judges are wholly at large. The judicial judgment in applying the Due Process Clause must move within the limits of accepted notions of justice and is not to be based upon the idiosyncrasies of a merely personal judgment. The fact that judges among themselves may differ whether in a particular case a trial offends accepted notions of justice is not disproof that general rather than idiosyncratic standards are applied. An important safeguard against such merely individual judgment is an alert deference to the judgment of the State court under review.

QUESTIONS FOR DISCUSSION

1. Does the "nationalization" of the Bill of Rights protect individual freedom?

2. If the Fourteenth Amendment *incorporated* the Bill of Rights, would that clarify the rights of the individual in relation to state and local government?

3. Can the states be trusted to protect individual rights?

4. Is federalism helpful in promoting diversity?

5. What rights are so fundamental that liberty could not survive if they were destroyed?

6. "If the framers of the Fourteenth Amendment had wanted to make the Bill of Rights applicable to the states, they would have said so." Discuss.

RECOMMENDED READINGS

BERGER, RAOUL. *Government by Judiciary: The Transformation of the Fourteenth Amendment.* Cambridge: Harvard University Press, 1977.

CORTNER, RICHARD C. *The Supreme Court and the Second Bill of Rights: The Fourteenth Amendment and the Nationalization of Civil Liberties.* Madison: University of Wisconsin Press, 1981.

DUNNE, GERALD T. *Hugo Black and the Judicial Revolution.* New York: Simon and Schuster, 1977.

FAIRMAN, CHARLES. "Does the Fourteenth Amendment Incorporate the Bill of Rights? The Original Understanding." 2 *Stanford Law Review* 5 (1949).

FRIENDLY, WILLIAM. "The Bill of Rights as a Code of Criminal Procedure." 53 *California Law Review* 929 (1965).

HENKIN, LOUIS. "Selective Incorporation of the Fourteenth Amendment." 73 *Yale Law Journal* 74 (1963).

KARST, KENNETH L. "Foreword: Equal Citizenship under the Fourteenth Amendment." 91 *Harvard Law Review* 1 (1977).

MARSHALL, BURKE. *Federalism and Civil Rights.* New York: Columbia University Press, 1964.

SCHAEFER, KARL. "Federalism and State Criminal Procedure." 70 *Harvard Law Review* 1 (1956).

Should the Supreme Court be limited by the Framers' intent?

YES THE BATTLE FOR THE CONSTITUTION: THE ATTORNEY GENERAL REPLIES TO HIS CRITICS

Edwin Meese III

A large part of American history has been the history of constitutional debate. From the Federalists and the Anti-Federalists, to Webster and Calhoun, to Lincoln and Douglas, we find many examples. Now, as we approach the bicentennial of the framing of the Constitution, we are witnessing another debate concerning our fundamental law. It is not simply a ceremonial debate, but one that promises to have a profound effect on the future of our Republic.

The current debate is a sign of a healthy nation. Unlike people of many other countries, we are free both to discover the defects of our laws and our governments through open discussion and to correct them through our political system.

This debate on the Constitution involves great and fundamental issues. It invites the participation of the best minds the bar, the academy, and the bench have to offer. In recent weeks, there have been important new contributions to this debate from some of the most distinguished scholars and jurists in the land. Representatives of the three branches of the federal government have entered the debate, journalistic commentators too.

Edwin Meese III, "The Battle for the Constitution: The Attorney General Replies to His Critics," *Policy Review*, no. 35 (Winter 1986), pp. 32–35.

A great deal has already been said, much of it of merit. But occasionally there has been confusion, and in some cases, even distortion. Caricatures and straw men, as one customarily finds even in the greatest debates, have made appearances. I've been surprised at some of the hysterical shrillness that we've seen in editorials and other commentary. Perhaps this response is explained by the fact that what we've said defies liberal dogma.

Still, whatever the differences, most participants are agreed about the same high objective: fidelity to our fundamental law.

It is easy to forget what a young country America really is. The bicentennial of our independence was just a few years ago; that of the Constitution is still two years off.

The period surrounding the creation of the Constitution is not a dark and mythical realm. The young America of the 1780s and 1790s was a vibrant place, alive with pamphlets, newspapers, and books chronicling and commenting upon the great issues of the day. We know how the Founding Fathers lived, and much of what they read, thought, and believed. The disputes and compromises of the Constitutional Convention are carefully recorded. The minutes of the Convention are a matter of public record. Several of the most important participants—including James Madison, the "father" of the Constitution—wrote comprehensive accounts of the convention. Others, Federalists and Anti-Federalists alike, committed their arguments for and against ratification, as well as their understandings of the Constitution, to paper, so that their ideas and conclusions could be widely circulated, read, and understood.

In short, the Constitution is not buried in the mists of time. We know a tremendous amount of the history of its genesis. The bicentennial is encouraging even more scholarship about its origins. We know who did what, when, and many times why. One can talk intelligently about a "founding generation."

With these thoughts in mind, I would like to discuss this administration's approach to constitutional interpretation, which has been led by President Reagan and which we at the Department of Justice and my colleagues in other agencies have advanced. But to begin, it may be useful to say what it is not.

Our approach does not view the Constitution as some kind of super-municipal code, designed to address merely the problems of a particular era—whether those of 1787, 1789, or 1868. There is no question that the Constitutional Convention grew out of a widespread dissatisfaction with the Articles of Confederation. But the delegates in Philadelphia moved beyond the job of patching that document to write a Constitution. Their intention was to write a document not just for their times but for posterity.

The language they employed clearly reflects this. For example, they addressed *commerce*, not simply shipping or barter. Later, the Bill of Rights spoke, through the Fourth Amendment, to "unreasonable searches and seizures," not merely the regulation of specific law enforcement practices of 1789. Still later, the framers of the 14th Amendment were concerned not simply about the rights of black citizens to personal security, but also about the equal protection of the law for all persons within the states.

The Constitution is not a legislative code bound to the time in which it was written. Neither, however, is it a mirror that simply reflects the thoughts and ideas of those who stand before it.

Our approach to constitutional interpretation begins with the document itself. The plain fact is, it exists. It is something that has been written down. Walter Berns of the American Enterprise Institute has noted that the central object of American constitutionalism was "the effort" of the founders "to express fundamental governmental arrangements in a legal document—to 'get it in writing.'"

Indeed, judicial review has been grounded in the fact that the Constitution is a written, as opposed to an unwritten, document. In *Marbury v. Madison,* John Marshall rested his rationale for judicial review on the fact that we have a written Constitution with meaning that is binding upon judges. "[I]t is apparent," he wrote, "that the framers of the Constitution contemplated that instrument as a rule for the government of *courts,* as well as of the legislature. Why otherwise does it direct the judges to take an oath to support it?"

A GOVERNMENT OF LAW

The presumption of a written document is that it conveys meaning. As Thomas Grey of the Stanford Law School has said, it makes "relatively definite and explicit what otherwise would be relatively indefinite and tacit."

We know that those who framed the Constitution chose their words carefully. They debated at great length the most minute points. The language they chose meant something. They proposed, they substituted, they edited, and they carefully revised. Their words were studied with equal care by state ratifying conventions.

This is not to suggest that there was unanimity among the framers and ratifiers on all points. The Constitution and the Bill of Rights, and some of the subsequent amendments, emerged after protracted debate. Nobody got everything they wanted. What's more, the framers were not clairvoyant—they could not foresee every issue that would be submitted for judicial review. Nor could they predict how all forseeable disputes would be resolved under the Constitution. But the point is that the meaning of the Constitution can be known.

What does this written Constitution mean? In places it is exactly specific. Where it says that Presidents of the United States must be at least 35 years of age, it means exactly that. Where it specifies how the House and Senate are to be organized, it means what it says.

The Constitution, including its 26 amendments, also expresses particular principles. One is the right to be free of an unreasonable search or seizure. Another concerns religious liberty. Another is the right to equal protection of the laws.

Those who framed these principles meant something by them. And the meaning can be found, understood, and applied.

The Constitution itself is also an expression of certain general principles. These principles reflect the deepest purpose of the Constitution—that of establishing a political system through which Americans can best govern themselves consistent with the goal of securing liberty.

The text and structure of the Constitution is instructive. It contains very little in the way of specific political solutions. It speaks volumes on how problems should be approached, and by whom. For example, the first three articles set out clearly the scope and limits of three distinct branches of national government. The powers of each are carefully and specifically enumerated. In this scheme, it is no accident to find the legislative branch described first, as the framers had fought and sacrificed to secure the right of democratic self-governance. Naturally, this faith in republicanism was not unbounded, as the next two articles make clear.

Yet the Constitution remains a document of powers and principles. And its undergirding premise remains that democratic self-government is subject only to the limits of certain constitutional principles. This respect for the political process was made explicit early on. When John Marshall upheld the act of Congress chartering a national bank in *McCulloch v. Maryland,* he wrote: "The Constitution [was] intended to endure for ages to come, and, consequently, to be adapted to the various crises of human affairs." But to use *McCulloch,* as some have tried, as support for the idea that the Constitution is a protean, changeable thing is to stand history on its head.

Justice Marshall was keeping faith in the original intention that Congress be free to elaborate and apply constitutional powers and principles. He was not saying that the Court must invent some new constitutional value in order to keep pace with the times. In Walter Berns's words: "Marshall's meaning is not that the Constitution may be adapted to the 'various crises of human affairs,' but that the legislative powers granted by the Constitution are adaptable to meet these crises."

The approach this administration advocates is rooted in the text of the Constitution as illuminated by those who drafted, proposed, and ratified it. In his famous *Commentary on the Constitution of the United States,* Justice Joseph Story explained:

> The first and fundamental rule in the interpretation of all instruments is to construe them according to the sense of the terms, and the intention of the parties.

Our approach understands the significance of a written document and seeks to discern the particular and general principles it expresses. It recognizes that there may be debate at times over the application of these principles. But it does not mean these principles cannot be identified.

Constitutional adjudication is obviously not a mechanical process. It requires an appeal to reason and discretion. The text and intention of the Constitution must be understood to constitute the banks within which constitutional interpretation must flow. As James Madison said, if "the sense in which the Constitution was accepted and ratified by the nation . . . be not the guide to expounding it, there can be no security for a consistent and stable, more than for a faithful exercise of its powers."

Thomas Jefferson, so often cited incorrectly as a framer of the Constitution, in fact shared Madison's view: "Our peculiar security is in the possession of a written Constitution. Let us not make it a blank paper by construction." Jefferson was even more explicit in his personal correspondence:

> On every question of construction [we should] carry ourselves back to the time when the Constitution was adapted; recollect the spirit manifested in the debates; and instead of trying [to find] what meaning may be squeezed out of the text, or invented against it, conform to the probable one, in which it was passed.

In the main, a jurisprudence that seeks to be faithful to our Constitution—a jurisprudence of original intention, as I have called it—is not difficult to describe. Where the language of the Constitution is specific, it must be obeyed. Where there is a demonstrable consensus among the framers and ratifiers as to a principle stated or implied by the Constitution, it should be followed. Where there is ambiguity as to the precise meaning or reach of constitutional provision, it should be interpreted and applied in a manner so as to at least not contradict the text of the Constitution itself.

Sadly, while almost everyone participating in the current constitutional debate would give assent to these propositions, the techniques and conclusions of some of the debaters do violence to them. What is the source of this violence? In large part, I believe that it is the misuse of history stemming from the neglect of the idea of a written constitution.

There is a frank proclamation by some judges and commentators that what matters most about the Constitution is not its words but its so-called "spirit." These individuals focus less on the language of specific provisions than on what they describe as the "vision" or "concepts of human dignity" they find embodied in the Constitution. This approach to jurisprudence has led to some remarkable and tragic conclusions.

In the 1850s, the Supreme Court under Chief Justice Roger B. Taney read blacks out of the Constitution in order to invalidate Congress' attempt to limit the spread of slavery. The *Dred Scott* decision, famously described as a judicial "self-infliction wound," helped bring on the Civil War. There is a lesson in such history. There is danger in seeing the Constitution as an empty vessel into which each generation may pour its passion and prejudice.

Our own time has its own fashions and passions. In recent decades, many have come to view the Constitution—more accurately, part of the Constitution, provisions of the Bill of Rights and the 14th Amendment—as a charter for judicial activism on behalf of various constituencies. Those who hold this view often have lacked demonstrable textual or historical support for their conclusions. Instead, they have "grounded" their rulings in appeals to social theories, to moral philosophies or personal notions of human dignity, or to "penumbras," somehow emanating ghostlike from various "provisions"—identified and not identified—in the Bill of Rights. The problem with this approach—as John Hart Ely, Dean of Stanford Law School, has observed with respect to one such decision—is not that it is bad constitutional law, but that it is not constitutional law in any meaningful sense.

Despite this fact, the perceived popularity of some results in particular cases has encouraged some observers to believe that any critique of the methodology of those decisions is an attack on the results. This perception is sufficiently widespread that it deserves an answer. My answer is to look at history.

When the Supreme Court, in *Brown v. Board of Education,* sounded the death knell for official segregation in the country, it earned all the plaudits it received. But the Supreme Court in that case was not giving new life to old words, or adapting a "living," "flexible" Constitution to new reality. It was restoring the original principle of the Constitution to constitutional law. The *Brown* Court was correcting the damage done 50 years earlier, when in *Plessy v. Ferguson,* an earlier Supreme Court had disregarded the clear intent of the framers of the Civil War amendments to eliminate the legal degradation of blacks, and had contrived a theory of the Constitution to support the charade of "separate but equal" discrimination. It is amazing how so much of what passes for social and political progress is really the undoing of old judicial mistakes.

Mistakes occur when the principles of specific Constitutional provisions—such as those contained in the Bill of Rights—are taken by some as invitations to read into the Constitution values that contradict the clear language of other provisions.

Acceptances to this illusory invitation have proliferated in recent decades. One Supreme Court justice identified the proper judicial standard as asking "what's best for this country." Another said it is important to "keep the Court out in front" of the general society. Various academic commentators have poured rhetorical gasoline on this judicial fire, suggesting that constitutional interpretation appropriately

be guided by such standards as whether a public policy "personified justice" or "comports with the notion of moral evolution" or confers "an identity" upon our society or was consistent with "natural ethical law" or was consistent with some "right of equal citizenship." These amorphous concepts, as opposed to the written Constitution, form a very poor base for judicial interpretation.

Unfortunately, navigation by such lodestars has in the past given us questionable economics, governmental disorder, and racism—all in the guise of constitutional law. Recently, one of the distinguished judges of one of our federal appeals courts got it about right when he wrote: "the truth is that the judge who looks outside the Constitution always looks inside himself and nowhere else." Or, as we recently put it before the Supreme Court in an important brief: "The further afield interpretation travels from its point of departure in the text, the greater the danger that constitutional adjudication will be like a picnic to which the framers bring the words and the judges the meaning."

In the *Osborne v. Bank of United States* decision 21 years after *Marbury,* Justice Marshall further elaborated this view of the relationship between the judge and the law, be it statutory or constitutional:

> Judicial power, as contra-distinguished from the power of the laws, has no existence. Courts are the mere instruments of the law, and can will nothing. When they are said to exercise a discretion, it is a mere legal discretion, a discretion to be exercised in discerning the course prescribed by law; and, when that is discerned, it is the duty of the Court to follow it.

Any true approach to constitutional interpretation must respect the document in all its parts and be faithful to the Constitution in its entirety.

What must be remembered in the current debate is that interpretation does not imply results. The framers were not trying to anticipate every answer. They were trying to create a tripartite national government, within a federal system, that would have the flexibility to adapt to face new exigencies—as it did, for example, in chartering a national bank. Their great interest was in the distribution of power and responsibility in order to secure the great goal of liberty for all.

A jurisprudence that seeks fidelity to the Constitution—a jurisprudence of original intention—is not a jurisprudence of political results. It is very much concerned with process, and it is a jurisprudence that in our day seeks to de-politicize the law. The great genius of the constitutional blueprint is found in its creation and respect for spheres of authority and the limits it placed on governmental power. In this scheme the framers did not see the courts as the exclusive custodians of the Constitution. Indeed, because the document posits so few conclusions, it leaves to the more political branches the matter of adapting and vivifying its principles in each generation. It also leaves to the people of the states, in the 10th Amendment, those responsibilities and rights not committed to federal care. The power to declare acts of Congress and laws of the states null and void is truly awesome. This power must be used when the Constitution clearly speaks. It should not be used when the Constitution does not.

In *Marbury v. Madison,* at the same time he vindicated the concept of judicial review, Justice Marshall wrote that the "principles" of the Constitution "are deemed fundamental and permanent," and except for formal amendment, "unchangeable." If we want a change in our Constitution or in our laws we must seek it through the formal mechanisms presented in that organizing document of our government.

At issue here is not an agenda of issues or a menu of results. At issue is a way of government. A jurisprudence based on

first principles is neither conservative nor liberal, neither right nor left. It is a jurisprudence that cares about committing and limiting to each organ of government the proper ambit of its responsibilities. It is a jurisprudence faithful to our Constitution.

By the same token, an activist jurisprudence, one which anchors the Constitution only in the consciences of jurists, is a chameleon jurisprudence, changing color and form in each era. The same activism hailed today may threaten the capacity for decision through democratic consensus tomorrow, as it has in many yesterdays. Ultimately, as the early democrats wrote into the Massachusetts Constitution, the best defense of our liberties is a government of laws and not men.

On this point it is helpful to recall the words of the late Justice Felix Frankfurter. As he wrote:

> [t]here is not under our Constitution a judicial remedy for every political mischief, for every undesirable exercise of legislative power. The framers carefully and with deliberate forethought refused to enthrone the judiciary. In this situation, as in others of like nature, appeal for relief does not belong here. Appeal must be to an informed, civically militant electorate.

As students of the Constitution are aware, the struggle for ratification was protracted and bitter. Essential to the success of the campaign was the outcome of the debate in the two most significant states: Virginia and New York. In New York, the battle between Federalists and Anti-Federalist forces was particularly hard. Both sides eagerly awaited the outcome in Virginia, which was sure to have a profound effect on the struggle in the Empire State. When news that Virginia had voted to ratify came, it was a particularly bitter blow to the Anti-Federalist side. Yet on the evening the message reached New York, an event took place that speaks volumes about the character of early America. The losing side, instead of grousing, feted the Federalist leaders in the taverns and inns of the city. There followed a night of good fellowship and mutual toasting. When the effects of good cheer wore off, the two sides returned to their inkwells, and the debate resumed.

There is a great temptation among those who view this debate from the outside to see in it a clash of personalities, a bitter exchange. But we and our distinguished opponents are carrying the old tradition of free, uninhibited, and vigorous debate. Out of such arguments come no losers, only truth.

It's the American way. And the Founders wouldn't want it any other way.

NO THE CONSTITUTION OF THE UNITED STATES: CONTEMPORARY RATIFICATION

Justice William J. Brennan, Jr.

I am deeply grateful for the invitation to participate in the "Text and Teaching" symposium. This rare opportunity to explore classic texts with participants of such wisdom, acumen and insight as those who have preceded and will follow me to this podium is indeed exhilarating. But it is also humbling. Even to approximate the standards of excellence of these vigorous and graceful intellects is a daunting task. I am honored that you have afforded me this opportunity to try.

It will perhaps not surprise you that the text I have chosen for exploration is the amended Constitution of the United States, which, of course, entrenches the Bill of Rights and the Civil War amendments, and draws sustenance from the bedrock principles of another great text, the Magna Carta. So fashioned, the Constitution embodies the aspiration to social justice, brotherhood, and human dignity that brought this nation into being. The Declaration of Independence, the Constitution and the Bill of Rights solemnly committed the United States to be a country where the dignity and rights of all persons

were equal before all authority. In all candor we must concede that part of this egalitarianism in America has been more pretension than realized fact. But we are an aspiring people, a people with faith in progress. Our amended Constitution is the lodestar for our aspirations. Like every text worth reading, it is not crystalline. The phrasing is broad and the limitations of its provisions are not clearly marked. Its majestic generalities and ennobling pronouncements are both luminous and obscure. This ambiguity of course calls forth interpretation, the interaction of reader and text. The encounter with the Constitutional text has been, in many senses, my life's work.

My approach to this text may differ from the approach of other participants in this symposium to their texts. Yet such differences may themselves stimulate reflection about what it is we do when we "interpret" a text. Thus I will attempt to elucidate my approach to the text as well as my substantive interpretation.

Perhaps the foremost difference is the fact that my encounters with the constitutional text are not purely or even primarily introspective; the Constitution cannot be for me simply a contemplative haven for private moral reflection. My relation to this great text is inescapably public. That is not

Justice William J. Brennan, Jr., "The Constitution of the United States: Contemporary Ratification," talk delivered at Text and Teaching Symposium, Georgetown University, Washington, D.C., Oct. 12, 1985.

to say that my reading of the text is not a personal reading, only that the personal reading perforce occurs in a public context, and is open to critical scrutiny from all quarters.

The Constitution is fundamentally a public text—the monumental charter of a government and a people—and a Justice of the Supreme Court must apply it to resolve public controversies. For, from our beginnings, a most important consequence of the constitutionally created separation of powers has been the American habit, extraordinary to other democracies, of casting social, economic, philosophical and political questions in the form of law suits, in an attempt to secure ultimate resolution by the Supreme Court. In this way, important aspects of the most fundamental issues confronting our democracy may finally arrive in the Supreme Court for judicial determination. Not infrequently, these are the issues upon which contemporary society is most deeply divided. They arouse our deepest emotions. The main burden of my twenty-nine Terms on the Supreme Court has thus been to wrestle with the Constitution in this heightened public context, to draw meaning from the text in order to resolve public controversies.

Two other aspects of my relation to this text warrant mention. First, constitutional interpretation for a federal judge is, for the most part, obligatory. When litigants approach the bar of court to adjudicate a constitutional dispute, they may justifiably demand an answer. Judges cannot avoid a definitive interpretation because they feel unable to, or would prefer not to, penetrate to the full meaning of the Constitution's provisions. Unlike literary critics, judges cannot merely savor the tensions or revel in the ambiguities inhering in the text—judges must resolve them.

Second, consequences flow from a Justice's interpretation in a direct and immediate way. A judicial decision respecting the incompatibility of Jim Crow with a constitutional guarantee of equality is not simply a contemplative exercise in defining the shape of a just society. It is an order—supported by the full coercive power of the State—that the present society change in a fundamental aspect. Under such circumstances the process of deciding can be a lonely, troubling experience for fallible human beings conscious that their best may not be adequate to the challenge. We Justices are certainly aware that we are not final because we are infallible; we know that we are infallible only because we are final. One does not forget how much may depend on the decision. More than the litigants may be affected. The course of vital social, economic and political currents may be directed.

These three defining characteristics of my relation to the constitutional text—its public nature, obligatory character, and consequentialist aspect—cannot help but influence the way I read that text. When Justices interpret the Constitution they speak for their community, not for themselves alone. The act of interpretation must be undertaken with full consciousness that it is, in a very real sense, the community's interpretation that is sought. Justices are not platonic guardians appointed to wield authority according to their personal moral predelictions. Precisely because coercive force must attend any judicial decision to countermand the will of a contemporary majority, the Justices must render constitutional interpretations that are received as legitimate. The source of legitimacy is, of course, a well-spring of controversy in legal and political circles. At the core of the debate is what the late Yale Law School professor Alexander Bickel labeled "the counter-majoritarian difficulty." Our commitment to self-governance in a representative democracy must be reconciled with vesting in electorally unaccountable Justices the power to invalidate the expressed desires of representative bodies on the ground of inconsistency with higher law. Because judicial power resides in the authority to give meaning to the Constitution, the debate is really a debate about how to read the text, about constraints on what is legitimate interpretation.

There are those who find legitimacy in fidelity to what they call "the intentions of the Framers." In its most doctrinaire incarnation, this view demands that Justices discern exactly what the Framers thought about the question under consideration and simply follow that intention in resolving the case before them. It is a view that feigns self-effacing deference to the specific judgments of those who forged our original social compact. But in truth it is little more than arrogance cloaked as humility. It is arrogant to pretend that from our vantage we can gauge accurately the intent of the Framers on application of principle to specific, contemporary questions. All too often, sources of potential enlightment such as records of the ratification debates provide sparse or ambiguous evidence of the original intention. Typically, all that can be gleaned is that the Framers themselves did not agree about the application or meaning of particular constitutional provisions, and hid their differences in cloaks of generality. Indeed, it is far from clear whose intention is relevant—that of the drafters, the congressional disputants, or the ratifiers in the states?—or even whether the idea of an original intention is a coherent way of thinking about a jointly drafted document drawing its authority from a general assent of the states. And apart from the problematic nature of the sources, our distance of two centuries cannot but work as a prism refracting all we perceive. One cannot help but speculate that the chorus of lamentations calling for interpretation faithful to "original intention"—and proposing nullification of interpretations that fail this quick litmus test—must inevitably come from persons who have no familiarity with the historical record.

Perhaps most importantly, while proponents of this facile historicism justify it as a depoliticization of the judiciary, the political underpinnings of such a choice should not escape notice. A position that upholds constitutional claims only if they were within the specific contemplation of the Framers in effect establishes a presumption of resolving textual ambiguities against the claim of constitutional right. It is far from clear what justifies such a presumption against claims of right. Nothing intrinsic in the nature of interpretation—if there is such a thing as the "nature" of interpretation—commands such a passive approach to ambiguity. This is a choice no less political than any other; it expresses antipathy to claims of the minority to rights against the majority. Those who would restrict claims of right to the values of 1789 specifically articulated in the Constitution turn a blind eye to social progress and eschew adaptation of overarching principles to changes of social circumstance.

Another, perhaps more sophisticated, response to the potential power of judicial interpretation stresses democratic theory: because ours is a government of the people's elected representatives, substantive value choices should by and large be left to them. This view emphasizes not the transcendent historical authority of the framers but the predominant contemporary authority of the elected branches of government. Yet it has similar consequences for the nature of proper judicial interpretation. Faith in the majoritarian process counsels restraint. Even under more expansive formulations of this approach, judicial review is appropriate only to the extent of ensuring that our democratic process functions smoothly. Thus, for example, we would protect freedom of speech merely to ensure that the people are heard by their representatives, rather than as a separate, substantive value. When, by contrast, society tosses up to the Supreme Court a dispute that would require invalidation of a legislature's substantive policy choice, the Court generally would stay its hand because the Constitution was meant as a plan of government and not as an embodiment of fundamental substantive values.

The view that all matters of substantive policy should be resolved through the majoritarian process has appeal under some circumstances, but I think it ultimately will not do. Unabashed enshrinement of majority will would permit the imposition of a social caste system or wholesale confiscation of property so long as a majority of the authorized legislative body, fairly elected, approved. Our Constitution could not abide such a situation. It is the very purpose of a Constitution—and particularly of the Bill of Rights—to declare certain values transcendent, beyond the reach of temporary political majorities. The majoritarian process cannot be expected to rectify claims of minority right that arise as a response to the outcomes of that very majoritarian process. As James Madison put it:

> The prescriptions in favor of liberty ought to be levelled against that quarter where the greatest danger lies, namely, that which possesses the highest prerogative of power. But this is not found in either the Executive or Legislative departments of Government, but in the body of the people, operating by the majority against the minority. (I Annals 437).

Faith in democracy is one thing, blind faith quite another. Those who drafted our Constitution understood the difference. One cannot read the text without admitting that it embodies substantive value choices; it places certain values beyond the power of any legislature. Obvious are the separation of powers; the privilege of the Writ of Habeas Corpus; prohibition of Bills of Attainder and ex post facto laws; prohibition of cruel and unusual punishments; the requirement of

just compensation for official taking of property; the prohibition of laws tending to establish religion or enjoining the free exercise of religion; and, since the Civil War, the banishment of slavery and official race discrimination. With respect to at least such principles, we simply have not constituted ourselves as strict utilitarians. While the Constitution may be amended, such amendments require an immense effort by the People as a whole.

To remain faithful to the content of the Constitution, therefore, an approach to interpreting the text must account for the existence of these substantive value choices, and must accept the ambiguity inherent in the effort to apply them to modern circumstances. The Framers discerned fundamental principles through struggles against particular malefactions of the Crown; the struggle shapes the particular contours of the articulated principles. But our acceptance of the fundamental principles has not and should not bind us to those precise, at times anachronistic, contours. Successive generations of Americans have continued to respect these fundamental choices and adopt them as their own guide to evaluating quite different historical practices. Each generation has the choice to overrule or add to the fundamental principles enunciated by the Framers; the Constitution can be amended or it can be ignored. Yet with respect to its fundamental principles, the text has suffered neither fate. Thus, if I may borrow the words of an esteemed predecessor, Justice Robert Jackson, the burden of judicial interpretation is to translate "the majestic generalities of the Bill of Rights, conceived as part of the pattern of liberal government in the eighteenth century, into concrete restraints on officials dealing with the problems of the twentieth century." (Barnette, 319 U.S., at 639).

We current Justices read the Constitution in the only way that we can: as Twentieth Century Americans. We look to the history of the time of framing and to the intervening history of interpretation. But the ultimate question must be, what do the words of the text mean in our time. For the genius of the Constitution rests not in any static meaning it might have had in a world that is dead and gone, but in the adaptability of its great principles to cope with current problems and current needs. What the constitutional fundamentals meant to the wisdom of other times cannot be their measure to the vision of our time. Similarly, what those fundamentals mean for us, our descendants will learn, cannot be the measure to the vision of their time. This realization is not, I assure you, a novel one of my own creation. Permit me to quote from one of the opinions of our Court, *Weems v. United States*, 217 U.S. 349, written nearly a century ago:

> Time works changes, brings into existence new conditions and purposes. Therefore, a principle to be vital must be capable of wider application than the mischief which gave it birth. This is peculiarly true of constitutions. They are not ephemeral enactments, designed to meet passing occasions. They are, to use the words of Chief Justice John Marshall, "designed to approach immortality as nearly as human institutions can approach it." The future is their care and provision for events of good and bad tendencies of which no prophecy can be made. In the application of a constitution, therefore, our contemplation cannot be only of what has been, but of what may be.

Interpretation must account for the transformative purpose of the text. Our Constitution was not intended to preserve a preexisting society but to make a new one, to put in place new principles that the prior political community had not sufficiently recognized. Thus, for example, when we interpret the Civil War Amendments to the charter—abolishing slavery, guaranteeing blacks equality under law, and guaranteeing blacks the right to vote—we must remember that those who put them in place had no desire to

enshrine the status quo. Their goal was to make over their world, to eliminate all vestige of slave caste.

Having discussed at some length how I, as a Supreme Court Justice, interact with this text, I think it time to turn to the fruits of this discourse. For the Constitution is a sublime oration on the dignity of man, a bold commitment by a people to the ideal of libertarian dignity protected through law. Some reflection is perhaps required before this can be seen.

The Constitution on its face is, in large measure, a structuring text, a blueprint for government. And when the text is not prescribing the form of government it is limiting the powers of that government. The original document, before addition of any of the amendments, does not speak primarily of the rights of man, but of the abilities and disabilities of government. When one reflects upon the text's preoccupation with the scope of government as well as its shape, however, one comes to understand that what this text is about is the relationship of the individual and the state. The text marks the metes and bounds of official authority and individual autonomy. When one studies the boundary that the text marks out, one gets a sense of the vision of the individual embodied in the Constitution.

As augmented by the Bill of Rights and the Civil War Amendments, this text is a sparkling vision of the supremacy of the human dignity of every individual. This vision is reflected in the very choice of democratic self-governance: the supreme value of a democracy is the presumed worth of each individual. And this vision manifests itself most dramatically in the specific prohibitions of the Bill of Rights, a term which I henceforth will apply to describe not only the original first eight amendments, but the Civil War amendments as well. It is a vision that has guided us as a people throughout our history, although the precise rules by which we have protected fundamental human dignity have been transformed over time in response to both transformations of social condition and evolution of our concepts of human dignity.

Until the end of the nineteenth century, freedom and dignity in our country found meaningful protection in the institution of real property. In a society still largely agricultural, a piece of land provided men not just with sustenance but with the means of economic independence, a necessary precondition of political independence and expression. Not surprisingly, property relationships formed the heart of litigation and of legal practice, and lawyers and judges tended to think stable property relationships the highest aim of the law.

But the days when common law property relationships dominated litigation and legal practice are past. To a growing extent economic existence now depends on less certain relationships with government—licenses, employment, contracts, subsidies, unemployment benefits, tax exemptions, welfare and the like. Government participation in the economic existence of individuals is pervasive and deep. Administrative matters and other dealings with government are at the epicenter of the exploding law. We turn to government and to the law for controls which would never have been expected or tolerated before this century, when a man's answer to economic oppression or difficulty was to move two hundred miles west. Now hundreds of thousands of Americans live entire lives without any real prospect of the dignity and autonomy that ownership of real property could confer. Protection of the human dignity of such citizens requires a much modified view of the proper relationship of individual and state.

In general, problems of the relationship of the citizen with government have multiplied and thus have engendered some of the most important constitutional issues of the day. As government acts ever more deeply upon those areas of our lives once marked "private," there is an even greater need to see that individual rights are not curtailed or cheapened in the interest of what may temporarily appear to be the "public good." And as government continues in its role of provider for so many of our disadvantaged citizens, there is an even greater need to ensure that government act with integrity and consistency in its dealings with these citizens. To put this another way, the possibilities for collision between government activity and individual rights will increase as the power and authority of government itself expands, and this growth, in turn, heightens the need for constant vigilance at the collision points. If our free society is to endure, those who govern must recognize human dignity and accept the enforcement of constitutional limitations on their power conceived by the Framers to be necessary to preserve that dignity and the air of freedom which is our proudest heritage. Such recognition will not come from a technical understanding of the organs of government, or the new forms of wealth they administer. It requires something different, something deeper—a personal confrontation with the well-springs of our society. Solutions of constitutional questions from that perspective have become the great challenge of the modern era. All the talk in the last half-decade about shrinking the government does not alter this reality or the challenge it imposes. The modern activist state is a concomitant of the complexity of modern society; it is inevitably with us. We must meet the challenge rather than wish it were not before us.

The challenge is essentially, of course, one to the capacity of our constitutional structure to foster and protect the freedom, the dignity, and the rights of all persons within our borders, which it is the great design of the Constitution to secure. During the time of my public service this challenge has largely taken shape within the confines of the interpretive question whether the specific guarantees of the Bill of Rights operate as restraints on the power of State government. We recognize the Bill of Rights as the primary source of express information as to what is meant by constitutional liberty. The safeguards enshrined in it are deeply etched in the foundation of America's freedoms. Each is a protection with centuries of history behind it, often dearly bought with the blood and lives of people determined to prevent oppression by their rulers. The first eight Amendments, however, were added to the Constitution to operate solely against federal power. It was not until the Thirteenth and Fourteenth Amendments were added, in 1865 and 1868, in response to a demand for national protection against abuses of state power, that the Constitution could be interpreted to require application of the first eight amendments to the states.

It was in particular the Fourteenth Amendment's guarantee that no person be deprived of life, liberty or property without process of law that led us to apply many of the specific guarantees of the Bill of Rights to the States. In my judgment, Justice Cardozo best captured the reasoning that brought us to such decisions when he described what the Court has done as a process by which the guarantees "have been taken over from the earlier articles of the federal bill of rights and brought within the Fourteenth Amendment by a process of absorption . . . [that] has had its source in the belief that neither liberty nor justice would exist if [those guarantees] . . . were sacrificed." (Palko, 302 U.S., at 326). But this process of absorption was neither swift nor steady. As late as 1922 only the Fifth Amendment guarantee of just compensation for official taking of property had been given force against the states. Between then and 1956 only the First Amendment guarantees of speech and

conscience and the Fourth Amendment ban of unreasonable searches and seizures had been incorporated—the latter, however, without the exclusionary rule to give it force. As late as 1961, I could stand before a distinguished assemblage of the bar at New York University's James Madison Lecture and list the following as guarantees that had not been thought to be sufficiently fundamental to the protection of human dignity so as to be enforced against the states: the prohibition of cruel and unusual punishments, the right against self-incrimination, the right to assistance of counsel in a criminal trial, the right to confront witnesses, the right to compulsory process, the right not to be placed in jeopardy of life or limb more than once upon accusation of a crime, the right not to have illegally obtained evidence introduced at a criminal trial, and the right to a jury of one's peers.

The history of the quarter century following that Madison Lecture need not be told in great detail. Suffice it to say that each of the guarantees listed above has been recognized as a fundamental aspect of ordered liberty. Of course, the above catalogue encompasses only the rights of the criminally accused, those caught, rightly or wrongly, in the maw of the criminal justice system. But it has been well said that there is no better test of a society than how it treats those accused of transgressing against it. Indeed, it is because we recognize that incarceration strips a man of his dignity that we demand strict adherence to fair procedure and proof of guilt beyond a reasonable doubt before taking such a drastic step. These requirements are, as Justice Harlan once said, "bottomed on a fundamental value determination of our society that it is far worse to convict an innocent man than to let a guilty man go free." (Winship, 397 U.S., at 372). There is no worse injustice than wrongly to strip a man of his dignity. And our adherence to the constitutional vision of human dignity is so strict that even after convicting a person according to these stringent standards, we demand that his dignity be infringed only to the extent appropriate to the crime and never by means of wanton infliction of pain or deprivation. I interpret the Constitution plainly to embody these fundamental values.

Of course the constitutional vision of human dignity has, in this past quarter century, infused far more than our decisions about the criminal process. Recognition of the principle of "one person, one vote" as a constitutional one redeems the promise of self-governance by affirming the essential dignity of every citizen in the right to equal participation in the democratic process. Recognition of so-called "new property" rights in those receiving government entitlements affirms the essential dignity of the least fortunate among us by demanding that government treat with decency, integrity and consistency those dependent on its benefits for their very survival. After all, a legislative majority initially decides to create governmental entitlements; the Constitution's Due Process Clause merely provides protection for entitlements thought necessary by society as a whole. Such due process rights prohibit government from imposing the devil's bargain of bartering away human dignity in exchange for human sustenance. Likewise, recognition of full equality for women—equal protection of the laws—ensures that gender has no bearing on claims to human dignity.

Recognition of broad and deep rights of expression and of conscience reaffirms the vision of human dignity in many ways. They too redeem the promise of self-governance by facilitating—indeed demanding—robust, uninhibited and wide-open debate on issues of public importance. Such public debate is of course vital to the development and dissemination of political ideas. As importantly, robust public discussion is the crucible in which personal political convictions are forged. In our democracy, such discussion is a political duty; it is the essence of self government. The constitutional vision of human dignity rejects the possibility of political orthodoxy imposed from above; it respects the right of each individual to form and to expresses political judgments, however far they may deviate from the mainstream and however unsettling they might be to the powerful or the elite. Recognition of these rights of expression and conscience also frees up the private space for both intellectual and spiritual development free of government dominance, either blatant or subtle. Justice Brandeis put it so well sixty years ago when he wrote: "Those who won our independence believed that the final end of the State was to make men free to develop their faculties; and that in its government the deliberative forces should prevail over the arbitrary. They valued liberty both as an end and as a means." (Whitney, 274 U.S., at 375).

I do not mean to suggest that we have in the last quarter century achieved a comprehensive definition of the constitutional ideal of human dignity. We are still striving toward that goal, and doubtless it will be an eternal quest. For if the interaction of this Justice and the constitutional text over the years confirms any single proposition, it is that the demands of human dignity will never cease to evolve.

Indeed, I cannot in good conscience refrain from mention of one grave and crucial respect in which we continue, in my judgment, to fall short of the constitutional vision of human dignity. It is in our continued tolerance of State-administered execution as a form of punishment. I make it a practice not to comment on the constitutional issues that come before the Court, but my position on this issue, of course, has been for some time fixed and immutable. I think I can venture some thoughts on this particular subject without transgressing my usual guideline too severely.

As I interpret the Constitution, capital punishment is under all circumstances

[the] cruel and unusual punishment prohibited by the Eighth and Fourteenth Amendments. This is a position of which I imagine you are not unaware. Much discussion of the merits of capital punishment has in recent years focused on the potential arbitrariness that attends its administration, and I have no doubt that such arbitrariness is a grave wrong. But for me, the wrong of capital punishment transcends such procedural issues. As I have said in my opinions, I view the Eighth Amendment's prohibition of cruel and unusual punishments as embodying to a unique degree moral principles that substantively restrain the punishments our civilized society may impose on those persons who transgress its laws. Foremost among the moral principles recognized in our cases and inherent in the prohibition is the primary principle that the State, even as it punishes, must treat its citizens in a manner consistent with their intrinsic worth as human beings. A punishment must not be so severe as to be utterly and irreversibly degrading to the very essence of human dignity. Death for whatever crime and under all circumstances is a truly awesome punishment. The calculated killing of a human being by the State involves, by its very nature, an absolute denial of the executed person's humanity. The most vile murder does not, in my view, release the State from constitutional restraints on the destruction of human dignity. Yet an executed person has lost the very right to have rights, now or ever. For me, then, the fatal constitutional infirmity of capital punishment is that it treats members of the human race as nonhumans, as objects to be toyed with and discarded. It is, indeed, "cruel and unusual." It is thus inconsistent with the fundamental premise of the Clause that even the most base criminal remains a human being possessed of some potential, at least, for common human dignity.

This is an interpretation to which a majority of my fellow Justices—not to mention, it would seem, a majority of my fellow countrymen—does not subscribe. Perhaps you find my adherence to it, and my recurrent publication of it, simply contrary, tiresome, or quixotic. Or perhaps you see in it a refusal to abide by the judicial principle of *stare decisis*, obedience to precedent. In my judgment, however, the unique interpretive role of the Supreme Court with respect to the Constitution demands some flexibility with respect to the call of *stare decisis*. Because we are the last word on the meaning of the Constitution, our views must be subject to revision over time, or the Constitution falls captive, again, to the anachronistic views of long-gone generations. I mentioned earlier the judge's role in seeking out the community's interpretation of the Constitutional text. Yet, again in my judgment, when a Justice perceives an interpretation of the text to have departed so far from its essential meaning, that Justice is bound, by a larger constitutional duty to the community, to expose the departure and point toward a different path. On this issue, the death penalty, I hope to embody a community striving for human dignity for all, although perhaps not yet arrived.

You have doubtless observed that this description of my personal encounter with the constitutional text has in large portion been a discussion of public developments in constitutional doctrine over the last quarter century. That, as I suggested at the outset, is inevitable because my interpretive career has demanded a public reading of the text. This public encounter with the text, however, has been a profound source of personal inspiration. The vision of human dignity embodied there is deeply moving. It is timeless. It has inspired Americans for two centuries and it will continue to inspire as it continues to evolve. That evolutionary process is inevitable and, indeed, it is the true interpretive genius of the text.

If we are to be as a shining city upon a hill, it will be because of our ceaseless pursuit of the constitutional ideal of human dignity. For the political and legal ideals that form the foundation of much that is best in American institutions—ideals jealously preserved and guarded throughout our history—still form the vital force in creative political thought and activity within the nation today. As we adapt our institutions to the ever-changing condi- tions of national and international life, those ideals of human dignity—liberty and justice for all individuals—will continue to inspire and guide us because they are entrenched in our Constitution. The Constitution with its Bill of Rights thus has a bright future, as well as a glorious past, for its spirit is inherent in the aspirations of our people.

QUESTIONS FOR DISCUSSION

1. What standards should guide the Supreme Court in its interpretation of the Constitution?
2. Is the intent of the Framers relevant today?
3. Should the Supreme Court be bound by various interpretations of the Constitution?
4. Does the meaning of the Constitution change with the times?
5. How can the Constitution be amended?

RECOMMENDED READINGS

ABRAHAM, HENRY J. *The Judiciary: The Supreme Court in the Governmental Process.* 6th ed. Newton, Mass.: Allyn and Bacon, 1983.

BLACK, CHARLES L., JR. *The People and the Court: Judicial Review in a Democracy.* New York: Macmillan, 1960.

FERRAND, MAX, ed. *The Records of the Federal Convention of 1787.* New Haven: Yale University Press, 1937; reprint. New Haven: Yale University Press, 1966.

HALPERN, STEPHEN C., and CHARLES M. LAMB, eds. *Supreme Court Activism and Restraint.* Lexington, Mass.: Heath, 1982.

KAUFMAN, IRVING R. "What Did the Founding Fathers Intend?" *New York Times Magazine,* Feb. 23, 1986, pp. 42, 59–60, 67–69.

KOCH, ADRIENNE. *Power, Morals and the Founding Fathers.* Ithaca: Cornell University Press, 1961.

LUSKY, LOUIS. *By What Right? A Commentary on the Supreme Court's Power to Revise the Constitution.* Charlottesville, Va.: Mitchie Co., 1976.

RADAR, RANDALL R. "Chaining the Court to the Constitution." *Modern Age* 25 (Summer 1981), pp. 243–48.

ROSSITER, CLINTON. *1787: The Grand Convention.* New York: Macmillan, 1966.

II CIVIL LIBERTIES

The first amendment to the Constitution states that "Congress shall make no law respecting an establishment of religion, or prohibiting the free exercise thereof; or abridging the freedom of speech, or of the press; or the right of the people peaceably to assemble, and to petition the government for a redress of grievances." These guarantees—freedom of conscience and freedom of expression—are fundamental to American life. They lie at the root of all other freedoms we cherish.

The First Amendment contains two references to religion: the *Establishment Clause* (prohibiting laws "respecting an establishment of religion") and the *Free Exercise Clause* (forbidding laws "prohibiting the free exercise thereof"). The two clauses are interrelated but protect values that sometimes compete with one another.

For example the Free Exercise Clause protects freedom of belief, while the Establishment Clause prohibits government support for religion. It is common practice throughout the United States to exempt church property used in church-related activities from taxation. Does this violate the Establishment Clause? Alternatively, would the *free exercise* of religion be unduly hindered if church property were not exempted from taxation? Or consider the claim of certain parents to exempt their children from reading particular textbooks because of religious belief. If the state must grant an exemption because of the Free Exercise Clause, is it not granting a preference to that particular religion in violation of the Establishment Clause?

It has been noted that the two religion clauses can be harmonized by recognizing that they serve a common purpose: to protect an individual's freedom of religious belief and practice. The Free Exercise Clause bars government from penalizing religion; the Establishment Clause prohibits government from rewarding it. Yet viewing the clauses as complementary does not remove potential tension. If all benefits are barred, undue burdens on religion may be the consequences. If all burdens are removed, undue benefits to religion may result. This dilemma suggests that an accommodation between the two clauses is essential.

Some have observed that the two clauses can best be reconciled if one adopts the theme of *neutrality*. Professor Philip Kurland of the University of Chicago proposes that "the freedom and separation clauses should be read as a single precept that *government cannot utilize religion as a standard for action or inaction* because these clauses prohibit classification in terms of religion either to control a benefit or to impose a burden."[1] Accordingly the Constitution should be read as *religion-blind*.

THE WALL BETWEEN CHURCH AND STATE

The arguments for the separation of church and state have deep roots in American history. An early advocate of separation was the pastor Roger Williams, who established the colony of Rhode Island and sought to protect the church from the state. In Williams's view, the church was a "garden" to be separated from the "wilderness" of the world, with its corrupt and secular influence.[2]

Thomas Jefferson, in his famous letter to the Danbury congregation, turned the argument around and claimed that religion would have a corrupting influence on the state. To prevent that, Jefferson counseled a "wall of separation between church and state."[3] James Madison pragmatically argued that the best guarantee against religious rivalries affecting political affairs was to keep religion and government rigorously separated.[4] This justification has become known as *strife-avoidance*.

Today it is generally assumed that the First Amendment commands the separation of church and state. But to translate that principle into action has given rise to some of the most contentious issues in American life. Some argue that the Establishment Clause does not forbid governmental support for religion in general but simply prohibits favoritism toward a particular religion.[5] But the Supreme Court has consistently rejected that view.[6] Nevertheless, as Justice Robert Jackson once stated, Jefferson's wall of separation between church and state has become "as winding as the famous serpentine wall" he designed for the University of Virginia.[7]

Currently the Supreme Court uses a three-part test to determine whether the Establishment Clause has been violated. First, the governmental action in question must have a secular purpose. Second, its primary effect must neither advance nor inhibit religion. Third, it must avoid "excessive government entanglement with religion."[8]

Consider the case of prayer. It is not unconstitutional to pray in a school building. What is unconstitutional is the requirement or encouragement by school (i.e., governmental) authorities to do so.

One of the more difficult areas involves the attempts by many states to provide financial assistance to parochial schools. The Supreme Court has tried to distinguish between public aid to students (which is permissible) and public aid to religion (which is not). This distinction is based on the *child benefit theory*.[9] At the college level the problem is relatively simple. Tax funds may be used to construct buildings and operate educational programs at church-related institutions so long as the money is not spent on buildings used for religious purposes or for teaching religious subjects. At the elementary school level the question is much more complicated. Pupils are younger and hence more susceptible to indoctrination. Moreover the secular and religious aspects of instruction at their level are most tightly interwoven. Thus aid given to church-operated elementary schools might become an aid to religion.

THE FREE EXERCISE OF RELIGION

The right to believe as one chooses—including the right to believe in no religion at all—is one of the unalienable rights Americans enjoy. The government cannot require a particular religious belief, nor can it discriminate against any person because of his or her religious beliefs or the lack of them. Religious oaths as a condition for government employment are explicitly unconstitutional.

But it is important to distinguish between religious belief and religious practice. The Supreme Court has made it abundantly clear that the absolute guarantee of religious freedom contained in the First Amendment pertains exclusively to religious belief. It does not protect the practices of a particular religion, if those practices should violate the law.

The constitutional distinction between belief and practice traces to *Reynolds v. United States* in 1878. The issue involved the Mormon church and the question of polygamy, which was a tenet of its faith. But Congress had outlawed polygamy in the territories (including Utah), and the Supreme Court upheld the statute. According to the Court, "It was never intended that the First Amendment . . . could be invoked as protection for the punishment of acts inimical to the peace, good order, and morals of society."[10] Accordingly religious convictions do not ordinarily exempt one from obeying laws that are otherwise valid.

In this context, a conscientious objector to military service enjoys no *constitutional* protection based on his religious creed. He may be granted deferred status, but if so, it is a matter of legislative choice and not a constitutional right.[11]

The question of what is a religion is understandably difficult. But it is clear that unconventional religions are entitled to the same constitutional protection for their beliefs as the more traditional ones. The determining factor for the Court has been that the belief must be "rooted in religion."[12] What the Supreme Court will not do is to examine and pass judgment on religious doctrine or decide which among rival claimants represents a true church.[13]

Should a Constitutional Amendment Restore the Right to Voluntary Prayer in the Public Schools?

In 1967 the Supreme Court held that a "non-denominational" prayer prepared by New York for use in the public schools was "wholly inconsistent with the Establishment Clause" of the First Amendment.[14] The following year in *School District of Abington Township v. Schempp* the Court decided that recitation of the Lord's Prayer and reading of the Bible were also unconstitutional.[15] Some religious leaders and certain newspapers defended the Court, but these comments scarcely balanced the volume and vigor of the critics of the two decisions. In fact, with the possible exception of the abortion issue, no decisions of the Supreme Court since the Civil War have aroused such lasting antipathy as the school prayer decisions.

One of the many responses has been to suggest a constitutional amendment that would authorize school prayer. Attempts to pass such an amendment received majority support in both houses of Congress in 1966 and 1971 but failed to obtain the necessary two-thirds majority required for a constitutional amendment. Another effort to overturn the Supreme Court's ruling sought to remove the question of prayer from the Court's appellate jurisdiction. (Under the Constitution the Congress determines the appellate jurisdiction of the Supreme Court.) This effort also failed.

But in the early 1980s efforts to amend the Constitution revived. The debate that follows pits two law professors on opposite sides of the question. Grover Rees of the University of Texas argues that the Supreme Court was wrong in its prayer decisions and, perhaps most important, that the First Amendment is simply not applicable to the states. The contrary position is taken by Norman Redlich of New York University. Redlich stresses the importance of the separation of church and state in the United States and notes how the Court's decision is consistent with that tradition. Both Rees's and Redlich's comments were made before the Senate Judiciary Committee in 1982 that was considering the proposed amendment. Once again it failed to receive the necessary congressional approval.

Are Federal Government Tax Credits to Parents Who Send Their Children to Private Religious Schools a Violation of the Separation of Church and State?

Public support for religious education is clearly prohibited by the Establishment Clause of the First Amendment. But it is equally clear that the boundaries of the "wall of separation" are difficult to draw with any precision. For example, the government cannot pay a salary supplement to teachers who teach secular subjects in parochial schools.[16] It cannot reimburse parents for the cost of parochial school tuition.[17] Neither can it give money to parochial schools for counselling[18] or to purchase instructional materials.[19]

But at the same time, the Supreme Court has upheld federal aid to construct buildings on denominational college campuses,[20] as well as state aid to provide for the loan of textbooks,[21] grant tax-exempt status to parochial schools,[22] and allow parents of parochial school children to deduct their tuition payments from state income tax returns.[23]

The question of whether a federal tax credit for parents of parochial school children would be permissible is considerably more contentious. In the debate on that subject, R. G. Puckett of Americans United for Separation of Church and State argues that such credit would not only violate the First Amendment, but it would place the public schools in considerable jeopardy since parents might remove their children to obtain the tax credit. Sister Renée Oliver, associate director of Citizens for Educational Freedom, argues that such support is consistent with the right of parents to choose the appropriate education for their children. Both statements were presented before the Senate Finance Committee when it was considering the tuition tax credit bill in 1983. The measure failed of passage.

Does Freedom of Religion Extend to Providing Sanctuary for Those Fleeing Political Persecution?

One of the fundamental rules of constitutional interpretation is that the guarantee of religious freedom contained in the First Amendment protects belief, not practice.[24] If action taken on religious principles violates a law that is otherwise valid, the perpetrator can be punished and the First Amendment will not provide a shield. Accordingly it appears equally clear that those who violate the immigration laws to shelter illegal aliens, even in a church and even in the name of religious principles, can be prosecuted and convicted—as they have been.

But is that the entire question? Is there a time when civil disobedience is justified, despite the clear holding of the law to the contrary? In "Sanctuary and the Law" the Center for Constitutional Rights argues that there are such occasions and suggests that the protection of the First Amendment may in fact apply. The article deals with the efforts of the Sanctuary movement to protect illegal immigrants whom it regards as refugees from political persecution. Law student Eletha Duffy states the case to the contrary and raises disturbing questions about the Sanctuary movement.

FREEDOM OF SPEECH, FREEDOM OF THE PRESS

The effective functioning of American democracy depends upon free speech, free press, and the right of all people to question the decisions of government and to campaign openly against them. As the late Judge Learned Hand of the U.S. Court of Appeals stated, the "right to criticize either by temperate reasoning, or by immoderate and indecent invective, [is] normally the privilege of the individual in countries dependent upon the free expression of opinion as the ultimate source of authority."[25]

The classic defense of free speech traces to John Milton, who wrote in 1644 to protest the oppressive censorship policies of King Charles I: "And though all the winds of doctrine were let loose to play upon the earth, so Truth be in the field, we do injuriously, by licencing and prohibiting, to misdoubt her strength. Let her and Falsehood grapple; who ever knew Truth put to the worst, in a free and open encounter."[26] Justice Oliver Wendell Holmes, Jr., expressed the same sentiment in *Abrams v. United States* when he said, "The best test of truth is the power of thought to get itself accepted in the competition of the market."[27]

Accordingly freedom of speech is not merely the freedom to express ideas that differ slightly from ours but, as Justice Robert Jackson noted, "freedom to differ as to things that touch the heart of the existing order."[28] Nevertheless the precise contours of the guarantees of free press and free speech remain debatable issues in American life. Even the intent of the Framers of the First Amendment is not completely clear. Some authorities, such as Professor Leonard Levy, argue that eighteenth-century Americans "did not believe in a broad scope for freedom of expression, particularly in the field of politics."[29] Others contend that freedom of expression was protected only against prior restraint; that is, against prepublication censorship.[30] But the most commonly accepted view is that the Framers of the First Amendment had more in mind. As expressed by Zechariah Chafee, Jr., in his influential work on free speech, the Framers "intended to wipe out the common law of sedition and make further prosecutions for criticism of the government . . . forever impossible in the United States of America."[31]

The broad interpretation of the First Amendment still leaves many problems unsettled. Do its guarantees protect only political speech, or are other forms of expression included? Does the First Amendment protect commercial advertising for example, or symbolic speech, such as the wearing of black arm bands to protest the war in Vietnam?[32] And what about obscenity and pornography? The definition of what is obscene is extremely difficult, for as Justice John Marshall Harlan noted, "One man's vulgarity is another's lyric."[33] An equally difficult issue involves suits for libel and slander. Are the punitive damages sometimes awarded by juries in such cases a threat to freedom of speech? These questions will be examined in the debates that follow.

Is Antipornography Legislation a Violation of Freedom of Speech?

Obscene publications enjoy no constitutional protection, but defining what is obscene is extremely difficult. The current criteria (adopted by the Supreme Court in 1973) hold that a work may be obscene if the average person, applying contemporary standards of the community, finds that the work, taken as a whole, appeals to a prurient interest in sex. The offending depiction of sexual conduct must be specifically defined by law. And the work, taken as a whole, must lack serious literary, artistic, political, or scientific value.[34]

Although the current test allows juries to determine whether a work appeals to prurient interests and is patently offensive, the criterion of artistic, literary, political, or scientific merit introduces a broader concept that is often more permissive. Finally the government must accurately and specifically define the types of sexual conduct whose depiction it wishes to forbid. And this is often difficult.

While the states are primarily responsible for regulating obscene literature, Congress has frequently exhibited a concern for the subject. It has adopted, and the Supreme Court has upheld, laws forbidding the importation of pornographic materials into the United States or the sending of such material through the mails or by means of interstate commerce—even to willing adults. Renewed efforts in Indianapolis, Indiana, and other communities to regulate what many deemed pornographic led the Senate to conduct hearings in 1984 on the effect of pornography on women and children. The two articles that follow—one by Barry W. Lynn, the legislative counsel of the American Civil Liberties Union; the other by Judy Goldsmith, former president of the National Organization for Women—present differing views as to whether antipornography legislation is constitutional. In reading both articles the student should carefully consider the problem of prior restraint and how it affects the issue. That and the elusive problem of definition make obscenity legislation one of the most volatile areas of constitutional debate.

Are Punitive Damages in Libel Cases a Threat to Free Speech?

In 1942 in *Chaplinsky v. New Hampshire* a unanimous Supreme Court held that libel and obscenity were not protected by the First Amendment.[35] But the Court scarcely anticipated the complex litigation that would arise relating to these kinds of speech. Not only are definitions of obscenity elusive, but how do you prove libel? How do you measure damages? And should public figures and public officials be treated differently from private citizens?

In the leading constitutional case of *New York Times v. Sullivan,* the Supreme Court held that public officials cannot collect damages for any statements made about them unless they can prove that the comments were made with knowledge that they were false—in other words, unless they can prove the comments were made with "actual malice."[36]

The constitutional standards for liberal actions brought by private persons are not so rigid. Individual citizens may collect damages without having to prove *actual malice.* They need only show that the statements were false, that there was negligence on the part of the media, and that as a result of the misstatements they suffered damage.

But whether the case involves a public official or a private person, the threats of libel suits and massive punitive judgments—that is, monetary damages that far exceed the harm caused and are intended to punish the offender—have an inevitable "chilling effect" on free speech and free press. As the Supreme Court has expressed it, "What is added to the field of libel is taken from the arena of debate, and democracy calls for robust, wide-open debate about public issues." The Court went on to say that libel "that deals with public affairs is not evil; it serves a socially useful function."[37]

In looking at the effect of punitive damages on the right of free speech and free press, the student should consider whether the First Amendment guarantees impose a limit on liability. Or, said differently, What remedies, especially with respect to damages, are constitutionally permissible to libel actions?

In the debate on that subject, John V. R. Bull of the *Philadelphia Inquirer* documents the chilling effect that massive damage judgments can inflict on a free press. He points out that not only is there no constitutional right to punitive damages, but that the concept itself is a relatively recent legal invention.

The case to the contrary is argued by Michael P. McDonald, the general counsel of the American Legal Foundation. McDonald argues that there is sufficient opportunity for judicial scrutiny of damage awards to ensure that they are not excessive. He stresses that high standards of journalistic accuracy are essential to free government and a newspaper that violates those standards should rightfully be punished.

Is Civil Disobedience an Act of Rebellion?

The First Amendment guarantees the right of all citizens "peaceably to assemble, and to petition the government for a redress of grievances." Does the right of peaceful assembly and petition include the right to violate a law deliberately but in a nonviolent manner? Civil disobedience is, after all, a deliberate violation of a law designed to call attention to, and prompt revision of, what is perceived to be an unjust law. In the general view of legal scholars, civil disobedience enjoys no constitutional protection, even if peacefully conducted. When the Rev. Martin Luther King, Jr., and his followers conducted a Good Friday protest march in Birmingham, Alabama, in 1963 in violation of a legal injunction forbidding the parade without a permit, the Supreme Court upheld the conviction. Said Justice Potter Stewart speaking for the Court:

> No man can be the judge in his own case, however exalted his station, however righteous his motives, and irrespective of his race, color, politics, or creed. . . . This Court cannot hold that the petitioners [King and others] were constitutionally free to ignore all the procedures of the law and carry their battle to the streets.[38]

But the Court's decision elicited a sharp dissent from Justice William J. Brennan, Jr., who insisted that the Supreme Court had elevated a "rule of judicial administration above the right of free expression."[39] Brennan, along with Chief Justice Earl Warren and Justices William O. Douglas and Abe Fortas, maintained that one does have the right to defy peacefully an obviously unconstitutional statute or injunction.

One of the most serious problems in cases of civil disobedience is the question of who is to judge the correctness of the act—or the unconstitutionality of the statute. For example, is it permissible for Dr. King to violate the ordinance in Birmingham forbidding parades without a permit, but improper for American Nazis to act in a similar manner in Skokie, Illinois? The courts have been quick to recognize the need for swift judicial review of such actions, precisely to maintain the authority of established legal procedures.

In the debate on this subject, Eugene V. Rostow, who was a law professor at the Yale Law School when he wrote the article reproduced here, examines the role of civil disobedience in a democratic society and argues that it has no place. In Rostow's words, "The idea of treating a right of civil disobedience as an aspect of personal liberty under the Constitution is at war with the moral principles on which this civilization, or any liberal civilization rest."

The argument in favor of civil disobedience is presented by Howard Zinn of Boston University. Zinn argues that the moral imperative of civil disobedience justifies it as a legitimate act of protest, regardless of constitutional or international law. In Zinn's view, "To urge the right of citizens to disobey unjust laws, and the duty of citizens to disobey dangerous laws, is of the very essence of democracy."

Are Laws Requiring Public Disclosure of Lobbying Activities a Violation of the Right to Petition?

Regulation of lobbying activities (defined broadly as the attempt to influence public officials and the policies they enact) treads dangerously close to infringing upon a citizen's right "to petition the Government" guaranteed by the First Amendment. The term *to lobby* derives from the lobby of the old Willard Hotel in Washington where representatives of various vested interests would congregate, hoping to encounter members of Congress or the executive branch and extol the virtues of their cause. Modern lobbying is far more extensive and sophisticated, but whether it is more effective is unclear.

There are thousands of lobbyists active in Washington today, and their activities run the gamut from routine announcements to the detailed consultation and advice that are a part of most legislation. In fact, the complexity of most legislation both permits and depends upon lobbyists to play a major role. Because members of Congress often have neither the time nor the expertise to grapple with highly technical matters, they frequently turn to lobbyists for information and advice. In short, lobbying is a vital part of the democratic process and without question enjoys the protection of the First Amendment.

But it is equally true that lobbying can be abused; that serious damage can be done to the democratic process through unscrupulous use of money and influence; and perhaps most significant, that it usually is not accountable to the body politic. The great Yazoo land fraud of the 1790s, in which the entire Georgia legislature was bribed into selling vast acreage owned by the state for a penny an acre, is perhaps the most flagrant example of the misuse of political lobbying. To control and regulate its excesses without doing damage to the right of citizens and groups to express their views freely is an important but often contentious problem.

The recent growth of political action committees (PACs) has greatly increased the impact of private interest groups and expanded the scope of traditional lobbying activity. It has also increased the clamor for their control. The Supreme Court has dealt cautiously with the issue. In *Buckley v. Valeo* the Court (in an extremely lengthy opinion) overturned as unconstitutional those portions of the Federal Elections Campaign Act of 1971 that sought to limit the amount of money a political group or association might spend during a campaign. Said the Court:

> The First Amendment denies government the power to determine that spending to promote one's political views is wasteful, excessive, or unwise. In the free society ordained by our Constitution it is not the government but the people— individually as citizens and candidates and collectively as associations and political committees—who must retain control over the quantity and range of debate on public issues in a political campaign.[40]

And while *Buckley* deals with campaign expenditures, it clearly indicates the skepticism the Supreme Court has traditionally assumed toward efforts to control and regulate the political process.

In the debate on this topic, Hope Eastman, formerly of the American Civil Liberties Union, argues against any revision in existing legislation that would require broadened public disclosure of lobbying activities. Ms. Eastman rests her case on the First Amendment.

Fred Wertheimer, president of Common Cause—another public interest group—disputes the constitutional barrier to further disclosure information and argues that additional public information is required to protect the integrity of the political process.

Is There a Constitutional Right to Abortion?

Perhaps no contemporary issue has been more vigorously contested or has generated more fervor than the question of abortion. In 1973 the Supreme Court delivered its landmark decision in *Roe v. Wade*, invalidating most antiabortion laws. The Court's decision was based on the right to privacy, which Justice Harry A. Blackmun acknowledged was not explicitly mentioned in the Constitution. But he pointed out that

> In varying contexts, the Court or individual Justices have, indeed, found at least the roots of that right in the First Amendment; in the Fourth and Fifth Amendments; in the penumbra of the Bill of Rights; in the Ninth Amendment; or in the concept of liberty guaranteed by the . . . 14th Amendment.[41]

Regardless of its source, Blackmun stated that the right of privacy was "broad enough to encompass a woman's decision whether or not to terminate her pregnancy."

The Supreme Court's decision has been attacked on two fronts. The most vociferous attack has been mounted by the opponents of abortion, who have raised profound moral questions pertaining to the life of the unborn fetus. Known broadly as the Right to Life movement, these critics have charged the Court with a failure to give due regard to the rights of the unborn.

A more pointed criticism has come from many legal scholars who are disturbed by the tendency of the Supreme Court to read new values and new rights into the Constitution—the *right of privacy* being the most notorious. From 1885 until 1937 the justices of the Supreme Court were inclined to read their own views of economic liberty into the Constitution.[42] The privacy decisions of the Court have been criticized as a modern example of similar judicial excess. The difference is that the earlier Supreme Courts sought to enlarge the protection of individual economic rights; the current Court has sought to expand individual civil liberties. But both, as Dean John Hart Ely of Stanford Law School suggests, involve writing contemporary values into the Constitution that simply are not there. As expressed by Ely, "The problem with *Roe* is not so much that it bungles the question it sets itself, but rather that it sets itself a question the Constitution has not made the Court's business."[43]

In the debate on this topic, Rhonda Copelon rejects the constitutional arguments of those who oppose the decision in *Roe v. Wade* and suggests that the decision "brought legal theory . . . closer to encompassing the existence of women." The arguments against the decision are marshaled by John T. Noonan, Jr., a professor of law at the University of California. Noonan's statement is contained in testimony that he gave to the Senate Judiciary Committee's Subcommittee on the Constitution. It traverses a much wider field than the limited objections offered by Ely.

NOTES

1. Philip Kurland, *Of Church and State and the Supreme Court,* 29 U. Chi. L. Rev. 1 (1961). Italics added.
2. See Mark DeWolfe Howe, *The Garden and the Wilderness: Religion and Government in American Constitutional History* (Chicago: University of Chicago Press, 1965).
3. Thomas Jefferson to the Danbury Baptist Association, 1802, in Andrew A. Lipscomb, ed., *The Writings of Thomas Jefferson* (Washington, D.C.: The Thomas Jefferson Memorial Association, 1983), xvi, 282.
4. James Madison, "Memorial and Remonstrance," 1785, in Galliaid Hunt, ed., *The Writings of James Madison* (New York: G.P. Putnam's Sons, 1900-1910), ii, 183.
5. Walter Berns, *The First Amendment and the Future of American Democracy* (New York: Basic Books, 1976), pp. 1–76.
6. *Committee for Public Education v. Nyquist,* 413 U.S. 756 (1973).
7. *Illinois ex rel. McCollum v. Board of Education,* 333 U.S. 203 (1948).
8. *Lemon v. Kurtzman,* 403 U.S. 602 (1971).
9. *Cochran v. Louisiana State Board of Education,* 281 U.S. 370 (1930); *Everson v. Board of Education,* 330 U.S. 1 (1947).
10. 98 U.S. 145 (1878).
11. The leading case remains the *Selective Draft Law Cases,* 245 U.S. 366 (1918). Also see *United States v. Seeger,* 380 U.S. 163 (1965).
12. *Thomas v. Review Board of Ind. Employment Service,* 450 U.S. 707 (1981).
13. *Watson v. Jones,* 3 Wall. 679 (1872).

14. *Engel v. Vitale,* 370 U.S. 421 (1967).

15. 374 U.S. 203 (1968).

16. *Lemon v. Kurtzman,* 403 U.S. 602 (1971).

17. *Committee for Public Education v. Nyquist,* 413 U.S. 756 (1973).

18. *Meek v. Pittenger,* 421 U.S. 349 (1975).

19. *Wolman v. Walter,* 433 U.S. 299 (1977).

20. *Tilton v. Richardson,* 407 U.S. 672 (1971).

21. *Board of Education v. Allen,* 392 U.S. 236 (1968).

22. *Walz v. Tax Commission,* 397 U.S. 664 (1970).

23. *Mueller v. Allen,* 103 S. Ct. 3062 (1983).

24. *Reynolds v. United States,* 98 U.S. 145 (1878).

25. *Masses Publishing Co. v. Patten,* 244 Fed. 535 (S.D. N.Y. 1917).

26. John Milton, *Areopagitica: A Speech for the Liberty of Unlicensed Printing* (1644).

27. 250 U.S. 616 (1919), Holmes dissenting.

28. *West Virginia State Board of Education v. Barnette,* 319 U.S. 624 (1943).

29. Leonard Levy, *Legacy of Suppression: Freedom of Speech and Press in Early American History* (Cambridge: Harvard University Press, 1960), p. 26.

30. See especially the opinion of Justice Oliver Wendell Holmes, Jr., in *Patterson v. Colorado,* 205 U.S. 454 (1907).

31. Zechariah Chafee, Jr., *Free Speech in the United States* (Cambridge: Harvard University Press, 1941), p. 21.

32. *Tinker v. Des Moines School District,* 393 U.S. 503 (1971).

33. *Cohen v. California,* 403 U.S. 15 (1971).

34. *Miller v. California,* 413 U.S. 15 (1973).

35. 315 U.S. 568 (1942).

36. 376 U.S. 254 (1964).

37. *Associated Press v. Walker,* 388 U.S. 130 (1967).

38. *Walker v. Birmingham,* 388 U.S. 307 (1967).

39. Two years later, in *Shuttelsworth v. Birmingham,* 394 U.S. 147 (1969), one of the demonstrators in the same march was successful in having his conviction reversed and the Birmingham ordinance overturned.

40. 424 U.S. 1 (1976).

41. 410 U.S. 113 (1973).

42. The leading case is *Lochner v. New York,* 198 U.S. 45 (1905), and the term often used critically to describe the process is *Lochnerizing* the Constitution.

43. John Hart Ely, *The Wages of Crying Wolf: A Comment on Roe v. Wade,* 82 YALE L. J. 920 (1973).

5 Should a constitutional amendment restore the right to voluntary prayer in the public schools?

YES THE CASE FOR VOLUNTARY PRAYER IN THE PUBLIC SCHOOLS

Grover Rees

Mr. Chairman and members of the Committee:

I am here to testify in support of S.J. Res. 199, a resolution proposing an amendment to the United Constitution [to] restore the right to voluntary prayer in public schools.

I have no particular qualifications to speak to the question whether school prayer is desirable. Indeed, I think it is important to emphasize that this amendment would not require that a single prayer ever be said by anyone in any school. It would simply provide that the decision be made by state and local education authorities—subject to the rights of individual conscience—rather than by the federal courts. As someone whose job it is to read and write about constitutional law and therefore about the federal courts, I think this transfer of decisionmaking power would be a good thing.

I also think it is important to observe what kind of a constitutional amendment we are talking about. This proposal would make no change at all in the Constitution as it was understood by those who framed and ratified it. Rather, it would have the effect of reversing certain decisions of the

United States Supreme Court, decisions that seem to have been based on the Justices' ideas about what was right for the country rather than on their construction of what the Constitution and its amendments meant to those who framed them.

The original understanding of the First Amendment was not that government could have nothing to do with religion. Rather, the Establishment Clause was intended to prohibit the *federal* government from establishing a national religion. This did not mean that prayer could not be a part of public life, and it imposed no restrictions whatever on state and local governments. The First Congress of the United States, the day after proposing the First Amendment, passed a resolution requesting that President Washington proclaim a day of national prayer and thanksgiving.[1] That Congress also reenacted the Northwest Ordinance, providing in part for public schools which were to advance "religion, morality, and knowledge."[2] Although Thomas Jefferson strongly opposed the establishment of religion in his own state of Virginia—and it [is] important not to confuse the views of individual framers on controversies within their own states with the intentions of all of

U.S. Cong., Senate, *Proposed Constitutional Amendment to Permit Voluntary Prayer,* **Hearings before the Committee on the Judiciary, 97th Cong., 2nd Sess., 1982, pp. 370–79.**

[1] 1 Annals of Congress 914 (1789).

[2] Act of Aug. 7, 1789, 1 Stat. 50, 51–52, n. (a).

them concerning what powers, if any, the federal constitution was to take away from the states[3]—Jefferson also wrote that he doubted whether "the liberties of a nation" could "be thought secure when we have removed their only firm basis, a conviction in the minds of the people that these liberties are the gift of God."[4] Jefferson's idea of what neutrality toward religion meant was perhaps best reflected in his plan to establish several seminaries at the University of Virginia, one for each of the several leading denominations in the state.[5]

The Supreme Court has held that the Fourteenth Amendment was intended to "incorporate" the Establishment Clause and make its prohibitions binding not only on the federal government but also on the states.[6] Constitutional historians, however, have generally been skeptical of the claim that the framers of the Fourteenth Amendment had any intention to "incorporate" the specific provisions of the Bill of Rights.[7] The case against incorporation of the Establishment Clause is particularly weak, since one of the purposes of that clause was almost certainly to prevent the federal government from interfering with the power of states to establish their own churches if they so desired.[8] How do you "incorporate" a states' rights provision and make it "binding" on the states?

Perhaps the most powerful piece of evidence against the proposition that those who framed and ratified the Fourteenth Amendment intended thereby to take away the power of state and local governments to provide for school prayer is the debate over the Blaine Amendment in 1876. This was a proposed constitutional amendment to prohibit the states from establishing religion or abridging the free exercise thereof.[9] Its proponents clearly did not believe that the Fourteenth Amendment already prevented the states from doing these things, and its opponents said they thought the matters should be left to state discretion.[10] This was eight years after the ratification of the Fourteenth Amendment. Many of those who were in Congress in 1876 had been in the Congress that proposed the Fourteenth Amendment.[11] Yet nobody suggested that the Blaine Amendment was superfluous because the Fourteenth Amendment already imposed its prohibitions on the states. Everyone assumed the states had the power to establish religion outright if they wanted to. And even the *proponents* of the Blaine Amendment—those who wanted to abolish state power to establish religion—explicitly provided that their amendment would not prevent Bible reading in the public schools.[12]

At the time of the school prayer cases in the early 1960s, the Blaine Amendment was cited as evidence that the Fourteenth Amendment did not make the Establishment Clause binding on the states, and that even if it did, the clause did not pro-

[3] *See* Engel v. Vitale, 370 U.S. 421, 445–56 (1962) (Stewart, J., dissenting).

[4] 4 Works of Thomas Jefferson 803 (Putnam, New York, 1904–05).

[5] 2 P. Bruce, History of the University of Virginia 367–69 (1920).

[6] Illinois ex rel. McCollum v. Board of Education, 333 U.S. 203 (1948).

[7] See, e.g., Fairman, *Does the Fourteenth Amendment Incorporate the Bill of Rights? The Original Understanding,* 2 Stan. L. Rev. 5 (1949); Morrison, *Does the Fourteenth Amendment Incorporate the Bill of Rights? The Judicial Interpretation,* 2 Stan L. Rev. 140 (1949).

[8] *See* [School District of] Abington Township v. Schempp, 374 U.S. 203, 309–10 (Stewart, J., dissenting); Snee, *Religious Disestablishment and the Fourteenth Amendment,* 1954 Wash. U.L.Q. 371.

[9] H. Res. 1, 44th Cong., 1st Sess. (1876), quoted in Illinois ex rel. McCollum v. Board of Education, 333 U.S. 203, 219 n. 6 (Frankfurter, J., concurring).

[10] *See* Meyer, *The Blaine Amendment and the Bill of Rights,* 64 Harv. L. Rev. 939 (1951).

[11] *See id.* at 941 n.14.

[12] See H. Res. 1, *supra* note 9: "This article shall not be construed to prohibit the reading of the Bible in any school or institution;. . . . "

hibit school prayer.[13] In Abington Township v. Schempp the Court rejected these arguments, making it clear that the original understanding was not as important to the Justices as their own recent precedents and their own views about the needs of modern society. Writing for the majority, Justice Clark observed that some people

> continue to question [the] history, logic and efficacy [of the Court's holdings that the Establishment Clause applies to the states and requires neutrality between religion and nonreligion.] Such contentions, in the light of the consistent interpretation in cases of this Court, seem entirely untenable and of value only as academic exercises.[14]

Justice Brennan, concurring, was even more explicit in rejecting arguments that the Court was bound by the intentions of those who proposed and ratified the provisions the Court claimed to be interpreting:

> Even if we assume that the draftsmen of the Fourteenth Amendment saw no immediate connection between its protections and the guarantees of the First Amendment, it is certainly too late in the day to suggest that their assumed inattention to the question dilutes the force of these constitutional guarantees in their application to the states. It is enough to conclude that the religious liberty embodied in the Fourteenth Amendment would not be viable if the Constitution were interpreted to forbid only establishments ordained by Congress.[15]

Justice Brennan was being somewhat disingenuous, for he was dealing not with evidence of "inattention" to a relationship between the Fourteenth Amendment and the Establishment Clause, but to evidence of an affirmative contemporaneous understanding that the amendment did *not* make the clause binding on the states. But he made it clear that the Justices' apprehension of the *Zeitgeist,* and not of the meaning attached to words by those who wrote and adopted them, was the basis of the school prayer opinions.

Among those who work in constitutional law it is considered naive to talk about the intentions of the framers. It is said that we cannot know what they intended, and that we might not want to know, so that the best the courts can do in "interpreting" the constitution is to divine and enforce the values that are important to Americans today.[16] For some of us at least, this attitude seems contrary to the whole rationale for recognizing the Supreme Court as the supreme interpreter of the Constitution. As articulated by Chief Justice John Marshall in *Marbury v. Madison,*[17] the doctrine of judicial review was grounded in the decision by the sovereign people to adopt a written constitution imposing restrictions on their legislature. That constitution, said Marshall, is supreme law. If a court is presented with a statute that conflicts with the meaning of the written constitution that was adopted by the people, then it is his *duty* (not just his power) to declare the law unconstitutional. But if it is impossible to tell what the Constitution really means, and if the Court is enforcing those policies and values that the Justices regard as fundamental, then there is no reason that their judgment should be superior to the judgment of Congress or of the state legislators. When the Court unfetters itself from the historical Constitution, it also unfetters the rest of us.

Yet, because the Court enforces its policies under the *rubric* of enforcing the Constitution, a constitutional amendment is the only effective way to reverse a

---

[13] *See* [School District of] Abington Township v. Schempp, 374 U.S. 203, 257–58 & n.21 (1963) (Brennan, J., concurring).

[14] *Id.* at 217 (majority opinion).

[15] *Id.* at 257–58 (Brennan, J., dissenting).

[16] *See, e.g.,* Sandalow, *Constitutional Interpretation,* 79 Mich. L. Rev. 1033 (1981).

[17] 1 Cranch 137 (1803).

Supreme Court opinion. When an amendment is proposed that would chip away at a piece of the twentieth-century judicial constitution and restore the original understanding, it strains the limits of honest advocacy to accuse supporters of the amendment of being radicals who are cluttering up our fundamental document with their particular causes and ideologies. Yet that has been the response to the school prayer amendment from many of its opponents, including some teachers of constitutional law. They keep two sets of books: Among the cognoscenti, judicial review is justified as a way of imposing on legislatures fundamental *contemporary* values that the legislatures stubbornly refuse to recognize.[18] But when the public becomes unhappy with a Supreme Court decision, we hear about the framers and the sanctity of the fundamental document. Yet the amending process—unlike the power of the judges to impose their own values on the public—is part of that document. Rhetoric about not cluttering up our fundamental document should be directed at the courts, not at those who seize the only available means of erasing judicial glosses on the original understanding. Constitutional scholars should remember that many Americans value the Constitution not simply for the sake of having one, but for what it says.

Finally, I would like to address myself briefly to some of the horror stories that have been told by opponents of the school prayer amendment. They speak as if it would force people to participate in prayer, yet the amendment explicitly provides that no such requirement can be imposed. Any person who for any reason objects to any prayer will have the right not to participate. The trick is that the definition of "coercion" has been expanded to

[18] *See, e.g.,* Sandalow, *supra* note 16; Wellington, *Common Law Rules and Constitutional Double Standards: Some Notes on Adjudication,* 83 Yale L.J. 221 (1973). *See generally* J. Ely, Democracy and Distrust 43–67 (1979).

include subliminal pressure to conform. This is a problem inherent not in the nature of prayer but in the nature of public education. Schools teach values as well as information: many people object to the particular things that are taught to their children, but even the most vehement opponents of such things as sex education and flag salutes seek only to have their children excused from participation, or perhaps to have their school boards exclude the offending programs from the curriculum. Nobody seeks to have the courts declare these things unconstitutional.

The other objection I have heard most frequently is that the amendment will empower governments to write their own prayers. It is true, of course, that the amendment will restore to state and local school authorities the power they had until 1962 to *choose* prayers that will be said in schools—always subject to the rights of individual students not to participate. It is also true that the power to choose a prayer might include the power to choose a prayer written by someone who is alive today. (I assume this is what is meant by "government writing prayers," since I don't imagine anyone believes the prayers will be composed on the floor of the state legislature.) I personally see no reason why school boards would want to commission new prayers; there are lots of perfectly good prayers that have been around for hundreds or thousands of years. But it is true that the amendment would allow this. The only response to those who object to this feature of the amendment is to ask what they would prefer; after all, *somebody* has to choose the content of any group prayer, or of any other group exercise. The two alternatives I can think of are to write a particular prayer into the Constitution, or to include a provision in the Constitution restricting the kinds of prayers that can be said. In either case, the government is still going to wind up choosing prayers; it is just that the power of choice will reside (as the power of prohibition now resides) in the federal courts rather than in state and local school authorities.

This is the answer to most of the horror stories: The power to do something invariably includes possible abuses of the power. To those who are convinced that state and local school authorities will abuse the power to provide for school prayer, I can only say that I trust the school boards more than I trust the federal courts. In applying their rule against prayer, the federal courts have forbidden not only "denominational" prayer, but also Bible reading,[19] student-initiated prayers in meetings after classes in school buildings,[20] posting of the Ten Command-

ments on classroom walls,[21] and school policies permitting students "to gather at the school . . . for any educational, moral, religious or ethical purposes."[22] One court even upheld a school principal's decision to deny kindergarten children the right to say grace before lunch—a decision based on the possibility that other children might have felt pressure to say grace, and that this would have been an establishment of religion within the courts' expansive definition.[23] We should trust our courts less and our communities more. The school prayer amendment will restore the decisionmaking power to the communities, where the framers of the Constitution intended it to reside.

[19] Abington Township v. Schempp, 374 U.S. 203 (1963).

[20] Brandon v. Board of Education of Guilderland Central School District, 635 F.2d 971 (2d Cir. 1980) (public school need not allow a student group to meet after school for voluntary prayers on the same terms as other student groups are allowed to meet, *since such meetings by the student prayer group would violate the Establishment Clause*); Lubbock Civil Liberties Union v. Lubbock Independent School District, 669 F.2d 1038 (5th Cir. 1982).

[21] Stone v. Graham, 441 U.S. 39 (1980).
[22] Lubbock Civil Liberties Union v. Lubbock Independent School District, 669 F.2d 1038 (5th Cir. 1982).
[23] Stein v. Oshinsky, 348 F.2d 999 (2d Cir. 1965). Although the court was not forced to decide whether the student-initiated prayers violated the Establishment Clause, it was on this basis that the principal had forbidden the prayers, and the court regarded the argument that to permit such prayers would violate the Establishment Clause as a serious one. *Id.* at 1001.

NO THE CASE AGAINST VOLUNTARY PRAYER IN THE PUBLIC SCHOOLS

Norman Redlich

My name is Norman Redlich. I am Dean and Professor of Law at the New York University School of Law where I have taught constitutional law for twenty-four years. I have been a member of the New York City Board of Education, and was Corporation Counsel of the City of New York from 1972 to 1974. I am the co-

U.S. Cong., Senate, *Proposed Constitutional Amendment to Permit Voluntary Prayer*, Hearings before the Committee on the Judiciary, 97th Cong., 2nd Sess., 1982, pp. 444–53.

author of a constitutional law casebook which will be published in November of 1982. From 1979 to 1981 I was co-Chairperson of the Lawyers' Committee for Civil Rights under Law.

Presently, I serve as co-Chairperson of the Commission on Law and Social Action of the American Jewish Congress and I am a member of the Board of Overseers of the Jewish Theological Seminary. I also served on that Seminary's special commission to study the question of the ordination of women in the Conservative Rabbinate. I mention the latter affiliations because while I appear here as a student of constitutional law, and in that capacity oppose the enactment of S.J.R. 199, my views on the subject are motivated in large part by a firm religious commitment. I consider myself a civil libertarian, and have been active in civil liberties and civil rights causes for many years. My opposition to this amendment, however, stems not only from my concern for civil liberties, but my abiding concern for the survival of religious freedom as we have known it in this country.

I recognize that in considering a constitutional amendment, such as is proposed by S.J.R. 199, the issue is not necessarily whether the Supreme Court's school prayer decisions have correctly interpreted the First Amendment, but rather whether, quite apart from that Amendment, religious exercises should be permitted in the public schools. The question, therefore, is not simply correctness of the interpretation of the Establishment Clause, but whether that interpretation, as set forth in *Engel v. Vitale* and *Abington School District v. Schempp* reflects those values and institutions best designed to promote both religion and liberty in this country. Because I believe profoundly in my religious faith, and in the absolute necessity of the government not imposing any religious faith, including my own, or anyone else, I oppose any attempt to tamper with values that underlie the Establishment Clause.

No other country has our commitment to the concept of separation of church and state. There is no country on earth that enjoys the religious pluralism and the religious freedom that has existed here, and there is no country which has been as free from religious strife as has been ours. This happy confluence of constitutional principles and religious liberty is no accident.

There are countries where established religions tolerate other religions; there are countries which are hostile to religions and where religions exist, if at all, by the sufferance of a despotic government and at great peril to those who would profess and practice their faith. To those of you on this committee, who share with me a religious faith, even if not my own, I ask whether you would exchange place in this country with citizens of any other country where principles of our First Amendment do not prevail.

The proposal you have before you does not deal with a fringe interpretation of the Establishment Clause. It deals not with questions of remedial reading taught to parochial school students, nor to the issue whether the singing of Christmas Carols is or is not a religious exercise. It does not concern textbooks or mathematics courses taught in religious schools. Nor does it even purport to establish a religious exercise which is non-denominational, perhaps because sponsors of the school prayer amendment realize that there is no such thing as a non-denominational prayer. No, this proposed amendment does not deal with peripheral questions under the Establishment Clause. This proposed amendment strikes at the very core of constitutional values that underlie our most precious guarantee of religious and political freedom. This amendment permits an avowedly religious exercise—a prayer—of whatever nature may be approved by the majority in any school district in the country. Whether it be Mormon prayers in Utah, Jewish prayers in Brooklyn, Catholic prayers in Boston, Baptist prayers in Georgia, Congregationalist prayers in parts of New England, religious prayers are to be permitted by this proposed amendment, subject only to the limitation that a person shall not be required to participate in prayer.

Scholars may disagree over the motivation of the Founders in prohibiting religious establishments. I happen to believe that the Supreme Court's interpretation of that history is correct. But even those who may disagree with the Court's view that all aid to religion is prohibited concede that government is not permitted to discriminate among religious sects. Even Justice Stewart, the sole dissenter in *Schempp,* agreed that school officials could not favor one religion over another. Most Americans conceive it as settled doctrine that religion is a private affair and that government may not favor one faith or the other. In my view, then, this proposal is not a conservative one, but rather a profoundly radical alteration of a basic precept of American life, the required neutrality of government among religious faiths. It will undo one of the proudest achievements of this republic.

It is too often assumed that the free exercise clause is the prime guarantee of religious liberty, that the Establishment Clause is, somehow, hostile to religion, designed to keep religion from becoming too powerful. This represents a profound misreading of history and a lack of appreciation of the Establishment Clause as itself a prime guarantor of religious liberty. There cannot be true religious liberty—the right of a person freely to choose those forms of religious belief and expression which represent that individual's innermost expression of faith—if the government is permitted to display favoritism to one faith or the other. It is our constitutional theory that the government, which represents all the people, has no business generating the pressure of any religious belief on any individual citizen. The First Amendment command that government make no law respecting an establishment of religion, which this proposed amendment would alter in a most fundamental sense, is an essential feature of a constitutional structure which guarantees that persons can conduct their religious practices, and express their religious beliefs, free

from pressure of government conformity.

What is different about this country—what distinguishes it from countries like England or Canada where establishments are permitted—is that in matters of faith we are all equal. I do not wish to be a religious stranger in my own country, and I do not wish any member of any faith to be a stranger in our midst. If there is an official prayer, of one religious denomination, everyone else is a stranger. Catholics in Jewish neighborhoods, or Jews in Catholic neighborhoods, have the right to assume that in this country there are no favorite religions. Take that away, and they become fearful minorities, practicing their faith because of the generosity of the majority. Persons then seek to advance their beliefs, to form coalitions, to protect their religious turf, lest they lose their right to worship. That is the kind of religious strife which the Founders sought to avoid. That concern was specifically articulated by James Madison when he wrote his remarkable document, the Memorial and Remonstrance against Religious Assessments, which was the intellectual forerunner to the Establishment Clause.

There is no merit to the claim that religious freedom is adequately protected by the language in this proposed amendment which prohibits requiring persons to participate in prayer. Stamping the imprimatur of government on any religious exercise is coercive. One does not solve the problem of coercion by stating that the person does not have to participate in prayer. As religious groups opposing this amendment have stated forcefully in their testimony, the evil comes from being part of a minority which does not participate in a ceremony which the government has established as the majority's will.

Nor is there merit to the claim, raised in almost every school prayer case, that the prohibition on publicly recited or officially chosen prayer violates the free exercise rights of those children who wish to pray. The Supreme Court has never held that students may not, on their own, recite prayers, say grace before or after meals, silently pray at the start of the day, or before exams, or before football games. Moreover, I think that former Chief Judge Irving Kaufman of the Second Circuit Court of Appeals was clearly correct in suggesting, in *Brandon v. Board of Education,* that, if a student can show that his or her religion requires prayer at set times, he or she must be permitted to do so. What is left of this free exercise claim, therefore, is that the clause somehow demands that students and teachers be permitted to invoke the authority of the state to promote their religion vis-à-vis others. That is not free exercise; it is precisely the evil which the Establishment Clause seeks to forbid, and it is precisely that which this amendment seeks to undo.

Let us think together for a moment about the role a written Constitution plays in a democratic society. The study of the American Constitution has been the principal focus of my professional life. The Constitution, if it does nothing else, must place certain limits on majority will. It is a profound truism that ours is a government of limited powers. To protect the rights of the states, Congress may not legislate in certain areas. And to protect certain rights of the people, the original Constitution limited the powers of both Congress and the states. The Bill of Rights, whose promised existence was necessary for ratification, imposed broad limitations on the power of the federal government. Constitutional scholars have debated at length particularly in recent years, the issue of the appropriate limitations which the Constitution, through the courts, may impose on democratic majorities. But I believe that virtually all constitutional scholars would agree that if there be one necessary limitation on majority will, it should be in those areas covered by the First Amendment, namely freedom of speech, assembly, petition, expression. These represent the basic fabric of democratic structure, of representative government. They should not be impaired merely because a majority, at any particular moment, wishes to impose its will.

Religious freedom is not simply a peripheral right placed in the First Amendment by accident. No portion of the First Amendment concerned James Madison more than the religion clauses. The founders recognized that political freedom and religious freedom always go hand-in-hand. Totalitarian governments either establish one religion, do away with religion, or subvert religion. The reason is that freedom of religion as we know it in this country, which includes the right to practice one's religion free from any imposed official faith, carries with it the recognition that there is an authority that the government cannot control. It is not surprising, upon reflection, that one of the demands of Solidarity in Poland was that the Catholic Mass be televised. Communist states will always be at war with religion because the one thing that a Communist state cannot tolerate is the notion that there is an institution people can believe in, and which the government cannot control.

The religion clauses of the Constitution, therefore, are an essential element of the fabric of political democracy. It is not by accident that the First Amendment begins with the words, "Congress shall make no law respecting an establishment of religion, or prohibiting the free exercise thereof." As the courts have expanded the protection of both the Free Exercise and Establishment Clauses, this country has enjoyed an increasing degree of religious freedom and peace. This proposed amendment seeks to undo all of the essential values that underlie the religion clauses. It permits the favoring of one religion over another; it permits the favoring of religions generally; and, despite its language and the intention of its sponsors, it necessarily sanctions coercion against religious minorities.

In recognition of the fact that the Bill of Rights has served this country well by protecting unpopular minorities against the abuses by transient majorities, over 500 professors of constitutional law and practicing attorneys, including almost all of the most prominent constitutional scholars in this country, have signed a statement which is appended to my testimony, urging that this amendment not be adopted.* I wish to quote here what I believe to be the essence of that statement:

> American liberties have been secure in large measure because they have been guaranteed by a Bill of Rights which the American people have until now deemed practically unamendable. If now, for the first time, an amendment to "narrow its operation" is adopted, a precedent will have been established which may prove too easy to follow when other controversial decisions interpreting the Bill of Rights are handed down. In the past, the Court has construed the provisions against infringement of the free exercise of religion and speech and assembly, or securing the privilege against self-incrimination, or requiring fair trial procedures, in a manner deemed by many at the time to be unduly restrictive of the proper powers of government. It is certain that it will do so again in the future. If the first clause of the Bill of Rights, forbidding laws respecting an establishment of religion, should prove so easily susceptible to impairment by amendment, none of the succeeding clauses will be secure.

Constitutions are not written in stone; nor does history always provide an absolute

* The list containing signatures of over 500 professors of constitutional law and practicing attorneys urging that the amendment be not adopted is on file with the Committee on the Judiciary.

answer to new constitutional issues. Courts, as we know, perform the interpretative role in this country. From time to time we have all disagreed with judicial interpretations of constitutional provisions. But before we take the drastic step of amending a core provision of our constitutional framework—the Establishment Clause—by overturning a court decision interpreting that clause, it is incumbent on all of us, including those who may disagree with the interpretation, to ask whether that interpretation is so inconsistent with the underlying values which gave rise to the constitutional provision as to warrant the drastic step of changing the Bill of Rights.

That the Establishment Clause was designed to prevent the government from composing prayers or other religious exercises is, in my view, irrefutable. That the Clause was designed to prevent coercion on the basis of religion is, in my view, irrefutable. That the Clause was designed, at a minimum, to maintain government neutrality among religions is, in my view, irrefutable.

Some may think that in the school prayer decisions the Supreme Court carried these principles too far. If so, the most that can be said is that the Supreme Court, like Othello, loved our constitutional values not wisely, but too well. I believe that the Court loved both wisely and well. Surely, excessive concern with religious freedom is not a vice to be corrected; rather it is a virtue—to be praised by most and tolerated by all.

I urge the rejection of this proposed amendment.

OUR MOST PRECIOUS HERITAGE
(Appendix to Testimony of Norman Redlich)

Our Bill of Rights is America's most precious heritage. For a century and three-quarters it has spread the mantle of protection over persons of all faiths and creeds, political, cultural and religious.

Under our system, special responsibility for the interpretation and application of the Bill of Rights rests with the Supreme Court. In discharging this responsibility the Court has from time to time handed down decisions which have aroused considerable controversy. Some of the decisions have been subjected to strong criticism and even condemnation. There have, no doubt, been decisions which have been deemed by a majority of the American people to have been unwise, either in the conclusion reached by the Court or in the manner by which that conclusion was reached.

It may be that the Court's decisions against state-sponsored prayer in the public schools belong in this category. We are, nevertheless, convinced that it would be far wiser for our nation to accept the decisions than to amend the Bill of Rights in order to nullify them.

We recognize that the Constitution provides for its own amendment, and that no provision of it, including the Bill of Rights, is immune to repeal or alteration at the will of the people expressed through the medium of constitutional amendment. Yet, it is relevant to recall in this respect the concluding paragraph of Thomas Jefferson's great Virginia statute for Establishing Religious Freedom:

> And though we well know that this assembly, elected by the people for the ordinary purposes of legislation only, have no power to restrain the acts of succeeding assemblies, constituted with powers equal to our own, and that therefore to declare this act to be irrevocable would be of no effect in law, yet we are free to declare, and do declare, that the rights hereby asserted are of the natural rights of mankind, and that if any act shall be hereafter passed to repeal the present, or to narrow its operation, such act will be an infringement of natural right.

American liberties have been secure in large measure because they have been guaranteed by a Bill of Rights which the American people have until now deemed practically unamendable. If now, for the first time, an amendment to "narrow its operation" is adopted, a precedent will have been established which may prove too easy to follow when other controversial decisions interpreting the Bill of Rights are handed down. In the past, the Court has construed the provisions against infringement of the free exercise of religion and of speech and assembly, or securing the privilege against self-incrimination, or requiring fair trial procedures, in a manner deemed by many at the time to be unduly restrictive of the proper powers of government. It is certain that it will do so again in the future. If the first clause of the Bill of Rights, forbidding laws respecting an establishment of religion, should prove so easily susceptible to impairment by amendment, none of the succeeding clauses will be secure.

A grave responsibility rests upon the Congress in taking this "first experiment on our liberties." Whatever disagreements some may have with the Prayer decisions, we believe strongly that they do not justify this experiment. Accordingly, we urge that Congress approve no measures to amend the First Amendment in order to overrule these decisions.

QUESTIONS FOR DISCUSSION

1. Does the First Amendment protect the freedom not to believe in God?
2. Should church and state be separate? Why?
3. Would a moment of silence be an acceptable constitutional substitute for prayer in school?

4. Does the Constitution prohibit prayer in school?
5. Define freedom of conscience.

RECOMMENDED READINGS

CHOPER, JESSE H. "Religion in the Schools." 47 *Minnesota Law Review* 329 (1963).

GREENE, EVARTS B. *Religion and the State: The Making and Testing of an American Tradition.* New York: New York University Press, 1941.

HOWE, MARK DEWOLFE. *The Garden and the Wilderness: Religion and Government in American Constitutional History.* Chicago: University of Chicago Press, 1965.

KONVITZ, MILTON R. "Church and State: How Separate?" *Midstream* 30 (Mar, 1984), pp. 32–37.

KURLAND, PHILIP. "Of Church and State and the Supreme Court." 29 *University of Chicago Law Review* 1 (1961).

MALBIN, MICHAEL J. *Religion and Politics: The Intention of the Authors of the First Amendment.* Washington, D.C.: American Enterprise Institute, 1978.

MORGAN, RICHARD E. *The Supreme Court and Religion.* New York: Free Press, 1973.

"The School Prayer Controversy: Pro & Con." *Congressional Digest* 63 (May 1984), entire issue.

U.S. CONG., SENATE. *Proposed Constitutional Amendment to Permit Voluntary Prayer.* Hearings before the Committee on the Judiciary, 97th Cong., 2nd Sess., 1982.

———. *Voluntary School Prayer Constitutional Amendment.* Hearings before the Subcommittee on the Constitution of the Committee on the Judiciary, 98th Cong., 2nd Sess., 1984.

6 Are federal government tax credits to parents who send their children to private religious schools a violation of the separation of church and state?

YES TUITION TAX CREDITS AND THE SEPARATION OF CHURCH AND STATE

R. G. Puckett

My name is R. G. Puckett. I am executive director of Americans United for Separation of Church and State. We appreciate this opportunity to address the Senate Finance Committee on S.2673, the Educational Opportunity and Equity Act of 1982.

Americans United is a 35-year-old organization dedicated solely to the preservation of the religious liberty and church-state separation provisions of the First Amendment of the Constitution. We represent through our membership individuals of conservative and liberal political persuasions as well as the full spectrum of religious faiths and nonbelievers who are concerned with the preservation of religious freedom.

It is this concern and regard for the First Amendment guarantees of religious liberty that has prompted our request to testify on this proposed legislation. While our interests center primarily in the area of the constitutional aspects of this bill, I

R. G. Puckett, statement in U.S. Cong., Senate, *Tuition Tax Credit Proposals*, Hearings before the Committee on Finance, 97th Cong., 2nd Sess., 1982, pp. 239–46.

will also address the economic and public policy problems with it as well.

There are serious constitutional problems with S.2673 in our opinion. This conclusion is based on year after year of Supreme Court decisions establishing a clear legal record that tax aid, direct or indirect to parochial or church-related schools, is aid to religion and, therefore, unconstitutional.

The Court has allowed only incidental aids, or auxiliary aids, which directly benefit all children equally and not the institutions. Aid of this type includes loans of textbooks, diagnostic services, and school lunch programs under the theory that all children benefit from the program. There are currently suits pending in lower federal courts, however, which are challenging textbook loans.

Beginning with *Lemon vs. Kurtzman* 403 U.S. 602 (1971), the Court established a three-part test for constitutionality for any plan to aid a parochial or church-related school. The law in question must reflect a clearly secular legislative purpose; it must have a primary effect that neither advances nor inhibits religion, and it must avoid excessive government entanglement with religion.

In the case *Committee for Public Education and Religious Liberty vs. Nyquist,* 413 U.S. 756 (1973), the Court struck down a New York state tuition tax credit plan similar to that proposed in S.2673. It said that since the benefits go "to parents who send their children to sectarian schools, their purpose and inevitable effect is to aid and advance those religious institutions."

There is no question that this tax aid advances religion since at least 85 percent of the students in all nonpublic schools are in church-related schools. The fact that the aid may be viewed as incidental in amount in light of high tuition rates does not alter its intent—to aid religion.

Moreover, the fact that the aid would be routed through parents is irrelevent. Parents would serve merely as conduits of the aid, which eventually goes to the church schools. We believe the child benefit theory could not be used to prove constitutionality in this case because the only children benefited are those in private schools, not all the children in the country.

The genesis and promotion of this bill represents a certain confluence of religious and political interests. As the Supreme Court pointed out in the 1971 *Lemon* ruling, "in a community where such a large number of pupils are served by church-related schools, it can be assumed that state assistance will entail considerable political activity. Partisans of parochial schools, understandably concerned with rising costs and sincerely dedicated to both the religious and secular educational missions of their schools, will inevitably champion this cause and promote political action to achieve their goals. Those who oppose state aid, whether for constitutional, religious, or fiscal reasons, will inevitably respond and employ all of the usual political campaign techniques to prevail . . . .

"Ordinarily political debate and division, however vigorous or even partisan, are normal and healthy manifestations of our democratic system of government, but political division along religious lines was one of the principal evils against which the First Amendment was intended to protect."

This bill could so entangle religion and politics that two centuries of progress in First Amendment rights to religious liberty and church-state separation could be unalterably reversed.

Furthermore, to deny that denominational elementary and secondary schools do not discriminate by religion is to deny their very purpose—to remain religiously homogeneous. Giving public funds to such schools through the tuition tax credit proposal in S.2673 would result in federal government subsidization of sectarian division and divisiveness in education. The result of this could only be a decline in interfaith and community harmony and a socio-economic crisis in education.

Beyond the obvious constitutional problems this proposed bill presents, there are numerous other problems it could create. The cost of this program could reach almost $4.5 billion over the first three years of the program. This is lost revenues for nonstimulative credits, which are uncontrollable and inflationary. It seems unconscionable to us that Congress would pass such legislation at a time when such drastic cuts are being made in the education budget.

Further, no one has adequately answered the concern church school administrators have over regulation of their schools. While many of these schools, which in the past have refused government funds, are holding out their hands now for a piece of the tax pie, they are, at the same time, objecting strenuously to any kind of federal, state, or local regulations.

There is no amount of federal funds that can be taken by these schools that will not be accompanied by increased regulations. A primary example of the need for regulations is contained in the bill itself. It states that no credit shall be paid to an educational institution unless that school files with the Secretary a statement that "declares that such institution has not followed a racially discriminatory policy during such calendar year." This puts the burden of proof on the school instead of on the government and requires more paperwork by church schools.

That would require new policing efforts by some agency, such as the Department of Education or the Internal Revenue Service. Government bureaucracy and red tape would evolve around the inevitable regulations that would come with tuition tax credits and would entangle government with religion, precisely what the religion clause of the First Amendment was intended to prohibit.

Beyond that, there are glaring omissions in the bill, with no mention of other types of discrimination, such as by religion, by sex, and in other ways.

Furthermore, the discrimination clause of the bill would produce the opposite effect the Administration claims it wants— to get government out of our lives. Churches could not freely exercise their religious mission of educating their youth with government investigating the attendance and other records that they would be forced to keep. Barbara Morris, a conservative activist and writer, warned in the Pro-Family Newsletter of April, 1981, that the tuition tax credit plan is a "trap that will result in government control of *all* schools." Morris also noted that "providing information for such tax credits on 1040 or other tax forms will enable the government to identify every family with children enrolled in Christian schools as well as the schools they attend—information they do not presently have."

The public schools were founded on the concept of a free universal system of education for every child, regardless of economic status, race, religion, or ethnic background. The institution of public schools in this country has been the foundation that has helped to produce a strong middle class, one of the highest literacy rates in the world, and a chance for every citizen to better himself or herself.

This proposed legislation would completely upend that concept and tradition. The beneficiaries of this aid would be primarily upper income families, who can afford to send their children to expensive nonpublic schools.

Furthermore, how much of a tax credit is enough? Who is the final arbiter to decide that question? If parents can claim 50 percent of tuition costs to nonpublic schools, why can't they claim the full amount? If the lesser amount is permissible, then the full amount is as well.

The amounts of the credits would escalate because parents would be encouraged to remove their children from public schools and place them in nonpublic schools to take advantage of the tax credit. This could force the costs of programs in private schools to increase, thus encouraging those schools to ask for a greater tax credit. Those schools could also raise their tuition rates to take full advantage of the credit.

The result could be an educational civil war between the private and public schools vying for public funds. Public school funds that have already been drastically cut would be cut further to meet the budgetary needs of funding tuition tax credits. John Chapoton, assistant secretary for tax policy for the Department of Treasury, said in testimony before the House Education and Labor Committee that, "Tuition tax credits would be increased to the extent that direct student assistance programs are reduced or private school enrollments or tuitions increase."

At the same time the private schools would not be required to follow minimum educational standards established for public schools. This aid would foster an elitist caste system of education in this country, with the public schools becoming the dumping ground of those not acceptable to the private schools, such as the poor, the handicapped, and others.

That is why the idea that tuition tax credits would foster so-called needed competition between the public and private schools is false. The roles of the public and private sectors in education are very different. Private schools do not have to follow standards of teacher qualifications, salaries, curricula, services, etc.

Beyond that, the local citizenry would have no say in what happened to the private schools, which are controlled and operated far from the eye of open public meetings as with the boards of education of public schools.

Historically the American people have not shown much support for aid to parochial schools. For approximately the past 15 years Americans from Alaska to New York have consistently voted down such aid. The following are results of statewide referenda and initiatives of the past decade on government aid to parochial and private schools, elementary, secondary, and postsecondary.

State	Year	Vote Against	Vote For
New York	1967	72.5%	27.5%
Michigan	1970	57	43
Nebraska	1970	57	43
Oregon	1972	61	39
Idaho	1972	57	43
Maryland	1972	55	45
Maryland	1974	56.5	43.5
Washington	1975	60.5	39.5
Missouri	1976	60	40
Alaska	1976	54	46
District of Columbia	1982	88	12

We understand the problems that parents who choose to send their children to nonpublic schools have in paying high tuition rates. But the answer is not to provide public funds to those special interest schools. It is bad economic and public policy because it would create chaos in our educational system and destroy our long tradition of separation of church and state and the right to privately and freely exercise our religious beliefs. Americans United ask this Committee to oppose S.2673.

NO THE CASE FOR TUITION TAX CREDITS

Sister Renée Oliver

I am Sister Renée Oliver, Associate Director of Citizens for Educational Freedom. I wish to thank the members of the Committee for the opportunity to speak to you on the very important topic of parental rights in education.

Citizens for Educational Freedom is a national, nonsectarian and nonpartisan organization made up of parents who are

Sister Renée Oliver, statement in U.S. Cong., Senate, *Tuition Tax Credit–1983*, Hearing before the Committee on Finance, 98th Cong., 1st Sess., 1983, pp. 325–35.

concerned that their rights in education are not being recognized.

Members believe, as I am sure you do, that the educational responsibility does not originate with the state, but rather that the ultimate responsibility for children belongs to parents. In 1925, the United States Supreme Court upheld the right of parents to choose the education of their children. Likewise the United Nations Declaration on Human Rights, to which this country subscribes, also acknowledges the prior right of parents to choose the education they want for their children.

Scholars in many fields have been pointing out with increasing frequency that most democratic states throughout the world recognize the prior right of parents. Although the particular form and extent of an equitable, pluralistic system of education varies in different countries, most democratic states acknowledge the fundamental right of parents to choose the kind of education they desire for their children and do not discriminate in the allocation of public funds among individuals, groups, or institutions. With the exception of the United States, virtually every Western democracy provides some measure of government support for denominational and alternative schools. According to a study by Dr. Daniel McGarry of St. Louis University of some 75 free world countries, about 65 provide *Direct* public assistance for independent schools. In comparison, the United States has only a limited form of educational pluralism.

In the early days of this country, most education was private, church-sponsored, and tax-supported. All schools receiving money from the government were considered "public" schools—not because they were agencies of the government, but because their education was providing a public service. Only since the *Everson* case in 1947 has the Supreme Court decided to oppose relief to parents of non-government school children as a violation of the First Amendment. This has resulted in strengthening the government monopoly of education, paid for with taxes from all citizens, and thus creating a condition of second-class citizenship for children whose parents exercise their right of choice. In America a monopolistic church is not allowed, but in its place a monopolistic public school system has been established.

The Supreme Court has not been consistent in its pronouncements either. The Court has ruled that the state may provide textbooks to non-government schools but not charts or maps. (They have yet to rule on whether a book of maps is permissible.) The Court has also ruled that the state may reimburse the schools for mandated services, but reimbursement for education itself—which is compulsory—is not permissible.

Unfortunately, past debate over the constitutionality of relief to parents has focused upon the Establishment Clause of the First Amendment and ignored the Free Exercise Clause. Education is mandated by law in every state of the union. Parents are, therefore, required to educate their children despite their ability or inability to find and afford a school that agrees with their own personal values. In some instances the compulsory education law forces parents to act contrary to their own conscience, a clear violation of this Free Exercise Clause. In *Sherbert v. Verner* (374 U.S.398, 405-1963) the Supreme Court said, ". . . conditions upon public benefits cannot be sustained if they so operate, whatever their purpose, as to inhibit or deter the exercise of First Amendment freedoms." Therefore, no citizen should be required to give up one benefit (educational tax dollars) in order to enjoy another (free exercise of religion).

In addition, there are many parents who believe that limiting their access to educational tax dollars while requiring compulsory education is also a violation of the Fourteenth Amendment, which guarantees them equal protection under the law. Clearly the poor are effectively denied their right of choice because they can neither afford to exercise choice nor refuse to attend school. The state has created a category of parents who, solely by reason of their economic status, must subject their children to a type of education in which they might not believe. This dilemma has led to what we call the "Home-school Protest Movement." More and more parents who cannot in conscience send their children to the assigned public school but cannot afford the non-public school of their choice, are taking their children out of school to educate them at home. While it is obviously a poor solution, they see it as the lesser of two evils.

To those who argue that parents already have the freedom to choose, I point out that they may do so only at a loss of their educational tax dollars. If one is on food stamps, he need not go to a government store; if one is on Medicare, he need not go to a government hospital; a GI Bill need not be used at a state college or university. But if one wishes to benefit from his tax dollars for elementary and secondary education, he must do so in a government school. This is discriminatory, especially today when the cost of education is consuming more and more of the family budget.

According to the National Center for Educational Statistics, 62 percent of the families who send their children to non-government schools have incomes under $25,000, and only 10 percent earn over $50,000. According to another study by the Catholic League for Religious and Civil Rights on inner city nonpublic schools, 72 percent of these parents earn under $15,000. Obviously, these families must be under severe stress to come up with the tuition to these schools.

It is inconsistent that those supporters of public schools who view them as bastions of democracy cannot see the danger to that same democracy of a single educational system supported by—and hence basically controlled by—the state. If we follow their arguments to their logical conclusions, the result would be the elimination of all non-public schools except those for the most wealthy, an obvious danger to the democracy they seek to protect. Those who prize independence from state-directed thought must surely recognize that an alternative system of education for all who

desire it is an essential characteristic of any true democracy. Otherwise we are in danger of promoting an educational system that will result in an undifferentiated, homogeneous mass of citizens.

We also think it is time that we differentiate between public schools and public education. Every school that graduates well-educated students is participating in public education and should be treated equally as contributing to the common good. The state's concern should be that quality education is available to all, not where that education occurs.

There is a parallel here to the *Bradfield* v. *Roberts* case of 1899, where the Supreme Court viewed a hospital owned and operated by nuns as "a secular corporation being managed by people who hold to the doctrine of the Roman Catholic Church." The Court thought that as long as the hospital performed its purpose as stated in the articles of incorporation, the sectarian character of the hospital was of no matter. So it should be with schools that are doing a good job of educating the next generation of Americans.

Today there are approximately five million children in non-government schools in this country. At an average cost of $2,553 per child in a public school, the parents of private school children are saving the American taxpayer almost $13 billion a year.

We don't think a tuition tax credit for this kind of saving is asking too much, especially if you look at the tax credits already listed on the back of an income tax form: for a political contribution, for insulating your home, and even for day care at a church-supported facility. If I understand the purpose of these tax credits, it is to encourage the public to engage in activities which are directed toward the common good. Surely education should be foremost among them.

When fully implemented, S-528 will

represent a tax loss of only $800 million. (5,000,000 children × $300 = $1.5 billion. But all families will not be eligible for full credit. Usually less than 50 percent of those eligible claim a credit, so $800 million is a generous figure.) Let us compare this to the $99 billion public education budget, 100 percent of which is paid for by taxpayers. A tuition tax credit would mean that the parents of non-public school children would retain the equivalent of 8/10ths of 1 percent of the amount of money already allocated to public schools. This is hardly three times the federal money for public schools, as claimed by the report of the American Association of School Administrators. That report failed to take into consideration the $517 per pupil federal tax relief currently realized by public schools. Nor would tuition tax credit money come out of the public education budget any more than an energy credit comes out of the budget for the Department of Energy or a credit for a campaign contribution comes out of the Congressional budget. Public schools will continue to be funded at present levels, regardless of what happens to tuition tax credits. Nor will non-passage of tuition tax credits mean that public schools will get an additional $800,000,000. The two issues are mutually exclusive and should be viewed as such. But excellence in public and non-public schools is not mutually exclusive. This country should be able to maintain both. May I point out that there has been no destruction of public education in any of the other free countries of the world where dual support of both public and non-public education is practiced, nor did it happen in Minnesota during the 27 years when that state had an educational tax deduction in effect (a practice now being challenged before the Supreme Court).

We also think the argument that tuition tax credits will destroy public schools is an insult to the many excellent public schools we have in this country. It implies that people will continue to attend them only if forced to do so by financial penalty. We do not believe that we must build a financial Berlin Wall around public schools to keep students in. On the contrary we believe that public schools are, and will continue to be, the major source of education in this country. But we do not believe that any parent should be locked into a particular school or school system, especially if it results in a non-education for their children. Nor do we believe that a government monopoly of education is in the best interest of either government or education or children. Whenever you have a monopoly or a protective tariff, costs rise and quality declines. On the other hand, if parents are truly able to send their children where they will get the best education, that freedom of choice will generate the kind of competition that will lead to excellence in all schools, public and private.

To the argument that public schools will never be able to compete with non-public schools because the latter may refuse difficult students, I would like to interject a personal observation that as a teacher of many years in parochial schools I have had children with all types of problems: deaf, blind, retarded, emotionally disturbed, etc. Non-public schools have always accepted these children and will continue to do so whenever possible. The only reason such children are sometimes refused is that some schools simply lack the money for facilities and faculty to give them the kind of education they need.

One final argument against tuition tax credits that we would like to address is the accusation that they will encourage racial segregation. Although it is obvious to anyone who has visited an inner-city parochial school that the opposite is really the case, the Coleman research report should put that argument to rest once and for all. He says, ". . . we see that blacks and whites are substantially less segregated in the private sector than in the public sector." In fact Coleman states that those blacks with the means to pay for private schools have "higher enrollment rates in Catholic schools than do whites of the same religious group." This leads Coleman to the conclusion that those most likely to benefit from a program such as tuition tax credits would be lower income minorities. The report also shows that there is a higher percentage of minorities in private schools in states such as New York and California which have large minority populations than in public schools. The minority enrollment in New York's private schools alone exceeds 60 percent.

Another point which we think has been ignored in this area is the fact that almost every private school—even the most prestigious—provides scholarships to poor and minority students, thus achieving a racial mixture not possible in an all-white suburban school.

In other areas, the number of minority students who have been refused admission because of discriminatory policies in a few schools is infinitesimal when compared to the vast numbers of minority children who have been prohibited from attending the schools of their choice because they could not afford the tuition.

Furthermore, all present legislation states quite clearly that no credit will be allowed to parents who send their children to schools that discriminate on the basis of race. This is in keeping with the strong stand against racial discrimination which CEF has always supported.

However, in spite of the number of pages in S-528 devoted to discrimination language, tuition tax credit legislation is not, and should not be, the vehicle to settle all the discrimination problems in our country, as laudable as that would be. We believe that there are other pieces of legislation that can better address those problems. Tuition tax credits, however, [are] the only means currently available to bring some measure of relief and justice to another civil rights issue: parents' basic right to choose the education of their own children.

In summary, while a tuition tax credit is not the final answer to the problems of equity and quality in education, CEF believes that it will foster parental rights in education. This in turn will promote the kind of competition that will encourage all schools and teachers to vie for excellence that can only be good for children, education, and the future of this great country. Therefore, CEF believes that a tuition tax credit involves a policy which should be pursued by this Congress.

If the federal government assists education in any way, it must do so in a manner that equalizes educational opportunity for all children.

QUESTIONS FOR DISCUSSION

1. Would federal tax credits for private school tuition encourage parents to remove their children from the public schools?
2. Would tax credits constitute an aid to religion by the federal government?
3. Is diversity in educational approaches constitutionally desirable?
4. Should parents have the right to choose the educational program for their children?
5. Should all religious schools be supported, or only those of major religions?
6. Who defines religion?

RECOMMENDED READINGS

BREEN, VINCENT D. "Tuition Tax Credits." *Journal for the Institute for Socioeconomic Studies,* 9 (Spring 1984), pp. 15–25.

KURLAND, PHILIP B. *Religion and Law: Of Church and State and the Supreme Court.* Chicago: Aldine, 1962.

MALBIN, MICHAEL J. *The Supreme Court and the Definition of Religion* (unpublished doctoral dissertation, Cornell University, 1973).

MORGAN, RICHARD E. *The Politics of Religious Conflict: Church and State in America,* 2nd ed. Washington, D.C.: University Press of America, 1980.

NEWMAN, SHAWN TIMOTHY. "Education Vouchers and Tuition Tax Credits: In Search of Viable Public Aid to Private Education." *Journal of Legislation,* 10 (Winter 1983), pp. 178–97.

PENDLETON, CLARENCE. "Education and Minorities." *Journal of Social, Political, and Economic Studies,* 9 (Spring 1984), pp. 72–78.

PFEFFER, LEO. *God, Caesar, and the Constitution.* Boston: Beacon Press, 1975.

SORAUF, FRANK. *The Wall of Separation: The Constitutional Politics of Church and State.* Princeton: Princeton University Press, 1976.

STOKES, ANSON PHELPS. *Church and State in the United States,* 3 vols. New York: Harper, 1950.

"Tuition Tax Credits: Pro & Con." *Congressional Digest,* 63 (Jan. 1984), whole issue.

U.S. CONG., SENATE. *Tuition Tax Credit–1983,* Hearing before the Committee on Finance, 98th Cong., 1st Sess., 1983.

———. *Tuition Tax Credit Proposals,* Hearings before the Committee on Finance, 97th Cong., 2nd Sess., 1982.

WEBER, PAUL J., and DENNIS A. GILBERT. *Private Churches and Public Monies: Church and State Fiscal Relations.* Westport, Conn.: Greenwood Press, 1981.

7 Does freedom of religion extend to providing sanctuary for those fleeing political persecution?

YES SANCTUARY AND THE LAW

Center for Constitutional Rights

The sanctuary movement was formed by church groups and other organizations to support and protect El Salvadoran and Guatemalan refugees from deportation by the U.S. government. U.S. officials maintain that these refugees enter this country seeking economic opportunity, not to escape grave danger, and therefore are deportable.

Deplorable human rights violations in El Salvador have been widely publicized. Up to 1 million Salvadorans have been displaced; more than 40,000 civilians have been killed. Military forces and government-sponsored death squads carry out torture and the "disappearance" of doctors, labor and religious workers, journalists, students, teachers, peasant leaders and even randomly selected people. The land and its people are endangered by bombing and the use of napalm.

In Guatemala, in 1954, the CIA organized the coup which overthrew the democratically elected, reformist government of Jacobo Arbenz. Since then, 86,000 people out of a population of 7 million have been killed by the army of paramilitary death squads. More than 35,000 have disappeared. More than 2,000 Indians have

been murdered by the current regime. Local church groups report that 500 people are killed every month.

THE U.S. GOVERNMENT'S RESPONSE

Under the U.S. Refugee Act of 1980, a refugee who demonstrates a "well-founded fear of persecution on account of race, religion, nationality, membership in a particular social group, or political opinion"[1] may not be deported back to the place of persecution.

Short of refugee or asylum status, "extended voluntary departure" (EVD) status or other temporary relief may be granted to persons fleeing from a country that U.S. officials designate as one that threatens to deny human rights or one where serious disturbances are taking place. In the past EVD status has been granted to people from Cuba, the Dominican Republic, Czechoslovakia, Chile, Cambodia, Vietnam, Laos, Iran and Nicaragua. Such status presently applies to Lebanon, Ethiopia, Afghanistan and Poland. The Attorney General, in consultation with the State Department, claims unfettered discretion in determining whether a group qualifies for EVD status.

Center for Constitutional Rights, "Sanctuary and the Law," *Engage/Social Action*, 14 (Jan. 1986), pp. 21–25. Copyright 1986 by The General Board of Church and Society of the United Methodist Church.

[1] According to the Act, a refugee is technically a person applying for asylum from outside the United States, while an asylum applicant is a person already within the U.S. borders.

U.S. officials have refused to recognize the plight of Salvadoran and Guatemalan refugees, denying them asylum and EVD status. In 1981 and 1982, for example, only 67 Salvadorans were granted asylum in the United States; 1,132 applications were denied. During this period, 11,637 Salvadorans were deported from the United States or accepted "voluntary departure."[2] In 1983, only two percent of the Salvadoran asylum applications were granted.

Approximately 500 Guatemalans and Salvadorans are deported each month from the United States, facing death and torture in their countries. Santana Chirino Amaya, a Salvadoran refugee, was deported by the U.S. government in June of 1981. In August his decapitated body was found at a crossroad where the Salvadoran army and right-wing death squads dump many of their victims. The political asylum project of the American Civil Liberties Union has collected evidence of 120 Salvadorans who have suffered murder, torture and imprisonment after being deported by the United States. Because of these dangers, Salvadoran and Guatemalan refugees deported from the United States often go into hiding upon return to their country.

Senator Edward Kennedy sought EVD status for Salvadorans in 1981, the U.S. Catholic Conference sought it in 1982, and 88 members of Congress tried, unsuccessfully, to achieve it in 1983. Currently, a bill pending in Congress would require the granting of EVD status to Salvadorans. The Administration, however, remains adamant in its denial of EVD status to Salvadorans and Guatemalans.

Contrary to law, immigration decisions concerning refugees from Guatemala and El Salvador are made on the basis of for-eign policy criteria, rather than humanitarian concerns. In order to qualify the El Salvador and Guatemala regimes for continued U.S. military and economic support, this country's immigration officials and politicians ignore the many reports which document the human rights abuses in those countries. This U.S. policy ignores numerous United Nations resolutions recognizing the plight of refugees from El Salvador and Guatemala. Even El Salvador's president, Jose Napoleon Duarte asked, in 1981, that Salvadorans then being deported from the United States be "allowed to remain in the United States until the turmoil is settled."

IS SANCTUARY LEGAL?

The legality of sanctuary has not as yet been finally determined by the U.S. courts. Many legal experts believe that there is a strong case for the legality of sanctuary. Immigration and Naturalization Service (INS) officials have begun the prosecution of sanctuary supporters for transporting foreign nationals. *Groups that are considering participation in the sanctuary movement are strongly advised to consult with a lawyer at the earliest possible moment.*

We at the Center believe that international law mandates the United States to protect people fleeing war crimes, human rights violations, or persecution. If the United States were performing its obligations under the principles recognized in the Geneva Conventions or international humanitarian law the refugee would not be here illegally. The charge of abetting an illegal presence in the United States is at the heart of the prosecution of sanctuary workers. Since we reject that charge of illegality, we believe that the indictments against sanctuary workers should be dismissed on that ground alone.

Moreover, we believe that religious sanctuary workers . . . are protected by the First Amendment which supports the free exercise of religion. In providing sanctu-

[2] "Voluntary departure" status requires people to leave the United States immediately—unlike "extended voluntary departure" status, which permits people to remain in the United States until it is safe for them to return home.

ary they are acting in accordance with religious doctrines which do not conflict with U.S. law.

In addition to assisting in the defense of sanctuary workers facing criminal charges, the CCR is developing an affirmative lawsuit which will seek to halt any further prosecution of sanctuary workers and deportation of Salvadoran refugees.

THE RIGHT TO TEMPORARY REFUGE

Three basic bodies of law require the United States to provide temporary refuge. They are: (1) international refugee law; (2) humanitarian law (the laws of war); and (3) international human rights law. Other countries are obeying these laws and do not deport Salvadorans and Guatemalans back to their countries.

1. International Refugee Law These refugee laws prohibit the deporting of persons to a country where their lives or freedom would be threatened on account of race, religion, nationality, political opinion, or membership in a particular social group. In part, this principle derives from the 1951 Convention Relating to the Status of Refugees (189 U.N.T.S. 137), and the 1967 Protocol Relating to the Status of Refugees (19 U.S.T. 6223). While the United States has placed the Refugee Act of 1980 on its statute books, and that law is in accord with the Convention and the Protocol, the lack of implementation by the Administration has effectively nullified it.

2. Humanitarian Law during Armed Conflict—The Geneva Convention of 1949 Humanitarian law protects the victims of war, including wounded and captured soldiers, civilians, refugees, and relief workers. This law has many sources, including custom, usage, and various international agreements. Its main codification is found in treaties to which the United States is a party—the Geneva Conventions of 1949.

Article 3 of the Convention Relative to the Protection of Civilian Persons in Time of War provides that murder, mutilation, cruel treatment, torture and other forms of violence to life and person are prohibited in armed conflict.

Article 1 of the Geneva Convention imposes on each party the responsibility to insure respect for the Convention in all circumstances.

Since the government of El Salvador violates Article 3 of the Convention, the United States is at the very least obligated not to return people to that country until the violations cease. This does not mean that persons affected are entitled to permanent residence in the United States. As explained above, the procedure of extended voluntary departure is available to satisfy U.S. obligations under the Convention.

3. International Human Rights Law Independently of the Geneva Conventions, international human rights law holds that no refugee may be returned to any country in which, due to the nature of the regime or particular situation in that country, basic human rights are grossly violated or entirely suppressed.

Violation of basic human rights is prohibited by customary international law; this refers to obligations so widely accepted by the world's nations as to be regarded as binding on all.

How Does International Law Protect Sanctuary Workers? If Salvadorans or Guatemalans have protected rights as outlined above, they are not "illegal aliens." They have a right to protection in the United States. Sanctuary workers who assist refugees are thus acting in a manner consistent with law. Proof of such a crime requires the government to show: (1) the illegal status of the protected alien, and (2) the knowledge of the sanctuary worker that the refugee was here illegally. If a sanctuary worker labors under a reasonable belief that the alien is in the United

States legally, that worker cannot be guilty of a crime which requires the government to prove an intent to oppose the U.S. immigration law.

CRIMINAL CHARGES RISKED

Sanctuary workers face potential prosecution under Section 274 of the Immigration and Nationality Act of 1952 (U.S.C. §1324). This Act defines the following crimes:

- Transporting an "alien" across the border into the United States, knowing that the alien was not duly admitted or lawfully entitled to reside here. This section requires active conduct on the part of a person accused of its violation.
- Transporting an alien within the United States, with the knowledge that the person is in the United States "in violation of law." The government must show that the alien entered this country less than three years prior to the alleged transportation, *and* that the transporting substantially furthered the refugee's violation of law.
- Concealing, harboring or shielding an alien, knowing that the refugee is illegally within the United States. This section applies, not only to clandestine activities, but also to public harboring. This harboring is defined broadly: it not only refers to the act of giving shelter, but covers any activity tending to substantially facilitate the ability of an illegal alien to remain in the United States. The crime of knowingly harboring an illegal alien might also include warning a person about the presence of an INS agent, devising an escape route, giving help in finding employment and filling out applications.
- Encouraging a refugee to enter the United States, knowing that such presence within the United States would be illegal.

If a person is convicted of violating the Immigration and Nationality Act the penalty that could be imposed is up to five years in prison or a fine not to exceed $2,000, for each separate instance of assisting an alien.

OTHER RELEVANT CRIMINAL STATUTES

Aiding and Abetting A federal law makes it a crime to aid in the commission of an offense against the United States (18 U.S.C. §2). Under this law the abettor is liable for punishment as if convicted as the principal.

Conspiracy Groups and individuals may be charged with conspiracy to commit an offense against the government (18 U.S.C. §371). For such conspiracy the penalty is imprisonment for up to five years and/or a fine of up to $10,000.

The First Amendment and international law defenses would apply to these charges as well.

NO   THE SANCTUARY MOVEMENT: ACT OF FAITH, CONSCIENCE, OR POLITICAL RESISTANCE?

Eletha Duffy

INTRODUCTION

Refugees harbored in sanctuaries all wear bandanas over their faces when out on the

Eletha Duffy, "The Sanctuary Movement: Act of Faith, Conscience, or Political Resistance?" Copyright ©1986 by Eletha Duffy. Reprinted by permission of the author. This article was specially written for this anthology.

streets. They spend weeks hiding in church basements, yet openly proclaim their fate on network television. Movement leaders notify the attorney general of their intention to violate federal immigration laws and then claim to be unjustly convicted for those very crimes. These are the actions of what has become known as Sanctuary.

The Sanctuary movement is the current U.S. church-sponsored action that involves harboring illegal aliens from El Salvador and Guatemala. Its leaders dramatically proclaim the invalidity of American immigration laws, and its advocates willingly violate these laws. The ideological foundation of the movement is liberation theology, which is based on a Marxist interpretation of the Gospels. The objective of the movement is to stop U.S. intervention in Latin America; it is not to change domestic immigration policy.

This assertion is evidenced by the actions of movement members as well as by the avoidance of legal alternatives to effect the necessary changes in the immigration laws. This group has made no substantial attempt to lobby for these changes; nor has it expressed its support for changes that have been proposed in Congress.

The movement intentionally functions outside the American legal and political systems. This is not because it wants to effect legal changes for the welfare of the persecuted illegal aliens. Rather, it functions illegally to encourage disrespect for the American legal system and, further, to subvert the validity of that system.

THE MOVEMENT'S LEADERS AND ESPOUSED AIMS

The founder of the movement is Jim Corbett, a Harvard-educated Quaker and former rancher. In 1981 he began sheltering Central American refugees in his home. Soon after, he joined forces with Rev. Jim Fife to organize a more cohesive form of Sanctuary. Rev. Fife has been the pastor of the Southside Presbyterian Church of Tucson, Arizona, for seventeen years. The coordinating body for the movement is the Chicago Religious Task Force. This group publishes papers advocating the ideas of the movement as well as coordinates its more bureaucratic functions.

Over the past four years the movement has gained the support of more than three hundred churches, nineteen cities, approximately twenty universities, and New Mexico (by state legislative action)—all of which have declared themselves sanctuaries. Sanctuary members have engaged in a variety of activities, ranging from harboring refugees to merely offering moral support.

The movement's leaders claim three separate levels of justification for their actions: theological, legal, and a form of civil disobedience. We will examine each argument so that we may evaluate their political behavior.

SANCTUARY AND THEOLOGY

Historical Evolution The original concept of sanctuary may be traced to the Bible. Leviticus establishes sanctuary for cities of refuge. This was to prevent blood vengeance targeted at those guilty of involuntary manslaughter. It was thereby established that the act of vengeance was to be God's act. Thus God's representative, the priest, acted as both protector and arbitrator. The purpose of this form of sanctuary was to prevent further acts of violence by aggrieved family members. It was not to protect a select group of people to make a political statement.[1]

In the Middle Ages there existed a limited form of ecclesiastical sanctuary—sanctuary permitted by the laws of the church. Sanctuary was available for most criminals with the exception of those accused of sacrilege or high treason. Those who were able to seek refuge in a church were to confess their wrongs and go into exile (or occasionally join the religious order), or they were brought before the authorities at the end of a forty-day period. The purpose of this period was to allow the defendant the time either to prepare a defense or to earn and save money for the repayment of debt. Sanctuary rights were limited, however, in 1591 by a papal bull

[1] Richard Feen, "How It All Began," *Washington Times,* Nov. 1, 1985, sec. D, p. 1.

issued by Pope Gregory XIV. As a result, by the end of the following century, debtors were the only ones extended sanctuary protection. The Reformation's early leaders held the concept of sanctuary to be invalid, moreover.

Although sanctuary remained in the canonical code books of the Roman Catholic Church, it was rarely practiced from the nineteenth century on.[2] In 1983 the revised Roman Catholic canon law abolished sanctuary altogether.[3] It therefore appears that sanctuary was an ailing relic of the Middle Ages that was laid to rest gradually, with careful thought.

Religious Justification   The proponents of the movement are aware of the status of the Judeo-Christian tradition and have thus turned to a more esoteric religious argument to justify their actions. In this regard Jim Corbett attempted to justify sanctuary on the basis of the central role of refugees in theology. He explains:

> Much of the Bible is by and about refugees. The word Hebrew itself traces back to an Egyptian word that can be translated refugee or illegal alien. The Hebrew prophets and the Gospel[s] are repetitively unambiguous about our obligation to protect and respect the "stranger." Within mainstream traditions he is Elijah and he is Christ.[4]

Mr. Corbett's fellow sanctuary workers, however, seem to consider only a select group of Salvadoran and Guatemalan refugees to be modern Elijahs. The vast majority of sanctuaries generally do not offer aid to refugees from Marxist or Communist countries like Cuba or Nicaragua. The "Statement of Faith"[5] of the

Chicago Religious Task Force repeatedly emphasizes that the goal of stopping U.S. intervention in Central America should be the primary end of the movement.

The Sanctuary movement's method of refugee selection has been described by Roy Huesca, a former intern for *Nation* magazine and former insider of the movement. He explained that potential refugees undergo extensive interviews while in El Salvador or Mexico. Only those who are endangered and who are political activists are offered sanctuary. Refugees attempting to prove persecution must also vociferously oppose American intervention in Central America. They must express a "willingness to relate their experiences publicly on arrival in the United States."[6]

As a result of the highly selective process involved in extending sanctuary to protect these "strangers" (to use Corbett's analogy), it is estimated that the 70,000-member movement harbors no more than five hundred illegal aliens.[7] These members are practicing a highly discriminatory form of religious behavior—a kind of behavior not mentioned in the Bible. Thus the actions of the Sanctuary movement cannot even be justified by this more ethereal religious argument.

SANCTUARY AND THE LAW

The United States has a generally lenient policy of policing church actions. The government will usually not swiftly enforce its laws when the church is the violator. This policy is best evidenced in this case by the fact that the federal government waited three years after the church notified the attorney general of its intent to violate federal immigration law before it began formal actions to prosecute. This post-

---

[2] Ibid., sec. D, p. 2.

[3] Daniel Ritchie, "Sanctuary," *Eternity,* June 1985, p. 28.

[4] Jim Corbett, "The Social Dynamics of the Sanctuary Movement," *World & I,* July 1986, p. 554.

[5] Holt Ruffin, "The Politics of Selective Compassion," *World & I,* July 1986, p. 602.

[6] Ibid.

[7] Rael Jean Isaac, "Sanctuary Scoundrels," *American Spectator,* Apr. 1986, p. 21.

poned action is especially tolerant given the fact that there has never been a legal right to sanctuary in the United States.

There is no law in the United States that grants or protects the church right to sanctuary. The only laws that govern this situation are those that involve the status of refugees. The municipal law is the U.S. Refugee Act of 1980, which sets forth the definitional rules regarding refugees and illegal aliens. It also bans the forceful repatriation of anyone who can be described as a refugee based on a well-founded fear of persecution for reasons of race, religion, nationality, political opinion, or membership in a particular social group. This law allows the regulation of the number of refugees that the United States will accept on the basis of geographical considerations. This last regulation permits the interjection of political bias for or against individuals from a particular region.

There are two fundamental problems associated with the administration of the U.S. law, aside from the potential for political abuse or geographical rationing. First, the act is unclear on the status of individuals fleeing from indirect harm, e.g., the threat of random execution in a state of guerrilla warfare and civil unrest. Second, in many cases it is extremely difficult to determine the individual's motive for seeking asylum. Political, but not economic, asylum may be granted. In the case of refugees from countries like El Salvador that suffer from both political unrest and economic hardship, the question of dominant motivation remains unclear. It is in part because of these problems with the administration of this binding federal law that Sanctuary members claim Salvadoran refugees are victimized.

Recent Convictions The movement has recently been involved in two federal cases to defend its actions and to claim that the government is violating its First Amendment right to free expression of religion. In the first case decided by the Ninth Circuit U.S. District Court in Arizona, eight of the most prominent Sanctuary leaders were found guilty of criminal offenses. Six were convicted of conspiring to smuggle Salvadorans and Guatemalans into the United States. The other two were found guilty of harboring illegal aliens. The defendants tried to argue that they had a religious duty to aid people who fear abuse in their homeland. However, the court refused to entertain that defense.

The Religious Duty Defense Though the notion of a religious duty defense may be appealing on an emotional level, it is in this case unacceptable under the law. It would be more reasonable to assert this defense for inaction (i.e., refusing to report knowledge of illegal aliens) than for the positive actions taken by the movement. There is clearly potential for abuse of an established "religious duty" defense for positive conduct. If a person could legally justify that religious duty compelled him to overtly violate a federal law like the 1980 Refugee Act, then the court would in effect be accepting the notion of a higher (divine) law that supersedes federal law. Furthermore, it would be accepting a highly subjective form of law that may be identified only by the individual conscience. This reasoning is not acceptable in a nonreligious society because no one set of higher law may be held supreme.

Pending Litigation Another Sanctuary federal suit is currently pending in California. In this case, the complainants (a coalition of eighty national and local religious groups) have two contentions: The first is that the United States is violating their First Amendment right of free exercise of religion. The second is that the movement is legal because the 1980 law grants asylum to refugees fleeing political persecution.

The 1980 law defines the limitations of refugee status. It does not empower any private group to evaluate the status of individuals seeking asylum, nor does it resurrect the establishment of church sanctuary. It seems highly unlikely, therefore, that the court will allow an implied right of sanctuary based on an act that has nothing to do with expanding the rights of religious groups.

First Amendment Claim The final claim is that the United States is violating the First Amendment right to free exercise of religion. It is important to first note that there is a distinction between the governmental interference with a belief and with an action. Under the law the freedom to hold religious beliefs is absolute.[8] Freedom to act out of religious belief, however, is not absolute. In this case a balancing test is used to determine the legitimacy of the law that is in conflict with religious actions. The court will weigh the severity of the burden on the individual against only the most compelling state interest. Also, if the state could achieve its ends by another means, then the statute will be stricken. For example, a statute that made polygamy an illegal act was upheld even though it applied to Mormons. This directly interfered with their religious practices. The court held that the state interest in abhorring polygamy outweighed the burden of an individual's free exercise of religion.[9]

Though this question is still pending before the District Court, it is likely that the court will find for the government. The government has a compelling interest in controlling immigration because of the many pressing domestic concerns surrounding the recent influx of aliens. The countervailing private interest in fulfilling one's religious duty to protect the persecuted is not at the core of one's religious existence. Not only may one still practice the Judeo-Christian ethic and live a moral life, but one also has the alternative of aiding these individuals while not violating federal law (i.e., providing legal assistance

or forming lobbying groups to advocate changes in current immigration law).

In conclusion, even Robert Drinan, a professor of law at Georgetown University and a proponent of the movement, states that "[a]lthough the term 'sanctuary' suggests some legal or historical validity for the concept, sanctuary as a legal doctrine was terminated by Henry VIII and ha[s] never held any real place in American law."[10] In sum the Sanctuary movement has neither a legal right nor a legal defense for its actions.

CIVIL DISOBEDIENCE AND SANCTUARY

Legal or theological grounds for sanctuary were the two possible forms of justification for the movement. As we now turn to the question of civil disobedience, we must note the following: Those engaging in acts of civil disobedience traditionally do not expect to avoid punishment. On the contrary, they acknowledge their deviance from the law and accept the imposition of sanctions.

There are three general categories of acts of disapproval.[11] Dissent and resistance are the two polar forms, while civil disobedience lies somewhere between the two. Dissent is the peaceful expression of disagreement. This form should always be protected by a government cherishing individual rights. Resistance is illegal action taken to undermine the law. For reasons of self-preservation and respect for law, the government will prosecute individuals for such illegal behavior.

Civil disobedience, the intermediate category, is quite broad in itself. Civil disobedients purposely violate a law, with the intent of changing that law by stirring pub-

---

[8] *Cantwell v. Connecticut*, 310 U.S. 296 (1940).

[9] *Reynolds v. United States*, 98 U.S. 145 (1878).

[10] Robert F. Drinan, "The Sanctuary Movement on Trial," *America*, Aug. 1985, p. 81.

[11] Herbert M. Levine, *Political Issues Debated: An Introduction to Politics* (Englewood Cliffs, N.J.: Prentice-Hall, 1987), 2nd ed., p. 132.

lic disapproval.[12] These actions are usually nonviolent and motivated by strong moral conviction. Those who commit such acts accept punishment.

The Sanctuary movement may be seen as engaging in civil disobedience because it is supposedly motivated by a religious belief that all refugees must be protected in this manner. Its actions, moreover, are illegal and nonviolent. This is not to say, however, that the movement totally complies with the accepted notions of civil disobedience. The movement is distinguished from the traditional form in two ways. First, the protagonists of the movement claim to have a constitutional right that justifies the purposeful violation of federal immigration laws. The movement claims it has the right to supersede the law and may publicly do so instead of using legal means to effect changes. Second, the movement does not clearly express its objectives, nor does it directly attack the perceived injustice. Most civil disobedients willingly proclaim their objectives and the basis for the illegal actions taken. Furthermore, there is usually a strong link between the laws targeted and the overall objectives of the particular movement. For example, the great Martin Luther King, Jr., professed the objective of attaining equal rights under the Constitution. He and his followers challenged laws that directly conflicted with any notion of equal protection.

The Sanctuary movement, however, explains its objectives and means in abstruse terms—intentionally clouding the issues. For various reasons (which will be more fully explained in the next section of this essay) it is evident that the political orientation of the movement is liberation theology, which is a Marxist-based ideology. The ultimate objective of the Movement is to stop U.S. intervention in Latin America. The attack on the validity of U.S. immigration laws cannot result in foreign policy changes. At best it may result in modification of these current domestic laws. The U.S. immigration laws reflect domestic policy concerns. They do not have great impact on foreign policy, nor does current foreign policy overwhelmingly mold the form of these laws. It is important to note at this point that this indirect attack on foreign policy marks a substantial and dangerous step beyond the traditional notions of civil disobedience.

Jim Corbett, the movement's founder, acknowledges that the movement goes far beyond actions of civil disobedience in this respect. He created the term *civil initiative* in an attempt to legitimize the movement's major stop from civil disobedience:

> The Sanctuary Movement is engaged in civil initiative rather than civil disobedience. . . . This constructive extension of the legal order calls for organization and procedures that *differ radically from civil disobedience* or other non-violent resistance designed to overturn specific laws or the legal order itself.[13]

We must examine why movement leaders are unwilling to clearly proclaim their objectives and ideological bases because of this deviation from the traditional form of civil disobedience. The result of this inquiry will become apparent through the examination of liberation theology and its influence on the movement.

THE POLITICAL MOTIVATION FOR THE SANCTUARY MOVEMENT

It is clear that the Sanctuary movement lacks firm theological and legal foundations. It therefore becomes necessary to scrutinize the motivations of those who advocate and indeed openly violate the law and manipulate religious tradition through sanctuary. To fully understand the movement for the purpose of deter-

---

12 Ibid.

13 Corbett, "Social Dynamics," p. 552.

mining which of the three above categories it best fits, it is necessary to examine its political-philosophical foundation. The ideological root for the movement is liberation theology. Liberation theology is a school of thought developed by the Left. It finds itself in conflict with traditional theology. In contradistinction to Judeo-Christian theology, liberation theology is a political ideology. It sees Christ as a political revolutionary dedicated to freeing the poor and the oppressed. It focuses on capitalism as the root of all evil. Liberation theology is itself a product of the Latin American community. It is viewed by one of its major proponents as playing a unique role in the course of history:

> We in Latin America are the only continent that is both Christian and underdeveloped, so we are in a special place. We will start a new understanding of the Faith because we belong to the churches, Catholic and Protestant, and we are living in a situation that makes them functional to the system. . . . The process of colonization, liberation and organization is best understood in Marxist terms.[14]

In a recent article, Jim Corbett twice denied that Sanctuary is motivated by liberation theology. He first rather graphically stated that the movement is not a "fifth column seducing U.S. churchgoers with Marxist/Leninist liberation theology in preparation for a Nicaraguan blitzkrieg that could . . . smash through the soft underbelly of U.S. defenses."[15] Later he went on to say that "we cannot accept the establishment of any overall creed or set of objectives for the Sanctuary Movement."[16]

In spite of Corbett's denials, both the writings of the movement's proponents and the actions taken by its members fully confirm its direct link with liberation theology. Corbett himself stated that "our message is simply that . . . the people of El Salvador and Guatemala are being tortured into resigning themselves to established patterns of subjugation—that is, to military rule of a wealthy elite that acts as the agent of U.S. domination."[17] Most poignantly, *Theology of Sanctuary,* a publication distributed by the movement's Chicago office, proclaims:

> This is the beginning of authentic solidarity. Liberation theology has crossed the border, not in books to be read and discussed, but in *praxis.* An insurgent faith is on the move, undertaken in hope and sustained by *resistance.* And the declaration of sanctuary is the pivotal act in this new religious solidarity movement.[18] (Italics added).

The movement's actions go far beyond civil disobedience to resistance by overtly challenging American law. A few examples will clarify this assertion:

1. Rev. Fife's Southside Presbyterian Church notified the Attorney General *by letter* of its specific intention to "publicly violate the Immigration Nationality Act 274 (a).[19]
2. The method of refugee selection previously discussed further aligns with the political objectives of liberation theology. The selective recruitment and support of political activists furthers the ideological attack of the American policy. It does nothing to aid illegal aliens or effect legal changes in ailing immigration policies and laws.
3. The main caucus of the movement verbally condemns those churches that universally offer sanctuary to anyone in need, especially if they harbor illegal aliens fleeing from Nicaragua or other Communist-controlled countries.[20]

[14] As quoted in Michael Novak, "Liberation Theology and the Pope," in *The Pope and Revolution,* ed. Quentin L. Quade (Washington, D.C.: Ethics and Public Policy Center, 1982), p. 77.
[15] Corbett, "Social Dynamics," p. 554.
[16] Ibid., p. 557.

[17] Isaac, "Sanctuary Scoundrels," p. 21.
Spectator, Apr. 1986, p. 21.
[18] "The Sanctuary Movement Sorting It Out," *Religion and Society* 2 (Apr. 1985), p. 5.
[19] As quoted in Isaac, "Sanctuary Scoundrels," p. 21.
[20] Ibid.

4. Those members who do ascribe to all the unwritten limitations of the movement exhibit a talent for public martyrdom. They make dramatic appeals to the public on an emotional level and use the media effectively to spread their word.

5. Finally, the 70,000-member movement harbors approximately only five hundred refugees. This is not because of a lack of support or even a lack of illegal aliens. This is because the movement's primary objective is political and not the welfare of illegal aliens.

These actions are a mere sampling of the steps taken by the Movement to further its political goals. The movement is using the immigration problem only as the publicized target of its actions. It focuses on deportation to stir memories of past atrocities and claims to be actively preventing the commission of current ones. All the actions taken, however, evidence that its primary objective is not the prevention of deportation, nor the effective change of U.S. immigration policy.

CONCLUSION

In summary the Sanctuary movement has neither legal nor theological justification. Its primary goal is not aiding refugees, and its illegal actions can be defended on no grounds rooted in our constitutional system. The movement relies on deceptive manipulation of immigrants and of legal and theological doctrines. Moreover, the movement cleverly seeks political and financial support from congregations—large groups of people who are inherently capable of accepting notions on faith. Many laymen are aware that sanctuary exists, yet are not aware that its purpose is anything more than assisting those in need. The congregations willingly proclaim their complicity to federal law violations because of their own moral convictions concerning the protection of the persecuted. Unfortunately, they are generally unaware of the dominant but less publicized goal of opposing U.S. intervention as well as U.S. law. Immigrants and church members alike are both pawns of a political battle that is tragically being fought in the wrong arena.

Most important, the ideological basis for the Sanctuary movement is fundamentally at odds with the Judeo-Christian doctrine, as well as with the American polity. The movement is not an act of religious defiance or of civil disobedience, but rather it is one of political resistance.

QUESTIONS FOR DISCUSSION

1. Why does the Constitution protect religious belief but not action based on belief?
2. Is religious belief *ever* a justification for breaking the law?
3. Is religion superior to the state?
4. Why is the right of sanctuary important?
5. Who should judge to whom sanctuary should be given?

RECOMMENDED READINGS

BAR, ROTEM. "If You Knew the Truth, Then Surely You Would Help Us." *Philadelphia Inquirer*, June 2, 1985, pp. 20–25 and 30–31.

COLLINS, SHEILA D. "The New Underground Railroad." *Monthly Review* 38 (May 1986), pp. 1–7.

CUMMINS, JOHN. "The Sanctuary Tradition." *Humanist* 46 (Mar.–Apr. 1986), pp. 8–9.

ISAAC, RAEL JEAN. "Sanctuary Scoundrels." *American Spectator* 19 (Apr. 1986), pp. 20–24.

NELSON, ALAN C. "The Sanctuary Movement: Humanitarian Action, Political Opposition or Lawlessness?" *Vital Speeches of the Day* 52 (June 1, 1986), pp. 482–85.

RITCHIE, DANIEL. "Sanctuary." *Eternity* 36 (June 1985), pp. 24–28 and 33.

"Sanctuary." *Engage/Social Action* 14 (Jan. 1986), entire issue.

SLIMP, FRED A., II. "Gimme Sanctuary: The Right of Asylum." *National Review* 37 (May 17, 1985), pp. 24–26 and 28.

QUAMMEN, DAVID. "Keepers of the Flame." *Esquire* 103 (June 1985), pp. 253–54, 256, 258–59, and 261.

ZALL, BARNABY W. "Asylum and Sanctuary: The American Dilemma." 72 *American Bar Association Journal* 66 (Aug. 1, 1986).

8 Is antipornography legislation a violation of freedom of speech?

YES PORNOGRAPHY AND FREEDOM OF SPEECH

Barry W. Lynn

My name is Barry W. Lynn. I am pleased to testify this morning on behalf of the American Civil Liberties Union. I serve as legislative counsel for the ACLU, a national non-partisan membership organization of 250,000 persons committed to the preservation and enhancement of the Bill of Rights and other constitutional guarantees.

We live in a country where the equality of men and women is neither generally portrayed nor routinely practiced. It is also a nation in which there is persistent violence against women by men who resent their achievements and the challenges they present to a male-dominated society. Against this volatile backdrop it is possible to reach for drastic proposals, including ones which could erode vital constitutional guarantees. One such flawed avenue is the new effort to curb sexually explicit material by creating broad new civil remedies so that individuals offended by it may hinder its use, sale, and distribution.

Many of the witnesses who have appeared during your previous two days of hearings, and several here today, have called for new legislative initiatives to regulate "pornography", which they erroneously assert can be objectively defined. They have made claims which would allegedly permit "pornography," now pro-

U.S. Cong., Senate, *Effect of Pornography on Women and Children,* Hearings before the Subcommittee on Juvenile Justice of the Committee on the Judiciary, 98th Cong., 2nd Sess., 1984, pp. 258–68.

tected by the Constitution, to be excised from First Amendment protection just as "obscenity" and "child pornography" have been.[1]

Unfortunately, this approach blurs critical distinctions between advocacy and action and between cause and symptom, distinctions which must be retained in order to preserve important First Amendment guarantees. It is clearly contrary to the guarantees of free speech and a free press, because it ultimately rests on the constitutionally-forbidden premise that governments can be parties to the suppression of offensive ideas and images.

The recently adopted Indianapolis ordinance which has been embraced by several witnesses makes actionable "the graphic sexually explicit subordination of women, whether in pictures or in words" if it also includes one or more specific elements, including, for example, the portrayal of women "as sexual objects . . . who enjoy humiliation" or the presentation of women "through postures of servility . . . or dis-

[1] "Obscenity" has been defined by the Supreme Court as requiring proof of three crucial elements: (1) that it appeals to the "prurient interest" as judged by the average person applying contemporary community standards; (b) that it describes or depicts, in a patently offensive way, specific sexual conduct defined by statute; (c) that, as a whole, it lacks serious literary, artistic, political, or scientific value. The ACLU believes this standard violates the First Amendment. However, "pornography" definitions would restrict even more material since there are no "average person" or "lacking value" tests.

play." Such language as "presented as sexual objects" lacks intrinsic or objective meaning. It either requires inquiry into the motive of the producer or allows even the most sensitive viewer's characterization to be the ultimate determination.

(The ACLU has filed an *amicus* brief in the case challenging the facial constitutionality of the Indianapolis ordinance. This is not a hearing on that ordinance *per se*. However, it is important to note that any approach to regulation of sexually explicit material which seeks to cover material not included within the Supreme Court's definition of "obscenity" in *Miller v. California,* 413 U.S. 15 (1973) or its description of "child pornography" in *United States v. Ferber* 458 U.S. 747 (1982) will face insurmountable constitutional "overbreadth" and "vagueness" problems.)

These phrases can in fact be construed by reasonable people to cover vast amounts of literative, art, and popular culture in today's marketplace. Novels by Norman Mailer, Erica Jong and John Irving, sex education "self-help" books, much "erotic" and even religious art of Eastern and Western cultures, and popular music videos could clearly be included. Likewise, many of the highest grossing films of 1984, including *Indiana Jones, Tightrope,* and *Purple Rain,* all contain sufficient graphic thematic messages about subordination of women to result in legal actions. It would not be simply the proprietor of the "Adam and Eve" bookstore who would have to wonder whether a court would find some of his sales items "pornographic"; it would be every movie exhibitor and every owner of a major bookstore chain.

That problem is the essence of a "chilling effect"—that persons will not write, or photograph, or sell because they do not want to risk that some particularly sensitive or particularly zealous individual will decide that their product is covered by the statutory language. Creating broad individual civil causes of action, particularly

ones which allow injunctions against continued distribution, will lead to "self-censorship." This can have as drastic an effect on the free flow of ideas as direct government censorship.

THE ALLEGED EFFECTS OF PORNOGRAPHY

The underpinning of new efforts to control "pornography" is that recently discovered and newly articulated factors take the material outside the scope of the First Amendment. However, the new framing of the argument against pornography, combined with the varieties of empirical research data, still meet no test ever articulated by the Supreme Court which would allow the state directly or its citizens indirectly to suppress this sexually explicit material.

The so-called "findings" section of the Indianapolis ordinance and other proposals notes that "Pornography is a discriminatory *practice* based on sex which denies women equal opportunities in society. Pornography is *central* in creating and maintaining sex as a basis for discrimination. . . . The bigotry and contempt it promotes, with the acts of *aggression it fosters,* harm women's opportunities for equality of rights . . ." (emphasis added). Many previous witnesses have made statements suggesting agreement with this analysis. However, these conclusions are unsupported by the actual evidence available.

(1) **Pornography as a "Practice"** Pornography includes words and pictures. It is "speech", not an act or a practice. The parallels between certain racist activity and pornography drawn by some pornography critics are inappropriate. Racial segregation is an "act" and it can be prohibited in spite of First Amendment claims of a "right of association". However, racist speech by the American Nazi Party or the

Ku Klux Klan which may, implicitly or explicitly, urge segregation cannot be barred. *Collin v. Smith* 578 F.2d 1197 (7th Cir. 1978), *cert. denied* 439 U.S. 916 (1978).

Even the vilest and most graphic sexist or racist speech is not transformed into action because of the intensity with which its critics detest it or the success it demonstrates in getting others to accede to its viewpoint. It is important to guarantee as a "civil right" that no person is denied a job, an education, or entry to a public facility on the basis of race or sex. This is true whether the decision to discriminate is based on listening to well-reasoned academic discourse, reading "hate literature," or watching old movies containing negative stereotypes. However, our "civil rights" laws do not, and may not, insulate individuals from the repugnant speech of others which urges the denial of such opportunities.

(2) Pornography as a Central Cause of Sex Discrimination Another "finding" is that pornography is "central" to maintenance of women's inequality. The "centrality" of pornography as a source of inequality is not empirically supportable. Unless one works in an adult bookstore, graphic, sexually explicit "pornography" is not a major source of sensory input for many people. However, if all that critics define as "pornography" were to disappear tomorrow, and it had *in fact* been central to subordination, the central position would then be taken up by other images from comic books, cartoon shows, jean advertising, television situation comedies, and dozens of other sources which assault our eyes and ears on a regular basis. Precisely the same arguments that undergird the efforts to eliminate graphic sexual images showing the subordination of women would then be applicable to a variety of remaining images which cast women in a demeaning light.

It may be popular to start the process of eliminating negative views of women by proceeding against graphic sexual images, since allies in such an effort could include those persons who see the issue simply as one of "indecency". However, there is no logical reason to stop there, given the vastly greater number of persons who are exposed to the concept of "subordination" in other, "non-explicit" media. Once we accept the premise upon which this "pornography" regulation is based—the eradication of contemptuous images—there is nowhere to stop the regulatory process.

In fact, once the decision to suppress "negative" portrayals is made, it is only a short trip to mandating "positive" portrayals. As Justice Brennan noted in his dissent in *Paris Adult Theatre I v. Slaton* 413 U.S. 49 (1973):

> For if a state may, in an effort to maintain or create a moral tone, prescribe what its citizens cannot read or cannot see, then it would seem to follow that in pursuit of that same objective a state could decree that its citizens must read certain books or must view certain films.

The sexually explicit messages labelled "pornographic" have not been demonstrated to be central to any discriminatory practices. However, even if such evidence was present, it would not dispose of the guarantees of the First Amendment.

(3) Pornography as Behavioral Stimulus, Not Advocacy There is also the claim that pornography is somehow different than other cultural expressions because it is not "speech". Professor Catherine MacKinnon, the co-author of several proposed anti-pornography ordinances, noted in the *amicus* brief she prepared in the Indianapolis case, that "unlike the 'literature' of other inequalities, pornography works as a behavioral conditioner, reinforcer and stimulus, not as idea or advocacy."

That assertion is simply incorrect. Sexually explicit material may communicate that the activity depicted is pleasurable and appropriate. It is often a rejection of ascetic lifestyles, rational analysis, and prudence. Women's studies professor Ann Barr Snitow notes that it promotes "the joys of passivity, of helpless abandon, of response without responsibility. . . ." According to *Village Voice* writer Ellen Willis the meaning of sexually explicit material is highly individual and complex:

> Sex in this culture has been so deeply politicized that it is impossible to make clear-cut distinctions between "authentic" sexual impulses and those conditioned by patriarchy. Between, say, *Ulysses* at one end and *Snuff* at the other, erotica/pornography conveys all sorts of mixed messages that elicit complicated and private responses.[2]

Of course, it also may communicate a more sinister message, that women do, or should, gain pleasure solely from subordination to men. Repulsive as that construct may be, it is a political philosophy which has been dominant in most civilizations since the beginning of human history. It is clearly an "idea" and much pornography serves as a tool for its advocacy.

Similarly, virtually all printed and visual material seeks not only to communicate ideas, but also to act as a "behavioral conditioner, reinforcer, and stimulus." Books and movies frequently: (1) teach people to view an issue in a certain way ("behavioral conditioner"), (2) legitimatize particular ways of thinking ("reinforcer"), or (3) urge people to act in accord with the images presented by the author ("stimulus"). The fact that pornography asserts an often repugnant world-view graphically or persuasively does not place it in a special category from other literature.

The Supreme Court recognized this in *Cohen v. California* 403 U.S. 1526 (1970), where it assessed the impact of Cohen entering the trial court wearing a jacket emblazoned with the words "Fuck the Draft."

> [M]uch linguistic expression serves a dual communicative function: it conveys not only ideas capable of relatively precise, detached explication, but otherwise unexpressible emotions as well. In fact, words are often chosen as much for their emotive as their cognitive force. We cannot sanction the view that the Constitution, while solicitous of the cognitive content of individual speech, has little or no regard for that emotive function which, practically speaking, may often be the more important element of the overall message sought to be communicated. . . .

There is yet another dimension of this false "stimulus-advocacy" dichotomy. A number of commentators have criticized the new effort to regulate pornography as an effort to totally rationalize human sexuality. Historian Alice Echols has lamented the rejection by some feminists of "the notion that fantasy is the repository of our ambivalent and conflictual feelings," which she says leads to "a highly mechanistic and behavioristic analysis that conflates fantasy with reality and pornography with violence".[3] Indeed, it is as dangerous for the state, directly or indirectly, to police fantasies as to police politics.

(4) Pornography as Cause of Sexual Violence Finally, much has been claimed about new data purporting to demonstrate a causal connection between certain types of pornography and sexual violence against women. Unfortunately, there is little recognition of distinctions between "causes" and "symptoms" in much of this discussion. This error is compounded by

---

[2] "Feminism, Moralism, and Pornography" in *Powers of Desire: The Politics of Sexuality,* eds. Ann Snitow, Christine Stansell, and Sharon Thompson (N.Y.: Monthly Review Press, 1983), p. 463.

[3] "The New Feminism of Yin and Yang" in *Powers of Desire,* p. 448.

drawing unwarranted implications from the evidence.

For example, at a previous hearing several researchers reported findings that in a sample of "serial murderers," 81 percent noted a "high interest" in pornography and that in another sample of persons arrested for various forms of child exploitation, all had at least some "pornography" (from *Playboy* on down) in their homes. However, the presence of two phenomena, criminal activity and pornography, does not necessarily demonstrate a causal connection between them; it is at least as likely to demonstrate that persons with certain abusive personalities are attracted to both crime and use of pornography.

It is also possible to misdirect the outrage against specific instances of sexual violence. It is undeniable that there are examples of media portrayals of sexual violence whose elements are replicated almost identically by persons during the commission of a criminal act. These occurrences do not permit broad intrusions into First Amendment rights, even if it were demonstrated that *but for* the media portrayals, no crime would have occurred (something which has not been proven in any case). Certainly, the results of psychological experiments on male college students which demonstrate only that some tend to react temporarily more aggressively under laboratory conditions after seeing "aggressive-erotic" films provides no basis for suppressing speech.[4] As Kate Ellis notes in "Pornography and the Feminist Imagination": "In all of these studies a single stimulus and response is being made to stand in for a long conditioning process."

The First Amendment may not be suspended because an image or an idea causes the most susceptible or most malleable person who hears it or sees it to behave in an anti-social manner. This was recognized by the Supreme Court in *Roth v. United States* 354 U.S. 476 (1957). An uncomfortable volume of previous testimony before this subcommittee suggests a return to this "most susceptible" standard. It is carried to its greatest extremes in some ordinance language permitting injunctions against the future distribution of a specific book or film if it can be linked to one act of violence.

An even more direct argument is that pornography is a form of "incitement" to violence against women. However, even sexually explicit material which implicitly advocates the subordination of women does not urge that viewers commit criminal activity. In the event that some piece of literature did urge criminal activity its possible suppression would be measured on the basis of well-established constitutional principles.

Supreme Court decisions on speech which allegedly incites listeners to criminal acts make it clear that mere speculative damage is insufficient to suppress speech and that only if there is a close and demonstrable causal nexus between speech and violence may speech be barred. This is the "clear and present" danger standard announced first in *Schenk v. United States* 249 U.S. 47 (1919). The Court has subsequently ruled that not even "advocacy" of "revenge" against public officials by Ku Klux Klan members carrying guns, *Brandenburg v. Ohio* 395 U.S. 444 (1969), or student revolutionaries' threat to "take the fucking street later," *Hess v. Indiana* 414 U.S. 105 (1973), could be suppressed. A violent criminal act was not likely to be the direct and imminent result of the speech in these cases. A review of the data on "incitement" to violence against women by pornography demonstrates nothing to meet the *Brandenburg* standard.

[4] See, for example, Edward Donnerstein and Leonard Berkowitz, "Victim Reactions in Aggressive Erotic Films as a Factor in Violence against Women", *Journal of Personality and Social Psychology,* Vol. 41, No. 4 (1981), pp. 710–724.

WHAT CAN BE DONE?

It is important to use the means of communication available to make it clear that remedies already exist for some of the conduct which has been previously described at your hearings. There has, for example, been testimony in regard to husbands forcing their spouses into sexual activity, described in "pornography," which they did not desire. That constitutes rape in most jurisdictions. The ACLU has been actively supporting elimination of "spouse" immunity in rape cases in those states where it still exists. We would not minimize the problem of getting prosecutors to charge in such cases, but that is no excuse for not empowering the public with the knowledge that such actions can be taken.

Similarly, at previous hearings, Ms. Linda Marchiano testified regarding her physical coercion into the production of the film "Deep Throat." It appears that the statute of limitations has run, precluding any criminal prosecution. Assuming the facts as she reported, however, she would seem to retain the possibility of civil actions without need for new ordinances or federal intervention.[5]

Privacy-related torts which could already cover Ms. Marchiano's situation include "public disclosure of private facts" (since there was the intimate portrayal of sexual activity), placing one in a "false light in the public eye" (since she could argue that the film gave the false impression that she was enjoying what was actually repugnant coerced activity) or "wrongful appropriation" (her unwanted activity was photographed and appropriated by the perpetrators of a crime for commercial advantage).

Damages or even injunctive relief could certainly be sought in such individual cases, but depending upon the precise facts elicited, First Amendment limitations on such actions could also arise. The

ACLU is exploring whether narrow legislation covering such coerced activities would be consistent with such constitutional concerns.

Obviously, this would be costly litigation, with substantial attendant problems of proof. However, any action brought under an Indianapolis-type statute would be similarly expensive, since there could be no statutory presumption of coercion in regard to all women appearing in pornography.

In addition, in a society which has the regard for openness and tolerance found in the United States, the ultimate answer to the existence of offensive images must be the production of "affirmative" alternative images. It means the replacement of images of female subordination with images of equality and authority. The First Amendment was designed to protect the "marketplace of ideas" because of a deeply rooted belief that when ideas and images compete, (even if they begin in "unequal" status), the "true" and "accurate" have the best chance to prevail.

No one could seriously suggest that women have an equal "voice" in institutions in the United States. On the other hand, there has already been an historically unprecedented increase in the number of women's voices speaking in every academic field, from law to medicine to theology, and in every artistic endeavor. Those are the sources for the positive views of women which will help shape the future.

In addition to the creation of alternative images, it is certainly constitutionally acceptable to work to create a "negative image" for pornography: to urge that our society would be healthier without it, to critique its moral and aesthetic value, and to urge its disuse by all persons.

CONCLUSION

It is unfortunate when the issues raised by the Indianapolis ordinance are couched as ones of "women's rights" versus "civil liber-

---

[5] The ACLU believes that some of these causes of actions, particularly when applied to a broad range of facts, may be inconsistent with the First Amendment.

ties." It is clearly possible to protect and enhance both. There is a right to be free from sexual coercion; however, there is no similar right to be free from offensive and insulting images. There may be instances where genuine constitutional claims will clash, where, for example, the constitutional right of privacy runs squarely into the free press guarantees of the First Amendment. The ACLU would be happy to review any statutory language in these delicate areas.

NO IN DEFENSE OF ANTIPORNOGRAPHY LEGISLATION

Judy Goldsmith

Good morning. I am Judy Goldsmith, President of the National Organization for Women, the nation's largest feminist organization.

As the representative of an organization dedicated to the elimination of all forms of discrimination against women, I welcome this opportunity to discuss the harmful effect of pornography on children and women.

NOW's position on pornography is summarized in the following resolution, adopted at our 1984 National Conference in June:

> RESOLVED, that NOW finds that pornography is a factor in creating and maintaining sex as a basis for discrimination. Pornography, as distinct from erotica, is a systematic practice of exploitation and subordination based on sex which differentially harms children and women. This harm includes dehumanization, sexual exploitation, forced sex, forced prostitution, physical injury, and social and sexual terrorism and inferiority [portrayed as enjoyable to its victims and] presented as entertainment. Pornography violates the civil rights of children and women.

U.S. Cong., Senate, *Effect of Pornography on Women and Children,* **Hearings before the Subcommittee on Juvenile Justice of the Committee on the Judiciary, 98th Cong., 2nd Sess., 1984, pp. 155–62.**

> BE IT FURTHER RESOLVED, that NOW supports education and action by the Chapters on this issue.

Pornography is a fast-growing problem calling for new solutions. Mounting statistics on domestic violence are demolishing the traditional excuse that pornography, like prostitution, can serve as a "catharsis" for men's aggressiveness that would otherwise be directed against their families and communities.[1] Instead, scientific research increasingly corroborates the reality to which victims have repeatedly testified: pornography is violence.[2]

As in the case of domestic violence, traditional legal boundary lines between public and private behavior are being redrawn because the damage in which pornography is implicated is becoming too extensive and severe to be concealed or disregarded.

In Minneapolis, police investigators testified that pornographic materials are commonly found at the site of sexual

[1] "Private Violence," *Time,* September 5, 1983, pages 19–29.

[2] Neil A. Malamuth, PhD, U.S. Senate Subcommittee on Juvenile Justice, Hearing, August 8, 1984, page 98. Also: Park Elliott Dietz, MD, and Barbara Evans, MSc, *American Journal of Psychiatry,* vol. 39, no. 11, November 1982, pages 1493–1495.

assaults, including assaults on children.[3] Women Organized Against Rape in Philadelphia reports intensification of brutality to rape victims treated at its rape crisis center[4] and cites pornography as an aggravating factor.[5] A recent Minneapolis police department analysis of crime frequency statistics established a disproportionate incidence of sexual assault in neighborhoods where outlets for pornography are clustered.[6] Moreover, increased use of questions about pornography on intake forms at treatment facilities for both perpetrators and victims of sexual violence is expected to confirm the direct correlation between pornography and violence that is already supported by a grim abundance of empirical data.

Increasing efforts by communities around the country to deal with pornography as a local problem are resulting in a growing recognition that pornography is a national dilemma.

The old "solutions"—censorship committees, obscenity laws, zoning regulations—were chiefly directed to keeping pornography underground and available only to adult men. Since pornography was not correctly identified as a menace to women's civil rights, these weak measures are proving inadequate to deal with the harmful impact of a nationwide industry with access to drugstores, supermarkets and living rooms and with sales volumes of $7 billion a year, amounting to $70 for every man in the United States and exceeding those of the film and record

[3] Public Hearings on Ordinance to Add Pornography as Discrimination against Women, Minneapolis City Council (Government Operations Committee), Minneapolis, Minnesota, December 12–13, 1983. Session II, page 11.

[4] Lynn Marks, Director of Women Organized Against Rape (WOAR), Philadelphia, personal communication, 8/84.

[5] Martha Burt and Janet Gornick, "Rape Crisis Centers after Ten Years," Urban Institute, 1984. Authors interviewed in *off our backs*, August-September, 1984.

[6] Supra note 3, Session III, page 124.

industries combined. Acknowledging the reality of that harm is the first requirement for constructive action against it. . . .

A psychotherapist who works with rapists quotes a patient as explaining, "I wanted to knock the woman off her pedestal, and I felt rape was the worst thing I could do to her. She wanted it, she was asking for it. She just said 'No' so I wouldn't think she was easy."[9]

The women who participate in the creation of pornography do so for a variety of reasons but rarely from entirely free choice. Psychological coercion, physical force, economic need, and the influence of drugs are all among the most common reasons why women become involved in pornography. The acts that are the core of pornography—the brutalization and depictions of dismemberment and murder of women on screen and in print—can lead to the execution of the acts in "real life." As with prostitution, few of its defenders would want the job themselves.[10]

$7.5 BILLION CAMPAIGN AGAINST WOMEN

Pornography is a $7.5 billion a year industry with roots in both "respectable" corporations and organized crime. It is larger than the movie and record industries combined. The sheer scale of this communications business is a measure of its influence on American society.

This influence can be seen in advertisements readily available to children in both electronic and print media. If children are able to learn from "Sesame Street," why wouldn't they absorb attitudes about women from exposure to violent and sexist images of women in advertising and news media?

Similarly, if advertisers spend millions of dollars on inches of print space or sec-

[9] Minneapolis Hearings, Session III, page 39.

[10] Caryn Jacobs, "Patterns of Violence: A Feminist Perspective on the Regulation of Pornography," *Harvard Women's Law Journal*, Vol. 7, page 21, 1984.

onds of time on electronic media to influence the behavior of consumers, it would be unreasonable to deny that exposure to pornographic images of behavior, communicated by the same media, also influences the consumer.

KNOCKING OUT THE COMPETITION

Women are statistically invisible as buyers of pornography. Men are the consumers who support this multi-billion dollar enterprise.[11] What does this product do for men?

If pornography were used only to blackmail and train newly recruited prostitutes or to stimulate rapists and child molesters, the pornography industry would not be as large and pervasive as it is. Moreover, if its "recreational" use by other men had no political force, pornography would hardly be as staunchly protected as it is by male authority in this country.

Pornography's function in our society, as well as the reason for its abundance and protected status, becomes glaringly obvious when we recognize that pornography defines women as inferior and subordinate to men. It gives men permission to devalue women or even to do violence to them. Like the girlie calendar in the construction shack or the painting of a nude woman above the bar in the saloon, pornography warns women to keep out.

By defining women as unqualified to participate in the men's world, except on men's terms and with their permission, pornography helps protect men from having to compete on their own merits with women. Just as racism eases competitive pressures for all whites, including those who consider themselves to be non-racist, pornography as an enforcer of sexism cuts down competition from women for the benefit of all men, including those who are not buyers of pornography.

11 Jacobs, op. cit., page 14.

What does pornography do to women? Apart from its direct use in crimes against them, pornography degrades women's self-image and undermines their sense of entitlement to equality with men. It mocks their humanity and individuality ("She wants it, they all do.") Pornography fosters a terrorist environment of psychological and physical intimidation from which no woman in our society is entirely immune. Women sense that pornography is power and that pornography displayed is power flaunted.

MEDIA CONTROL OF WOMEN'S IMAGE

Given pornography's function, it can hardly be regarded as coincidental that the explosive expansion of the pornography industry occurred during the same time period that saw an unprecedented movement of women into the paid workforce, as well as open resistance to sex discrimination and a renewed drive for recognition of women's right to legal equality.

From 1953 on, Hugh Hefner's successful merchandising of Playboy as coffee-table pornography bought respectability for pornographic images and attitudes in the news and entertainment media. When the women's movement opened new career opportunities to women in the early '70's, Hefner responded by demonstrating graphically that naked "career women" were indistinguishable from the naked "secretaries" that Playboy customarily featured. Well-publicized forays to college campuses not only offered reassuring evidence that women, educated or not, are all the same, but also gave many a fledgling journalist a chance to be a First Amendment hero by risking his editorship of the campus newspaper in a bold defense of Hefner's right to photograph "the Girls of the Big 10," the Ivy League, etc. (Hefner's pioneering idea has since been developed by other pornographers into a hardcore genre featuring photographs of bound, gagged, and tortured "college girls.")

Playboy's portrayal of women as "happy hookers" continues to undercut women's ability to be taken seriously in their professions. Sex harassment in the workplace is encouraged by the view of women as objects, not co-workers.

In a memo to Playboy staff members, Hefner offered his view of how the magazine should portray the women's movement and pornography: "These chicks are our natural enemy. . . . It is time we do battle with them. . . . What I want is a devastating piece that takes the militant feminists apart. . . . They are unalterably opposed to the romantic boy-girl society that Playboy promotes. . . ."[12]

The reality behind Playboy's "romantic boy-girl society" is described by Linda Marchiano who experienced it during her period of enforced participation as pornographic film star "Linda Lovelace": "Mr. Traynor and Mr. (Hugh) Hefner sat around discussing what they could do with me, all kinds of different atrocities. And it seemed that Mr. Hefner and Mr. Traynor both enjoyed seeing a woman used by an animal. And so Mr. Hefner had Mr. Traynor's dog flown in from Florida to the L.A. Mansion."[13]

Meanwhile, the Playboy Foundation was applying a thin veneer of respectability to its pornographic empire by contributing money to women's organizations and seeking to place Playboy employees on their governing boards. And establishing awards for First Amendment advocacy.

Today, with pornography routinely advertised on newspaper movie pages, the casual pornography and everyday misogyny of the comics and editorial pages is scarcely noticed. Where, for example, does the news business end and pornography begin when Playboy founder Hugh Hefner is interviewed as an objective source on the Miss America firing and Playboy president Christie Hefner rates a feature article in the *Washington Post* as an outstanding young businesswoman and expert on feminism? It would be naive to deny that this institutionalization of pornography in the news media negatively influences news coverage of women and women's issues.

The effect of this hit-and-run intrusion of pornography into the everyday experience of women is merely suggested by such examples as an Atlanta law firm's combination of a bathing suit contest for women interns with refusal of partnerships to qualified women attorneys on its staff. Or the publication in *Screw* of a purloined photograph of a former Miss America engaged in simulated sexual activity with another woman whose head has been replaced by a photograph of the first woman candidate for vice-president of the United States.[14]

PUBLIC POLICY RESPONSE TO PORNOGRAPHY

Increasingly, efforts by communities around the country to deal with pornography as a local problem are resulting in recognition that pornography is a national dilemma.

The traditional "solutions"—censorship boards, obscenity laws, zoning regulations—were chiefly intended simply to keep pornography underground where it would be available only to adult men. Since pornography was not correctly identified as a menace to women's civil rights, these measures are now proving inadequate to deal with the harmful impact of a nationwide industry with access to drugstores,

---

[12] Jacobs, op. cit., page 31.

[13] Minneapolis Hearings, Session I, page 54. Also Linda Marchiano, *Ordeal*, Citadel Press, 1980, pages 189–191.

[14] *Washington Post*, 8/15/84, B3.

supermarkets, and living rooms and annual sales amounting to $70 for every man in the United States. . . .

No longer intimidated by pornographers' aggressive use of First Amendment absolutism to shield their business activities, citizens' organizations and elected officials are beginning to explore innovative legislative strategies to combat what is increasingly recognized as incitement to violence and a threat to public welfare.

Clearly needed are laws to protect children from pornographic exploitation and to empower women harmed by pornography to seek civil remedies. Not needed is more obscenity law, which amounts to a moral judgement call by community leaders and does not address the harm done to women by pornography. Nor can an effective strategy focus narrowly on pornography's involvement in specific aberrant behavior.

The integrity of the First Amendment is not at issue in this discussion. The civil rights approach does not involve bans, censorship, or criminal sanctions, but provides a civil remedy for those who have suffered harm.[19]

Defenses of the pornographic status quo tend to rely on appeals to First Amendment guarantees of freedom of speech for pornographers.

"Pornographers," Professor A. Catharine MacKinnon points out "have historically rested their claim to immunity from interference on the alleged difficulty of distinguishing what they publish from any other form of expression. The civil rights definition of pornography draws a line that makes this distinction clear. The pornographers' argument that their freedom is everyone's freedom has previously obscured the essential fact that the freedom of the pornographers enforces the subordination of women."[20]

The First Amendment right to speech has never been absolute, however. In the one case where the Supreme Court has balanced a municipal sex discrimination ordinance (barring sex segregation in employment advertising) against the First Amendment, the ordinance won (1973).[21]

More recently the Supreme Court, recognizing child pornography to be a form of child abuse, allowed states to make it a crime to exclude its speech from First Amendment protection. (The American Civil Liberties Union, on the other hand, defended child pornography as protected speech throughout the litigation.)[22]

The Minneapolis City Council hearings on pornography showed a similar level of harm done to women in adult pornography, as well as the integral role adult pornography plays in child abuse.

To women, whose constitutional rights are the subject of 200 years of unresolved debate and are still uniquely subject to legislative and judicial whim in the absence of the Equal Rights Amendment, there is considerable irony in the civil libertarian claim that pornographers' license to libel women as a class is protected by the Constitution's First Amendment. Without a right of equal access to free speech, freedom of speech defined in terms of the absence of government prohibitions is likely to benefit only those who can afford to claim it.[23] Women are entitled to freedom from the threat of pornography.

---

[19] Andrea Dworkin and Catharine A. MacKinnon. Memo: "Proposed Ordinance on Pornography: Frequently Asked Questions" to Minneapolis City Council, December 26, 1983, page 8.

[20] Ibid., page 9.
[21] Ibid., page 9.
[22] Ibid., page 9.
[23] Jacobs, op. cit., page 45.

QUESTIONS FOR DISCUSSION

1. What is pornography?
2. When does the protection of morality become a threat to freedom of expression?
3. Is there a constitutional distinction between public and private use of pornographic material?
4. Can morality be legislated?
5. "I can't define it [pornography], but I know it when I see it." Discuss.

RECOMMENDED READINGS

BLAKELY, MARY KAY. "Is One Woman's Sexuality Another Woman's Pornography?" *Ms.* 13 (Apr. 1985), pp. 37–38, 40, 44, 46–47, 120, 123.

BRYDEN, DAVID. "Between Two Constitutions: Feminism and Pornography." *Constitutional Commentary* 2 (Winter 1985), pp. 147–80.

CLOR, HARRY M. *Obscenity and Public Morality.* Chicago: University of Chicago Press, 1969.

COX, ARCHIBALD J. *Freedom of Expression.* Cambridge: Harvard University Press, 1981.

DEGRAZIA, EDWARD, and ROGER K. NEWMAN. *Movies, Censors and the First Amendment.* New York: R. R. Bowker, 1983.

DWORKIN, ANDREA. "Against the Male Flood: Censorship, Pornography, and Equality." 8 *Harvard Women's Law Journal* 1 (Spring 1985).

HOFFMAN, ERIC. "Feminism, Pornography, and Law." 133 *University of Pennsylvania Law Review* 497 (Jan. 1985).

MACKINNON, CATHARINE A. "Pornography, Civil Rights, and Speech." 20 *Harvard Civil Rights–Civil Liberties Law Review* 1 (Summer 1985).

PALLY, MARCIA. "Ban Sexism, Not Pornography." *Nation* 240 (June 29, 1985), pp. 794–97.

PILPEL, HARRIET E. *Obscenity and the Constitution.* New York: R. R. Bowker, 1973.

PRESS, ARIC. "The War against Pornography." *Newsweek* 105 (Mar. 18, 1985), pp. 58–62, 65–66.

U.S. CONG., SENATE. *Effect of Pornography on Women and Children.* Hearings before the Subcommittee on Juvenile Justice of the Committee on the Judiciary, 98th Cong., 2nd Sess., 1984.

9 Are punitive damages in libel cases a threat to free speech?

YES PUNITIVE DAMAGES: CAN THE PRESS SURVIVE?

John V. R. Bull

Next August, we will observe a remarkable event—the 250th anniversary of the acquittal of John Peter Zenger on libel charges. In its 1735 Decision, a jury established the principle that truth is a defense to libel.

And until recently, we all thought that principle was an inviolate tenet of American democracy, a bedrock on which our unique form of free society could rest.

But unless something unexpected happens, our celebration next year could well turn into a wake, for truth is no longer a defense to libel—indeed, the truth or falsity of a story is often irrelevant—and multi-million-dollar jury verdicts are threatening the very existence of newspapers, broadcast stations and syndicates.

As Gene Roberts, executive editor of *The Philadelphia Inquirer,* expressed it recently: "You don't have to look closely at many libel cases in the last three years to know that the First Amendment may be in more jeopardy than at any time in its nearly 200 years of existence."

And that is hardly an overstatement.

While the number of libel cases brought against the press in recent years has risen to alarming proportions, the initial success rate of these suits is even more startling:

* We lose 83 percent of all libel cases that go to a jury. True, through appeals and reduced

John V. R. Bull, "Punitive Damages: Can the Press Survive?" *Vital Speeches of the Day* 51 (Oct. 15, 1984), pp. 11–13.

awards, we end up "winning"—if that is the word—90 percent of these cases, but the cost of that protracted defense is immense—in terms of money, manpower, time, the incalculable effect on our staffs, and our institutional willingness to tackle difficult stories.

* The average jury award in libel actions is now more than $2 million, according to a recent survey by the Libel Defense Resource Center. Compare that to the $750,000 average award against manufacturers in products liability cases, and the $700,000 average medical malpractice award.

In percentages, the press loses 83 percent of its cases before juries, manufacturers lose 38 percent, and doctors lose only 33 percent. At the moment, there are at least 15 multi-million-dollar awards against the press—more in the past 10 years than in the preceding 200.

* As the stakes get higher, our defenses are being diminished: In 28 states, we cannot even insure against punitive damages, and other states may soon swell that number. In state after state, courts are deciding that punitive means punishment, and a newspaper, broadcaster or syndicate is not truly punished if the cost is borne by its insurance company.

* The "chilling effect" on papers willing to do investigative reporting is showing signs of becoming a penetrating deep-freeze as reporters fear the effect of a lawsuit on their careers—even if they eventually win the case. And only the bold publisher or editor will brave the legal thickets as freely as he or she used to do.

* The very people who have traditionally protected the press—the judges—are now,

125

themselves filing libel suits against us. My own paper, *The Philadelphia Inquirer,* is being sued by two members of the Pennsylvania state supreme court, a former U. S. attorney, a former district attorney, a former chief assistant district attorney, and a state superior court judge.

And these cases are getting tough: Just last week, in an incredible display of judicial arrogance, the Pa. supreme court refused to remove itself from ruling on motions in the very cases brought by their two colleagues against *The Inquirer.*

In each such suit against *The Inquirer,* the paper was guilty only of printing stories or editorials critical of the official's public conduct.

Now we are facing suits galore from public officials who, keenly aware of their 90 percent chance of success, at least on the first round, are looking for a public relations "quick fix" to their problems.

And even though they may lose their case on appeal, these officials likely will be able to tell their friends and neighbors that a jury of fine, upstanding citizens heard their case and vindicated them.

As the size of jury awards increases, a new crop of good, high-powered lawyers rushes like magpies to the matterhorns of cash. Sam Klein, the lawyer for the First Amendment Coalition in Pennsylvania, has noticed a high-quality plaintiff's lawyer facing him in the courtroom in recent years, lawyers working on contingency fees clearly attracted by the potential pot of gold at the end of the libel rainbow.

And who can blame them when they see awards of $26.5 million against *Penthouse* magazine; $40 million awards against *Hustler* magazine, a "mere" $2.05 million against the *Washington Post,* $1.6 million for Carol Burnett, and $9.1 million against the Alton (Ill.) *Telegraph?*

And higher awards encourage others to file suit.

Worse, insurance companies are increasingly pressuring us to settle and avoid the risk of big judgments. What this means for first amendment principles is obvious, but few papers can withstand this kind of pressure.

Moreover, these punitive damage awards usually have little relation to the seriousness of the offense, but have more to do with the financial condition of the newspaper's ownership and profitability.

Juries are told that the owner is a big, rich corporate conglomerate to which $4 million or so will mean little in the long run. And, being human, jurors are apt to feel they are being compassionate by awarding some of those vast millions to "the little guy" whose feelings were hurt, even if he sustained precious little other "damage."

The Libel Defense Resource Center has noted the bitter irony that while "libel damages are typically based on speculative harm to reputation and hurt feelings, only rarely is specific economic injury entailed."

Punitive damages are, in essence, a penalty for free speech—a fine almost like a criminal penalty, for speech that some may find unpopular—and one that is imposed way out of proportion to the "crime," even if a libel *was* committed.

Yet we are not bank embezzlers, swindlers of old folks' life savings, evil-minded charlatans or flim-flam artists. *They* can steal money and sometimes get off with a light sentence.

But let a newspaper question an elected official's public actions, and it can be fined literally millions of dollars, not for crimes against the people, but for practicing free speech.

Gene Roberts has found a fascinating parallel: A few months ago, a federal grand jury indicted Metropolitan Edison Co., the utility that runs the Three Mile Island Nuclear Reactors, of deliberately falsifying safety records in the months before the notorious accident at the firm's Unit #1 reactor.

If the 11-count indictment leads to a

conviction, Met-Ed faces a maximum fine of $85,000.

Meanwhile, the press is routinely the target of multi-million-dollar fines, or higher.

So we get these big verdicts.

Fortunately, most are still overturned on appeal.

But some day, inevitably, one of them is going to be upheld and when that happens to a small newspaper or struggling broadcaster with limited resources, that paper or station may well be forced out of business.

It nearly happened to the Alton *Telegraph*. It *could* happen to one of us one of these days, for with rulings such as the U.S. Supreme Court's Herbert vs. Lando which permits examination of the internal workings of a newsroom, the potential for damage is almost limitless.

Ironically, the very institutional safeguards we have built over the past several years against sloppy journalism—codes of conduct and professional standards, for instance—are now proving to be our own worst enemy.

A prudent editor will think twice before committing any firm rules to paper, for the slightest infraction—understandable or not—may be just the opening a sharp plaintiff's attorney needs to win a multi-million-dollar judgment.

The time newspaper people spend on the witness stand, while considerable, is inconsequential when compared to the potential damage from a libel suit.

Of greater danger in the long run is the undeniable chilling effect this has on a newsroom, for while it may be difficult to point to specific examples, there inevitably will be a reporter, a good reporter, who will try to duck a story he just *knows* will end up in court.

And surely, few lengthy, serious investigative efforts can stand up to the relentless cross-examination of a good plaintiff's lawyer. My own editor spent six days on the witness stand earlier this year

in a case that was 10 years old. More than half that time was taken up by the opposing lawyer reading our reporter's notes into the record, implying that by not including every word in his notes in the finished story, that the reporter had duped his editors and the public, as well.

And all my editor's explanations about the distilling process that goes into every news story and all his illustrations of how every fact, statement and quote is weighed for relevance and pertinence—none of this was persuasive with a jury unsophisticated in the ways of journalism and they returned a $4.4 million verdict against the *Inquirer*.

In an increasingly litigious society, there's little reason to hope our problems will diminish.

Indeed, the Libel Defense Resource Center has identified three conservative "public interest" groups that deliberately and blatantly promote libel actions.

We all know about Reed Irvine's Accuracy in Media, but compared with the American Legal Foundation and the Capital Legal Foundation, Irvine is almost a gadfly.

The Capital Legal Foundation sees libel litigation as a "splendid solution" to what it calls the "abuse [of] individual rights" by "large commercial [media] units."

"The answer . . . is not regulation, but litigation," the CLF has proclaimed, adding that "the only fair, effective and flexible check on media unfairness and concentration" is through the courts and jury system.

Shortly after issuing that policy statement, CLF took on the representation of Gen. William Westmoreland in his libel suit against CBS.

The American Legal Foundation has a similar goal of seeking to "offset the disproportionate influence wielded by the media." Accordingly, the ALF provided in-kind legal support to Dr. Carl Galloway in his libel action against "60 Minutes" and is reported to have offered financial assistance to two New Jersey police officers also suing "60 Minutes."

With all this activity, it is clear the problem facing us is immense, with many facets—all of which spell TROUBLE for newspapers, broadcasters and syndicates, alike.

What can we do about it?

The most drastic solution is to stop publishing, but ironically, even that may not help. As you remember, the Alton *Telegraph* got in trouble even though it never published a word about the case that resulted in that $9.1 million verdict.

And we probably ought to recognize that ultimately, reporters and editors cannot avoid being sued; nothing, really, can prevent us from coming under legal attack.

"We're just a handy, attractive target and we should recognize it," Alex Mac-Leod, assistant managing editor of the Seattle *Times*, said in a recent story in the *ASNE Bulletin*. "A goal of avoiding being sued is both futile and dangerous journalistically."

But there *ARE* things we can do to lessen the blow.

Some defense lawyers urge abolishing punitive damages entirely, on grounds they grossly over-compensate for whatever hurts and psychic injuries are suffered by libel victims.

And surprisingly, says Mark Peterson of the Rand Corp's Institute for Civil Justice in Santa Monica, only a small number of product liability cases involve punitive damages, although when they do occur, they attract a lot of press attention.

Indeed, Adrian Foley of Newark, N.J., chairman of the American Bar Association's Litigation section, has appointed a special blue-ribbon committee to make a thorough study of the punitive damages doctrine.

Another approach—seeking protective legislation on a state-by-state basis—is

favored by Jack Landau, director of the Reporter's Committee for Freedom of the Press.

Noting that eight states already prohibit punitive damages (although in four of those states the prohibition applies only to defamation cases), Landau suggests the grounds for collecting a libel award should be severely limited in the "I can't sleep at night" cases.

Since there is no constitutional right to punitive damages (indeed, the concept has been in existence only since the turn of the century), Landau suggests damages could be limited in four ways:

1. By re-establishing truth as an absolute defense.
2. By not permitting damages where there is no malice.
3. By not permitting them when a retraction is published.
4. By limiting damages to a specific dollar amount, say $25,000.

Two other avenues may be worth considering:

1. Amend the rules of civil procedure to force judges to make a preliminary assessment as to whether the story is true or false. If true, dismiss the case. If false, proceed to the lengthy, costly and intrusive pre-trial discovery proceedings we all love so much.
2. Permit the recovery of legal fees if the jury does not return an award against the paper or broadcaster.

In Pennsylvania, we are about to embark on a public education campaign among all segments of the communications industry to alert editors and broadcasters to the dangers.

We specifically are aiming at the small papers and stations that seem most vulnerable to big libel awards.

We don't know what will come of these regional informational meetings, but at least we'll be able to make an informed, collective judgment whether to seek protective legislation.

Yes, I know that many of us have long

held firmly to the belief we should not seek legislation, relying instead on Constitutional protections.

But I suggest that the time may have arrived when the threat to our future survival may be so great that we may be forced to put such concerns on ice.

Relying as we have on the judiciary may no longer be viable. We may have to get to work to save our own necks.

NO SHOULD PUNITIVE DAMAGE AWARDS IN DEFAMATION SUITS BE ABOLISHED?

Michael P. McDonald

Punitive damages occupy an anomalous position among the remedies available to a plaintiff at law. A hybrid legal concept—part civil fine, part an expression of a jury's indignation—the doctrine has been the subject of a controversy that has long raged over the continued need for and indeed justification of a remedy that "plac[es] in private hands the use of punishment to deter."[1]

Nowhere has this debate been waged with greater intensity than in the context of libel litigation.[2] Though punitive damages have been firmly entrenched in the American common law of defamation since the nation's founding,[3] this has done little to silence critics who view the remedy as fundamentally at odds with the First Amendment's guarantee of free speech.[4]

It might appear as though those favoring the retention of punitive damages in defamation cases have little to fear. Despite the wholesale federalization and impairment of major aspects of state libel law that have occurred since *New York Times v. Sullivan*,[5] the Supreme Court explicitly has sanctioned awards of punitive damages to both private and public figures provided that the "actual malice" standard of liability of *New York Times* is met.[6]

Furthermore, the overwhelming majority of state courts and legislatures to consider the issue of punitive damages in light

Michael P. McDonald, "Should Punitive Damage Awards in Defamation Suits Be Abolished?" *National Law Journal* 7 (Nov. 19, 1984), pp. 22–23.

[1] Jones v. Fisher, 42 Wisc. 2d 209, 166 N.W. 2d 175 (1969).

[2] At common law, three types of damages are available to libel plaintiffs: general, special and punitive. General damages are awarded without proof of injury when libel per se is proven. Special damages are awarded for other special forms of libel. Punitive damages are awarded in addition to general or special damages upon a showing of spite, ill will or intent to injure the plaintiff, i.e., common law "actual malice." The primary purpose of awarding punitive damages in libel litigation is to provide a deterrent to wrongful conduct so as to "safeguard all those similarly situated against like abuse." Curtis Publishing Co. v. Butts, 388 U.S. 130, 161 (1967).

[3] See, Gertz v. Robert Welch Inc., 418 U.S. 323, 398 (1974) (White, J., dissenting) ("For almost 200 years, punitive damages and the First Amendment have peacefully coexisted.")

[4] See, e.g., Rosenbloom v. Metromedia Inc., 403 U.S. 29, 84 (1971) (Marshall, J., dissenting) (punitive damages involve a threat "to society's interest in freedom of the press.")

[5] 376 U.S. 254 (1964).

[6] Gertz v. Robert Welch Inc., 418 U.S. 323, 349 (1974). "Actual malice" has been defined in New York Times as publishing a false factual defamatory statement with knowledge of falsity or reckless disregard as to truth or falsity. 376 U.S. at 280.

of the high court's most recent pronouncements have strongly reaffirmed the doctrine's continuing validity in the protection of reputation and privacy interests.[7] Only eight states have abolished the doctrine.[8]

Yet this appearance of broad acceptance is deceptive. Judging by the spate of legal articles that has appeared over the last decade condemning the award of punitive damages to successful defamation plaintiffs, one is forced to conclude that the academic community remains as hostile to the doctrine as ever.[9]

What effect the cumulative weight of negative scholarly opinion will have on the Supreme Court as it attempts to forge a consensus in *Dun & Bradstreet v. Greenmoss*,[10] which was argued before the court Oct. 3 and raises the issue of punitive damages in the context of a non-media defendant, is an additional reason for concern about the longevity of the current status quo.

Finally, in apparent reaction to the number of large punitive damage awards against media defendants at several recent and well-publicized libel trials,[11] it is noteworthy that several elements of the media defense bar have announced publicly their intention to go on the offensive to "limit the libel damages madness."[12]

Specifically, a sustained nationwide crusade to have newspapers lobby their state legislatures to abolish punitive damages was launched earlier this year with the backing of major media groups.[13] Consequently, the prospect of seeing judicial or legislative modifications in the doctrine of punitive damages in the imminent future remains a very real possibility.

There are normally four principal arguments advanced by those opposed to the continued retention of punitive damages in libel litigation involving the media.[14] How successful they are in limiting or altogether abolishing such awards depends in large measure on just how carefully the merits of each of these arguments is scrutinized.

Objections to punitive damages against media defendants in libel actions begin with an examination of the vital role the press plays in our political process and the special constitutional status that has been conferred upon it by the First Amendment.[15]

According to this view, since the Founding Fathers believed that democracy is dependent on a free flow of information

---

[7] See, generally, Collins and Drushal, The Reaction of the State Courts to Gertz v. Robert Welch Inc., 28 Case W. Res. 306 (1978); Comment, Defamation and State Constitutions: The Search for a State Law-Based Standard After Gertz, 19 Will. L. R. 665 (1983).

[8] They are Louisiana, Massachusetts, Michigan, Montana, Nebraska, New Hampshire, Oregon and Washington state.

[9] See, generally, Anderson, Libel and Press Self-Censorship, 53 Tex. L. Rev. 442 (1975); Jollymore, The Constitutionality of Punitive Damages in Libel Actions, 45 Ford. L. Rev. 1382 (1977); Franklin, Good Names and Bad Law: A Critique of Libel Law and a Proposal, 18 Univ. San Fran. L. Rev. 1, 39 (1983) ("[Abolition of punitive damages] may be the most common proposal in all discussions of what is wrong with libel law.")

[10] 83–18. The lower court opinion is reported unofficially at 461 A.2d 414 (1983).

[11] E.g., Burnett v. National Enquirer, 7 Med. L. Rptr. 1321 (Cal. Super. Ct. L.A. Cty., 1981), vacated in part and remanded 193 Cal. Rptr. 206, 9 Med. L. Rptr. 1921 (Cal. App. 1983).

[12] Statement of Jack Landau of the Reporter's Committee for Freedom of the Press. Reporter's Committee Proposal Gains Supporters, Editor and Publisher, May 26, 1984, at 45.

[13] In a related development, "[T]he Communications Law Committee of the New York City Bar Association has formed a special subcommittee to propose eliminating punitive damages from New York State's libel laws." Id.

[14] This article does not address the wisdom or constitutionality of assessing punitive damages against non-media defendants.

[15] The First Amendment provides in pertinent part that "Congress shall make no law . . . abridging the freedom of speech, or of the press." U.S. Const. Amend. I. The words "press" and "media" are used interchangeably throughout this article.

and since the First Amendment was designed specifically to safeguard the rights of those who write and disseminate ideas and information, the press must be shielded "from governmental interference . . . [as well as from] repression of that freedom by private interests."[16]

As Justice William O. Douglas once wrote in dissent: "The press has a preferred position in our constitutional scheme not to enable it to make money; not to set newsmen apart as a favored class, but to bring fulfillment to the public's right to know."[17]

Vigorous prosecution of the media for libelous publications, so this line of reasoning runs, backed by the threat of excessive punitive damages, may vindicate an individual's private reputational interest but it does so at the expense of the larger social good in receiving information.[18] Fidelity to the First Amendment demands that the press be immunized from the threat of large libel damage awards.

The principal problem with this argument, which viewed broadly amounts essentially to affording the press absolute immunity from all tort liability having the potential to be costly, is that it has been rebuffed on several prior occasions by the Supreme Court.

As Justice Byron R. White pointed out in dissent in *Gertz v. Welch,* it can hardly be contended that the First Amendment was intended to immunize the press from libel liability.[19] Despite the vital role that the framers foresaw the press as playing in our democratic society and the obvious protec-

tions the First Amendment offers, "scant, if any, evidence exists" that the press was to be granted a "license to defame."[20]

Moreover, an unbroken line of Supreme Court decisions has held that "a business is not immune from regulation because it is an agency of the press. The publisher of a newspaper has no special immunity from the application of general laws. He has no special privilege to invade the rights and liberties of others."[21]

Although states may be required "to use finer regulatory tools where dealing with the press,"[22] they retain the power to hold the press accountable whenever it invades the legitimate rights of others, particularly in the area of defamation law.[23]

If it were otherwise, it would be equally plausible to argue that "if an automobile carrying a newsman to the scene of a history-making event ran over a pedestrian . . . the size of the verdict [would] . . . have to be assessed against the probability that it would deter broadcasters from news-gathering before it would pass muster under the First Amendment."[24] This "press exceptionalism" argument amounts to an untenable construction of the First Amendment.[25]

A second criticism frequently made against punitive damages is that the award of enormous and "unregulated" damages by characteristically "anti-media" juries

[16] Associated Press v. U.S., 326 U.S. 1, 20 (1945) cited with approval in Miami Herald Publishing Co. v. Tornillo, 418 U.S. 241, 252 (1974).

[17] Branzburg v. Hayes, 408 U.S. 665. 721 (1972) (Douglas, J., dissenting).

[18] Cf. Sweeney v. Patterson, 128 F.2d 457, 458 (1942) ("Whatever is added to the field of libel is taken away from the field of free debate."); cited with approval in New York Times v. Sullivan, 376 U.S. at 272.

[19] Gertz v. Robert Welch Inc., 418 U.S. at 380–81.

[20] Id. at 381 and 387.

[21] Associated Press v. NLRB, 301 U.S. 103, 132–133 (1937), cited with approval in Rosebloom v. Metromedia Inc., 403 U.S. 29, 67 (Harlan, J., dissenting).

[22] Rosenbloom v. Metromedia Inc., 403 U.S. at 67.

[23] "It is a fallacy . . . to assume that the First Amendment is the only guidepost in the area of state defamation laws. It is not. . . . The protection of private personality, like the protection of life itself, is left primarily to the individual states under the Ninth and Tenth Amendments." Rosenblatt v. Baer, at 92 (Stewart, J., concurring).

[24] Rosenbloom v. Metromedia Inc., 403 U.S. at 67.

[25] See, Lewis, A Preferred Position for Journalism?, 7 Hof. L. Rev. 595 (1979).

amounts to little more than an unwarranted windfall to the libel plaintiff.[26]

In addition, abolitionists contend that
while the doctrine's supporters may claim
that the amount of money a jury awards in
punitive damages must legally bear some
"reasonable relationship" to the actual
damage the plaintiff has suffered, in fact,
the huge awards that are currently being
assumed against "deep pocket" media
defendants amply indicate that no such
"reasonable relationship" standard is being
employed.[27]

Admittedly, assigning an economic
value to a person's interest in his or her
good reputation is a difficult task. Nevertheless, the value of one's good name
always has been highly prized.

As Justice Potter Stewart once put it:
"The right of a man to the protection of
his own reputation from unjustified invasion and wrongful hurt reflects no more
than our basic concept of the essential
worth of every human being—a concept at
the root of any decent system of ordered
liberty."[28]

The common law of defamation treated
an individual's reputational interest as
being at least the equivalent of a property
interest. The common law practice of
allowing juries to settle upon a monetary
equivalent in damages for the harm
inflicted through the publication of defamatory falsehoods has been followed in this
country since its inception.[29]

In light of the fact that *compensatory*
damages may be enormous and similarly
awarded by juries to redress the harm
done to an intangible interest, it is difficult
to see how a large punitive damage award
constitutes a "windfall" to the plaintiff.
Additionally, in making an award of
punitive damages the jury must necessarily
consider the wealth of the defendant. Otherwise the amount assessed in punitive
damages may not be sufficiently high
enough to deter that defendant from
engaging in similar tortious conduct in the
future.

As for the argument that "anti-media"
juries are awarding "unregulated" punitive damages, this contention simply
ignores two important facts. Juries are
selected by *both* parties after extensive voir
dire hearings. And even if the punitive
damage verdict rendered by a jury bears
no reasonable relationship to the amount
of actual harm suffered, post-trial judicial
nullification of large jury awards regularly
operates to reduce those awards.[30]

As Prof. Charles McCormick noted:
"The danger . . . of immoderate [punitive
damage] verdicts is certainly a real
one. . . . Nevertheless the verdict may be
twice submitted by the complaining defendant to the common sense of trained judicial minds, once on motion for new trial
and again on appeal, and it must be a rare
instance when an unjustifiable award
escapes correction."[31]

Finally, even though an award of
punitive damages may constitute a windfall to a particular plaintiff, if it deters that
particular defendant or other media
organizations from engaging in similarly
offensive acts in the future, it serves a public good.[32]

---

[26] Rosenbloom v. Metromedia Inc., 403 U.S. at 84
(Marshall, J., dissenting) ("These awards are not to
compensate victims; they are only windfalls.")

[27] For example, in Curtis Publishing Co. v. Butts,
388 U.S. 130 (1967) the jury returned a verdict of
only $60,000 in general damages, but $3 million in
punitive damages. However, it should be noted that
the court upheld that award of punitive damages.

[28] Rosenblatt v. Baer, 383 U.S. 75, 92 (1966) (Stewart, J, concurring).

[29] See, Comment, The Constitutionality of Punitive
Damages and the Present Role of "Common Law
Malice" in the Modern Law of Libel and Slander, 10
Cumb. L. Rev. 487 (1979).

[30] See, Murphy, Comments on Judicial Nullification
of Jury Awards in Public Official and Public Figure
Libel Suits, 86 W.Va. L. Rev. 269 (1983).

[31] C. McCormick, Law of Damages, Sec. 118 at 431
(1935).

[32] Rosenbloom v. Metromedia Inc., 403 U.S. at 74.

The third and perhaps most widely accepted argument for abolishing punitive damages stems from the belief that such awards necessarily have an unconstitutional "chilling effect" on free speech.[33]

Central to this argument is the proposition that controversial news stories are less likely to be written if their subsequent publication could result in liability for millions of dollars in punitive damages. According to those people familiar with the workings of the newsroom, important stories are regularly "spiked" for just that reason.

Yet despite the argument's currency and surface plausibility, problems abound. On the contrary, what little evidence does exist suggests that only a very small percentage of newsrooms are deterred by the threat of large punitive damage verdicts from pursuing news stories.

For example, last summer, more than one-third of all TV station news departments were questioned regarding how the rise in libel suits was affecting their policies and operations. Only 3.6 percent of those responding said that they were purposefully "avoiding certain kinds of stories."[34] As one news manager remarked, "[w]e are not backing off from stories at all. Investigative reporting is part of our approach, and there is probably even a little more now than in the past."[35]

Second, although some "speech" in the everyday sense of the word inevitably is being "chilled" through the potential

assessment of punitive damages, that "speech" is not constitutionally protected by the First Amendment. Punitive damages exist precisely in order to chill speech that should not be spoken.

Accordingly, if there is a chilling effect and "if the claimed inhibition flows from the fear of damages liability for publishing knowing or reckless falsehoods, those effects are precisely what *New York Times* and other cases have held to be consistent with the First Amendment. Spreading false information in and of itself carries no First Amendment credentials. '[T]here is no constitutional value in false statements of fact.'"[36]

The final objection normally raised to awarding punitive damages in libel suits is the fear that such awards, because of their large nature, may have the unfortunate effect of putting small publishers out of business.[37] While a large metropolitan newspaper may be able to absorb a large punitive damages judgment, smaller papers simply do not have the financial resources to survive a "megaverdict."

Consequently, the marketplace of ideas would be dramatically homogenized if punitive damage awards—which fall with particular oppressiveness on small or unpopular papers—are retained. The example most frequently referred to whenever this argument is raised is the case of the Alton Telegraph.[38]

The Alton Telegraph is a small southern Illinois daily with a circulation of just under 40,000. In 1969, two reporters working for the paper on a local corrup-

[33] The phrase "chilling effect" made its debut in Gibson v. Florida Legis. Invest. Comm., 372 U.S. 539, 556–57 (1963). By 1967, however, the term had already become "ubiquitous" in First Amendment cases. Zwickler v. Kooter, 389 U.S. 241, 256 n.2 (1967) (Harlan, J., concurring).

[34] See Silverman, Impact of Libel Cases Being Felt at Station Level, Television/Radio Age, Sept. 12, 1983, at 41. The "impact" the title of the article refers to is the fact that because of the potential for libel litigation, station news departments are more careful editing, checking facts and consulting with station counsel now than in the past.

[35] Id.

[36] Herbert v. Lando, 441 U.S. 153, 171 (1979) quoting Gertz v. Robert Welch Inc., 481 U.S. 323, 340 (1974).

[37] See, Jollymore, The Constitutionality of Punitive Damages in Libel Actions, 45 Ford. L. Rev. 1382 (1977).

[38] 'Chilling Effect': How Libel Suit Sapped the Crusading Spirit of a Small Newspaper, Wall St. J., Sept. 29, 1983, at 1, col. 1.

tion story sent a memo to the Justice Department in which they stated that a source had linked a local building contractor to the underworld.

The charge was never printed in the paper; however, when the contractor found out about the memo, he sued the Telegraph. In 1980, a jury rendered a $9.2 million libel judgment against the paper in actual and punitive damages that forced it into bankruptcy court.[39] The Alton Telegraph, so this argument runs, stands as a constant reminder of what could happen to other small investigative newspapers around the nation unless the threat of punitive damages is abolished.

While one can sympathize with the fact that small and financially weak media may need protection, we should hesitate before using their delicacy as a pretext for rewriting the law of defamation.[40] The newspaper business is, after all, a business. Just as public officials have assumed the risk of being defamed that a public career entails,[41] so too newspapers assume the risk that a negligently or maliciously set printing press may harm an individual's reputation and that they will be brought to bear for the consequent harm they have inflicted.

Theory aside, the number of libel suits that have been brought against small media in the past has been extremely small.[42] Furthermore, small media, like large media, are able to obtain libel insurance, which, in certain instances, covers punitive damages for very modest premiums.[43]

Finally, it bears emphasizing that small papers can inflict as much harm to a person's good name as large ones. The press in this country generally does an excellent job of providing news and information to the public. Like any human institution, however, it oftentimes makes mistakes.

On some occasions the mistakes are attributable to simple negligence. On others, however, false factual assertions may have been made with the knowledge that they were false or with reckless disregard for their truth.

When the latter situation occurs and when, as a direct result, a person's good name is severely impaired, that individual should be allowed to recover compensatory damages for the harm. Furthermore, punitive damages should be assessed against the news organization just as they are assessed against other businesses found to have engaged in wanton misconduct that harms another.[44]

"For [more than] 200 years, punitive damages and the First Amendment have peacefully coexisted."[45] They should continue to do so until such time as more weighty arguments in favor of the abolition of this doctrine are developed.

[39] The suit was eventually settled for $1.4 million. The paper remains in business.
[40] In Buckley v. Valeo, 424 U.S. 1, 49 (1976) (per curiam), the Supreme Court properly stated: "The First Amendment protection against governmental abridgement of free expression cannot properly be made to depend on a person's financial ability to engage in public discussion."
[41] "An individual who decides to seek governmental office must accept certain necessary consequences of that involvement in public affairs. He runs the risk of closer public scrutiny than might otherwise be the case." Gertz v. Welch, 418 U.S. at 344.
[42] See, Jollymore, supra at 1419.
[43] Employers Reinsurance Corp. (ERC) offers libel insurance to newspapers that explicitly cover punitive damages. Up to a $10 million libel insurance policy may be obtained for a premium of several hundred dollars depending on the circulation and frequency of the paper. Information taken from ERC literature.
[44] See, e.g., Durrill v. Ford Motor Co., 79 3203 (28th D. Ct. Tx.) (jury award of $6.8 million in actual damages and $100 million in punitive damages to parents whose daughter died following a rear-end collision involving a 1974 Ford Mustang II.)
[45] Gertz v. Welch, 418 U.S. at 398 (White, J., dissenting).

QUESTIONS FOR DISCUSSION

1. Does the possible award of punitive damages cause the press to be more responsible?
2. Is freedom of the press unduly inhibited by the fear of libel litigation?
3. Should the press be immune from libel laws when dealing with public figures?
4. Do libel and slander laws restrict political debate?
5. When someone enters public political life, does he or she surrender the right to privacy?

RECOMMENDED READINGS

ADLER, RENATA. *Reckless Disregard: Westmoreland v. CBS et al.; Sharon v. Time.* New York: Knopf, 1986.

BARNEY, ARTHUR L. "Libel and the First Amendment—A New Constitutional Privilege." 51 *Virginia Law Review* 1 (1965).

BRILL, STEVEN. "Redoing Libel Law." 6 *American Lawyer* 1 (Sept. 1984).

COOPER, R. JOHN, and BRUCE W. SANFORD, eds. *First Amendment and Libel: The Experts Look at Print, Broadcast, and Cable.* New York: Harcourt Brace Jovanovich, 1983.

"Defamation and the First Amendment: New Perspectives." 25 *William and Mary Law Review* (1983–84), entire issue.

GARBUS, MARTIN. "Abolish Libel—The Only Answer." *Nation,* 237 (Oct. 8, 1983), pp. 302–3.

HENRY, WILLIAM A., III. "Libel Law: Good Intentions Gone Awry." *Time* 125 (Mar. 4, 1985), pp. 93–94.

JOLLYMORE, NICHOLAS. "The Constitutionality of Punitive Damages in Libel Actions." 45 *Fordham Law Review* 1382 (May 1977).

KAUFMAN, IRVING R. "Press, Privacy and Malice: Reflections on New York Times v. Sullivan." 56 *New York State Bar Journal* 10 (July 1984).

NEIER, ARYEH. "The Case for a Right of Reply." *Nation* 237 (Oct. 8, 1983), pp. 299–302.

NIMMER, ALFRED. "The Right to Speak from Times to Time: First Amendment Theory Applied to Libel and Misapplied to Privacy." 56 *California Law Review* (1968).

REDISH, MARTIN H. "The Value of Free Speech." 130 *University of Pennsylvania Law Review* 591 (Jan. 1982).

SMOLLA, ROD. "Self-Love and Libel." *Washington Monthly* 15 (Nov. 1983), pp. 44–49.

10 Is civil disobedience an act of rebellion?

YES NO RIGHT TO CIVIL DISOBEDIENCE

Eugene V. Rostow

Our society—as a society of consent—should not, and indeed cannot acknowledge a right of civil disobedience; the moral and philosophical arguments advanced in support of such a right are in error; and the analogies invoked in its behalf are inapplicable.

My major premise is the corollary of Jefferson's magisterial sentence, which echoes Locke, Rousseau, and a long line of philosophers stretching back to Plato at least: The "just Powers" of government derive from "the consent of the governed." It follows that in a society of consent the powers of government are just in Jefferson's sense, that is, they are legitimate, because authorized and renewed by procedures of voting all must respect.

As a consequence, such citizen owes his fellow citizens, and the state they have established together, a moral duty to obey valid laws until they are repealed, or fall into disuse. I stress the word "valid" in the preceding sentence, to distinguish situations—of the utmost importance for our legal system—where the citizen is testing the constitutionality of a statute, an ordinance, or an official act.

This proposition is the beginning, not the end, of the problem. The individual owes other moral duties in his life—to his God, his family, his work, his conscience.

Eugene V. Rostow, "No Right to Civil Disobedience," *Trial Magazine* 6 (June–July 1970), pp. 16–19. © 1970 Association of Trial Lawyers of America. Reprinted with permission.

Sometimes—often—there is conflict among the moral claims upon a man. But if man lives in a society of consent, and above all in a society of equality and of liberty, his relation to the valid laws of that society should be regarded as moral in character, because it is rooted in his consent and promises to others. Therefore it is entitled to great weight in the hierarchy of moral claims he must face in the course of his life.

If a man decides to commit an act of civil disobedience, for example, because he feels that what the law requires would breach his obligation to God, our culture would acknowledge at most his naked power, but not his right or privilege to do so. But then he should in turn acknowledge that if he does decide to violate the law, he thereby breaches a covenant with moral dimensions, and is not committing a purely technical offense. To be sure, he would contend that he is breaking the law in order to avoid what he would regard as a greater sin.

But the law, too, has a moral content; it represents the moral judgment of the majority, and its sense of justice. Under such circumstances, the individual should at least respect his duty to the law he has helped to make by accepting its penalties.

The modern, secular world has long since rejected the Divine Right of Kings. The proudest claim of the legal tradition we inherited is that the king too is under the law. Locke's theory of the social compact has become the prevailing political theory of modern times, and the only modern rival for the doctrine that power proceeds from the barrel of a gun. As Professor Alexander P. d'Entrèves has said, "the principle of equality, together with the related notion of consent as the foundation of power, is the essential component of the idea of legitimacy in the modern world."

The notion of the social compact is of course a metaphor. The social contract is hardly a formal document to be interpreted like a deed. But the phrase embodies the idea of an understanding, nonetheless; the core of ideas, values and customs, defining the ultimate norms of the society, and binding all who share its culture. That body of shared values is the foundation on which any community is built. It involves a commitment on the part of each citizen to play the game according to the moral code of the community as a whole, and to respect the equal rights of all his fellow citizens.

The social contract binds the state as well as the citizen. The two sets of obligations are reciprocal. Neither can exist without the other. But the citizen's obligation continues as long as the state remains faithful to the fundamental rules.

Even the most perfect of democratic societies is capable of error, and indeed capable of law which violates its own code of social morality, or higher ideals urged by individuals in the name of moral advance. But unless such errors breach the essential terms of the social contract itself, and destroy the capacity of democracy to correct its errors, they do not weaken the citizen's moral obligation to obey valid law.

The question is always one of degree. If, for example, a President should dismiss the Supreme Court and the Congress, and attempt to rule by decree, all would concur, I should suppose, that the United States had become a different country, and that the social compact itself was broken.

But an individual is not justified in concluding that the state has abrogated the social contract because he feels, and feels passionately, that injustices are unremedied, or not remedied fast enough. Human society has never achieved utopia, and it is not likely to do so soon.

The test proposed by Jefferson is still sufficient. Governments are instituted among men, he argued, to secure the unalienable rights of man. It follows, he said, that men are justified in altering the form of their government when it becomes destructive of these ends, and in revolution itself when "a long train of abuses and usurpations, pursuing invariably the same object, evinces a design to reduce them under absolute Despotism."

As Professor Rawls has remarked:

"Even under a just Constitution, unjust laws may be passed and unjust policies enforced. Some form of majority principle is necessary, but the majority may be mistaken, more or less wilfully, in what it legislates. . . . Assuming that the Constitution is just and that we have accepted and plan to continue to accept its benefits, we then have both an obligation and a natural duty (and in any case the duty) to comply with what the majority enacts even though it may be unjust. In this way we become bound to follow unjust laws, not always, of course, but provided the injustice does not exceed certain limits."

The purely legal tradition is that each person is bound by ties of allegiance to the sovereignty of a nation, to its laws and to its social code, by the fact of residence or citizenship. Allegiance, the law books have said for centuries, is the reciprocal of the protection each person receives through living in an organized community.

The most famous and most influential denial of this concept is that of Thoreau. His "Essay on Civil Disobedience," and his "Speech in Defense of John Brown," assert the theory that a citizen of superior virtue—the rare man of conscience, a member of the "wise minority"—has the right and indeed is under a duty to disobey valid laws, like tax laws.

Professor Rawls, who approaches this subject very much as I do, would, however, justify narrowly limited forms of civil disobedience "in a reasonably just (though of course not perfectly just) democratic regime" when they are entirely peaceful; when the actors fully accept the rightness of their punishment; when acts of disobedience are limited to dissent on fundamental questions of internal policy; and when they consist of "political action which addresses the sense of justice of the majority in order to urge reconsideration of the measures protested and to warn that in the firm opinion of the dissenters the conditions of social cooperation are not being honored."

In Professor Rawls' sense of the term, civil disobedience is "disobedience to law within the limits of fidelity to law"—that is, disobedience as a means of appealing to the majority, or to the courts, in the name of the sense of justice of the community as a whole.

But how are we to determine whether the "firm" and "sincere" minority is right in its view that the measures adopted by the majority violate the sense of justice of the community as a whole?

Presumably, the majority has already decided the contrary; it has not as yet been persuaded by the arguments of the minority. I find no substance in Professor Rawls' distinction between grounds for civil disobedience that society should respect and purely individual views of social justice, or views based on considerations of interest.

I can understand the difference between the opinions of an individual about the morality and justice of a given measure, and the view of it that would be taken under the code of morality of society as a whole, as applied and interpreted by mass public opinion, by elections, by the President, by governors, by legislators, by

courts, and ultimately by 12 men in a jury box.

I can also understand that the dissenting individual would claim—with complete sincerity—that he was interpreting the community's sense of justice more correctly than the majority. But if the majority does not come to agree, how can Professor Rawl's distinction justify civil disobedience in the one case—where the minority appeals to the community's sense of justice—but not in the other, where dissent rests explicitly on individual ethical views? Aren't the minority views quite as "individual" in the one case as in the other? I can find no halfway house, or Third Thing, between the two concepts.

I conclude that while Professor Rawls would not allow civil disobedience to go as far as Thoreau, he would, like Thoreau, condone civil disobedience when the individual, and the individual alone, firmly, earnestly and sincerely decides that he is right, and the majority wrong, in interpreting the community's justice.

The American community, permeated by Jefferson's ideals, can never stress enough the need to respect the autonomy of the iconoclast, nor do too much to protect freedom of thought from repression at the will of the majority.

But no society of consent could live according to Thoreau's principle, and no other society would care enough about the rights of a nonconformist to consider it. It would allow each man to decree himself elect—a claim at odds with the rule of equality which is the essence of democracy.

If the premise I have just stated is accepted—and even Thoreau conceded its moral force, although he sought an exception to it for himself—then the arguments for civil disobedience fall into place.

Our tradition recognizes no general "right" of revolution. On the contrary, we rejected that claim on the battlefields of the Civil War. For a society of consent, there can be no claim of a "right" to revolt, unless and until the social compact itself is threatened by destruction.

Nor is the case for civil disobedience supported in any way by the experience of the civil rights movement, and the philosophy of the Rev. Martin Luther King, Jr. By far the larger and more significant part of the struggle for Negro equality was and is an invocation of law, and an appeal to it.

Socrates spoke of the laws of Athens as having given him "a share in every good which . . . [they] had to give." That statement could not come from a black man in America, without sharp qualifications.

Does the burden of the past exempt the Negro from the obligations of the social compact?

He now helps, more and more genuinely, to make the laws.

But no man can say with conviction that we have yet come half, or quarter, of the way.

It is true that error, or the presence of injustice, do not of themselves void the social compact. But when error and injustice become the rule, not the exception; when the democratic process itself is suspended; when minority rights and personal freedom are denied—then, surely, the society ceases to be one of consent; the social contract could be regarded as breached; and the power to wage war against society could be claimed as right.

I do not believe the black American today is in this position, or believes himself to be. It is apparent that society, led by its system of law, is seeking to achieve and guarantee his equality.

Thus, I do not believe the American Negro can or should be regarded as exempted from the obligation to obey constitutionally valid laws, nor that his dark history justifies violence by black citizens today.

Students justify university rioting based on a similar exclusion from the social contract. They say they have a right to disobey the rules of their colleges or universities, or to disrupt their operations, because they do not participate in their management.

There is no doubt that universities suffer the ailments of other institutions—bureaucracy, conservatism, timidity, and occasional failures of responsibility. But these are the normal problems of all organized social life. The shortcomings of a particular university at a particular moment of its history, however irritating, can hardly be put forward to justify illegal programs intended to destroy the university, or to bring about reform, or what claims to be reform, by methods of coercion rather than of democracy.

By the same token, those who disagree with the nation's policy in Viet Nam have every right to employ all the methods of democratic political freedom to persuade their fellow citizens to accept their views. But, I should contend, they have no moral right to disrupt the draft; to interfere with the freedom of those who believe they are preaching national suicide; to break up universities or public meetings; to burn the files of draft boards; or to engage in other acts of violence and illegality.

The same issues arise, with far less color of right, when the ends sought in demonstrations are changes in university policies, or welfare policies, or policies with regard to the administration of educational systems. In the conflicts which have so profoundly disturbed and weakened our universities in recent years, for example, demonstrators have claimed a "right" to engage in tactics of disruption, the occupation of buildings, and even more extreme forms of coercion. They do not claim that the laws governing the organization of universities are "unconstitutional." They undertake such tactics, and undertake to justify them, simply as means to persuade those who could not be persuaded otherwise to change policies about ROTC, university research programs, and the internal organization of universities.

What is the possible source of such a

right? Not the laws which establish the authority of university officials. Not the Constitution, which defines the rights of freedom of speech and of the press, and of peaceable assembly to petition for the redress of grievances. Not Divine Right, surely, or some impalpable right of man not articulated in the Constitution.

Society should recognize the moral and legal propriety of such tactics, it is urged, when the violations of law are "minor" ones committed by men who are loyal to our own political and moral traditions, and who are sincerely convinced that in pursuing a particular policy the nation has not kept faith with the principles on which its legal and political system purports to rest.

But the law cannot and should not distinguish between the rights of protest of those who do and those who do not generally accept the rightness of our constitutional system. The history of attempts to condemn or to restrict the civil rights of those deemed "disloyal" or "un-American" is not a happy one, and I cannot believe it is wise or practicable for this purpose to distinguish between appeals to the conscience of the nation made by those who in their hearts are attached to the fundamental principles of the Constitution, and those who would gladly destroy it. The distinction is subjective.

Ample and depressing experience attests to the difficulties of applying such a test. Our legal order has generally, and in my view, rightly addressed itself in large part to actions, and sought to avoid distinctions as to legal rights based on distinctions of attitude.

Good men and bad men, anarchists and conservatives, men of all faiths and of no faith, are equally protected by the Constitution and its Bill of Rights, and equally bound by valid laws enacted through constitutional procedures. All are equally free to appeal to the conscience of the nation, and to its traditional values, whether their appeal is made in good faith or in bad.

Three more general arguments have been put forward to justify illegal action, including some use of "minor" violence:

1. that violating laws, and some recourse to violence, should be regarded as a permissible way to dramatize a point of view, and gain access to newspapers and television that would otherwise have been difficult to obtain; an illegal and violent act, it is urged, can shock into a state of reflection some men who would not otherwise consider the problem;
2. that such tactics induce desirable changes in policies or institutions that might not have come, or come so soon, through democratic persuasion alone; and
3. that violence is sometimes "forced" on militants by the stubborness and inactivity of those who direct legitimate institutions, and who have not been persuaded by arguments in which militants passionately believe.

These contentions all rest, in effect, on the thesis that the end does indeed justify the means, at least if the means are not "too" damaging. Convinced of the rightness of their own views, men of this outlook claim the right to seek changes in society against the will of the majority through tactics of planned disobedience which sometimes include the use of force.

But there is no ethical case for revolution in a working and effective democracy, however beset it may be with the difficult problems of social transition. In such societies, laws can be changed legitimately only by the deliberate processes of elections and of parliamentary action: by votes after hearings, reports and debates. Recourse to illegal methods of political and social action can have the most corrosive effect on society, especially if they are employed by the well-educated and the well-established, in the name of moral right. Violations of law by the leadership of a community have more impact on society than ordinary crime.

As for the thoughtless argument that tactics of violence and coercion have forced change at a more rapid pace than could have been achieved by persuasion alone, they recall the classic justifications of Fascism: that Mussolini made the trains run on time.

Those who justify acts of disruption and coercion in the name of a utilitarian theory of civil disobedience have no way of knowing, or predicting, that their behavior has a reasonable chance of achieving more good than harm. By acting on their own decision, without the backing of any majority, they necessarily function not as rational utilitarians, but on impulse and instinct. They cannot find a ground for denying the same privilege to others who feel quite as strongly about the rightness of their views. Thus they degrade the quality of public discourse, from which public opinion flows, for they necessarily reduce the level of rationality, and increase the level of passion and violence, in the process of making decisions of social policy.

The arguments used to justify illegality as a political tactic in contemporary controversies parallel those employed in the worst and most prolonged experience of the nation with civil disobedience—the resistance of the South to the enforcement of the Fourteenth Amendment for nearly a century after 1868.

The hardest task for law, always, is to achieve a change in custom. And the most difficult legal task our society has ever undertaken is the enforcement of the Fourteenth Amendment. There is always some difference between positive law and the living law of customary behavior. Sometimes the written law lags behind custom, as it does when laws become obsolete, like statutes proscribing contraception. Sometimes the law collides with custom, and has to retreat—the case of Prohibition comes to mind. Often the law seeks to affect a change in custom. The Fourteenth Amendment is the most ambitious example of such an attempt in our history. Another is the field of labor

relations, where, after years of frustration and of struggle, the law declared the right of workers to organize and bargain collectively.

If the social revolutions of the last 40 years are viewed in perspective, they appear as among the greatest historic achievements of our political system. Responding to the stresses of its experience with depression and war, the nation deeply altered its conception of social justice, through programs carried out by judicial and parliamentary means, and conceived in terms which confirmed and fulfilled its own aspirations. Violence played a minimal part in these events, and often a negative one.

Those who have recently pursued experiments in disorder have discovered how easy it is to paralyze a society based on consent. Such societies are not police states. They are organized on the assumption that citizens normally obey the law. It has been intoxicating for young militants to realize that, for a moment, they can paralyze cities and institutions, and provoke situations of riot and siege. But they discover too that even the most tolerant and permissive societies do not submit to their own destruction. We are slow to anger, but hardly meek. Every government and every society has an inherent right to insist on obedience to its laws, to restore order, and to assure its own survival.

The idea of treating a right of civil disobedience as an aspect of personal liberty under the Constitution is at war with the moral principles on which this civilization, and any liberal civilization rest; and it is equally at war with the possibility of social peace, and of personal liberty.

Individual liberty can be respected and protected only in a society based on a shared understanding as to the broad aspirations of the law. Social concord in this sense requires a general acceptance of the citizen's moral obligation to obey valid law.

Respect for the agreed limits of social conflict is essential if men are to live in liberty, and not, in Hobbes' phrase, as wolves.

A prolongation of today's riot tactics would have tragic consequences, if fear comes to dominate the political atmosphere and policy turns to a reliance on repression rather than on social progress as the primary method of order. Repudiating the principle of majority rule, as Jefferson said long ago, can lead only to military despotism. Violence and counter-violence, sooner or later, generate forces that demand social peace, even at the price of personal liberty.

It could happen here. We cannot expect to be immune from the experience of all mankind if we defy the principle of democratic consent, which thus far has been the essence of our destiny, and of our freedom.

The social compact of the United States is an unusual one. The power of the majority is checked and restrained in many ways, not least through the Supreme Court, enforcing a written Constitution. Our notion is that freedom is a corollary of agreed restraints on freedom; that man cannot be free, especially in a democratic society, unless the state, and the majority, are not free—unless they can be compelled to respect rights which are "subject to no vote," in Justice Jackson's vivid phrase—rights essential to the dignity of man in a free society, and to the vitality of its public life.

I do not suggest that all is well with our society, and that the social tensions we feel all about us are an illusion. Not at all. Like every other period of rapid progress in history, hope based on the experience of progress has generated a deep and urgent restlessness—a desire to press forward more rapidly still, for more progress. Explosive and even revolutionary impatience in societies, as many students of the phenomenon of revolution have remarked, usually develops not in situations of hopelessness, of poverty, and of hunger, but at times when social conditions are improving.

The agenda for social action in the United States is formidable. The process of change has generated its own momentum. Many institutions and arrangements have been left behind by the uneven pace of change in different sectors of society.

But nothing in our experience should lead us to suppose that the agenda is beyond the capacity of our social order.

NO   DISOBEDIENCE AND DEMOCRACY

Howard Zinn

. . . 1. Civil disobedience is the deliberate, discriminate, violation of law for a vital social purpose. It becomes not only justifiable but necessary when a fundamental human right is at stake, and when legal channels are inadequate for securing that right. It may take the form of violating an

Excerpted from Howard Zinn, *Disobedience and Democracy: Nine Fallacies on Law and Order* (New York: Random House, 1968), pp. 119–24.

obnoxious law, protesting an unjust condition, or symbolically enacting a desirable law or condition. It may or may not eventually be held legal, because of constitutional law or international law, but its aim is always to close the gap between law and justice, as an infinite process in the development of democracy.

2. There is no social value to a general obedience to the law, any more than there is value to a general disobedience to the

law. Obedience to bad laws as a way of inculcating some abstract subservience to "the rule of law" can only encourage the already strong tendencies of citizens to bow to the power of authority, to desist from challenging the status quo. To exalt the rule of law as an absolute is the mark of totalitarianism, and it is possible to have an atmosphere of totalitarianism in a society which has many of the attributes of democracy. To urge the right of citizens to disobey unjust laws, and the duty of citizens to disobey dangerous laws, is of the very essence of democracy, which assumes that government and its laws are not sacred, but are instruments, serving certain ends: life, liberty, happiness. The instruments are dispensable. The ends are not.

3. Civil disobedience may involve violation of laws which are not in themselves obnoxious, in order to protest on a very important issue. In each case, the importance of the law being violated would need to be measured against the importance of the issue. A traffic law, temporarily broken, is not nearly as important as the life of a child run over by a car; illegal trespass into offices is nowhere as serious as the killing of people in war; the unlawful occupation of a building is not as sinful as racism in education. Since not only specific laws, but general conditions may be unbearable, laws not themselves ordinarily onerous may need to be violated as protest.

4. If a specific act of civil disobedience is a morally justifiable act of protest, then the jailing of those engaged in that act is immoral and should be opposed, contested to the very end. The protester need be no more willing to accept the rule of punishment than to accept the rule he broke. There may be many times when protesters *choose* to go to jail, as a way of continuing their protest, as a way of reminding their countrymen of injustice. But that is different than the notion that they *must* go to jail as part of a rule connected with civil disobedience. The key point is that the spirit of protest should be maintained all the way, whether it is done by remaining in jail, or by evading it. To accept jail penitently as an accession to "the rules" is to switch suddenly to a spirit of subservience, to demean the seriousness of the protest.

5. Those who engage in civil disobedience should choose tactics which are as nonviolent as possible, consonant with the effectiveness of their protest and the importance of the issue. There must be a reasonable relationship between the degree of disorder and the significance of the issue at stake. The distinction between harm to people and harm to property should be a paramount consideration. Tactics directed at property might include (again, depending on efficacy and the issue): depreciation (as in boycotts), damage, temporary occupation, and permanent appropriation. In any event, the force of any act of civil disobedience must be focused clearly, discriminately on the object of protest.

6. The degree of disorder in civil disobedience should not be weighed against a false "peace" presumed to exist in the status quo, but against the real disorder and violence that are part of daily life, overtly expressed internationally in wars, but hidden locally under that facade of "order" which obscures the injustice of contemporary society.

7. In our reasoning about civil disobedience, we must never forget that we and the state are separate in our interests, and we must not be lured into forgetting this by the agents of the state. The state seeks power, influence, wealth, as ends in themselves. The individual seeks health, peace, creative activity, love. The state, because of its power and wealth, has no end of spokesmen for its interests. This means the citizen must understand the need to think and act on his own or in concert with fellow citizens.

A few words in conclusion. I have argued strenuously against what I consider the fallacious thinking of Mr. Fortas. I have done so because I think it urgent for American democracy that citizens should not relinquish the vital weapon of civil disobedience against the already-frightening power of the state.

I do not think civil disobedience is enough; it is a way of protest, but in itself it does not construct a new society. There are many other things that citizens should do to begin to build a new way of life in the midst of the old, to live the way human beings should live—enjoying the fruits of the earth, the warmth of nature and of one another—without hostility, without the artificial separation of religion, or race, or nationalism. Further, not all forms of civil disobedience are moral; not all are effective.

However, when one looks around and sees the condition of the black person, the existence of poverty, the continued stupidity of war, the growing blight of an unnatural life in malodorous, crowded cities or inhuman suburbs—and when one considers the impotence of our existing political institutions in affecting this, we know that not just mild, petty, gradual steps, but revolutionary changes are needed. We also suspect that classical revolutionary war in our country is not feasible.

We are thus led to the conclusion that the only way to escape the twin evils of stagnation and chaotic violence at home, and to avoid devastating wars abroad, is for citizens to accept, utilize, control the disorder of civil disobedience, enriching it with countless possibilities and tactics not yet imagined, to make life more human for us and others on this earth.

It is very hard, in the comfortable environment of middle-class America, to discard the notion that everything will be better if we don't have the disturbance of civil disobedience, if we confine ourselves to voting, writing letters to our Congressmen, speaking our minds politely. But those outside are not so comfortable. Most people in the world are hungry, have no decent place to sleep, no doctor when they are sick; and some are fleeing from attacking airplanes. Somehow, we must transcend our own tight, air-conditioned chambers and begin to feel their plight, their needs. It may become evident that, despite our wealth, we can have no real peace until they do. We might then join them in battering at the complacency of those who guard a false "order," with that healthy commotion that has always attended the growth of justice.

QUESTIONS FOR DISCUSSION

1. Is it ever justifiable to disobey the law?
2. Who is to decide whether a law is just or unjust?
3. Should those who violate unjust laws be punished?
4. Is the individual above the law?
5. Does belief in a just cause authorize acting illegally?
6. What is a just cause?
7. Is the issue of civil disobedience peculiarly applicable to democracies rather than to dictatorships?
8. Which, if any, of the following situations would justify acts of civil disobedience in the United States: the investment by an American corporation in South Africa; the establishment of an office committed to providing humanitarian assistance to the Contras fighting against the Sandinista government in Nicaragua; the building of a nuclear power plant for peaceful

purposes; the construction of a ballistic missile silo; the opening of an abortion clinic; the establishment of a Palestine Liberation Organization office; the doubling of tuition at a state university?

RECOMMENDED READINGS

BEDAU, HUGO A., ed. *Civil Disobedience: Theory and Practice.* New York: Pegasus, 1969.

BERRIGAN, DANIEL. *The Dark Night of Resistance.* Garden City, N.Y.: Doubleday, 1971.

CARLIN, DAVID R., JR. "Civil Disobedience, Self-Righteousness and the Antinuclear Movement." *America* 147 (Sept. 25, 1982), pp. 152–54.

COHEN, CARL. *Civil Disobedience: Conscience, Tactics, and the Law.* New York: Columbia University Press, 1971.

FORTAS, ABE. *Concerning Dissent and Civil Disobedience.* New York: New American Library, 1968.

HALL, ROBERT TOM. *The Morality of Civil Disobedience.* New York: Harper and Row, 1971.

KENT, EDWARD ALLEN, ed. *Revolution and the Rule of Law.* Englewood Cliffs, N.J.: Prentice-Hall, 1971.

LENS, SIDNEY. "The Irrelevant Ballot Box." *Progressive* 44 (Sept. 1980), pp. 39–41.

LEVINE, GEORGE DANZIG. "Should Civil Disobedience Be Legalized?: Reflections on Coercive Protest and the Democratic Regime of Law." 31 *Southwestern Law Journal* 617 (Summer 1977).

LEVINE, HERBERT M. "Is Civil Disobedience Justified in a Representative Democracy?" in his *Political Issues Debated: An Introduction to Politics.* 2nd ed. Englewood Cliffs, N.J.: Prentice-Hall, 1987. Pp. 138–45.

MURPHY, JEFFRIE G., ed. *Civil Disobedience and Violence.* Belmont, Calif.: Wadsworth, 1971.

WEBER, DAVID R., ed. *Civil Disobedience in America: A Documentary History.* Ithaca: Cornell University Press, 1978.

11 Are laws requiring public disclosure of lobbying activities a violation of the right to petition?

YES LOBBYING AND THE FIRST AMENDMENT

Hope Eastman

My name is Hope Eastman. I am a lawyer in private practice in Washington, D.C. For eight years I was the assistant director of the Washington Office of the American Civil Liberties Union and have written and testified over the years on government regulation of lobbying. I am delighted to appear here today on behalf of the American Civil Liberties Union to communicate its views on this subject.

Repeatedly throughout the last decade, Congress has been asked to pass sweeping legislation requiring the disclosure of lobbying activities. The ACLU has opposed these proposals because they conflict with fundamental First Amendment principles. Our position remains unchanged. Proponents of legislation perceive an evil to be regulated by the government. We see the constitutional right under the First Amendment to petition the government for redress of grievances which must be protected.

Many practices which could be included under the rubric of lobbying have long been banned by federal laws on bribery and buying influence. The proposals now under consideration do not directly prohibit any lobbying activity. They regulate by disclosure, with enforcement by sub-

U.S. Cong., Senate, *Oversight of the 1946 Federal Regulation of Lobbying Act,* Hearings before the Committee on Governmental Affairs, 98th Cong., 1st Sess., 1983.

poena power, fines, and criminal penalties. In this way, the government becomes the monitor of the right to petition.

The Supreme Court has articulated a stiff test against which regulation must be measured in *Buckley v. Valeo,* 424 U.S. 1 (1976). Although the ACLU would support a stiffer test, the *Buckley* test is a demanding one:

> We long have recognized that significant encroachments on First Amendment rights of the sort that compelled disclosure imposes cannot be justified by a mere showing of some legitimate governmental interest. Since *Alabama* [*NAACP v. Alabama,* 357 U.S. 449 (1958)] we have required that the subordinating interest of the State must survive exacting scrutiny. We also have insisted that there be a "relevant correlation" or "substantial relation" between the governmental interest and the information required to be disclosed.

Two post-*Buckley* decisions of the Supreme Court must be kept in mind when applying the *Buckley* standard to lobbying disclosure. In *Brown v. Socialist Workers '74 Campaign Committee,* 103 S.Ct. 416 (1982), the Court held unconstitutional application of a campaign expenditure disclosure law to minor political parties that would subject the persons identified to the reasonable probability of threats, harassment, or reprisals. In so doing, the Court affirmed the recognition in *Buckley* that the government's interests supporting disclosure are weaker and the danger to First Amendment values greater when disclosure laws are applied to minor parties (*Id.* at 421). The loss of such minor parties or political movements from government regulation affects us all:

> The public interest also suffers if that result comes to pass, for there is a consequent reduction in the free circulation of ideas both within and without the political arena. (*Buckley v. Valeo,* 424 U.S. at 71)

The other case which must be borne in mind is *First National Bank of Boston v. Bellotti,* 435 U.S. 765 (1978). In that case a criminal statute prohibited business corporations from making contributions or expenditures to influence voter referenda on issues not materially affecting the corporation's business. Finding the statute unconstitutional, the Court stated:

> The inherent worth of the speech in terms of its capacity for informing the public does not depend upon the identity of its source, whether corporation, association, union or individual. (*Id.* at 777).

This case reminds us of several fundamentals. First, the kind of speech involved in lobbying is "at the heart of the First Amendment's protection" (*Id.* at 776), "the type of speech indispensable to decision making in a democracy" (*Id.* at 777). Second, it is impermissible under the First Amendment to regulate speech in "an attempt to give one side of a debatable public question an advantage in expressing its views" (*Id.* at 785). Third, only where "advocacy threatened imminently to undermine democratic processes, thereby denigrating rather than serving First Amendment interests" would the Court even look at the argument that regulation was proper under the constitution (*Id.* at 789).

In *Buckley,* the governmental interests on which the Court relied when upholding campaign finance disclosure were voter knowledge about a candidate's allegiances, deterrence of corruption, and enforcement of campaign contribution limits.

What are the Government interests here? At the outset, it is necessary to deal with the image of the lobbyist and the kinds of lobbying techniques they use which greatly influence the drive for regulation.

In the early days of the congressional effort to control lobbying, attention was focused on the all-powerful lobbyist, who, on the eve of the final vote, could by-pass the regular channels for influencing the legislative process and, by a simple well-placed phone call, turn around the whole process through extralegal means. Whether this image was accurate or not, it was the catalyst for regulatory efforts. Congress responded to an unarticulated belief that lobbying is evil—that lobbyists are rather paunchy individuals who carry bags of money and smoke cigars.

In later years, the "evil" image shifted to focus on enormous corporations or trade associations generating thousands of letters from unwitting citizens whose views thereby are somehow illegitimately used by an organization to make a point.

The common elements in these pictures are secrecy and the expenditure of vast sums of money. The primary targets of the reformers' zeal are the amount of money spent to stimulate grass-roots communications to Congress, huge advertising and public relations campaigns, and the use of "armies of lobbyists." Senator Kennedy perhaps expressed best this attitude some years ago: "Vast amounts of money and influence are spent in secret ways for secret purposes" (Lobby Reform Legislation: Hearings before the Senate Committee on Government Operation, 94th Cong., 1st Sess, 8, 1975, Statement of Senator Edward Kennedy).

What kind of secret expenditure of vast sums are we talking about in the context of lobbying laws? It is not bribes. It is not campaign contributions. It is not campaign expenditures. It is not the provision of election-year manpower. It is no longer even expensive lunches, dinners, and other direct gifts.

Lobbying laws are aimed elsewhere. Congress seeks disclosure of groups spending money to send people to talk to members of Congress and other government officials, institutions communicating information to citizens—by direct solicitation or by indirect advertising campaigns—in order to get them to communicate their views to those government officials. The reformers have downplayed the important function organizations which lobby are playing in the political process:

> [L]obbyists do on many occasions perform extremely useful functions in the national interest. They can be tapped for expert information on problems, they can analyze the impact of proposed legislation on their areas of concern, and they are an effective vehicle for representation of the interest group they represent. (*Id.* at 3, Statement of Senator Charles Percy)

And they ignore entirely that these very activities are the essence of the American system: petitioning government for redress of grievances. A lobbyist's true function is to bring information to the government and take away information from the government, thereby facilitating the flow of knowledge and understanding and participation of the grass roots—individuals or companies who operate far from the nation's capital. With more information about what the government is up to, people are better able to attempt to influence policy—something which in our system of government is both legitimate and desirable.

The proposals for reform have taken the form of highly refined disclosure statutes which would require all lobbyists to register, to file with the government detailed information on their identities, the size of their organizations, the issues upon which they are active, and the mechanisms through which they attempt to influence public opinion. The mechanisms to be identified have ranged from identifying all executive or legislative officials with whom the lobbyist talks within a given week to listing in a government report every occasion on which they have urged their grass roots members to write or to have letters sent to their members of Congress.

When these proposals have been subjected to scrutiny, it has become clear what Congress does *not* wish to do. It does not wish to impede the flow of information to the citizenry which the skilled lobbyist provides. It does not want the record-keeping burden of regulation to put smaller grass-roots organizations out of business. It does not want to rob contributors to controversial organizations of their anonymity. It does not want to deter the citizen from communicating his or her true feelings on an issue to members of Congress. What is left is a wish on the part of some members to distinguish between a national campaign and an individual's true feelings. Several observations are necessary. First, most of the members I have talked to say that their political experience enables them to make that judgment without any new information. Second, when a well-financed national lobbying campaign is underway, the major organizations that might be seeking to encourage people to write letters to Congress are doing so openly and are themselves visably engaged in lobbying activities. Third, the idea that an individual letter stimulated by an organization is not a reflection of an individual's true feelings is false. The lobbyist can only bring information to the individual. The individual decides whether to write or whether to let the organization write on his or her behalf. The fact that a busy person has not chosen to sit down and write an individualized letter, but has chosen to draw on the lobbyist's help does not mean that the individual cares less.

It is clear from the foregoing that the ACLU believes that no governmental interest exists to justify new lobbying disclosure legislation. We urge Congress to

respond to the cries for legislation with an effort to distinguish fact from fantasy. Justice Brennan wrote of a profound national commitment to the principle that "debate on public issues should be uninhibited, robust and wide-open" (*New York Times Co. v. Sullivan,* 376 U.S. 254, 270, 1969). Essential to preservation of that debate is that Congress pay more than lip service to the fact that lobbying is indeed that First Amendment right to petition for redress of grievances.

NO LOBBYING AND LOBBY DISCLOSURE LEGISLATION

Fred Wertheimer

I would like to thank you, Mr. Chairman and Members of the Committee, for the opportunity to testify on the role of lobbying in our political process and on ways of improving that role.

I appear on behalf of a registered national citizens' lobbying organization with 250,000 members. Common Cause strongly believes that lobbying has an important and very valuable role to play in our democracy, a role rooted in our Constitution.

I appear also as an individual who has been a registered and paid lobbyist since 1971. I take great pride and satisfaction in the way I've been able to spend my time professionally during the past twelve years.

Lobbying can enhance and benefit the legislative process in a number of ways. It can provide information, and facilitate the

exchange of ideas. It can expand citizen participation and encourage government responsiveness and accountability. It can educate and aid in the development of public policy. It can contribute to the building of consensus and help turn theory into reality. It can play an essential role in making our political system work.

Lobbying, however, can also fundamentally undermine our system of government and public confidence in it. This can occur when the methods and tools used to lobby result in improper or inappropriate influence or the appearance of such influence being exercised on government decisions and decision makers.

It can occur when citizens conclude that, as a result of the activities of lobbyists and lobbying organizations, money has too much influence on decisions, representatives are too obligated to private interests to properly represent their constituents, public concerns and views are being distorted, and government decisions aren't being made on the merits.

U.S. Cong., Senate, *Oversight of the 1946 Federal Regulation of Lobbying Act,* **Hearings before the Committee on Governmental Affairs, 98th Cong., 1st Sess., 1983.**

In listing the concerns of this Committee, Mr. Chairman, in your letter of invitation to testify, you state, "[W]e are also concerned with portraying the lobbyist as a legitimate actor in the legislative process and removing some of the anxiety and suspicion with which the public views the lobbying profession."

We share this goal, Mr. Chairman, and believe that in order to accomplish it, Congress must be prepared to deal with the underlying causes that create public anxiety and suspicion about lobbying. Principal among these causes are the role of money in the lobbying process and the secrecy and lack of accurate information that frequently surrounds lobbying.

Congress has already recognized, to some extent, that public concerns about lobbying practices are not without merit. There are limits and restrictions on the gifts and fees that Members of Congress may receive from lobbyists and lobbying organizations. Public disclosure of personal finances for Members allows the public to determine, among other things, whether financial relationships between public officials and lobbying groups are affecting policy decisions.

Limits on campaign contributions from individuals and groups demonstrate Congress's recognition that the campaign contribution can be an effective vehicle for private interests to obtain influence with public officials. The Federal Regulation of Lobbying Act establishes that Members of Congress and the public have the right and the need to know how much money is being spent by whom to influence congressional decisions.

Congress has dealt with public concerns about legislative decision making, however, with varying degrees of effectiveness. The single most important factor today, for example, in undermining public confidence in the integrity of Congress and its ability to make decisions on the merits is the role being played by PAC contributions.

PACs are generally tied to groups that regularly conduct organized lobbying efforts, and campaign contributions are an integral part of these efforts. As Republican Representative W. Henson Moore (La.) has observed, "[A Member] may be polite to you, but if you really want to see him perk up and be interested in what you say, let him know you represent a political action committee that is going to be active in the next election."

PACs, through campaign contributions, are creating a higher obligation for our representatives, an obligation to serve PAC interests, first and foremost. Citizens understand this, and they also understand that representatives are becoming so dependent upon these contributions for their political existence that they are rapidly losing their ability to adequately represent the constituents that have elected them.

In a recent speech, former Representative Richard Bolling, a thirty-year veteran and highly regarded leader of the House of Representatives, outlined his deep concern about what special interest money is doing to Congress:

> During my service in Congress I witnessed Congressmen's need for funds and interest groups' desires for influence increase and combine in a way that steadily began to undermine policy, undermine representation and undermine the institution of Congress. . . . What I fear today is that special interest money is damaging Congress to the same scandalous degree as it damaged the executive branch during Watergate; the only difference is that the means now being used are legal.

From across the political spectrum we find similar concerns being raised by Senator Barry Goldwater, who recently said in a statement entitled "Unlimited Campaign Spending—A Crisis of Liberty,"

> The public does not have any doubt about the power of money. Every poll taken

shows that the vast majority of Americans believe campaign spending is "a very serious problem" and that "those who contribute large sums of money have too much influence over the government."

If in fact we are to help remove the anxiety and suspicion with which the public views the lobbying profession, the PAC problem and its impact on Congress must be dealt with.

We would like to focus our testimony today, however, on another area where Congress has been ineffective in dealing with lobbying practices, the issue of public disclosure of significant lobbying activities.

THE GROWTH OF LOBBYING

Increasingly, citizen groups, economic interest groups, industries, and other interests have been discovering the usefulness of lobbying in influencing legislative outcomes. The result has been an enormous explosion during the past decade in lobbying activities, both in Washington and at the level of the grass roots.

Time magazine has estimated that the number of lobbyists in Washington almost doubled—from 8,000 to 15,000—between 1977 and 1982. Contributing to that swell, the number of corporations with Washington representatives increased 500 percent in the last decade. And the size of lobbying staffs grew as well. The Ford Motor Company, for example, which kept 3 representatives in Washington in the early 1960s, last year maintained a full-time Washington staff of 40.

The increase in grass-roots lobbying has been equally explosive, and its growth can be expected to continue. In addition to established grass-roots lobbying organizations such as the Chamber of Commerce, the National Rifle Association, and Common Cause, major businesses, industries, and other associations are learning how to lobby Congress through the American public. These latter groups can be especially effective at grass-roots lobbying because of their access to very substantial resources and an extensive network of employees, shareholders, members, and customers. The banking industry, for example, was able to mobilize millions of its customers to write to Congress against tax withholding on interest and dividends—a law the industry opposed—and eventually succeeded in having that law repealed. Other groups, such as the insurance industry, public utilities, and oil companies, serve an equally extensive network and have the resources and technology to reach them. Lately, more and more groups have shown a willingness to do so . . . .

THE DISCLOSURE OF LOBBYING

Under the Federal Regulation of Lobbying Act, we require disclosure of lobbying expenditures, just as we require disclosure of campaign contributions, payments of honoraria, and other factors that significantly affect the political process in the absence of disclosure, lobbying has the potential to misrepresent the political pressure being brought to bear, and to distort the context in which political decisions are made.

Unfortunately, we operate today under a law, enacted in 1946, that does not effectively compel disclosure of lobbying activities and expenditures. The growing boom in lobbying—especially stimulated by lobbying based on new technologies—provides graphic examples of how the lobby disclosure system does not work, and provides a compelling illustration of the need to strengthen and revise that system.

NONDISCLOSURE OF LOBBYING IS EXTENSIVE

If one looks only at the lobby disclosure reports filed quarterly with the Congress, Common Cause often appears to be the highest-spending lobbying entity in the country. This fact, however, reveals more about what other groups disclose—or do not disclose—than it does about Common Cause's ranking in expenditures as a lobbying organization. Press accounts and Common Cause studies have turned up numerous expenditure campaigns greater than Common Cause's that have gone undisclosed under the lobby disclosure law. A few examples of lobbying undisclosed under the Act follow:

The Insurance Industry One recent Common Cause study . . . found that at least ten insurance companies, trade associations, and state regulatory associations across the nation have been lobbying heavily against unisex insurance legislation now before the Congress. Our study documented extensive grass-roots lobbying activities (and estimated expenditures of over $600,000) by these groups over a period of four months. None of those grass-roots lobbying activities were disclosed in quarterly lobbying reports.

The Banking Industry Last year and this year, thousands of banks and savings and loans participated in a grass-roots lobbying campaign to repeal tax withholding on interest and dividends. Together they distributed millions of statement stuffers to their customers, stimulating a flood of anti-withholding mail on Capitol Hill and the eventual repeal of the tax provision. A Common Cause investigation of the lobby reports revealed that only four banks filled lobby reports during that campaign, and no banks reported any grass-roots expenditures on the withholding issue. . . .

The Securities Industry Reports in the press have been tracking the efforts of a group of businessmen, known as "The Coalition," that is now waging an intense grass-roots lobbying campaign against a tax bill that would limit the use of tax-exempt bond financing for private development. According to the press accounts, The Coalition has made a great deal of progress toward its goal of generating 5,000 letters and 10 personal constituent visits to every member of the House Ways and Means Committee, in hopes of stopping the tax provision. No estimates of the group's lobbying expenditures are available, and so far, The Coalition has not registered a lobbying organization or filed lobby disclosure reports.

The Phone Company Two recent articles in *The Wall Street Journal* noted, first, that AT&T is waging a multimillion dollar lobbying campaign against congressional efforts to delay phone rate increases that may result from deregulation, and second, that none of the Bell System's lobbyists are registered as such in Congress.

Defense Contractors The General Accounting Office (GAO) conducted an investigation into defense contractor lobbying activities, revealing an extensive amount of nonreporting. In connection with the proposed purchase of C-5B cargo planes, GAO found lobbying expenditures of $496,000 by Lockheed and $21,000 by Boeing—a total of $517,000 during three months in 1982. The two contractors, however, disclosed less than 10 percent of that figure for all of calendar 1982.

There are other examples of unreported lobbying. The U.S. Chamber of Commerce does not register as a lobbying organization. (The expenses reported by the registered agents of those organizations gives no clue as to the magnitude of total organizational lobbying.) The National Rifle Association does not report its considerable grass-roots lobbying expenditures. It is quite clear that unreported lobbying activities are extensive, and that accurate disclosure is more the exception than the rule.

NONDISCLOSURE OF LOBBYING IS A PROBLEM

The question is sometimes asked, "Why should Congress be concerned about undisclosed lobbying? Can't Congress and the public learn from the press and other sources where the lobbying pressure originates?"

Hidden Lobbying To begin with, the source of lobbying pressure is *not* always apparent. Especially where grass-roots lobbying is concerned, increasingly sophisticated techniques can effectively mask the interests at work and the extent to which they represent the views of the public. The direct-mail industry, for example, has achieved such precision in targeting that it can reach well-defined segments of the population (e.g., persons of similar income group, geographic location, race, age, sex, occupation and level of educational attainment) that are most likely to respond to a particular grass-roots appeal. (A congressman receiving extensive communications resulting from a carefully cultivated direct mailing may not be able to tell the extent to which the response was spontaneous or an orchestrated reaction.) Members and the public should know the source of political pressure, and the amount spent to generate that pressure, in order to evaluate it.

Grass-roots lobbyists have discovered other state-of-the-art methods to generate constituent mail on a given issue. High-speed computers and laser printers will create a constituent letter, printed on what appears to be personalized stationery, for individuals to sign and mail to their representatives. Disguised in this way, an artificially generated mail campaign becomes even less distinguishable from a spontaneous expression of constituents' views.

The lobbyists can also skip completely the process of urging individuals to write to Congress on particular issues by simply securing blanket permission to communicate on their behalf. Similar to writing a blank check, the individual agrees to let the lobbying group select issues and positions and then communicate to Congress,

under the individual's name, expressing whatever position the lobbying group deems appropriate. In this way a trade or professional association can amass a bank of names that can be used and reused to generate telegrams to Members on any given issue. And Congress would not necessarily know the actual involvement by the person whose name appears on the communication.

The use of these lobbying techniques is growing, and with it grows the ability of lobbyists to obscure the source and extent of the political pressure they bring to bear. Without effective lobby disclosure, Members of Congress may find themselves less and less able to discern a general expression of public opinion from one that is artificially stimulated.

Unconcealed Lobbying Of course, as the Senators well know, having received hundreds of thousands of bank-prompted letters and postcards opposing withholding, the source of lobbying pressure is not always hidden. Even when the interest behind lobbying pressure is known, however, more precise information is helpful. For example, did all of the banks in your states participate in the anti-withholding statement stuffer campaign? Or just the small banks? Or just the big banks? Was the lobbying more intense among banks serving primarily elderly, or low-income, or unemployed communities? Would it have been useful to know which financial institutions did *not* participate in the campaign and why they did not participate? Exactly how much was spent in this campaign? Without accurate and complete lobby disclosure, Congress and the public are deprived of information that may have important bearing on public policy decision making.

The Public's Right to Know Citizens' need for information about lobbying is also important. The public has a right to know how their government works, and particularly how government decisions are influenced by the activities of organizations heavily engaged in the legislative process. Disclosure of lobbying expenditures provides the public with a valuable measure of the money and influence being brought to bear on political decisions. As the Washington State Supreme Court stated in rendering a judgment affirmed by the U.S. Supreme Court:

> The electorate, we believe, has a right to know of the sources and magnitude of financial and persuasional influences upon government. The voting public should be able to evaluate the performance of their elected officials in terms of representation of the electors' interest in contradistinction to those interests represented by lobbyists. Public information and the disclosure . . . required of lobbyists and their employers may provide the electorate with a heretofore unavailable perspective regarding the role that money and special influence play in government decision making. . . . (*Fritz v. Gorton*, 517 P.2d 911; 931, *appeal dismissed*, 417 U.S. 902, 1974)

THE "REASONS" FOR NONDISCLOSURE

There has been much debate and confusion over the provisions of the lobby disclosure law. Many interpret the law to contain loopholes which exempt them from registering or from disclosing all of their lobbying activities. In particular, three reasons are often given to justify nondisclosure or incomplete disclosure of lobbying.

"Principal Purpose" One loophole frequently cited is that the law requires disclosure only from individuals and organizations whose principal purpose is lobbying. Thus, some would argue that even though insurance companies or trade associations might spend millions of dollars lobbying, they need not disclose those expenditures because their principal purpose, in the case of companies, is to sell insurance, or, in the case of associations, is

to provide services to members. That argument, though often used, is incorrect. The Supreme Court said of it in *U.S. v. Harriss:*

> the 'principal purpose' requirement does not exclude . . . a person whose activities *in substantial part* are directed to influencing legislation. . . . If it were otherwise—if an organization, for example, were exempted because lobbying was only one of its main activities—the Act would in large measure be reduced to a mere exhortation against abuse of the legislative process. (347 U.S. at 622-23). (Emphasis added.)

Thus the Court ruled that if one of the main purposes of an organization is to influence legislation, the requirements of the lobby disclosure law apply.*

"Direct Influence on Congress Another loophole cited is that the law, as interpreted by the Supreme Court, requires disclosure only of "direct" efforts to influence Congress, and not "indirect" efforts such as grass-roots lobbying. This is a misreading of the *Harriss* case. The Supreme Court in *Harriss* explicitly included grass-roots lobbying in its definition of "direct communication with members of Congress."**

The legislative history of the Act makes clear that, at the very least, Congress sought

---

* In its "Outline of Instructions for Filing Reports," the Clerk of the House of Representatives—with whom all lobby disclosure reports are filed—offers a similar interpretation of the "principal purpose" rule:
Organizations and individuals are required to report receipts and expenditures in connection with legislative interests, regardless of the nature and extent of their nonlegislative activities—even where the very great bulk of their activity is nonlegislative. (p.3)
** The instructions of the Clerk of the House agree on this point as well:
Frequently, [organizations] direct campaigns to spur activity on issues. In some cases . . . [they] send communications to the membership in general, urging them to write or wire Congress. . . . [O]rganizations of this type should register and file reports pursuant to the act. (p. 7)

disclosure of such direct pressures, exerted by the lobbyist themselves or through their hirelings *or through an artificially stimulated letter campaign.* (347 U.S. at 620) (Emphasis added.)

Enforcement Another reason for nondisclosure is that the common misinterpretations of the law described above go unchallenged. Prosecution under the lobby disclosure law is rare. In the 37 years since it was passed, there have been only five prosecutions, two of which resulted in convictions. Because of the many loopholes—both real and perceived—officials at the Justice Department have said the Act is too vaguely drawn and its criminal penalties are too strict to allow them to prosecute successfully suspected violations.*** The Department will, when it receives a complaint, write a letter to the party suspected of noncompliance asking them to register. However, no one is required to forward such complaints to the Justice Department on a regular basis. Although the Clerk of the House and the Secretary of the Senate see that they are filed promptly and correctly, these offices are not authorized to perform any further audit of lobbying expenditures. Within this environment, disregard for the law will almost certainly go unchallenged, and many are hard pressed to take the law seriously.

WHAT CAN BE DONE?

In spite of the apparent invalidity of these perceived "loopholes," confusion about the law's provisions persists. The disclosure law, now almost 40 years old, does contain obscure language; and decades of nondisclosure have reinforced the notion that the law is weak and ineffective. In

*** Violation of the lobby disclosure law is a criminal offense and can be punished by a fine of up to $5,000, imprisonment of up to one year, or both. Repeated violation of the law is a felony, leading to even more severe punishment.

addition, a general lack of enforcement allows many to disregard the law with impunity. In practice, the current law simply does not produce the kind of complete information needed by Congress and the public to understand and evaluate political issues.

This Committee is to be commended for taking a fresh look at the lobbying industry and the system that is supposed to provide lobby disclosure. We believe your efforts should culminate in the enactment of an effective lobby disclosure law that responds to the political realities of today's lobbying. Such a law would include the following features:

1. A Time and/or Dollar Expenditure Threshold The present lobby disclosure law requires registration by those whose "principal purpose" is to lobby. As mentioned earlier, the Supreme Court has interpreted this to cover those "whose activities in substantial part are directed to influencing legislation" (*U.S. v. Harriss*, 347 U.S. 612 at 622). Nonetheless, numerous organizations principally engaged in some non-lobbying activity—such as producing oil or selling insurance—refuse to register, even though they also spend millions of dollars on lobbying.

To avoid this problem, Congress should enact a time and/or dollar expenditure threshold which, when crossed, would require an individual or organization to register. For example, an organization would have to register if it spent more than x dollars on lobbying, and/or if its employees spent more than y hours on lobbying in a calendar quarter.

2. Coverage of Grass Roots Lobbying In 1954 the Supreme Court interpreted the current lobbying law to require disclosure of only "direct" efforts to influence Congress (*U.S. v. Harriss*, 347 U.S. at 620). Although the Court explicitly included grass roots lobbying in its definition of "direct" lobbying, many organizations have failed to disclose their grass roots lobbying expenditures.

Congress should remedy this by making clear that grass roots lobbying—such as direct mail or advertising appeals—is a covered lobbying activity. Again, a threshold amount should be used to ensure that substantial grass roots lobbying efforts are covered and distinguished from individual or small-scale letter writing efforts. The threshold could be set in terms of dollars spent on grass roots lobbying, or in terms of the number of solicitations distributed, or both.

3. Contributor Disclosure It is important that Congress and the public know the identity of those providing significant contributions to a lobbying organization and the amount they have given. The current lobbying law requires disclosure of contributors, and this principle was found by the Supreme Court to serve the legitimate purpose of "maintain[ing] the integrity of a basic governmental process" (*U.S. v. Harriss*, 347 U.S. at 625). In the absence of contributor disclosure, lobbying interests can hide behind deceptive names. For example, the name "Committee For Fair Insurance Rates" does not itself reveal the members it represents—some 90 contributing insurance companies opposed to gender-neutral insurance rates. Because this organization has disclosed the names of its contributors under the present law, however, its true nature and purpose is apparent. A new or revised lobbying law should continue to require disclosure of this kind of information.

4. Civil Enforcement Provisions More than ten years ago, the Congress came to grips with the need to reform an antiquated, loophole-ridden campaign finance law whose criminal enforcement machinery had seldom been put to use. To make that important law work, Congress enacted clear requirements for comprehensive campaign disclosure and established auditing, investigatory and civil enforcement provisions (Federal Election Campaign Act of 1971, Pub. Law 92-225). The importance of a strong enforcement provision is underscored by the fact that Congress went back and amended the campaign finance law three years later, moving the responsibility for enforcement to a new agency that would be independent of those covered by the regulations, the President and Members of Congress (Federal Election Campaign Act Amendments of 1974, Pub. Law 93-443).

Today there is effectively no review of compliance with the lobby disclosure law, and prosecution of violations is virtually nonexistent. Although there is some review of lobbying reports by the Clerk of the House and the Secretary of the Senate, there is no regular review of lobbying expenditures. Officials at the Justice Department have said the Act is too vaguely drawn and its criminal penalties are too strict to allow them to prosecute successfully suspected violations.

Congress should grant specific authority to an oversight agency, such as the General Accounting Office, to review disclosure reports and investigate suspected noncompliance. In addition, Congress should also add civil enforcement provisions to the lobby disclosure law to provide a wider range of sanctions to enforcers of the law. The Justice Department would retain jurisdiction over formal proceedings, both civil and criminal.

CONCLUSION

Organized lobbying is a significant and growing factor in influencing public policy decisions. We believe that enactment of a carefully drawn lobby disclosure law will provide Congress and the public with the opportunity to better understand the nature of the pressures being exerted on government officials, and will help to protect the integrity of the political process.

We are encouraged that this subcommittee is taking up the lobby disclosure issue. We hope that a workable and effective lobby disclosure law can be enacted, and we look forward to working with the subcommittee to achieve that end.

QUESTIONS FOR DISCUSSION

1. Are lobbies a threat to democracy?
2. Why do lobbies enjoy constitutional protection?
3. What public functions do lobbyists serve?
4. Can lobbying be regulated?
5. Is the "public interest" in the eye of the beholder?

RECOMMENDED READINGS

CIGLER, ALLAN J., and BURDETT A. LOOMIS, eds. *Interest Group Politics*. Washington, D.C.: Congressional Quarterly Press, 1983.

CONGRESSIONAL QUARTERLY. *The Washington Lobby*, 4th ed. Washington, D.C.: Congressional Quarterly Press, 1982.

DREW, ELIZABETH. *Politics and Money: The New Road to Corruption*. New York: Macmillan, 1983.

ETZIONI, AMITAI. *Capital Corruption: The New Attack on American Democracy*. San Diego, Calif.: Harcourt Brace Jovanovich, 1984.

GLEN, MAXWELL. "Raising Money." *National Journal*, 17 (Sept. 14, 1985), pp. 2066–68 and 2073–76.

KOSTERLITZ, JULIE, and PATRICIA THEILER. "Money on Their Minds." *Center Magazine*, 10 (July/Aug. 1984), pp. 16–23.

LEVITAN, SAR, and MARTHA R. COOPER. *Business Lobbies: The Public Good and the Bottom Line*. Baltimore, Md.: Johns Hopkins University Press, 1984.

LYNN, BARRY. "Lobby Disclosure and Religious Liberty." *Church and State*, 32 (Nov. 1979), pp. 20–22.

U.S. CONG., SENATE. *Oversight of the 1946 Federal Regulation of Lobbying Act*. Hearings before the Committee on Governmental Affairs, 98th Cong., 1st Sess., 1983.

WOOTON, GRAHAM. *Interest Groups: Policy and Politics in America*. Englewood Cliffs, N.J.: Prentice-Hall, 1985.

12 *Is there a constitutional right to abortion?*

YES ABORTION AND THE CONSTITUTION

Rhonda Copelon

Mr. Chairman and members of the subcommittee: I appreciate the Subcommittee's invitation to appear and discuss the implications of the proposed amendments to overturn the Supreme Court's recognition of the right to abortion in *Roe* v. *Wade*,[1] by restoring state power or creating federal power to restrict abortion legislatively.

I will address my remarks to the constitutional foundations and significance of the *Roe* v. *Wade* decision and the inefficacy as well as the dangers of the proposed effort to repeal it. I have been asked to focus on Senator Eagleton's proposal to reempower the states to restrict abortion. Much of what I will say, however, applies as well to Senator Hatfield's so-called "federalism" amendment.

No decision of the Supreme Court has meant more to the lives, the health, the well-being, the freedom and the dignity of women than the decision in *Roe* v. *Wade*. While this decision alone can hardly remedy the inequality of women, recognition of the right to make childbearing decisions is fundamental to the attainment of equality and the realization of women's full capacities as human beings.

Roe v. *Wade* ranks with other landmark decisions that have moved this nation forward on the path toward liberty and equal-

ity. Like *Brown* v. *Board of Education*,[2] it has drawn much criticism and wrought great, but long overdue change.

Roe v. *Wade* is not, as some of its critics like to contend, a departure from constitutional tradition. Rather applied to women some of the basic concepts upon which this nation was founded. It repudiated the historic disregard for the dignity and personhood of women and the relegation of women to a separate sphere and second-class citizenship. It brought legal theory, developed by and for men, closer to encompassing the existence of women.

Consider for a moment, the relation of some of our most fundamental constitutional principles to the issue of compulsory pregnancy and childrearing:

We all hold as sacred the physical privacy of the home. If we guard so jealously our physical environment and possessions from intrusion by the state, how can we accord lesser status to the dominion and control over the physical self? Indeed, the right of bodily integrity is one of the foundations of the right to privacy.[3] We insist on the right to informed consent to medical treatment; we recognize each individual's right to refuse to donate organs to

U.S. Cong., Senate, *Legal Ramifications of the Human Life Amendment,* **Hearings before the Subcommittee on the Constitution of the Committee on the Judiciary, 98th Cong., 1st Sess., 1983, pp. 131–35.**

[1] 410 U.S. 113 (1973)

[2] *Brown* v. *Board of Education*, 347 *U.S.* 483 (1954).

[3] In *Union Pacific R.R. Co.* v. *Botsford,* the Court wrote: "No right is held more sacred, or is more carefully guarded, by the common law than the right of every individual to the possession and control of his own person, free from all restraint or interference of others, unless by clear and unquestionable authority of law. . . ." 11 S. Ct. 1000, 1001.

save the life of another person;[4] we consider the forcible extraction of the contents of a suspect's stomach to be conduct that "shocks the conscience."[5] And yet, those who criticize *Roe* v. *Wade* show little concern for massive invasion of physical integrity and privacy that forced pregnancy entails.

The constitutional right of association embraces the right to form a family, to choose our most intimate associates and guide the raising of children. This is an aspect of privacy protected by both due process and the first amendment. The state cannot fix marriages nor even force an unwilling parent to care for a child. It is not for the state to mandate intimate association; and yet the power to block abortion denies to women an aspect of this right accorded to others.

The first amendment protects our thoughts, beliefs, and verbal as well as symbolic expression. We can neither be restrained from speech nor forced to break silence. The Constitution protects these rights not only because of a utilitarian view that a marketplace of ideas serves the public good, but also because of the place of expression in the development of individual identity and the fulfillment of human aspirations. Is not the commitment to bring a child into the world and to raise it through daily love, nurture and teaching an awesome form of expression, a reflection of one's beliefs, thoughts, identity and notion of what is meaningful? Men and women speak with their bodies on the picket line and in demonstrations; women likewise "speak" in childbearing.

The first amendment also protects the right to follow religious and conscientious convictions. It demands that the state respect diverse beliefs and practices that involve worship, ritual, and decisions about everyday life.[6] We recognize as religious, matters of life and death and of ultimate concern. The decision whether to bear a child, like conscientious objection to military service, is one of conscientious dimension.[7] The religions and people of this country are deeply divided over the propriety and, indeed, necessity of abortion. While for some any consideration of abortion is grave evil, others hold that a pregnant woman has a religious and moral obligation to make a decision and to consider abortion where the alternative is to sacrifice her well-being of her family's or that of the incipient life.[8] The right to abortion is thus rooted in the recognition that women too make conscientious decisions.

Few would dispute that the constitution recognizes the right to work as part of fundamental liberty. And although we have failed to properly implement that right by providing jobs for millions of unemployed people, we deem fundamental the principle, enshrined in the thirteenth amendment, that no person should be forced into involuntary servitude as a result either of private conspiracy or public law. Does this right not extend to woman, entitling her to say "no" to the unparalleled labor demanded by pregnancy, childbirth and childbearing and to the expropriation of her body and service for the sake of another? If we strip away the sentimentalism that has rendered invisible the work of childbearing and rearing,[9] forced preg-

---

[4] *McFally* v. *Shimp* (unpublished, Ct. 51 Common Pleas, Allegheny County, Pa., Civil Division, July 26, 1978).

[5] *Rochin* v. *California,* 342 U.S. 165, 172 (1952).

[6] *Wisconsin* v. *Yoder,* 406 U.S. 205 (1972).

[7] Compare, e.g., *United States* v. *Seeger,* 380 U.S. 163 (1965); *Welsh* v. *United States,* 398 U.S. 333 (1970).

[8] For a description of different religious positions, see *McRae* v. *Califano,* 491 F. Supp. 630, 690–702, 741–42 (E.D.N.Y. 1980).

[9] As the Court said in *Frontiero* v. *Richardson:* "There can be no doubt that our Nation has had a long and unfortunate history of sex discrimination. Traditionally, such discrimination was rationalized by an attitude of "romantic paternalism" which, in practical effect, put women, not on a pedestal, but in a cage." 411 U.S. 685 (1973).

nancy must surely be recognized as a form of involuntary servitude.[10]

And what of the equality of women? Not to apply the foregoing constitutional principles to the question of the liberty to choose abortion is to deny to women equal personhood and dignity in the most fundamental sense. At the same time, to deny the right to abortion ensures that women will be excluded from full participation in society. Without the ability to decide whether and when to bear children, women lack essential control over their lives. Unexpected pregnancy and involuntary motherhood can preclude education, shatter work patterns and aspirations, and make organizational and political involvement impossible. A woman is no more biologically required to remain pregnant than a cardiac patient is to die of a treatable heart condition. Pregnancy is not natural or necessary but is rather legally imposed by denying access to safe technology which, in myriad other spheres, we applaud as enhancing the possibility for human freedom and endeavor.

In sum, the criticism of *Roe* v. *Wade* has less to do with judicial excess, than with a view of woman as less than a whole person under the constitution; as someone whose self and aspirations can and should be legally subordinated to the service of others. The criticism reflects a failure to understand the gravity with which women view the responsibility of childbearing, and the violence of forced pregnancy to human dignity.

To the extent that the effort to overturn *Roe* v. *Wade* stems from religious convictions about the personhood and supremacy of the fetus, it imperils a pluralistic society which demands of us all respect for differing and often mutually abhorrent views. One of the nation's greatest jurists, Judge John F. Dooling, Jr., was right when he said "[t]he irreconcilable conflict of deeply and widely held views on this issue of individual conscience excludes any legislative intervention except that which protects each individual's freedom of conscientious decision and conscientious non-participations."[11]

Thus to give to Congress or the states the power to dictate what shall be orthodox on a matter of this dimension is anathema to our constitutional tradition.[12] Fundamental liberty and respect for individual conscience transcend geographical and political boundaries. That is the meaning of being one nation.

Moreover, it could not possibly satisfy opponents of the right to abortion to have their claims on behalf of the fertilized egg or the fetus determined on a state-by-state basis or subject to political compromise in Congress. It is totally inconsistent with the claim that the fetus is a person to allow what they see as murder to occur in some places and under some conditions. The testimony previously given before this subcommittee demonstrates that Senator Eagle-

---

[10] In *Bailey* v. *Alabama* Justice Hughes summarized the purpose of the Thirteenth Amendment: "The plain intention [of the thirteenth amendment] was to abolish slavery of whatever name and form. . . . to make labor free, by prohibiting the control by which the personal service of one man is disposed of or coerced for another's benefit which is the essence of involuntary servitude." 219 U.S. 219, 241 (1911).

[11] *McRae* v. *Califano*, 491 F. Supp. 630, 742 (E.D.N.Y., 1980).
[12] As Justice Jackson wrote in *West Virginia State Board of Education* v. *Barnette*, Struggles to coerce uniformity of sentiment in support of some and thought essential to their time and country have been waged by many good as well as evil men. Nationalism is a relatively recent phenomenon but at other times and places the ends have been racial or territorial security, support of a dynasty or regime and particular plans for saving souls. . . . Those who begin the coercive elimination of dissent soon find themselves exterminating dissenters. Compulsory unification of opinion achieves only the unanimity of the graveyard. [F]reedom to differ is not limited to things that do not matter much. That would be a mere shadow of freedom. The test of its substance is the right to differ as to things that touch the heart of the existing order. If there is any fixed star in our constitutional constellation, it is that no official, high or petty, can prescribe what shall be orthodox in politics, nationalism, religion, or other matters of opinion, or force citizens to confess by work or act their faith therein. 391 U.S. 624, 641–42.

ton's proposal lacks principle and is acceptable to no one. It should also be clear that just as it will satisfy no one, it will not put to rest or remove from Congress the abortion issue.

It is also not at all clear that the proposed amendment can accomplish even the checkered goal it sets for itself. The declaration that "[a] right to abortion is not secured by this Constitution" cannot undo the entire foundation of the right to abortion. Privacy, bodily integrity, the rights of conscience, the rights of women to life, liberty and equal treatment under law, and the right to due process, if only in the procedural sense—these rights would not be disturbed by an amendment negating the right to abortion itself.

For example, assuming there is no right to abortion secured by the Constitution, can a state pass a law wholly outlawing abortion? I doubt it. Even Justice Rehnquist, dissenting in *Roe* v. *Wade*, considers it rational to prefer the life of the pregnant woman over that of the fetus.[13]

Or to ask the next question: can a state pass a law which permits abortion only to save the life of a woman? I think there would be great doubt on that score as well. The other dissenter in *Roe* v. *Wade*, Justice White, indicated that where abortion is needed to preserve health the rationality of outlawing abortion is in question.[14] For the Court to require that abortion be available where a woman's life and health is at stake is not grounded on the right to abortion; it has rather to do with the right of self-preservation, and, even more fundamentally, with the right to be treated within the bounds of reason.

To limit abortion to life-saving circumstances would also raise other questions under the due process clause. The abortion law at issue in *Roe* v. *Wade,* which allowed abortion only where a woman's life was at stake, was invalidated by the district court on vagueness grounds.[15] Can a meaningful distinction be made between life and health, or between physical and mental health?[16] I think not.

Last week, Mr. Chairman, you asked Senator Eagleton, a series of questions about the impact of his amendment. He answered these in the affirmative. Today I suggest, precisely because *Roe* v. *Wade* is so deeply grounded in our fundamental constitutional traditions, that Senator Eagleton's confidence about the restrictive impact of his amendment is misplaced.

For example, you asked, Mr. Chairman, whether the amendment would permit a state to condition abortion on the consent of a woman's husband. The answer is far from clear. A woman's right, married or single, to determine what medical care is necessary and what shall be done to her body, is not grounded on the right to abortion, but on the right of bodily integrity and on the principle that law cannot enforce personal service. A husband has no right to compel the birth of a child, just as he has no right to the law's assistance in compelling his wife's sexual submission to satisfy this or any other desire. And unless the hypothetical consent law were to give the wife a concomitant right to insist on insemination, or veto her husband's vasec-

---

[13] "If the Texas statute were to prohibit an abortion even where the mother's life is in jeopardy, I have little doubt that such a statute would lack a rational relation to a valid state objective under the test stated in *Williamson, supra*" 410 U.S. 113, 174 (1973) (Rehnquist, j. dissenting)

[14] 410 U.S. 113, 223 (1973) (White, j. dissenting)

[15] *Roe* v. *Wade*, 314 F. Supp. 1217 (N.D. Texas, 1970) The *per curiam* opinion stated that, "It is apparent that there are grave and manifold uncertainties in the application of Article 1196. How *likely* must death be? Must death be certain if the abortion is not performed? It is enough that the woman could not undergo birth without an ascertainably higher possibility of death than would normally be the case? What if the woman threatened suicide if the abortion was not performed? How *imminent* must death be if the abortion is not performed? Is it sufficient if having the child will shorten the life of the woman by a number of years? These questions simply cannot be answered." *id* at 1223.

[16] In *United States* v. *Vuitch*, 402 U.S. 62 (1971) a statute was saved from vagueness by recognizing that "health" encompasses both physical and mental health.

tomy, sexual affairs or financial decisions, all of which equally affect the marriage, spousal consent to abortion would present equal protection problems wholly apart from whether a right to abortion is secured by the Constitution.

You also asked whether this amendment would permit states to pass the so-called "informed consent" statutes. This issue, which is presently before the Supreme Court,[17] would also raise serious constitutional questions apart from the right to abortion. For a state, in the guise of informed consent, to require as the Akron ordinance does, that doctors tell women that the fetus is "human life" raises issues about forced speech and propagation of belief under the first amendment that are not likely to be affected by the proposed amendment. Moreover, the absence of a right to abortion cannot empower a state to require that women be given false, misleading and one-sided information about the risks and benefits of abortion and childbirth. If in the abortion context, a state could compel the telling and hearing of lies, what dangerous power would we have ceded to the state in other areas?

You asked further whether a state would be able to protect the life of a viable fetus or shield doctors and nurses from compelled participation in abortion. No amendment is necessary to accomplish these purposes. The federal government and at least 42 states protect the right of individual conscience to refuse participation in abortion, and the Court has made clear that under a properly drawn statute (and not one that is vague or overbroad) a viable fetus, born as a consequence of an abortion procedure, can be protected.[18]

All this is not to say that I think that

your amendment or that of Senator Eagleton will have no effect. To take away the right to abortion, to permit a patchwork quilt of abortion laws, to empower medical committees or courts to second-guess the decisions of a woman and her doctor—any or all of these would deny the fundamental humanity and equal personhood of women.

The practical effect will be devastating—although it will not stop abortions. The wealthy will find legal abortions at added risk to their health by travelling to states or countries that recognize the right to abortion, or by paying the layers of doctors that restrictive laws would resurrect. The tragic impact of the amendment would fall on the poor, who are disproportionately black and third world, on the working class, and on the young, because they would not have the wherewithal to obtain safe, legal abortions. The amendment and the legislation it would spawn would consign hundreds of thousands of women each year to the life-threatening risks of illegal abortion, to desperate measures of self-abortion, to life-and-death struggles against complications, and to lifelong health damage, emotional scars and sterility created by criminalization. Others would be relegated to the life-shattering, and life- and health-threatening prospect of forced pregnancy and involuntary motherhood.

It is also possible that the proposed amendment will undo more of our constitutional tradition than many of its sponsors and supporters might wish. If the amendment revokes the right to privacy insofar as it involves abortion, then what of the right to obtain contraceptives to prevent pregnancy? The most common forms

[17] *City of Akron* v. *Akron Center for Reproductive Health*, Nos. 81–746 and 81–1623. *sub judice.*
[18] *See, Planned Parenthood of Central Missouri* v. *Danforth*, 428 U.S. 52 (1976), where the Supreme Court distinguished between criminal penalties for neglect

of a live-born infant and that of a non-viable fetus. *See also, Colautti* v. *Franklin*, 439 U.S. 379 (1979) where a standard for fetal protection was struck down on the grounds of vagueness and overbreadth, not because protection of a viable fetus is impermissible.

of contraceptive—the low-estrogen birth control pill, the IUD and morning after pills—might be outlawed. Could privacy be further invaded by compulsory pregnancy surveillance and reporting requirements for physicians? Will basic concepts like due process, notice, equal protection and the like be swept aside wherever abortion is at issue?

Never before has this nation—despite great outcry against certain decisions of the Supreme Court—passed a constitutional amendment that took away a fundamental constitutional right. Once before, with the Eighteenth Amendment, we approved an amendment that invaded the private sphere. Prohibition was a disaster: it bred violence, death and disrespect for law; it created huge profits that built a criminal trade; it made criminals of decent people, and it caused the watering down of other constitutional safeguards. To amend the constitution to augment rather than limit the power of government over the personal aspects of people's lives invites these dire consequences. And to do so in an area which is not simply a matter of lifestyle, but affects the right which is a cornerstone of liberty and equality for women, can only produce massive resistance and unforgiveable carnage.

In sum the effort to recriminalize and thereby stop abortion must ultimately fail because it can alter neither the conviction of women that abortion is our inalienable right, nor the fact that it is a necessity in our lives. I urge, Mr. Chairman and members of the subcommittee, that you recognize that any amendment which seeks to deny the right to abortion will consign women to enormous suffering and threaten the foundations of our pluralistic society. No amendment will put the issue to rest or take it out of the halls of Congress. It can only assure its supporters a place of ignominy in the annals of history.

NO RESTORING THE PROTECTION OF LIFE TO THE CONSTITUTION

John T. Noonan, Jr.

I propose to address three topics:

1. The right to an abortion as it existed in the Constitution, American traditions, and judicial precedent before *Roe* v. *Wade.*
2. The radical right to abortion established by *Roe* v. *Wade.*
3. The social dimensions of this right.

In conclusion, I shall say something about the Amendment before you.

U.S. Cong., Senate, *Constitutional Amendments Relating to Abortion,* Hearings before the Subcommittee on the Constitution of the Committee on the Judiciary, 97th Cong., 1st Sess., 1981, vol. I, pp. 39–50.

I. THE CONSTITUTIONAL RIGHT TO AN ABORTION BEFORE JANUARY 22, 1973

Before January 22, 1973, the date of the decision of *Roe* v. *Wade,* no right to an abortion existed in the Constitution.

The explicit text of the Constitution, as everyone knows, does not mention abortion. The Ninth Amendment, reserving unenumerated rights by the Constitution to the people, appeared to guarantee to the people the right to protect life, and in fact the fifty states did protect life outside the womb and within the womb. The Fourteenth Amendment expressly declaring that no state shall "deprive any person of life" without due process of law appeared to guarantee the protection of all human beings. The Supreme Court in a stirring dictum had declared that "one's right to life" depends on "the outcome of no election."[1] The right to life, put beyond electoral caprice, appeared to be secured by the due process clause. No student of language, no one faithful and attentive to the words of the Constitution, could have supposed that the very clauses which seemed to secure life could be turned inside out to mandate destruction of the states' life-protective measures.

Nothing in the traditions of the American people suggested that abortion was a constitutional right. Since the beginning of the republic, abortion had been a crime at common law. In the nineteenth century it became a crime by statute.[2] The congressmen who proposed and ratified the Fourteenth Amendment approved legislation banning abortion in the federal territories.[3] The State legislatures which ratified the Fourteenth Amendment enacted or left in force strict statutes against abortion.[4] How amazed these congressmen and legislatures would have been to have told that the Amendment they adopted could be read to eradicate the criminal laws safeguarding life! From the date of the adoption of the Fourteenth Amendment in 1868 until January 22, 1973 the traditions of the American people assured the protection of life in the womb by criminal statutes.

No precedents of the Supreme Court indicated that there was any constitutional right to abortion. The Digest of Supreme Court Cases is bare of citation to abortion cases before 1971. In that year the Court sustained the constitutionality of the District of Columbia abortion law.[5] The right to privacy as a constitutional right had only been discovered or created in 1965 in *Griswold* v. *Connecticut,* and in the language of its discoverer or creator, Justice Douglas, was a right based on the immunity of "the sacred precincts of the marital bedroom."[6] The right to privacy as enunciated in 1965 supported the sanctity of marriage; it did not subvert it. Thousands of cases interpreted the Constitution before *Roe* v. *Wade* was argued. Not a single precedent in the Supreme Court held that there was any such thing as the right to abortion in the Constitution. Only, in the year *Roe* v. *Wade* was argued, the Court in *Eisenstadt* v. *Baird* stood the right of privacy on its head to include the rights of the unmarried and to hint in a dictum that the decision "to bear" children fell within its ambit.[7] But *Eisenstadt* v. *Baird* was decided with *Roe* v. *Wade* in view. It was a bit of bootstrapping by the Court, creating a half-precedent for a decision it was ready to make. In terms of almost two centuries of constitutional adjudication, the right to abortion proclaimed in 1973 was a right created out of the air by the will of a majority of the Court in 1973. It was without basis in the text of the Constitution, without basis in the traditions of the American people, and without basis in judicial precedent. Its creation was by fiat. Its creation was, in the words of Justice Byron White, an act of "raw judicial power."[8] By the

---

[1] *West Virginia State Board of Education* v. *Barnette* 319 U.S. 624 (1943) at 638.

[2] Louisell and Noonan, "Constitutional Balance," in Noonan, ed., *The Morality of Abortion* (Cambridge: Harvard University Press, 1970) 225.

[3] *E.g., The Compiled Laws of Wyoming* (1876), chapter xxxv, sec. 25; see also Noonan, *A Private Choice* (New York: The Free Press, 1979) 5–6.

[4] *E.g., Laws of Vermont* (1867) Public Act, no. 57.

[5] *United States* v. *Vuitch* 402 U.S. 62 (1971); see *Digest of United States Supreme Court Reports* (1969) at "Abortion."

[6] *Griswold* v. *Connecticut* 381 U.S. 479 (1965) at 486.

[7] *Eisenstadt* v. *Baird* 405 U.S. 438 (1972) at 453.

[8] *Roe* v. *Wade* 410 U.S. at 222 (dissenting opinion).

power of the Court's majority the constitutional protection of life was, in effect, repealed; the Constitution was, in effect, amended; and a new constitutional provision was, in effect, written: "The right to abortion is conferred by this Constitution."

II. THE EXTENT OF THE RIGHT TO ABORTION

How extensive was the right to abortion created in 1973? The media have so consistently palliated and disguised the character of the right that it is necessary to be particularly exact in answering this question. The proper answer is that the right was the most radical in the civilized world.

The Court said that for the first three months of pregnancy no governmental authority of any kind could intervene in the decision to obtain an abortion from a licensed physician.[9] In the second stage of pregnancy, the state was permitted to require abortions to be performed within hospitals or other licensed facilities in order to safeguard the health of the pregnant woman; no protection was permitted during this period for the unborn child.[10] No recognition of the existence of the unborn child was accorded by the Court during the first two phases of pregnancy.

In the third and final phase of pregnancy, reached at viability (reckoned by Justice Blackmun to occur ordinarily at seven months), the zero which the unborn child was in the Court's eyes graduated to recognition as "potential life." At this stage, the state was permitted to protect the life of the child, subject however to a remarkable exception.[11] The exception was that no law could restrict an abortion performed for the health of the mother;

and health was defined by the Court in the companion case of *Doe* v. *Bolton* in terms of "all factors—physical, emotional, psychological, and the woman's age—relevant to well-being."[12]

That definition and the health exception effectively negated the state's power to protect life in the womb after viability. There is not, I should suppose, a single abortion performed that cannot claim justification in terms of the emotional and psychological well-being of the person requesting the abortion. When the Constitution, as effectively amended and interpreted by the Court, declares that it is a person's constitutional right to be free of the restraint of any law interfering with emotional or psychological well-being when abortion is in question, there is no way that a state can effectively legislate to prevent abortion. Abortion on demand—although Chief Justice Burger in a concurring opinion made a valiant attempt to deny it[13]—is in reality the law of the land. Liberty of abortion, as a constitutional right, is, for practical purposes, virtually unlimited.

Because almost no governmental restriction on abortion is permitted in the first months of pregnancy, gross abuses have developed of the kind investigated by the Chicago *Sun Times* and reported in its issues of November 1978: fashionable, modern abortion clinics in the heart of the Chicago shopping district where "dozens of abortions" were performed on persons who were not pregnant; where abortions were performed on screaming women without anesthesia; where one successful operator billed Medicaid in a single year for $720,000; and where "an alarming number of women" suffered severe and permanent damage to their reproductive organs. These thoroughly legal clinics were the beneficiaries of the nearly abso-

---

[9] *Roe* v. *Wade* at 163; cf. *Connecticut* v. *Menillo* 423 U.S. 9 (1975).

[10] *Roe* v. *Wade* at 164.

[11] *Roe* v. *Wade* at 163–164.

[12] *Doe* v. *Bolton* 410 U.S. 179 at 192.

[13] *Roe* v. *Wade* at 208 (concurring opinion).

lute right to abortion created by the Court.[14]

Because no governmental restriction on abortion is effective in the late stages of pregnancy, there has been a rash of cases around the country involving the death of children after their abortion has failed. To cite three well-known examples, California prosecuted Dr. Wardell, Massachusetts prosecuted Dr. Edelin, South Carolina prosecuted Dr. Floyd, each for the post-abortion death of a child whose abortion the doctor had attempted; in each case the intersection of the constitutional right to abortion with the facts of the case resulted in the doctor's acquittal.[15] That these cases involving children born alive should occur at all is symptomatic of a situation in which late abortions are permitted and not unfrequently occur.

Unregulated early abortion, late abortion risking infanticide, abortion for any reason related to the emotional well-being of the abortion seeker, these are the practices which fall within the scope and demonstrate the extent of the court-created, radical, constitutional right to abortion.

III. THE SOCIAL CONSEQUENCES OF THE CONSTITUTIONAL RIGHT TO ABORTION

The right to abortion was said by the Court to be part of the right to privacy; and the exercise of the right is said to be a private choice. Was there ever a right less exactly described? Was there ever a slogan more misleading? What is private is what can be done alone, or at home, or within one's family. The right to abortion is exercised with the help of a trained professional, a doctor, and often with the participation of a clinical or hospital staff. Its existence does not depend on personal volition but on pushing physicians to perform abortions and on pushing hospitals to make them available and on pushing medical schools to select students willing to perform them. The enforcement of this right of privacy has required constant litigation and the judicial overruling of dozens of municipal ordinances and state laws. A favorite contention of champions of this private right has been that its exercise cannot be effective without public funding! And this bizarre conclusion was enforced by a federal district judge for four years and is still the law of California and Massachusetts. The development of this form of privacy has led to the most deliberate and most serious intrusions by the state into the truly private realms of marriage and the family. It has resulted in an abortion epidemic of enormous proportions. Few constitutional rights in our country's history have had such massive social consequences as this offshoot of the right to privacy.

The right to abortion has resulted in the threat of malpractice suits against doctors that have not wished to perform or advise abortion.[16] It has resulted in litigation against hospitals that have declined to provide abortion.[17] It has led to the screening out of medical school candidates with conscientious objection against abortion.[18] It has led the judiciary to strike down legislation intended to avoid by zoning the ugly urban blight of abortion clinics;[19] to strike down legislation attempting to protect the child in a late abortion who might be born alive;[20] to strike down legislation attempting to afford a minimal amount of information and a minimal time of deliberation to the abortion-seeker.[21] It has been the banner

---

[14] The Chicago *Sun Times* November 12–November 18, 1978; see also Noonan, *A Private Choice* 164–165.

[15] See, e.g., *Commonwealth* v. *Edelin* (Mass.) 359 N.E. 2d 4 (1976).

[16] See Noonan, *A Private Choice* 84.

[17] E.g., *Doe* v. *Charleston Area Medical Center Inc.* 529 F.d. 638 (4th Cir. 1975).

[18] See Noonan, *A Private Choice* 86.

[19] *Framingham Clinic Inc.* v. *Board of Selectmen of Southborough* (Mass.) 367 N.E. 2d 606 (1977).

[20] *Colautti* v. *Franklin* 439 U.S. 379 (1979).

[21] E.g., *Women's Services, P.C.* v. *Thorne* 483 F. Supp. 1022 at 1049 (D. Neb. 1979).

under which almost the entire federal judiciary has enlisted with a zeal for social engineering and the re-shaping of state law that would do them credit as crusaders. I do not stop to dwell on the grievous error, now corrected, by which a single federal judge in Brooklyn, in contravention of the Article I of the Constitution, arrogated to himself the power to appropriate money from the Treasury which the Constitution allocates to Congress and ordered the payment of millions of dollars in the federal funding of abortion—an order that stayed in effect for four years until finally held invalid.[22]

Most significantly of all, the constitutional right to abortion has permitted the courts to invade the family sphere and to hold, first, that parents have no final authority over their minor children in this matter which so deeply involves the physical and psychological and moral health of the child;[23] and to hold, second, that a father—although he has a constitutional right to share in procreating, per *Skinner* v. *Oklahoma*[24]—has no right whatsoever to protect the unborn child he has joined in procreating.[25] No greater intrusion could be introduced into the legal structure of the family than these changes which allow the minor child to be autonomous in the abortion decision and the female progenitor to be solely responsible for the decision whether unborn offspring shall live or die.

The greatest social consequence of all has been the destruction of human life that has followed on the establishment of the constitutional right. No one doubts that the life in the womb—conceived by two human beings, possessed of the human chromosomal code, possessed of every genetic feature of human beings—is a human boy or a human girl. These lives

[22] *Harris* v. *McCrae* 448 U.S. 297 (1980).
[23] *Bellotti* v. *Baird* 443 U.S. 622 (1979) (plurality opinion at 644).
[24] *Skinner* v. *Oklahoma* 315 U.S. 535 (1942).
[25] *Planned Parenthood* v. *Danforth* 428 U.S. 52 (1976).

are now being taken at the rate of over one million a year. This is a massive increase in abortion in America. This is an epidemic. Proponents of abortion are fond of bringing up tragic cases where abortion would resolve a heartbreaking situation. There are such tragic cases, and everyone sympathizes with persons caught in them. But these tragic cases cannot compare in number or in tragedy with the terrible social fact that Americans are now killing their own offspring on a scale exceeding that of any war.

A choice cannot be private which affects another's life. The child in the womb has blood and brains, a respiratory system, a circulatory system, a urinary system that is not those of his or her mother. The child in the womb is not the property of her or his parent. The body of the child in the womb is not that of her or his parent. Sexuality may be private, reproduction may be private, but the taking of the life of the unborn cannot be private. It is a social act. Multiplied one million times a year, it is a social act amounting to atrocity.

IV. THE PROPOSED AMENDMENT

The Amendment before you is extraordinarily simple and extraordinarily direct. It denies that the Constitution contains the kind of right which fiat created nine years ago. At one stroke it demolishes *Roe* v. *Wade* and the unhappy sequelae of *Roe* v. *Wade*. With a few words it performs surgery by which the judicial amendment to the Constitution made nine years ago is excised. It restores to Congress and to the States the power to protect life.

The Amendment does not make abortion into murder—that would be untraditional in both morals and in law. The Amendment does not confer any power over contraception. A favorite red herring of the supporters of abortion is the pretense that contraceptive rights are involved in what is done with abortion. It is time to call this confusion of contraception with abortion what it is—a lie. The Amendment uses the term traditionally used by criminal statutes "abortion." The Amendment uses the term as it was employed in *Roe* v. *Wade* to mean the taking of life at any time in the womb; and the Amendment denies the right to take such unborn life.

The Amendment does not attempt to solve, magically as it were, every problem associated with abortion by language frozen into the Constitution. There are those who believe that only language affirming the personhood of the unborn will suffice to staunch the wound *Roe* v. *Wade* created. But any language about "persons" is likely to involve the due process clause, a clause whose meaning has shifted again and again with judicial opinion. The life of a person cannot be taken without due process of law; but due process of law, as interpreted by the judiciary, is not a firm foundation on which to rely. Moreover, any attempt to provide in the Constitution against private action taking the life of the unborn must allow for the traditional exception by which abortion is permitted where the mother's life is at stake. There is grave danger that any exception to save life or to prevent death will be interpreted judicially to permit abortion for health reasons; and abortion for health reasons is easily turned into the equivalent of abortion on demand.[26] We cannot risk a constitutional exception that gives such latitude to the courts.

The Amendment puts power to protect life where it had been from the inception of the Republic until January 22, 1973, and it makes one change. Because the Supreme Court acted nationally to legalize

[26] See *United States* v. *Vuitch* 402 U.S. 62 (1971).

abortion, the Amendment gives Congress the power to establish a national standard of protection for unborn life. At the same time the Amendment recognizes the historic role and historic primacy of the States in the protection of life and commands that the more protective state laws shall prevail over the federal minimum.

After nine years of experience in attempting to draft language corrective of *Roe* v. *Wade* and in participating in the drafting efforts of others, I am convinced that there is no magic formula, no perfect form of Amendment, that is immune from misinterpretation or criticism. The Amendment before you is a very good Amendment. It accomplishes what must be accomplished. I offer by way of suggestion only the following changes in the draft:

> Sec. 1 *No* right to abortion is *conferred* by this Constitution.
>
> Sec. 2. Congress and the several States shall have power to restrict or prohibit *abortion;* provided that the more *protective* law shall prevail.

"No" instead of "the," so that the right is comprehensively denied. "Conferred" instead of "secured," because "secured" has too benign a flavor. "Abortion" in the singular, because it is a general evil, like slavery. "Protective," because it has a more positive flavor than "restrictive."

Whatever technical corrections are made in the Amendment, I urge you to accept it in substance. About it the lovers of life can unite. With its enactment the great goal of restoring the protection of life in the United States will have been achieved.

QUESTIONS FOR DISCUSSION

1. In a constitutional sense, when does life begin?
2. Is there a constitutional right to privacy?

3. Why can a state prevent abortion in the third trimester of pregnancy, but not in the first?
4. Should a fetus be considered a person (under the Fourteenth Amendment)?
5. What is the "right to life"?

RECOMMENDED READINGS

BOPP, JAMES, JR.., ed. *Restoring the Right to Life.* Provo, Utah: Brigham Young University Press, 1984.

DIONISPOULOS, P. ALLAN, and CRAIG R. DUCAT. *The Right to Privacy.* St. Paul: West, 1976.

DORSEN, NORMAN. "Crushing Freedom in the Name of Life." *Human Rights* 10 (Spring 1982), pp. 18–21, 46–47.

GARFIELD, JAY L., and PATRICIA HENNESSEY. *Abortion: Moral and Legal Perspectives.* Amherst: University of Massachusetts Press, 1984.

HEKMAN, RANDALL J. *Justice for the Unborn: Why We Have "Legal" Abortion, and How We Can Stop It.* Ann Arbor: Servant Books, 1984.

LUKER, KRISTIN. *Abortion and the Politics of Motherhood.* Berkeley: University of California Press, 1984.

MATTEO, MELISSA A. "Governmental Abortion Policies and the Right to Privacy: The Rights of the Individual and the Rights of the Unborn." 11 *Brooklyn Journal of International Law* 103 (Winter 1985).

O'CONNOR, JOHN J. "Human Lives, Human Rights." *Human Life Review* 11 (Winter–Spring 1985), pp. 41–65.

STEINER, GILBERT Y., ed. *The Abortion Dispute and the American System.* Washington, D.C.: Brookings Institution, 1983.

U.S. CONG., SENATE. *Constitutional Amendments Relating to Abortion.* Hearings before the Subcommittee on the Constitution of the Committee on the Judiciary, 97th Cong., 1st Sess., 1981.

III CIVIL RIGHTS

The idea of individual human dignity is fundamental to Western society, but it is in the United States that the idea has become an organizing principle of government. As the Declaration of Independence proclaims, "We hold these truths to be self-evident, that all men are created equal." To be sure, the Framers of the Declaration were speaking primarily of white male Americans, but the inexorable growth of our democracy has permitted those words to be read broadly to include all Americans within their ambit.

But the struggle for equality has not been easy; nor is it complete. Black slavery remained constitutionally protected until the adoption of the Thirteenth Amendment in 1865. Women were denied the right to vote in most elections until 1920, when the Nineteenth Amendment was ratified. And racial segregation enjoyed the support of the Supreme Court until 1954.[1]

In retrospect it may seem curious that neither the Constitution nor the Bill of Rights contains a specific reference to equality. But that defect was corrected by adoption of the Fourteenth Amendment in 1868. That amendment provides that "No State shall . . . deny to any person within its jurisdiction the equal protection of the laws." It is unmistakably clear that the Fourteenth Amendment, passed after the Civil War, was intended to grant equality to the newly freed slaves and to prevent state and local governments from discriminating against them. In recent years the Supreme Court has held that the Equal Protection Clause also applies to the national government,[2] although it does not apply to individual social behavior.[3] Nevertheless, when individuals act outside their own homes, clubs, or social surroundings—for example, when they provide goods and services to the general public—the government may act to forbid racial, religious, or sex discrimination.[4]

Ironically, the Supreme Court's original interpretation of the Fourteenth Amendment was exceedingly narrow. In the *Slaughter-House Cases* of 1873, a case in which black rights were not at issue, the Court held that it was not "the purpose of the Fourteenth Amendment . . . to transfer the security and protection of . . . civil rights . . . from the States to the federal government." In the view of Justice Samuel Freeman Miller, who spoke for the majority, to hold otherwise would "constitute this court a perpetual censor upon all legislation of the States, on the civil rights of their own citizens."[5]

Coming just eight years after the Civil War, the *Slaughter-House Cases* can be seen as an attempt by the Supreme Court to redress the balance of federalism in favor of the states and to limit the growth of national power that the victory of the Union had produced. The determination of the Court to limit the scope of the Fourteenth Amendment became abundantly clear in 1883 when the justices for the first time confronted congressional legislation intended to guarantee blacks the equal protection of the laws. In the *Civil Rights Cases* the Supreme Court declared unconstitutional most of the provisions of the Civil Rights Acts of 1866 and 1875 prohibiting racial discrimination in public facilities (e.g., hotels, restaurants, and public conveyances). According to the Court the Fourteenth Amendment applied only to state action and did not authorize Congress to forbid discrimination by private individuals (such as innkeepers). Once again the Court's reasoning emphasized the preservation of states' rights at the expense of the equal protection of the laws.[6]

By the 1890s state-enforced racial segregation had become a way of life in the South. Blacks were disenfranchised, and all-white legislatures enacted sweeping segregation ordinances, known as Jim Crow laws, making it a crime for blacks and whites to use the same public facilities.[7] When the constitutionality of these laws was tested before the Supreme Court in 1896, the Court, in the leading case of *Plessy v. Ferguson*, endorsed the view that racial segregation did not violate the Equal Protection Clause provided the segregated facilities were of equal quality. The Fourteenth Amendment, said the Court, mandated equality, not the commingling of the races. Thus was born the constitutional doctrine of *separate but equal*, which sustained legal segregation of the races in the United States for more than fifty years. (Separate but equal proved to be a convenient legal fiction, for the fact is that states invariably provided blacks with inferior facilities.) Interestingly, the only Southerner on the Supreme Court, Justice John Marshall Harlan of Kentucky, registered a vigorous dissent in *Plessy*. In Harlan's words:

> Our Constitution is color-blind, and neither knows nor tolerates classes among citizens. In respect of civil rights, all citizens are equal before the law. The humblest is the peer of the most powerful. The law regards man as man, and takes no account of his surroundings or of his color when his civil rights as guaranteed by the supreme law of the land are involved. It is, therefore, to be regretted that this high tribunal . . . has reached the conclusion that it is competent for a State to regulate the enjoyment by citizens of their civil rights solely upon the basis of race.

Denouncing the formula of separate but equal adopted by the Court, Harlan predicted that the "judgment this day rendered will, in time, prove to be quite as pernicious as the decision made . . . in the Dred Scott Case."[8]

Justice Harlan's prophecy proved correct, and in 1954 in the landmark case of *Brown v. Board of Education* a unanimous Supreme Court held that separate but equal was a contradiction in terms: that segregated educational facilities were inherently unequal and thus violated the equal protection clause of the Fourteenth Amendment.[9] The following year in the second *Brown* case the Court ordered school boards to proceed "with all deliberate speed to desegregate public schools at the earliest practicable date."[10] Citing the *Brown* cases as precedent, the Supreme Court then moved on a broad front to desegregate public beaches,[11] buses,[12] golf courses,[13] parks,[14] and all other public facilities.[15]

But the Court's orders were not complied with uniformly. Massive resistance to desegregation broke out in many Southern states. In 1964, ten years after the *Brown* decision, only about 2 percent of the black pupils in the eleven states of the old Confederacy were attending schools with whites, and mostly in Virginia and Texas.[16] By 1970, however, the dual school system of the South was a thing of the past. The combination of resolute federal judges determined to uphold the Supreme Court's decision, the willingness of Presidents Dwight D. Eisenhower and John F. Kennedy to employ military force, if necessary, to enforce judicial decisions, and the passage of the Voting Rights Act of 1965, which once again made it possible for blacks to vote throughout the United States, caused the last vestiges of segregation to crumble. Of the roughly 2,700 school districts in the South, more than 97 percent had been desegregated by 1970.[17]

FROM DESEGREGATION TO INTEGRATION

The decision of the Supreme Court in *Brown v. Board of Education* was premised on the idea that the Constitution was color-blind: that race could not be used as a criterion in assigning pupils to particular schools. The Civil Rights Act of 1964 expressed a similar view and noted that children should not be assigned to schools to achieve any particular racial balance. But by the late 1960s the federal courts were beginning to view the matter differently. In 1966 the Court of Appeals for the Fifth Circuit (that is, for the Deep South) held that the words *desegregation* and *integration* meant the same thing and that schools had a constitutional duty to *integrate*, by which it meant the "racial mixing of students."[18] The Supreme Court declined to review that holding and indeed, two years later, in overturning a "freedom of choice" plan of school attendance in New Kent County, Virginia, stated that the "ultimate end to be brought about" is a "unitary, nonracial system of public education."[19] In 1971 the Court ordered busing imposed in Charlotte, North Carolina, to achieve greater racial balance. (Prior to that, pupils had been assigned to the nearest school without regard to race.) Speaking through Chief Justice Warren G. Burger, the Court said that any school system that had once practiced segregation could be ordered to use racial quotas and mandatory busing to remedy past discrimination. In effect the Court had departed from the original 1954 holding in *Brown v. Board of Education* that local government could *not* use race as a criterion in assigning pupils to a particular school. By 1973 school boards *must* use race as a factor. Desegregation had yielded to integration, causing many legal scholars to question the basis of the Supreme Court's reasoning, if the Constitution was "color-blind."[20] The Court has taken the position that producing racially balanced schools is a necessary corrective to previous government action that had required segregated schools. Critics countered that if racial balancing was to be a redress for past discrimination, the burden of it should not fall on members of the present generation, who were not guilty of that discrimination.

Is Affirmative Action Reverse Discrimination?

There is little doubt that the legacy of segregation has left a large number of black Americans disadvantaged and unable to compete for openings in universities, for skilled jobs, and for competitive contracts. Is a policy of governmental neutrality on the question of race sufficient to assure the equality of opportunity upon which American democracy depends? William T. Coleman, Jr., a civil rights advocate, for example, argues that it is not and that temporary remedial action, commonly referred to as *affirmative action,* is required. According to Coleman: "The ultimate goal of affirmative action . . . is not to set up a permanent system of proportional representation for all racial and ethnic groups. Rather, it is to break the cycle of discrimination and to achieve equality of opportunity which is not illusory."[21]

By contrast, Professor Thomas Sowell, a black economist at Stanford University, argues that affirmative action does not work and that it rests on a false premise: namely, that most differences between groups is based on past discrimination—which he doubts. Sowell contends that affirmative action is unconstitutional and that "what the masses of blacks get from affirmative action . . . is mainly the resentment of the rest of society."[22] Recent presidential administrations have sided with Coleman; the Reagan administration agrees with Sowell. And the Supreme Court has been sharply divided on the issue.

When Allen Bakke, a white male and a top engineering student at Minnesota and Stanford universities (and a Vietnam veteran) was twice denied admission to the medical school at the University of California, Davis, he brought suit, charging that the university had unconstitutionally set aside sixteen places in the entering class for minority students. The California Supreme Court agreed with Bakke and ordered the university to admit him. The university appealed to the Supreme Court, and the Court, with no single opinion commanding a majority, overturned the California plan as unconstitutional, ordered Bakke admitted, but at the same time held that a university may take race into account in its admission process providing that it does not become the single decisive factor.[23] The Supreme Court's seeming inability to reconcile the conflicting viewpoints on affirmative action illustrates the complexity of the issue.

The following year, in *United States v. Weber* the Court upheld (5–2) a collective-bargaining arrangement that reserved for black employees 50 percent of the openings in a company training program "until the percentage of black craft workers in the plant is commensurate with the percentage of blacks in the local labor force." Justice William J. Brennan, Jr.'s, majority opinion held that employers and unions in the private sector were "free to take such race-conscious steps to eliminate manifest racial imbalances in traditionally segregated job categories." But in an extensive and vehement dissent, Justice William H. Rehnquist (joined by Chief Justice Burger) accused the Court of a logical flight of fancy "reminiscent not of jurists such as [Lord] Hale, [Oliver Wendell] Holmes, and [Charles Evans] Hughes, but of escape artists such as Houdini."[24]

In 1980 the Court returned to the issue of affirmative action in *Fullilove v. Klutznick,* and by a vote of 6–3 upheld a provision of the Public Works Act of 1977 requiring at least 10 percent of federal funds granted to local public works projects be set aside for minority business enterprises.[25] Nevertheless the Supreme Court has not consistently permitted preferential treatment for blacks. For example, when Memphis, Tennessee, was forced to lay off fire fighters for budgetary reasons, the Court rejected the Memphis plan to discharge white firemen first in order to enhance racial balance. The fire department's seniority system (last hired, first fired) was held to be nondiscriminatory and therefore to be used, even if that meant discharging many recently hired black firemen.[26]

The Reagan administration has sought to extend the implications of the Memphis decision by arguing that any type of quota system is wrong. The Supreme Court, recognizing the complexity of the issue of affirmative action, has continued to follow an ambiguous pattern. It has continued to uphold preferential treatment for minorities in initial hiring and some promotion decisions but has rejected plans that would penalize nonminority employees already on the job.

Because of the great constitutional importance of the issue of affirmative action, the articles chosen for the debate below are two classic opinions by justices of the Supreme Court on opposite sides of the issue. The concurring opinion of Justice Thurgood Marshall in the *Bakke* case presents a moving justification for affirmative action by the Court's first black justice. Marshall had represented the plaintiffs before the Supreme Court in the first desegregation case, *Brown v. Board of Education,* and his opinion from the bench in *Bakke* traces the history of racial discrimination in the United States.

Justice Potter Stewart, who dissented from the Court's holding in *Fullilove v. Klutznick,* argues in equally convincing fashion that the Constitution is colorblind and that affirmative action runs squarely against that principle. Stewart sees affirmative action as a new form of racism and argues that if the Equal Protection Clause means anything, it means that governments cannot individually discriminate "not even 'temporarily' and not even as an 'experiment.'"

SEX DISCRIMINATION AND THE EQUAL PROTECTION CLAUSE

The struggle for equal rights for women has been closely connected with the movement for black equality. But whereas blacks were fighting against a legal tradition designed to keep them in an inferior status, women confronted a tradition that claimed to protect them. Both women and blacks were denied the right to vote, but women were always held to be citizens. The nineteenth-century Supreme Court simply did not believe that citizenship conferred the right to vote.[27] The Court's supposed deference to women can be seen in decisions that upheld Vermont's laws banning women from the legal profession (a "man's vocation")[28] and in the 1908 decision in *Muller v. Oregon* upholding that state's maximum ten-hour workday for women who worked in laundries and factories. Said Justice David J. Brewer, "Woman has always been dependent upon man," and it was obvious that "woman's physical structure" placed her "at a disadvantage in the struggle for subsistence." But in words of significant importance the Court held that legislation to protect women "seems necessary to secure a real equality of right."[29] And in 1908 that was a considerable concession.

The feminist movement—which traces its origins to the Seneca Falls Women's Rights Convention in 1848—disputes the claim that the differences between women and men justify a different legal status, and in recent years Congress has been sympathetic to that position. It has enacted legislation requiring equal pay for men and women doing the same jobs;[30] prohibited discrimination on the basis of sex in employment and in all schools and universities receiving federal funds;[31] and banned discrimination against pregnant women in the workplace.[32]

The Supreme Court has also reexamined the legal practices that treated men and women differently. The traditional view of "protecting" women from the rigors of contemporary life has been rejected. In 1971, for example, the Court overturned an Idaho statute that gave preference to men as administrators of children's estates. In a unanimous decision the Court held that any law that classifies people on the basis of sex "must be reasonable, not arbitrary, and must rest on some ground of difference having a fair and substantial relation to the object of the legislation so that all persons similarly circumstanced shall be treated alike." Unlike laws that distinguish on the basis of race (which are "inherently suspect"), laws based on sex are held to a standard of "reasonableness," and are somewhat less difficult to sustain.[33]

As a result the holdings of the Supreme Court on the issue of female equality are mixed. For example, a state cannot set different ages at which men and women become legal adults.[34] It cannot set different ages for buying beer. (Oklahoma permitted women to purchase beer at age eighteen but required men to be twenty-one—one argument being that a young woman would usually be in the company of an older man who could drive her home.)[35] Neither can women be barred for jobs because of arbitrary height and weight requirements;[36] nor can they be excluded from membership in the Junior Chamber of Commerce (a quasi-public organization);[37] nor can girls be barred from Little League baseball teams.[38]

On the other hand, all-boy and all-girl public schools are permitted if enrollment is voluntary and quality is equal;[39] states can provide a property tax deduction for widows but not for widowers;[40] and the U.S. Navy may allow female officers more time in grade before being separated from the service than it allows men.[41] Similarly, in the leading case of *Rostker v. Goldberg* the Court has held that it is permissible for Congress to draft men into the military, but not women, without violating the Due Process Clause of the Constitution.[42] (Congress had previously barred women from serving in combat roles.)[43]

The proposed Equal Rights Amendment (ERA) to the Constitution would have overturned *Rostker v. Goldberg* and would have required complete equality for men and women, including full service in the military. The key position of the amendment (which was first introduced in 1923) provided that "Equality of rights under the law shall not be denied or abridged by the United States or any State on account of sex."

The Equal Rights Amendment precipitated broad public debate concerning the rights of women. When it was passed by Congress in 1972 and sent to the states for ratification, few anticipated any difficulty. (The amendment had been endorsed by all presidents since Harry Truman and by both political parties and had sailed through the Senate 84–8 and the House of Representatives 354–24.) But optimism soon faded as it became apparent that the required thirty-eight states might not ratify. By 1978 the ratification effort was stalled at thirty-five—three short of the necessary three-quarters of the states. Congress extended the original 1979 deadline by three years but to no avail. The amendment had bogged down in a sea of controversy. Opponents charged that the amendment would require that women be drafted for combat duty and that it would eliminate laws that protected women in the workplace (such as maximum-hour and minimum-wage laws). The Mormon Church and the National Council of Catholic Women came out in opposition, and in 1980 the Republican party withdrew its support. (President Ronald Reagan had long opposed the amendment.) When the time for ratification expired in 1982, it was clear that the measure was dead, at least for the moment.

The defeat of the ERA illustrates the complexity of the issue of equal rights for women. While no one would agree with Sen. James K. Vardaman of Mississippi, who said in opposing the woman suffrage amendment in 1915 that the United States should be a government "by white men, of white men, for all men,"[44] there are many who believe that there are rational reasons for treating women differently from men in certain circumstances. The Supreme Court, for example, has upheld legislation that punishes males but not females for statutory rape, holding that men and women are not "similarly situated" with respect to sexual relations.[45] This suggests that the issue will continue to generate considerable controversy.

The issue of affirmative action for women was addressed by the Supreme Court in *Johnson v. Transportation Agency, Santa Clara County*. In a 6–3 decision, written by Justice William J. Brennan, Jr., the Court upheld the preferential promotion of a woman deemed slightly less qualified than a male competitor under a Santa Clara County, California, plan to increase the percentage of women in jobs traditionally held by men. The Court's decision removed whatever legal clouds there may have been that affirmative action was less justifiable for women than for racial minorities or that the only basis for affirmative action was to redress a past practice of discrimination. In a vigorous dissent, Justice Antonin Scalia (joined by Chief Justice William H. Rehnquist and Justice Byron R. White) suggested that the Court had replaced "the goal of a discrimination-free society with the quite incompatible goal of proportional representation."[46] The debate continues.

Would "Comparable Worth" Laws Enhance Equality for Women?

Today women constitute more than 42 percent of the work force. But their median hourly earnings are only 72 percent of their male counterparts. These results cannot be explained by lower educational levels. Since 1970 more women than men have graduated from high school and college, yet women college graduates earn (on average) $400 less per year than men who have had no education beyond elementary school.

The fact is, four-fifths of all women are concentrated in low-paying clerical, sales, domestic, and machine-operator jobs. They constitute 70 percent of retail clerks and 87 percent of cashiers, but only 1.4 percent of carpenters and 1.7 percent of electricians. In corporate America 97 percent of the typists, 99 percent of the secretaries, and 86 percent of the file clerks are women.[47] This occupational disparity (in which "women's work," it is alleged, is undervalued) has caused many to advocate a scheme of remuneration based on *comparable worth:* namely, jobs that require similar education and training and entail similar responsibility should pay the same. This scheme supposedly would end the practice of paying female librarians, nurses, and teachers less than male ambulance drivers, window cleaners, and parking lot attendants.

The difficulties are twofold: How does one measure comparable worth, and does the Constitution require it? Should the marketplace, or should government, determine whether one job is worth as much as another? In the debate that follows, Joy Ann Grune, former executive director of the National Committee on Pay Equity, argues that comparable worth, which she defines as *pay equity*, is an idea whose time has come. She illustrates how existing pay schemes discriminate unfairly against women and suggests that governmental action is required to correct that discrimination. The *contra* position is put forward by June O'Neill of the Urban Institute. O'Neill argues that current pay differentials reflect "differences in the roles of women and men in the family and the effect these role differences have on the accumulation of skills and other job choices that affect pay," rather than on employer discrimination. She suggests that comparable worth is essentially capricious, and fails to provide an adequate substitute for marketplace judgments.

Is the Exclusion of Women from Influential Men's Clubs a Denial of Civil Rights for Women?

The Equal Protection Clause of the Fourteenth Amendment and the Due Process Clause of the Fifth Amendment protect the individual from discrimination by government, whether it is local, state, or national. But the issue of individual discrimination in purely social surroundings triggers no constitutional prohibition. In fact the right to privacy, which the Supreme Court has found in the Constitution, arguably protects an individual's right to associate with whomever he or she chooses. The issue becomes more complicated when dealing with formal clubs and related social organizations. If those clubs enjoy governmental support or sanction, they may be properly required to practice non-discriminatory policies. Similarly national clubs of a quasi-official character, such as Junior Chambers of Commerce (or Jaycees), have been brought under the protective cover of the Fourteenth Amendment.[48] And in 1987 a unanimous Supreme Court decision (7–0) extended that ruling to Rotary Clubs, which the Court did not consider "sufficiently personal or private to warrant constitutional protection."[49] But what about purely social organizations such as golf clubs or the traditional men's club in major cities? Generally the courts have held that *purely* social organizations are free to admit or to refuse to admit whomever they choose.

In the debate on this subject, Sydney H. Schanberg, a former columnist for the *New York Times*, argues that the exclusion of women from influential men's clubs, such as the Century Club, the Union League, and the University Club, represents a denial of full equality. He contends that membership in such clubs is often a necessity for career advancement. He asserts, moreover, that private clubs are nothing more than extensions of the workplace.

The justification of selective membership policies is provided by writer Lewis H. Lapham, who is a member of the Century Club. He argues that the character of private men's clubs would change if women were allowed membership. He denies that women are entitled to membership because of career necessities.

Judicial precedents are cited by partisans on either side of the subject of club membership. The issue ultimately reduces to whether the club is a purely private, social body or has a public character on account of its activities. By and large the Supreme Court has been reluctant to intervene in merely private matters.

NOTES

1. *Brown v. Board of Education,* 347 U.S. 483 (1954).
2. *Bolling v. Sharpe,* 347 U.S. 497 (1954).
3. *Moose Lodge v. Irvis,* 407 U.S. 163 (1972).

4. See *Jones v. Mayer*, 393 U.S. 409 (1968), invoking the Thirteenth Amendment to support federal action.

5. 16 Wallace 36 (1873).

6. 109 U.S. 3 (1883).

7. See especially C. Vann Woodward, *The Strange Career of Jim Crow* (New York: Oxford University Press, 1968).

8. 163 U.S. 537 (1896). In *Dred Scott v. Sandford*, 19 Howard 393 (1857), a bitterly divided Supreme Court held that blacks were not citizens of the United States and therefore had no access to the federal courts. The Court's decision is widely believed to have been one of the proximate causes of the Civil War.

9. 347 U.S. 483 (1954).

10. 349 U.S. 294 (1955).

11. *Mayor of Baltimore v. Dawson*, 350 U.S. 877 (1955).

12. *Gayle v. Browder*, 352 U.S. 903 (1956).

13. *Holmes v. City of Atlanta*, 350 U.S. 879 (1955).

14. *New Orleans City Park Imp. Association v. Detiege*, 358 U.S. 54 (1958).

15. *Johnson v. Virginia*, 373 U.S. 61 (1963).

16. Francis M. Wilhoit, *The Politics of Massive Resistance* (New York: George Braziller, 1973), p. 289.

17. Frederick S. Mosteller and Daniel P. Moynihan, eds., *On Equality of Educational Opportunity* (New York: Random House, 1972), pp. 60–62.

18. *United States v. Jefferson County Board of Education*, 372 F.2d 836 (1966).

19. *Green v. County School Board of New Kent County*, 391 U.S. 430 (1968). Freedom of choice meant that pupils could go to the school of their choice in the county, regardless of race or residence.

20. See, for example, Edmund W. Kitch, "The Return of Color-Consciousness to the Constitution," 1979 *Supreme Court Review* 1.

21. William T. Coleman, Jr., "Statement," in U.S. Cong., Senate, *Affirmative Action and Equal Protection*, Hearing before the Subcommittee on the Constitution of the Committee on the Judiciary, 97th Cong., 1st Sess., 1981, p. 234.

22. Thomas Sowell, *Weber and Bakke and the Presuppositions of Affirmative Action*, 26 WAYNE L. REV. 1336 (1980).

23. *University of California Regents v. Bakke*, 438 U.S. 265 (1978).

24. 443 U.S. 193 (1979).

25. 448 U.S. 448 (1980).

26. *Firefighters Local 1784 v. Stotts*, 104 S. Ct. 2576 (1984).

27. *Minor v. Happersett*, 88 U.S. (21 Wall.) 162 (185).

28. *Bradwell v. State*, 83 U.S. (16 Wall.) 130 (1872).

29. 208 U.S. 412 (1908).

30. Equal Pay Act of 1963.

31. Civil Rights Act of 1964, as amended.

32. Education Act of 1972.

33. *Reed v. Reed*, 404 U.S. 71 (1971).

34. *Stanton v. Stanton*, 421 U.S. 7 (1975).

35. *Craig v. Boven*, 429 U.S. 191 (1976).

36. *Dothard v. Rawlinson*, 433 U.S. 321 (1977).

37. *Roberts v. United States Jaycees*, 104 S. Ct. 3244 (1984).

38. *Fortin v. Darlington Little League*, 514 F. Id. 344 (1975).

39. *Vorchheimer v. School District of Philadelphia*, 430 U.S. 703 (1977).

40. *Kahn v. Shevin*, 416 U.S. 351 (1974).

41. *Schlesinger v. Ballard*, 419 U.S. 498 (1975).

42. 453 U.S. 57 (1981). The issue, pertaining to the federal government, and not the states, invoked the Fifth, not the Fourteenth, Amendment.

43. 10 United States Code, sections 6015 and 8549.

44. Quoted in Alan P. Grimes, *Democracy and the Amendments to the Constitution* (Lexington: Lexington Books, 1978) p. 91.

45. *Michael M. v. Superior Court,* 450 U.S. 464 (1981).

46. Supreme Court docket, 85–1129 (decided Mar. 25, 1987).

47. Nancy F. Rytina, "Earnings of Men and Women: A Look at Specific Occupations," *Monthly Labor Review,* Apr. 1982, pp. 42–48.

48. *Roberts v. United States Jaycees,* 104 S. Ct. 3244 (1984).

49. *Board of Directors of Rotary International v. Rotary Club of Duarte,* Docket No. 86-421 (decided May 4, 1987).

13 Is affirmative action reverse discrimination?

YES DISSENTING OPINION: FULLILOVE V. KLUTZNICK

Justice Potter Stewart

"Our Constitution is color-blind, and neither knows nor tolerates classes among citizens. . . . The law regards man as man, and takes no account of his surroundings or of his color. . . ." Those words were written by a Member of this Court 84 years ago. *Plessy* v. *Ferguson,* 163 U. S. 537, 559 (Harlan, J., dissenting). His colleagues disagreed with him, and held that a statute that required the separation of people on the basis of their race was constitutionally valid because it was a "reasonable" exercise of legislative power and had been "enacted in good faith for the promotion [of] the public good. . . ." *Id.,* at 550. Today, the Court upholds a statute that accords a preference to citizens who are "Negroes, Spanish-speaking, Orientals, Indians, Eskimos, and Aleuts," for much the same reasons. I think today's decision is wrong for the same reason that *Plessy* v. *Ferguson* was wrong, and I respectfully dissent.

A

The equal protection standard of the Constitution has one clear and central meaning—it absolutely prohibits invidious discrimination by government. That standard must be met by every State under the Equal Protection Clause of the Fourteenth Amendment. *Loving* v. *Virginia,* 388 U. S.

Excerpted from *Fullilove v. Klutznick,* 448 U. S. 448 (1980).

1, 10; *Hill* v. *Texas,* 316 U. S. 400; *Strauder* v. *West Virginia,* 100 U. S. 303, 307–308; *Slaughter-House Cases,* 16 Wall. 36, 71–72. And that standard must be met by the United States itself under the Due Process Clause of the Fifth Amendment. *Washington* v. *Davis,* 426 U. S. 229, 239; *Bolling* v. *Sharpe,* 347 U. S. 497.[1] Under our Constitution, any official action that treats a person differently on account of his race or ethnic origin is inherently suspect and presumptively invalid. *McLaughlin* v. *Florida,* 379 U. S. 184, 192; *Bolling* v. *Sharpe, supra,* at 499; *Korematsu* v. *United States,* 323 U. S. 214, 216.[2]

The hostility of the Constitution to racial classifications by government has been manifested in many cases decided by this Court. See, *e.g., Loving* v. *Virginia, supra; McLaughlin* v. *Florida, supra; Brown* v. *Board of Education,* 347 U. S. 483; *Missouri ex rel. Gaines* v. *Canada,* 305 U. S. 337. And our cases have made clear that the Constitution is wholly neutral in forbidding such racial discrimination, whatever

[1] "Equal protection analysis in the Fifth Amendment area is the same as that under the Fourteenth Amendment." *Buckley* v. *Valeo,* 424 U. S. 1, 93.

[2] By contrast, nothing in the Constitution prohibits a private person from discriminating on the basis of race in his personal or business affairs. See *Steelworkers* v. *Weber,* 443 U. S. 193. The Fourteenth Amendment limits only the actions of the States; the Fifth Amendment limits only the actions of the National Government.

the race may be of those who are its victims. In *Anderson* v. *Martin,* 375 U. S. 399, for instance, the Court dealt with a state law that required that the race of each candidate for election to public office be designated on the nomination papers and ballots. Although the law applied equally to candidates of whatever race, the Court held that it nonetheless violated the constitutional standard of equal protection. "We see *no relevance,*" the Court said, "in the State's pointing up the race of the candidate as bearing upon his qualifications for office." *Id.,* at 403 (emphasis added). Similarly, in *Loving* v. *Virginia, supra,* and *McLaughlin* v. *Florida, supra,* the Court held that statutes outlawing miscegenation and interracial cohabitation were constitutionally invalid, even though the laws penalized all violators equally. The laws were unconstitutional for the simple reason that they penalized individuals solely because of their race, whatever their race might be. See also *Goss* v. *Board of Education,* 373 U. S. 683; *Buchanan* v. *Warley,* 245 U. S. 60.[3]

[3] *University of California Regents* v. *Bakke,* 438 U. S. 265, and *United Jewish Organizations* v. *Carey,* 430 U. S. 144, do not suggest a different rule. The Court in *Bakke* invalidated the racially preferential admissions program that had deprived Bakke of equal access to a place in the medical school of a state university. In *United Jewish Organizations* v. *Carey,* a state legislature had apportioned certain voting districts with an awareness of their racial composition. Since the plaintiffs there had "failed to show that the legislative reapportionment plan had either the purpose or the effect of discriminating against them on the basis of their race," no constitutional violation had occurred. 430 U. S., at 179–180 (concurring opinion). No person in that case was deprived of his electoral franchise.

More than 35 years ago, during the Second World War, this Court did find constitutional a governmental program imposing injury on the basis of race. See *Korematsu* v. *United States,* 323 U. S. 214; *Hirabayashi* v. *United States,* 320 U. S. 81. Significantly, those cases were decided not only in time of war, but also in an era before the Court had held that the Due Process Clause of the Fifth Amendment imposes the same equal protection standard upon the Federal Government that the Fourteenth Amendment imposes upon the States. See *Bolling* v. *Sharpe,* 347 U. S. 497.

This history contains one clear lesson. Under our Constitution, the government may never act to the detriment of a person solely because of that person's race.[4] The color of a person's skin and the country of his origin are immutable facts that bear no relation to ability, disadvantage, moral culpability, or any other characteristics of constitutionally permissible interest to government. "Distinctions between citizens solely because of their ancestry are by their very nature odious to a free people whose institutions are founded upon the doctrine of equality." *Hirabayashi* v. *United States,* 320 U. S. 81, 100, quoted in *Loving* v. *Virginia, supra,* at 11.[5] In short, racial discrimination is by definition individious discrimination.

The rule cannot be any different when the persons injured by a racially biased law are not members of a racial minority. The guarantee of equal protection is "universal in [its] application, to all persons . . . without regard to any differences of race, of color, or of nationality." *Yick Wo* v. *Hopkins,* 118 U. S. 356, 369. See *In re Griffiths,* 413 U. S. 717; *Hernandez* v. *Texas,* 347 U. S. 475; *Truax* v. *Raich,* 239 U. S. 33, 39–43; *Strauder* v. *West Virginia,* 100 U. S., at 308.

[4] A court of equity may, of course, take race into account in devising a remedial decree to undo a violation of a law prohibiting discrimination on the basis of race. See *Teamsters* v. *United States,* 431 U. S. 324; *Franks* v. *Bowman Transportation Co.,* 424 U. S. 747; *Swann* v. *Charlotte-Mecklenburg Board of Education,* 402 U. S. 1, 18–32. But such a judicial decree, following litigation in which a violation of law has been determined, is wholly different from generalized legislation that awards benefits and imposes detriments dependent upon the race of the recipients. See text in Part B, *infra.*

[5] As Mr. Justice Murphy wrote in dissenting from the Court's opinion and judgment in *Korematsu* v. *United States, supra,* at 242: "Racial discrimination in any form and in any degree has no justifiable part whatever in our democratic way of life. It is unattractive in any setting but it is utterly revolting among a free people who have embraced the principles set forth in the Constitution of the United States." See also *DeFunis* v. *Odegaard,* 416 U. S. 312, 331–344 (Douglas, J., dissenting); A. Bickel, The Morality of Consent 132–133 (1975).

The command of the equal protection guarantee is simple but unequivocal: In the words of the Fourteenth Amendment: "No State shall . . . deny to *any* person . . . the equal protection of the laws." Nothing in this language singles out some "persons" for more "equal" treatment than others. Rather, as the Court made clear in *Shelley* v. *Kraemer*, 334 U. S. 1, 22, the benefits afforded by the Equal Protection Clause "are, by its terms, guaranteed to the individual. [They] are personal rights." From the perspective of a person detrimentally affected by a racially discriminatory law, the arbitrariness and unfairness is entirely the same, whatever his skin color and whatever the law's purpose, be it purportedly "for the promotion of the public good" or otherwise.

No one disputes the self-evident proposition that Congress has broad discretion under its spending power to disburse the revenues of the United States as it deems best and to set conditions on the receipt of the funds disbursed. No one disputes that Congress has the authority under the Commerce Clause to regulate contracting practices on federally funded public works projects, or that it enjoys broad powers under § 5 of the Fourteenth Amendment "to enforce by appropriate legislation" the provisions of that Amendment. But these self-evident truisms do not begin to answer the question before us in this case. For in the exercise of its powers, Congress must obey the Constitution just as the legislatures of all the States must obey the Constitution in the exercise of their powers. If a law is unconstitutional, it is no less unconstitutional just because it is a product of the Congress of the United States.

B

On its face, the minority business enterprise (MBE) provision at issue in this case denies the equal protection of the law. The Public Works Employment Act of 1977 directs that all project construction shall be performed by those private contractors who submit the lowest competitive bids and who meet established criteria of responsibility. 42 U. S. C. § 6705 (e) (1) (1976 ed., Supp. II). One class of contracting firms—defined solely according to the racial and ethnic attributes of their owners—is, however, excepted from the full rigor of these requirements with respect to a percentage of each federal grant. The statute, on its face and in effect, thus bars a class to which the petitioners belong from having the opportunity to receive a government benefit, and bars the members of that class solely on the basis of their race or ethnic background. This is precisely the kind of law that the guarantee of equal protection forbids.

The Court's attempt to characterize the law as a proper remedial measure to counteract the effects of past or present racial discrimination is remarkably unconvincing. The Legislative Branch of government is not a court of equity. It has neither the dispassionate objectivity nor the flexibility that are needed to mold a race-conscious remedy around the single objective of eliminating the effects of past or present discrimination.[6]

But even assuming that Congress has the power, under § 5 of the Fourteenth Amendment or some other constitutional provision, to remedy previous illegal racial discrimination, there is no evidence that Congress has in the past engaged in racial discrimination in its disbursement of federal contracting funds. The MBE provision thus pushes the limits of any such justification far beyond the equal protection standard of the Constitution. Cer-

---

[6] See n. 4, *supra*. In *McDaniel* v. *Barresi*, 402 U. S. 39, the Court approved a county's voluntary race-conscious redrafting of its public school pupil assignment system in order to eliminate the effects of past unconstitutional racial segregation of the pupils. But no pupil was deprived of a public school education as a result.

tainly, nothing in the Constitution gives Congress any greater authority to impose detriments on the basis of race than is afforded the Judicial Branch.[7] And a judicial decree that imposes burdens on the basis of race can be upheld only where its sole purpose is to eradicate the actual effects of illegal race discrimination. See *Pasadena City Board of Education* v. *Spangler*, 427 U. S. 424.

The provision at issue here does not satisfy this condition. Its legislative history suggests that it had at least two other objectives in addition to that of counteracting the effects of past or present racial discrimination in the public works construction industry.[8] One such purpose appears to have been to assure to minority contractors a certain percentage of federally funded public works

contracts.[9] But, since the guarantee of equal protection immunizes from capricious governmental treatment "persons"—not "races"—it can never countenance laws that seek racial balance as a goal in and of itself. "Preferring members of any one group for no reason other than race or ethnic origin is discrimination for its own sake. This the Constitution forbids." *University of California Regents* v. *Bakke*, 438 U. S. 265, 307 (opinion of Powell, J.). Second, there are indications that the MBE provision may have been enacted to compensate for the effects of social, educational, and economic "disadvantage."[10] No race, however, has a monopoly on social, educational, or economic disadvantage,[11] and

---

[7] Section 2 of the Thirteenth Amendment gives Congress the authority to "enforce" the provisions of § 1 of the same Amendment, and § 5 of the Fourteenth Amendment provides that "[t]he Congress shall have power to enforce, by appropriate legislation, the provisions of this article." Neither section grants to Congress the authority to require the States to flout their obligation under § 1 of the Fourteenth Amendment to afford "the equal protection of the laws" or the power to enact legislation that itself violates the equal protection component of the Fifth Amendment.

[8] The legislative history of the MBE provision itself contains not one mention of racial discrimination or the need to provide a mechanism to correct the effects of such discrimination. From the context of the Act, however, it is reasonable to infer that the program was enacted, at least in part, to remedy perceived past and present racial discrimination. In 1977, Congress knew that many minority business enterprises had historically suffered racial discrimination in the economy as a whole and in the construction industry in particular. See H. R. Rep. No. 94–1791, pp. 182–183 (1977); H. R. Rep. No. 94–468, pp. 1–2 (1975); To Amend and Extend the Local Public Works Capital Development and Investment Act: Hearings on H. R. 11 and Related Bills before the Subcommittee on Economic Development of the House Committee on Public Works and Transportation, 95th Cong., 1st Sess., 939 (1977) (statement of Rep. Conyers). Some of this discrimination may well, in fact, have violated one or more of the state and federal antidiscrimination laws.

[9] See 123 Cong. Rec. 5327 (1977) (Rep. Mitchell) ("all [the MBE provision] attempts to do is to provide that those who are in minority businesses get a *fair share of the action* from this public works legislation") (emphasis supplied). Moreover, sponsors of the legislation repeatedly referred to the low participation rate of minority businesses in federal procurement programs. See *id.*, at 5331 (Rep. Biaggi); *id.*, at 5327–5328 (Rep. Mitchell); *id.*, at 5097–5098 (Rep. Mitchell); *id.*, at 7156 (Sen. Brooke).

[10] See *id.*, at 5330 (Rep. Conyers) ("minority contractors and businessmen who are trying to enter in on the bidding process . . . get the 'works' almost every time. The bidding process is one whose intricacies defy the imaginations of most of us here"). That the elimination of "disadvantage" is one of the program's objectives is an inference that finds support in the agency's own interpretation of the statute. See U. S. Dept. of Commerce, Economic Development Administration, EDA Minority Business Enterprise Technical Bulletin (Additional Assistance and Information Available to Grantees and Their Contractors In Meeting The 10% MBE Requirement) 9–10 (1977) (Technical Bulletin) ("a [minority] subcontractor's price should not be considered unreasonable if he is merely trying to cover his costs because the price results from *disadvantage* which affects the MBE's costs of doing business *or* results from *discrimination*" (emphasis added)).

[11] For instance, in 1978, 83.4% of persons over the age of 25 who had not completed high school were "white," see U. S. Dept. of Commerce Bureau of the Census, Statistical Abstract of the United States 145 (1979), and in 1977, 79.0% of households with annual incomes of less than $5,000 were "white," see *id.*, at 458.

any law that indulges in such a presumption clearly violates the constitutional guarantee of equal protection. Since the MBE provision was in whole or in part designed to effectuate objectives other than the elimination of the effects of racial discrimination, it cannot stand as a remedy that comports with the strictures of equal protection, even if it otherwise could.[12]

C

The Fourteenth Amendment was adopted to ensure that every person must be treated equally by each State regardless of the color of his skin. The Amendment

[12] Moreover, even a properly based judicial decree will be struck down if the scope of the remedy it provides is not carefully tailored to fit the nature and extent of the violation. See *Dayton Board of Education* v. *Brinkman,* 433 U. S. 406, 419–420; *Milliken* v. *Bradley,* 418 U. S. 717. Here, assuming that the MBE provision was intended solely as a remedy for past and present racial discrimination, it sweeps far too broadly. It directs every state and local government covered by the program to set aside 10% of its grant for minority business enterprises. Waivers from that requirement are permitted, but only where insufficient numbers of minority businesses capable of doing the work at nonexorbitant prices are located in the relevant contracting area. No waiver is provided for any governmental entity that can prove a history free of racial discrimination. Nor is any exemption permitted for nonminority contractors that are able to demonstrate that they have not engaged in racially discriminatory behavior. Finally, the statute makes no attempt to direct the aid it provides solely toward those minority contracting firms that arguably still suffer from the effects of past or present discrimination.

These are not the characteristics of a racially conscious remedial decree that is closely tailored to the evil to be corrected. In today's society, it constitutes far too gross an oversimplification to assume that every single Negro, Spanish-speaking citizen, Oriental, Indian, Eskimo, and Aleut potentially interested in construction contracting currently suffers from the effects of past or present racial discrimination. Since the MBE set-aside must be viewed as resting upon such an assumption, it necessarily paints with too broad a brush. Except to make whole the identified victims of racial discrimination, the guarantee of equal protection prohibits the government from taking detrimental action against innocent people on the basis of the sins of others of their own race.

promised to carry to its necessary conclusion a fundamental principle upon which this Nation had been founded—that the law would honor no preference based on lineage.[13] Tragically, the promise of 1868 was not immediately fulfilled, and decades passed before the States and the Federal Government were finally directed to eliminate detrimental classifications based on race. Today, the Court derails this achievement and places its imprimatur on the creation once again by government of privileges based on birth.

The Court, moreover, takes this drastic step without, in my opinion, seriously considering the ramifications of its decision. Laws that operate on the basis of race require definitions of race. Because of the Court's decision today, our statute books will once again have to contain laws that reflect the odious practice of delineating the qualities that make one person a Negro and make another white.[14] Moreover, racial discrimination, even "good faith" racial discrimination, is inevitably a two-edged sword. "[P]referential programs may only reinforce common stereotypes holding that certain groups are unable to achieve success without special protection based on a factor having no relationship to individual worth." *University of California Regents* v. *Bakke, supra,* at 298 (opinion of Powell, J.). Most importantly, by making race a relevant criterion once again in its own affairs the Government implicitly teaches the public that the apportionment

[13] The Framers of our Constitution lived at a time when the Old World still operated in the shadow of ancient feudal traditions. As products of the Age of Enlightenment, they set out to establish a society that recognized no distinctions among white men on account of their birth. See U. S. Const., Art. I, § 9, cl. 8 ("No Title of Nobility shall be granted by the United States"). The words Thomas Jefferson wrote in 1776 in the Declaration of Independence, however, contained the seeds of a far broader principle: "We hold these truths to be self-evident: that all men are created equal. . . ."

[14] See Technical Bulletin, *supra,* n. 10, at 1. Cf. Ga. Code § 53–312 (1937); Tex. Penal Code, Art. 493 (Vernon 1938).

of rewards and penalties can legitimately be made according to race—rather than according to merit or ability—and that people can, and perhaps should, view themselves and others in terms of their racial characteristics. Notions of "racial entitlement" will be fostered, and private discrimination will necessarily be encouraged.[15] See *Hughes* v. *Superior Court,* 339

---

[15] "Our Government is the potent, the omnipresent teacher. For good or for ill, it teaches the whole people by its example." *Olmstead* v. *United States,* 277 U. S. 438, 485 (Brandeis, J., dissenting).

U. S. 460, 463–464; T. Eastland & W. Bennett, Counting by Race 139–170 (1979); Van Alstyne, Rites of Passage: Race, the Supreme Court, and the Constitution, 46 U. Chi. L. Rev. 775 (1979).

There are those who think that we need a new Constitution, and their views may someday prevail. But under the Constitution we have, one practice in which government may never engage is the practice of racism—not even "temporarily" and not even as an "experiment."

For these reasons, I would reverse the judgment of the Court of Appeals.

NO CONCURRING OPINION: *UNIVERSITY OF CALIFORNIA REGENTS V. BAKKE*

Justice Thurgood Marshall

I agree with the judgment of the Court only insofar as it permits a university to consider the race of an applicant in making admissions decisions. I do not agree that petitioner's admissions program violates the Constitution. For it must be remembered that, during most of the past 200 years, the Constitution as interpreted by this Court did not prohibit the most ingenious and pervasive forms of discrimination against the Negro. Now, when a State acts to remedy the effects of that legacy of discrimination, I cannot believe that this same Constitution stands as a barrier.

I: A

Three hundred and fifty years ago, the Negro was dragged to this country in chains to be sold into slavery. Uprooted from his homeland and thrust into bond-

Excerpted from *University of California Regents* v. *Bakke,* 438 U. S. 265 (1978).

age for forced labor, the slave was deprived of all legal rights. It was unlawful to teach him to read; he could be sold away from his family and friends at the whim of his master; and killing or maiming him was not a crime. The system of slavery brutalized and dehumanized both master and slave.[1]

The denial of human rights was etched into the American Colonies' first attempts at establishing self-government. When the colonists determined to seek their independence from England, they drafted a unique document cataloguing their grievances against the King and proclaiming as "self-evident" that "all men are created equal" and are endowed "with certain

---

[1] The history recounted here is perhaps too well known to require documentation. But I must acknowledge the authorities on which I rely in retelling it. J. Franklin, From Slavery to Freedom (4th ed. 1974) (hereinafter Franklin); R. Kluger, Simple Justice (1975) (hereinafter Kluger); C. Woodward, The Strange Career of Jim Crow (3d ed. 1974) (hereinafter Woodward).

unalienable Rights," including those to "Life, Liberty and the pursuit of Happiness." The self-evident truths and the unalienable rights were intended, however, to apply only to white men. An earlier draft of the Declaration of Independence, submitted by Thomas Jefferson to the Continental Congress, had included among the charges against the King that

[h]e has waged cruel war against human nature itself, violating its most sacred rights of life and liberty in the persons of a distant people who never offended him, captivating and carrying them into slavery in another hemisphere, or to incur miserable death in their transportation thither. Franklin 88.

The Southern delegation insisted that the charge be deleted; the colonists themselves were implicated in the slave trade, and inclusion of this claim might have made it more difficult to justify the continuation of slavery once the ties to England were severed. Thus, even as the colonists embarked on a course to secure their own freedom and equality, they ensured perpetuation of the system that deprived a whole race of those rights.

The implicit protection of slavery embodied in the Declaration of Independence was made explicit in the Constitution, which treated a slave as being equivalent to three-fifths of a person for purposes of apportioning representatives and taxes among the States. Art. I, § 2. The Constitution also contained a clause ensuring that the "Migration or Importation" of slaves into the existing States would be legal until at least 1808, Art. I, § 9, and a fugitive slave clause requiring that when a slave escaped to another State, he must be returned on the claim of the master, Art. IV, § 2. In their declaration of the principles that were to provide the cornerstone of the new Nation, therefore, the Framers made it plain that "we the people," for whose protection the Constitution was designed, did not include those whose

skins were the wrong color. As Professor John Hope Franklin has observed, Americans "proudly accepted the challenge and responsibility of their new political freedom by establishing the machinery and safeguards that insured the continued enslavement of blacks." Franklin 100.

The individual States likewise established the machinery to protect the system of slavery through the promulgation of the Slave Codes, which were designed primarily to defend the property interest of the owner in his slave. The position of the Negro slave as mere property was confirmed by this Court in *Dred Scott* v. *Sandford,* 19 How. 393 (1857), holding that the Missouri Compromise—which prohibited slavery in the portion of the Louisiana Purchase Territory north of Missouri—was unconstitutional because it deprived slave owners of their property without due process. The Court declared that under the Constitution a slave was property, and "[t]he right to traffic in it, like an ordinary article of merchandise and property, was guarantied to the citizens of the United States. . . ." *Id.,* at 451. The Court further concluded that Negroes were not intended to be included as citizens under the Constitution but were "regarded as beings of an inferior order . . . altogether unfit to associate with the white race, either in social or political relations; and so far inferior, that they had no rights which the white man was bound to respect. . . ." *Id.,* at 407.

B

The status of the Negro as property was officially erased by his emancipation at the end of the Civil War. But the long-awaited emancipation, while freeing the Negro from slavery, did not bring him citizenship or equality in any meaningful way. Slavery was replaced by a system of "laws which imposed upon the colored race onerous disabilities and burdens, and curtailed their rights in the pursuit of life, liberty, and property to such an extent that their freedom was of little value." *Slaughter-House Cases*, 16 Wall. 36, 70 (1873). Despite the passage of the Thirteenth, Fourteenth, and Fifteenth Amendments, the Negro was systematically denied the rights those Amendments were supposed to secure. The combined actions and inactions of the State and Federal Governments maintained Negroes in a position of legal inferiority for another century after the Civil War.

The Southern States took the first steps to re-enslave the Negroes. Immediately following the end of the Civil War, many of the provisional legislatures passed Black Codes, similar to the Slave Codes, which, among other things, limited the rights of Negroes to own or rent property and permitted imprisonment for breach of employment contracts. Over the next several decades, the South managed to disenfranchise the Negroes in spite of the Fifteenth Amendment by various techniques, including poll taxes, deliberately complicated balloting processes, property and literacy qualifications, and finally the white primary.

Congress responded to the legal disabilities being imposed in the Southern States by passing the Reconstruction Acts and the Civil Rights Acts. Congress also responded to the needs of the Negroes at the end of the Civil War by establishing the Bureau of Refugees, Freedmen, and Abandoned Lands, better known as the Freedmen's Bureau, to supply food, hospitals, land, and education to the newly freed slaves. Thus, for a time it seemed as if the Negro might be protected from the continued denial of his civil rights and might be relieved of the disabilities that prevented him from taking his place as a free and equal citizen.

That time, however, was short-lived. Reconstruction came to a close, and, with the assistance of this Court, the Negro was rapidly stripped of his new civil rights. In the words of C. Vann Woodward: "By narrow and ingenious interpretation [the Supreme Court's] decisions over a period of years had whittled away a great part of the authority presumably given the government for protection of civil rights." Woodward 139.

The Court began by interpreting the Civil War Amendments in a manner that sharply curtailed their substantive protections. See, *e.g., Slaughter-House Cases, supra; United States* v. *Reese*, 92 U.S. 214 (1876); *United States* v. *Cruikshank*, 92 U. S. 542 (1876). Then in the notorious *Civil Rights Cases*, 109 U. S. 3 (1883), the Court strangled Congress' efforts to use its power to promote racial equality. In those cases the Court invalidated sections of the Civil Rights Act of 1875 that made it a crime to deny equal access to "inns, public conveyances, theatres and other places of public amusement." *Id.*, at 10. According to the Court, the Fourteenth Amendment gave Congress the power to proscribe only discriminatory action by the State. The Court ruled that the Negroes who were excluded from public places suffered only an invasion of their social rights at the hands of private individuals, and Congress had no power to remedy that. *Id.*, at 24–25. "When a man has emerged from slavery, and by the aid of beneficent legislation has shaken off the inseparable concomitants of that state," the Court concluded, "there must be some stage in the progress of his elevation when he takes the rank of a mere citizen, and ceases to be the special favorite of the laws. . . ." *Id.*, at 25. As Mr. Justice Harlan noted in dissent, however, the Civil War Amendments and Civil Rights Acts did not make the Negroes the "special favorite" of the laws but instead "sought to accomplish in reference to that race . . . —what had already been done in every State of the Union for the white race—to secure and protect rights belonging to them as freemen and citizens; nothing more." *Id.*, at 61.

The Court's ultimate blow to the Civil War Amendments and to the equality of

Negroes came in *Plessy* v. *Ferguson,* 163 U. S. 537 (1896). In upholding a Louisiana law that required railway companies to provide "equal but separate" accommodations for whites and Negroes, the Court held that the Fourteenth Amendment was not intended "to abolish distinctions based upon color, or to enforce social, as distinguished from political equality, or a commingling of the two races upon terms unsatisfactory to either." *Id.,* at 544. Ignoring totally the realities of the positions of the two races, the Court remarked:

> We consider the underlying fallacy of the plaintiff's argument to consist in the assumption that the enforced separation of the two races stamps the colored race with a badge of inferiority. If this be so, it is not by reason of anything found in the act, but solely because the colored race chooses to put that construction upon it. *Id.,* at 551.

Mr. Justice Harlan's dissenting opinion recognized the bankruptcy of the Court's reasoning. He noted that the "real meaning" of the legislation was "that colored citizens are so inferior and degraded that they cannot be allowed to sit in public coaches occupied by white citizens." *Id.,* at 560. He expressed his fear that if like laws were enacted in other States, "the effect would be in the highest degree mischievous." *Id.,* at 563. Although slavery would have disappeared, the States would retain the power "to interfere with the full enjoyment of the blessings of freedom; to regulate civil rights, common to all citizens, upon the basis of race; and to place in a condition of legal inferiority a large body of American citizens. . . ." *Ibid.*

The fears of Mr. Justice Harlan were soon to be realized. In the wake of *Plessy,* many States expanded their Jim Crow laws, which had up until that time been limited primarily to passenger trains and schools. The segregation of the races was extended to residential areas, parks, hospitals, theaters, waiting rooms, and bathrooms. There were even statutes and ordinances which authorized separate phone booths for Negroes and whites, which required that textbooks used by children of one race be kept separate from those used by the other, and which required that Negro and white prostitutes be kept in separate districts. In 1898, after *Plessy,* the Charlestown News and Courier printed a parody of Jim Crow laws:

> If there must be Jim Crow cars on the railroads, there should be Jim Crow cars on the street railways. Also on all passenger boats. . . . If there are to be Jim Crow cars, moreover, there should be Jim Crow waiting saloons at all stations, and Jim Crow eating houses. . . . There should be Jim Crow sections of the jury box, and a separate Jim Crow dock and witness stand in every court—and a Jim Crow Bible for colored witnesses to kiss. Woodward 68.

The irony is that before many years had passed, with the exception of the Jim Crow witness stand, "all the improbable applications of the principle suggested by the editor in derision had been put into practice—down to and including the Jim Crow Bible." *Id.,* at 69.

Nor were the laws restricting the rights of Negroes limited solely to the Southern States. In many of the Northern States, the Negro was denied the right to vote, prevented from serving on juries, and excluded from theaters, restaurants, hotels, and inns. Under President Wilson, the Federal Government began to require segregation in Government buildings; desks of Negro employees were curtained off; separate bathrooms and separate tables in the cafeterias were provided; and even the galleries of the Congress were segregated. When his segregationist policies were attacked, President Wilson responded that segregation was "'not humiliating but a benefit'" and that he was "'rendering [the Negroes] more safe in their possession of office and less likely to be discriminated against.'" Kluger 91.

The enforced segregation of the races continued into the middle of the 20th century. In both World Wars, Negroes were for the most part confined to separate military units; it was not until 1948 that an end to segregation in the military was ordered by President Truman. And the history of the exclusion of Negro children from white public schools is too well known and recent to require repeating here. That Negroes were deliberately excluded from public graduate and professional schools— and thereby denied the opportunity to become doctors, lawyers, engineers, and the like—is also well established. It is of course true that some of the Jim Crow laws (which the decisions of this Court had helped to foster) were struck down by this Court in a series of decisions leading up to *Brown* v. *Board of Education,* 347 U. S. 483 (1954). See, *e.g., Morgan* v. *Virginia,* 328 U. S. 373 (1946); *Sweatt* v. *Painter,* 339 U. S. 629 (1950); *McLaurin* v. *Oklahoma State Regents,* 339 U. S. 637 (1950). Those decisions, however, did not automatically end segregation, nor did they move Negroes from a position of legal inferiority to one of equality. The legacy of years of slavery and of years of second-class citizenship in the wake of emancipation could not be so easily eliminated.

II

The position of the Negro today in America is the tragic but inevitable consequence of centuries of unequal treatment. Measured by any benchmark of comfort or achievement, meaningful equality remains a distant dream for the Negro.

A Negro child today has a life expectancy which is shorter by more than five years than that of a white child.[2] The Negro child's mother is over three times more likely to die of complications in child-

birth,[3] and the infant mortality rate for Negroes is nearly twice that for whites.[4] The median income of the Negro family is only 60% that of the median of a white family,[5] and the percentage of Negroes who live in families with incomes below the poverty line is nearly four times greater than that of whites.[6]

When the Negro child reaches working age, he finds that America offers him significantly less than it offers his white counterpart. For Negro adults, the unemployment rate is twice that of whites,[7] and the unemployment rate for Negro teenagers is nearly three times that of white teenagers.[8] A Negro male who completes four years of college can expect a median annual income of merely $110 more than a white male who has only a high school diploma.[9] Although Negroes represent 11.5% of the population,[10] they are only 1.2% of the lawyers and judges, 2% of the physicians, 2.3% of the dentists, 1.1% of the engineers and 2.6% of the college and university professors.[11]

The relationship between those figures and the history of unequal treatment afforded to the Negro cannot be denied. At every point from birth to death the impact of the past is reflected in the still disfavored position of the Negro.

In light of the sorry history of discrimination and its devastating impact on the

---

[2] U. S. Dept. of Commerce, Bureau of the Census, Statistical Abstract of the United States 65 (1977) (Table 94).

[3] *Id.,* at 70 (Table 102).

[4] Ibid.

[5] U. S. Dept. of Commerce, Bureau of the Census, Current Population Reports, Series P–60, No. 107, p. 7 (1977) (Table 1).

[6] *Id.,* at 20 (Table 14).

[7] U. S. Dept. of Labor, Bureau of Labor Statistics, Employment and Earnings, January 1978, p. 170 (Table 44).

[8] Ibid.

[9] U. S. Dept. of Commerce, Bureau of the Census, Current Population Reports, Series P-60, No. 105, p. 198 (1977) (Table 47).

[10] U. S. Dept. of Commerce, Bureau of the Census, Statistical Abstract, *supra* at 25 (Table 24).

[11] *Id.,* at 407–408 (Table 662) (based on 1970 census).

lives of Negroes, bringing the Negro into the mainstream of American life should be a state interest of the highest order. To fail to do so is to ensure that America will forever remain a divided society.

III

I do not believe that the Fourteenth Amendment requires us to accept that fate. Neither its history nor our past cases lend any support to the conclusion that a university may not remedy the cumulative effects of society's discrimination by giving consideration to race in an effort to increase the number and percentage of Negro doctors.

A

This Court long ago remarked that

> in any fair and just construction of any section or phrase of these [Civil War] amendments, it is necessary to look to the purpose which we have said was the pervading spirit of them all, the evil which they were designed to remedy. . . . *Slaughter-House Cases,* 16 Wall., at 72.

It is plain that the Fourteenth Amendment was not intended to prohibit measures designed to remedy the effects of the Nation's past treatment of Negroes. The Congress that passed the Fourteenth Amendment is the same Congress that passed the 1866 Freedmen's Bureau Act, an Act that provided many of its benefits only to Negroes. Act of July 16, 1866, ch. 200, 14 Stat. 173; see *supra,* at 391. Although the Freedmen's Bureau legislation provided aid for refugees, thereby including white persons within some of the relief measures, 14 Stat. 174; see also Act of Mar. 3, 1865, ch. 90, 13 Stat. 507, the bill was regarded, to the dismay of many Congressmen, as "solely and entirely for the freedmen, and to the exclusion of all

other persons. . . ." Cong. Globe, 39th Cong., 1st Sess., 544 (1866) (remarks of Rep. Taylor). See also *id.,* at 634–635 (remarks of Rep. Ritter); *id.,* at App. 78, 80–81 (remarks of Rep. Chanler). Indeed, the bill was bitterly opposed on the ground that it "undertakes to make the negro in some respects . . . superior . . . and gives them favors that the poor white boy in the North cannot get." *Id.,* at 401 (remarks of Sen. McDougall). See also *id.,* at 319 (remarks of Sen. Hendricks); *id.,* at 362 (remarks of Sen. Saulsbury); *id.,* at 397 (remarks of Sen. Willey); *id.,* at 544 (remarks of Rep. Taylor). The bill's supporters defended it—not by rebutting the claim of special treatment—but by pointing to the need for such treatment:

> The very discrimination it makes between "destitute and suffering" negroes, and destitute and suffering white paupers, proceeds upon the distinction that, in the omitted case, civil rights and immunities are already sufficiently protected by the possession of political power, the absence of which in the case provided for necessitates governmental protection. *Id.,* at App. 75 (remarks of Rep. Phelps).

Despite the objection to the special treatment the bill would provide for Negroes, it was passed by Congress. *Id.,* at 421, 688. President Johnson vetoed this bill and also a subsequent bill that contained some modifications; one of his principal objections to both bills was that they gave special benefits to Negroes. 8 Messages and Papers of the Presidents 3596, 3599, 3620, 3623 (1897). Rejecting the concerns of the President and the bill's opponents, Congress overrode the President's second veto. Cong. Globe, 39th Cong., 1st Sess., 3842, 3850 (1866).

Since the Congress that considered and rejected the objections to the 1866 Freedmen's Bureau Act concerning special relief to Negroes also proposed the Fourteenth Amendment, it is inconceivable that the Fourteenth Amendment was intended to prohibit all race-conscious relief measures. It "would be a distortion of the policy manifested in that amendment, which was adopted to prevent state legislation designed to perpetuate discrimination on the basis of race or color," *Railway Mail Assn.* v. *Corsi,* 326 U. S. 88, 94 (1945), to hold that it barred state action to remedy the effects of that discrimination. Such a result would pervert the intent of the Framers by substituting abstract equality for the genuine equality the Amendment was intended to achieve.

B

As has been demonstrated in our joint opinion, this Court's past cases establish the constitutionality of race-conscious remedial measures. Beginning with the school desegregation cases, we recognized that even absent a judicial or legislative finding of constitutional violation, a school board constitutionally could consider the race of students in making school-assignment decisions. See *Swann* v. *Charlotte-Mecklenburg Board of Education,* 402 U. S. 1, 16 (1971); *McDaniel* v. *Barresi,* 402 U. S. 39, 41 (1971). We noted, moreover, that a

> flat prohibition against assignment of students for the purpose of creating a racial balance must inevitably conflict with the duty of school authorities to disestablish dual school systems. As we have held in *Swann,* the Constitution does not compel any particular degree of racial balance or mixing, but when past and continuing constitutional violations are found, some ratios are likely to be useful as starting points in shaping a remedy. An absolute prohibition against use of such a device—even as a starting point—contravenes the implicit command of *Green* v. *County School Board,* 391 U. S. 430 (1968), that all reasonable methods be available to formulate an effective remedy." *Board of Education* v. *Swann,* 402 U. S. 43, 46 (1971).

As we have observed, "[a]ny other approach would freeze the status quo that is the very target of all desegregation processes." *McDaniel* v. *Barresi, supra,* at 41.

Only last Term, in *United Jewish Organizations* v. *Carey,* 430 U. S. 144 (1977), we upheld a New York reapportionment plan that was deliberately drawn on the basis of race to enhance the electoral power of Negroes and Puerto Ricans; the plan had the effect of diluting the electoral strength of the Hasidic Jewish community. We were willing in *UJO* to sanction the remedial use of a racial classification even though it disadvantaged otherwise "innocent" individuals. In another case last Term, *Califano* v. *Webster,* 430 U. S. 313 (1977), the Court upheld a provision in the Social Security laws that discriminated against men because its purpose was "'the permissible one of redressing our society's longstanding disparate treatment of women.'" *Id.,* at 317, quoting *Califano* v. *Goldfarb,* 430 U. S. 199, 209 n. 8 (1977) (plurality opinion). We thus recognized the permissibility of remedying past societal discrimination through the use of otherwise disfavored classifications.

Nothing in those cases suggests that a university cannot similarly act to remedy past discrimination.[12] It is true that in both *UJO* and *Webster* the use of the disfavored classification was predicated on legislative or administrative action, but in neither case had those bodies made findings that there had been constitutional violations or that the specific individuals to be benefited had actually been the victims of discrimination. Rather, the classification in each of those cases was based on a determination

---

[12] Indeed, the action of the University finds support in the regulations promulgated under Title VI by the Department of Health, Education, and Welfare and approved by the President, which authorize a federally funded institution to take affirmative steps to overcome past discrimination against groups even where the institution was not guilty of prior discrimination. 45 CFR § 80.3 (b)(6)(ii) (1977).

that the group was in need of the remedy because of some type of past discrimination. There is thus ample support for the conclusion that a university can employ race-conscious measures to remedy past societal discrimination, without the need for a finding that those benefited were actually victims of that discrimination.

IV

While I applaud the judgment of the Court that a university may consider race in its admissions process, it is more than a little ironic that, after several hundred years of class-based discrimination against Negroes, the Court is unwilling to hold that a class-based remedy for that discrimination is permissible. In declining to so hold, today's judgment ignores the fact that for several hundred years Negroes have been discriminated against, not as individuals, but rather solely because of the color of their skins. It is unnecessary in 20th-century America to have individual Negroes demonstrate that they have been victims of racial discrimination; the racism of our society has been so pervasive that none, regardless of wealth or position, has managed to escape its impact. The experience of Negroes in America has been different in kind, not just in degree, from that of other ethnic groups. It is not merely the history of slavery alone but also that a whole people were marked as inferior by the law. And that mark has endured. The dream of America as the great melting pot has not been realized for the Negro; because of his skin color he never even made it into the pot.

These differences in the experience of the Negro make it difficult for me to accept that Negroes cannot be afforded greater protection under the Fourteenth Amendment where it is necessary to remedy the effects of past discrimination. In the *Civil Rights Cases, supra,* the Court wrote that the Negro emerging from slavery must cease "to be the special favorite of the laws." 109 U. S., at 25; see *supra,* at 392. We cannot in light of the history of the last century yield to that view. Had the Court in that decision and others been willing to "do for human liberty and the fundamental rights of American citizenship, what it did . . . for the protection of slavery and the rights of the masters of fugitive slaves," 109 U. S., at 53 (Harlan, J., dissenting), we would not need now to permit the recognition of any "special wards."

Most importantly, had the Court been willing in 1896, in *Plessy* v. *Ferguson,* to hold that the Equal Protection Clause forbids differences in treatment based on race, we would not be faced with this dilemma in 1978. We must remember, however, that the principle that the "Constitution is color-blind" appeared only in the opinion of the lone dissenter, 163 U. S., at 559. The majority of the Court rejected the principle of color blindness, and for the next 60 years, from *Plessy* to *Brown* v. *Board of Education,* ours was a Nation where, *by law,* an individual could be given "special" treatment based on the color of his skin.

It is because of a legacy of unequal treatment that we now must permit the institutions of this society to give consideration to race in making decisions about who will hold the positions of influence, affluence, and prestige in America. For far too long, the doors to those positions have been shut to Negroes. If we are ever to become a fully integrated society, one in which the color of a person's skin will not determine the opportunities available to him or her, we must be willing to take steps to open those doors. I do not believe that anyone can truly look into America's past and still find that a remedy for the effects of that past is impermissible.

It has been said that this case involves only the individual, Bakke, and this University. I doubt, however, that there is a computer capable of determining the number of persons and institutions that may be affected by the decision in this case. For example, we are told by the Attorney General of the United States that at least 27 federal agencies have adopted regulations requiring recipients of federal funds to take "'*affirmative action* to overcome the effects of conditions which resulted in limiting participation . . . by persons of a particular race, color, or national origin.'" Supplemental Brief for United States as *Amicus Curiae* 16 (emphasis added). I cannot even guess the number of state and local governments that have set up affirmative-action programs, which may be affected by today's decision.

I fear that we have come full circle. After the Civil War our Government started several "affirmative action" programs. This Court in the *Civil Rights Cases* and *Plessy* v. *Ferguson* destroyed the movement toward complete equality. For almost a century no action was taken, and this nonaction was with the tacit approval of the courts. Then we had *Brown* v. *Board of Education* and the Civil Rights Acts of Congress, followed by numerous affirmative-action programs. *Now,* we have this Court again stepping in, this time to stop affirmative-action programs of the type used by the University of California.

QUESTIONS FOR DISCUSSION

1. Does the Equal Protection Clause bar preferential treatment for blacks and women?
2. Is affirmative action fair?
3. Does past discrimination justify affirmative action?
4. What is *equality* in the admission to competitive programs or employment?
5. Is affirmative action good for blacks and women?
6. Does the Constitution require affirmative action?
7. Who are the beneficiaries of affirmative action? Who are its victims?
8. "The real problems affecting the minority underclass of the United States can in no way be affected by affirmative action." Discuss.

RECOMMENDED READINGS

COHEN, CARL. "Why Racial Preference Is Illegal and Immoral." *Commentary* 67 (June 1979), pp. 40–52.

DREYFUSS, JOEL, and CHARLES LAWRENCE III. *The Bakke Case: The Politics of Inequality.* New York: Harcourt Brace Jovanovich, 1979.

GLAZER, NATHAN. *Affirmative Discrimination: Ethnic Inequality and Public Policy.* New York: Basic Books, 1978.

HEANEY, GERALD W. "Busing, Timetables, Goals, and Ratios: Tombstones of Equal Opportunity." 69 *Minnesota Law Review* 735 (Apr. 1985).

LIVINGSTON, JOHN C. *Fair Game: Inequality and Affirmative Action.* San Francisco: W. H. Freeman, 1979.

NAGEL, THOMAS. "A Defense of Affirmative Action." *QQ* 1 (Fall 1981), pp. 6–9.

SCHNAPPER, ERIC. "Affirmative Action and the Legislative History of the Fourteenth Amendment." 71 *Virginia Law Review* 753 (June 1985).

SCHWARTZ, HERMAN. "In Defense of Affirmative Action." *Dissent* 31 (Fall 1984), pp. 406–14.

SOWELL, THOMAS. "A Dissenting Opinion about Affirmative Action." *Across the Board* 18 (Jan. 1981), pp. 65–72.

THOMPSON, WALTER G. "Affirmative Action." *Journal of Social, Political and Economic Studies* 7 (Winter 1982), pp. 377–86.

U. S. CONG., SENATE. *Affirmative Action and Equal Protection.* Hearing before the Subcommittee on the Constitution of the Committee on the Judiciary, 97th Cong., 1st Sess., 1983.

14 *Would "comparable worth" laws enhance equality for women?*

YES PAY EQUITY IS A NECESSARY REMEDY FOR WAGE DISCRIMINATION

Joy Ann Grune

INTRODUCTION

The entry of working women into the U.S. labor force is one of the most significant developments of the 20th century. Although most women work because they need to and many because they want to, the most powerful explanation for the extraordinary movement of women into the paid work force is the accelerated demand for their labor. The transformation of the U.S. economy, particularly since World War II, would not have been possible without women's response to the call for new workers, to fill new jobs, in growing industries. This is the terrain that gives birth to pay equity.

As a historical development, pay equity is a direct response to the societal importance—so often denied and ridiculed—of females and female-dominated jobs in today's economy. Women demand pay equity as they reject their trivialization as workers.

Culture, history, psychiatry, and social relations all have a role in wage discrimination, as they do in other legal rights issues. They contribute to the creation and maintenance of a gender-based division of labor

U.S. Commission on Civil Rights, *Comparable Worth: Issues for the 80's. A Consultation of the U. S. Commission on Civil Rights,* June 6–7, 1984 (Washington, D.C.: Commission on Civil Rights, 1984), vol. I, pp. 165–73.

in the market economy that is old, pronounced, and pays women less. But the focus of pay equity is on the translation of theory into practice, which occurs when an employer sets discriminatory wages for a job classification because of the sex, or race or ethnicity, of a predominant number of its occupants.

This paper defines pay equity as a matter of discrimination and shows why affirmative action is not a substitute. It examines five fallacies behind market-based arguments against pay equity and assesses the question of cost. Recent activities of Federal, State, and local governments are described; the Federal Government's lack of enforcement of the 1964 Civil Rights Act is reviewed; and recommendations are offered for effective government involvement.

PAY EQUITY IS A NECESSARY REMEDY FOR WAGE DISCRIMINATION

The principle of pay equity requires the elimination of discrimination in pay within a firm that has operated to depress the wages of entire job classifications because of the sex of the overwhelming majority of occupants. The goal of pay equity is accomplished by raising the wages of predominantly female jobs in a workplace to match the wages of similarly valued male jobs.

The challenge of pay equity is deliberate and focuses directly on the wage-setting process. It does not rely on indirect or laissez faire overtures such as affirmative action programs or the market, which have shown themselves historically to be inadequate to the task of significantly reducing overall wage bias.

Pay equity is an essential remedy for wage discrimination based on sex. It is uniquely capable of reaching deeply structured patterns of wage discrimination associated with job segregation.

The majority of pay equity initiatives have been efforts to reach sex-based discrimination. When patterns of job segregation and wage depression in a workplace are associated with race or ethnicity, the principle of pay equity also can be applied. In New York State, for example, the pay equity job evaluation study now taking place is studying race and sex. U.S. House Resolution 239 introduced by Congresswoman Olympia Snowe (R-Me.) in 1984 calls for a pilot pay equity job evaluation study of the Federal sector that is not restricted to sex.

The U.S. Supreme Court, in *Gunther v. County of Washington,* has decided that wage discrimination involving jobs that are comparable, though not equal, is illegal. Such violations of Title VII of the Civil Rights Act must be stopped if women, and the men who work with them in predominantly female jobs, are to be released from employment discrimination.

The persistence of the wage gap and job segregation; the findings of virtually every pay equity job evaluation study showing that predominantly female jobs are paid less than male jobs of comparable worth; favorable court decisions in *Gunther, Washington State,* and *IUE v. Washington;* and growing research and understanding of how the labor market operates—all indicate that wage discrimination is at work in creating consistently low pay for female-dominated jobs.

EQUAL PAY FOR EQUAL WORK AND THE ELIMINATION OF DISCRIMINATION IN HIRING AND PROMOTION ARE NOT SUBSTITUTES FOR PAY EQUITY

A comprehensive program to eliminate employment discrimination against women needs to include provisions for pay equity, equal pay for equal work, and the elimination of discrimination in hiring and promotion. These are complementary, but analytically distinct approaches to related, but different problems encountered in a workplace. All are required by law.

Equal Pay for Equal Work With few exceptions, equal pay for equal work is accepted by the public as a fundamental right of working people. The Equal Pay Act, passed by the U.S. Congress in 1963, mandates equal pay for equal work performed by men and women.

In 1962, 1 year before the Equal Pay Act was passed, full-time, year-round working women earned 59.5 cents for each dollar earned by their male counterparts. Today, the figure is 61 cents.[1] The inability of the act to significantly reduce the wage gap should not be misconstrued. For example, 6 years ago Daniel Glisberg, then Assistant Secretary of Labor, reported in a speech to the Coalition of Labor Union Women that the Equal Pay Act "has obtained $164 million for some 272,000 employees, nearly all women. These figures do not include the $150 million settlement obtained for 13,000 employees of AT&T. In 1978 alone, we were able to restore income or other compensation to more than 15,000 workers for a total of $8.7 million."[2]

Enforcement of the Equal Pay Act has brought higher wages to many women. Stronger enforcement is still needed, par-

[1] *The Wage Gap: Myths and Facts* (National Committee on Pay Equity, 1983).

[2] Joy Ann Grune, *Manual on Pay Equity: Raising Wages for Women's Work* (Conference on Alternative State and Local Policies and National Committee on Pay Equity, 1980), p. 61.

ticularly since greater numbers of women are slowly assuming jobs equal to men's.

Unfortunately, however, the vast number of employed women do not hold jobs equal to those held by men, and, therefore, the right to a nondiscriminatory wage afforded by the Equal Pay Act does not apply to their situation. In addition, the movement of women into nontraditional jobs over the last 20 years has been outpaced by the movement of women into the work force through low paying, mostly female jobs.

In 1982 over 50 percent of working women were found in 20 out of a total of 427 occupations.[3] It is estimated that two-thirds of all women and men would have to change jobs to achieve equality of distribution by sex.[4] The degree of occupational segregation by sex is as severe today as it was over 80 years ago.[5]

Women of all colors are concentrated in low paying, overwhelmingly female jobs. Although the employment distributions of different ethnic and racial groups of women are converging, there are still differences. For example, in 1979, clerical work employed more than 35 percent of all working women, including 35.9 percent of white women, 29 percent of black women, 31.1 percent of Mexican women, 38.4 percent of Puerto Rican women, and 31.2 percent of Cuban women.[6] Two out of 12 occupational groups—service and clerical work—employ about 60 percent of black women and 53 percent of white women.[7]

Increasingly, women of color are moving into the same occupations as those in which White women work, so that:

[3] *The Wage Gap: Myths and Facts.*
[4] Heidi Hartmann, "The Case for Comparable Worth," *Equal Pay for Unequal Work* (Eagle Forum Education and Legal Defense Fund, 1984), p. 14.
[5] Ibid.
[6] *Women of Color and Pay Equity* (National Committee on Pay Equity, 1984).
[7] Ibid.

- Clerical work now accounts for almost one-third of women workers in nearly every racial and ethnic group;
- Only Cuban, Chinese and Native American women have slightly higher percentages in operative, blue-collar work than in clerical;
- The jobs held by Black women have shifted significantly from blue-collar, operative work to white-collar work: clerical, professional, technical, managerial and sales;
- Mexican American and Puerto Rican women remain concentrated in operative occupations, although this occupational category is second for both of these populations to clerical work.[8]

The facts indicate that the vast majority—perhaps 80 percent—of women work in predominantly female jobs. The wage discrimination they experience is more often and more directly in reference to predominantly male jobs that are comparable, not equal. Thus, the Equal Pay Act is limited in its ability to help them.

The Elimination of Discrimination in Hiring and Promotion Women workers are moving into predominantly male, white-collar and blue-collar jobs. This movement has not seriously reduced the index of job segregation or the wage gap because simultaneously even more women have entered the work force through predominantly female jobs with low wages.

The entry of women into nontraditional jobs with nondiscriminatory wages is in large measure due to the Equal Pay Act, Civil Rights Act, and Executive Order 11246. If these laws had not been in place, it is likely that the degree of job segregation and the wage gap would have dramatically increased over the last 20 years because the entry of women into feminized jobs with low wages, particularly into the expanding clerical and service sectors, would have even more outpaced their movement into nontraditional work with higher wages.

The elimination of discriminatory ob-

[8] Ibid.

stacles that impede or prevent women from moving into jobs is required by law. It is one essential component of an anti-discrimination program that can allow women to operate as workers without being victimized by illegal acts. However, this approach is no substitute—legally or pragmatically—for requiring the elimination of sex-based wage discrimination.

First of all, the law is already clear in stating that wage discrimination is illegal and must be eliminated whether it occurs between jobs that are equal or between jobs that are comparable. The availability of an affirmative action program does not transform an illegal act of wage discrimination into a legal one. Similarly, a woman's decision to enter or stay in a job—regardless of her reasons for so deciding—does not give the employer license to discriminate. This is the case in equal pay for equal work situations and in situations with comparable jobs. Finally, employer efforts to stop discrimination against women who try to move into male-dominated jobs do not, under any circumstances, permit the employer to reduce wages for other jobs because they are held by women.

A nurse has the right to an opportunity to be a doctor, and a secretary has the right to an opportunity to be an executive or a management analyst. To tell a nurse that she must be a doctor to escape discrimination in employment is to blame the victim and to turn antidiscrimination laws inside out.

Along similar lines, it has been suggested that pursuing job integration through affirmative action can take the place of pay equity. It is argued that if typists, nurses, secretaries, and librarians, for example, were to leave their fields and find jobs in higher paying, traditionally male jobs, the wage gap would close. This approach cannot legally substitute for pay equity, for the reasons offered above. It is an important complement, but has difficulties.

First, as indicated earlier, it is estimated that two-thirds of men and women would have to change jobs for equality of occupational distribution to occur. Given these numbers, closing the wage gap through job integration and affirmative action would take a very long time, perhaps forever.

Second, this approach calls on women to forsake years or decades of experience and training. Some women may want to; many may not. But in any event, such an employment policy makes little sense because its success would depend on millions of skilled women deserting the service sector infrastructure of the economy.

Third, an employment policy whose goal is to place millions of women into industries and occupations that are male dominated presents the problem of training and attracting men to replace them. Finally, although the service sector has numerous predominantly female jobs and contains some of the fastest growing occupations, many traditionally male jobs, especially in basic industry, are suffering growing rates of unemployment. A wage gap reduction policy that tries to move growing numbers of women from high growth jobs to shrinking, predominantly male jobs is doomed to failure.

It is distinctly possible that the implementation of pay equity will do as much as or more than any other policy to promote job integration, affirmative action, and the elimination of discrimination in hiring and promotion:

- The empowerment of women, which is already a frequently visible accompaniment to pay equity, will result in more determined women seeking new types of work;
- There will be much less of an incentive to employers for maintaining sex-segregated jobs once pay equity is implemented;
- Affirmative action will be used by employers to integrate jobs so as to avoid financial and legal liability in pay equity cases; and
- Higher wages in predominantly female jobs will attract men.

THE FAILURE OF MARKET ARGUMENTS AGAINST PAY EQUITY

Great confusion is being created around pay equity and the market. It has been alleged that pay equity would destroy the market and is unnecessary and impossible because of the market. These arguments are not accurate and are based on five fallacies:

(a) The market is free and operates without interventions.
(b) The market will eliminate discrimination.
(c) Pay equity requires the setting of wages outside of a market economy and is an alternative to market-based wage determination.
(d) Employers currently respond directly and uniformly to market forces.
(e) Wages are currently set almost exclusively and directly on the basis of market wage rates.

The Market Is Free and Operates without Interventions There are few political tendencies today which claim that the market is or should be completely free. For the sake of employers, children, and adult workers, government has long intervened in the economy with legislation, Executive orders, appropriations, tax codes, etc. These steps are taken because of the belief that some principles take precedence over the right of a market to be free. Child labor laws, collective bargaining laws, anti-discrimination laws, health and safety laws, environmental laws, tax breaks, and targeted subsidies to ailing companies are examples of the belief in action.

In addition to government, companies have also intervened in market behavior. In the employment area, for example, 9 to 5: National Association of Working Women has claimed that "large employers in major cities form consortia to discuss wage rates and benefits. Working Women believes that such groups have been influential in holding down clerical salaries over the years."[9] Nine to 5 has specifically

[9] Grune, *Manual on Pay Equity,* p. 145.

identified the Boston Survey Group, a group of large employers that has met for the purpose of setting clerical salaries.

The Market Will Eliminate Discrimination The market has not eliminated discrimination, and there is nothing to indicate that it will. In fact, according to the National Academy of Sciences, "market wages incorporate the effects of many institutional factors, including discrimination."[10]

When an employer sets wages directly on the basis of market rates for predominantly female jobs, it incorporates prior discrimination by other employers. Without efforts to remove bias from market rates, this type of reliance on the market becomes one of the most damaging transmitters of discrimination because it serves to carry discrimination from employer to employer.

Pay Equity Requires the Setting of Wages outside of a Market Economy and Is an Alternative to Market-Based Wage Determination Pay equity does not mean the destruction of an external, market-based, salary-setting scheme that will be replaced by a purely internal one. The goal of pay equity is to eliminate bias and discrimination in wage setting. This bias may operate through market rates, through the way the employer responds to or relies on the market, through biased job evaluation systems, or through purely subjective judgments made by employers. The objective of pay equity is not to overturn the market, but merely to eliminate bias, whatever its sources.

The Comparable Worth strategy can be seen as an attempt to bring wages of female-dominated jobs up to the going market wage rates for similar type work that is not female-dominated. Wages for female-dominated

[10] Heidi Hartmann and Don Treiman, *Women, Work, and Wages: Equal Pay for Jobs of Equal Value* (National Academy of Sciences, 1981), p. 65.

jobs are seen to be artificially depressed by discrimination. In this view it is not Comparable Worth that interferes with a free market, but discrimination. Given that there is discrimination in the labor market, which depresses the wages of women's jobs, intervention is necessary to remove discrimination and its effects. It is therefore unnecessary to have an alternative to market wages; it is necessary only to adjust them. A variety of mechanisms, particularly job evaluation systems, exist that can be used to adjust wages to remove the effects of discrimination.[11]

It would be virtually impossible for firms to establish wages with no reliance on the market, and pay equity activists have not asked employers to do so. They usually suggest that wages for predominantly male jobs be derived from prevailing market rates and be used as the baseline. Under this approach, wages for predominantly female jobs are raised to match those of similarly valued, predominantly male jobs. This, for example, was the remedy that Judge Jack Tanner ordered in Washington State.

For all of these reasons, it is incorrect to characterize pay equity as necessarily a full substitute for or alternative to market-based wages. Pay equity requires a wage structure that is not consistently marred or dented by wage depressions that are tied to gender or race. On top of such an equitable structure, it is possible to build in contingencies that permit an employer to respond legitimately and fairly to real shortages, to seniority requirements, to employment needs of a labor pool. But in its essence, the structure needs to be nondiscriminatory and, therefore, cannot be entirely market dependent.

Employers Respond Automatically and Uniformly to Market Forces Pay equity advocates are beginning to believe that

[11] Hartmann, "The Case for Comparable Worth," p. 11.

employers rely on and respond to market forces differently depending on the sex composition of the job for which wages are being set. In the area of supply and demand, an employer has choices in how to respond to a shortage of workers. The choices—relative to a shortage of nurses, for example—include temporarily absorbing the shortage, hiring temporary nurses, having the nurses who are employed work overtime, redesigning the workload, changing recruitment techniques, or possibly, raising wages. Pay equity advocates fear that the last choice—raising wages—is less likely to be used or will be used less quickly when the job is mostly female. They also fear that wages will be raised a smaller amount. The nurse shortage of several years ago was experienced by numerous metropolitan areas and led to a great variety of innovative recruitment techniques, including international forays to the Philippines and elsewhere. But wages did not increase as much or as quickly as might be expected.

The use of surveys to calculate prevailing wage rates is another example of how employers can incorporate bias into their reliance on the market. In West Virginia, for example, clerical workers are concerned that their large employer tends to survey lower paying firms in a smaller geographical area when the job in question is predominantly female or minority.

As pay equity activists begin to research seriously the wage-setting procedures in their places of employment, they are finding that employers have latitude in responding to and relying on the market and that it is too often exercised to the disadvantage of the predominantly female jobs.

Wages Are Set by Employers Exclusively and Directly on the Basis of Prevailing Wage Rates Many employers use a combination of standards to determine wages. These include prevailing wage rates, job evaluation systems, and subjective judgments about the worth of a job. Some employers, such as Washington State, select a limited number of jobs whose wages are directly tied to the market. These are called benchmarks, and other jobs are then slotted into place. Slotting is sometimes accomplished formally through the use of a job evaluation system and sometimes informally through the personal judgments of those doing the slotting. The number of employers who tie every job classification directly to the market is probably a distinct minority.

It has been estimated that 60–65 percent of all public and private employers use job evaluation systems. They are standard management tools that permit the internal ranking of job classifications on the basis of worth for purposes of salary setting. They have been used by public and private employers to meet considerations of internal equity, to provide rationality and justification to the wage hierarchy, and to make it unnecessary to perform wage surveys for every job classification.

Some employers rely primarily on their own judgments concerning the value of a job. The judgments determine wages when there is no formal system, but sometimes the subjective judgment takes precedence over formal findings. In *IUE v. Westinghouse,* for example, the court ruled that Westinghouse had discriminated because it ignored the findings of its own point ratings and reduced wages for women's jobs, offering stereotypic judgments about women as justification.

THE COST OF IMPLEMENTING AND NOT IMPLEMENTING PAY EQUITY

There are no sound estimates of the overall implementation costs of pay equity in the United States. As individual employers begin to implement pay equity and to complete pay equity job evaluation studies,

workplace by workplace costs and most estimates are becoming known.

In Minnesota, implementation will cost 0.3 percent of the total biennial budget. It costs 4 percent of the State's annual payroll budget, and the State determined it could afford this at 1 percent a year for each of 4 years. In spring 1983, $21.8 million was appropriated for the first 2 years.

In Washington State, the implementation ordered by Judge Tanner will cost approximately 1 percent of the State's budget. However, on top of this will be the backpay award ordered by the court of approximately $500 million.

The primary reason for the cost difference between the two States is that Minnesota voluntarily identified discrimination in its civil service system and voluntarily decided to eliminate it. Washington State also voluntarily identified discrimination in its civil service system. This was first done in 1974. Unfortunately, despite several followup studies with the same findings of discrimination, the State refused to implement pay equity. It risked a lawsuit, lost, and was ordered to raise wages and provide backpay.

Given that wage discrimination is illegal, the most fiscally responsible route for an employer to take is voluntary compliance. This avoids long, expensive court battles and backpay awards. It allows an employer to stay in more control of the process and more effectively plan for orderly implementation.

It should be noted that because so little is known about the cost of implementing pay equity, the National Committee on Pay Equity is surveying all employers who have begun implementation and all employers who have estimates of cost based on completed pay equity job evaluation studies.

In 1982 full-time, year-round working women were paid 61 cents relative to every dollar of their male counterparts. In 1980 the equivalent figures were 56 cents in the private sector, 62.8 cents in the Federal

TABLE 1
Mean Earnings of Year-Round, Full-Time Workers by Work Exprience, Sex, and Race as a Percentage of the Earnings of Men of All Races, 1980
Mean earnings as a percentage of the earnings of all men

Work experience	All men	White men	Black men	Hispanic men	All women	White women	Black women	Hispanic women
Federal government	$24,050	103.1	80.8	90.7	62.8	63.1	62.2	N/A
State & local government	18,748	102.5	76.0	82.8	71.5	72.7	64.8	62.9
Private wage & salary	21,011	102.9	68.1	72.1	56.0	56.8	50.2	47.9

SOURCE: *The Wage Gap: Myths and Facts*, National Committee on Pay Equity, 1983.

sector, and 71.5 cents in State and local government.[12] In Table 1, these figures are broken down by race and ethnicity.

These statistics indicate that the greatest expense, on the average, will be in private firms, followed by the Federal Government and then by State and local governments. But cost will vary workplace by workplace. For example, according to the Communications Workers of America (CWA), AFL-CIO, women earned 78 cents for every man's dollar at AT&T in the late 1970s. A Midwestern State preparing for a possible job evaluation study found that full-time, year-round women in State employment earn approximately 85 cents for every man's dollar.

The elimination of wage discrimination against women and men who work in predominantly female jobs will cost money. The single most important step an employer can take to contain costs is to act quickly and voluntarily. But in any case, to paraphrase Winn Newman, the cost of correcting discrimination is no excuse or defense for breaking the law. Society makes regular judgments through the laws it makes about which corners may and may not be cut to save money. It has decided that money cannot be taken from the paychecks of women and used in other ways.

[12] *The Wage Gap: Myths and Facts.*

THE ROLE OF GOVERNMENT IN ELIMINATING WAGE DISCRIMINATION

Federal Government Activities   The Civil Rights Act forbids discrimination in compensation when the jobs in question are equal and when they are comparable. The law, which celebrates its 20th anniversary this year, is sufficient. No new Federal legislation of this sort is necessary.

Unfortunately, however, the Equal Employment Opportunity Commission (EEOC) is not adequately meeting its statutory obligation to enforce the law. Pay equity charges have been warehoused; no litigation is taking place in this area; and existing EEOC policy, first adopted in September 1981, which gives guidelines on how to investigate wage discrimination charges, is not being followed or enforced. The National Committee on Pay Equity has recommended that the EEOC take concrete steps in these directions . . . .

About the time of the congressional oversight hearings on the EEOC and pay equity that were held by Congressman Barney Frank (D-Mass.) in 1984, EEOC Chair Clarence Thomas announced that he had established a task force in headquarters that would review the backlog of charges, search for a litigation vehicle, and develop policy. The review of charges, assuming it is thorough and accurate, is long overdue, as are efforts to litigate in this important area. The development of new policy may be unnecessary, given that Commission policy already exists, and could easily become another excuse for postponing antidiscrimination actions.

These failures on the part of the executive branch of the Federal Government have provoked Congress, private citizens, and private organizations to take initiatives. Members of Congress have held hearings on the EEOC's role, introduced a resolution criticizing Federal enforcement agencies, and introduced legislation to give specific direction to enforcement agencies. Of particular note are House and Senate resolutions that call for a pilot pay equity job evaluation study of the Federal Government.

Private individuals and organizations are lobbying the EEOC and Congress for more enforcement. They are also assuming the expense of filing their own pay equity charges and lawsuits. Discrimination charges have been filed against Illinois, Hawaii, Los Angeles, Chicago, Philadelphia, Fairfax County (Va.), St. Louis Post-Dispatch, and elsewhere. Lawsuits have been filed against Michigan Bell and Nassau County (N.Y.).

State and Local Government Activities In large part because of the inaction of the Federal Government, the balance of pay equity activities shifted to State and local levels over the past 3 to 4 years. They have become the most productive areas. Well over 100 efforts have taken place in more than 30 States, with more now on the way.[13] The overwhelming majority of these apply only to the employers of the government taking action. They have occurred through collective bargaining, executive order, legislative action, and personnel department action. State, county,

[13] *Who's Working for Working Women: A Survey of State and Local Government Initiatives* (National Committee on Pay Equity, 1984).

municipal, and school board governments have:

- Held hearings and collected data on job segregation and the wage gap;
- Mandated and funded pay equity job evaluation studies;
- Amended civil service policies to require pay equity; and
- Enforced existing laws, such as equal and fair employment practice laws, to provide pay equity.

Pennsylvania is the only State seriously considering an amendment to State law specifically to forbid wage discrimination among comparable jobs in the private sector. This is still pending. Minnesota is the only State to pass legislation requiring that local governments move to pay equity. This passed in April 1984.

All of these victories have made pay equity activists determined to move more often and more quickly from pay equity policies and studies to implementation. Minnesota is the only State to adopt fully an implementation plan. New Mexico's legislation allocated $33 million to upgrade the 3,000 lowest paid jobs in the State government, 86 percent occupied by women, before the results of its job evaluation study. Connecticut public employee unions have negotiated small pay equity funds pending study results. Washington State has been ordered to implement pay equity by a judge. Months before the trial, and 9 years after the first study, the Washington Legislature allocated $1.5 million to begin upgrading. There are additional partial and full implementations that have taken place at the municipal level.

What the Government Should Do Many people may think that the most effective, fiscally sound, and least disruptive approach to eliminating discrimination is voluntary compliance. But if voluntary compliance is to work, the Federal Government must provide strict law enforcement.

A few public employers are now taking this route, but virtually no private employers appear to be. AT&T and CWA negotiated a joint labor-management committee that developed and field tested a job evaluation system in 1980–83. The 1983 contract calls for joint committees in all operating and other AT&T companies to develop systems. But no implementation of the plan or pay equity has yet occurred. Westinghouse, General Electric, and Charley Brothers have begun to implement pay equity because of lawsuits that they lost or that led to settlements. If private employers are engaging in voluntary compliance, they are keeping it a big secret. Employers have stated that voluntary compliance requires incentive and that the best incentive is strict enforcement of the law. Since this is not taking place, it should come as no surprise that there are so few private sector initiatives.

With the accumulation of preliminary victories in cities and States, activists will be turning to the EEOC directly and through their elected representatives for assistance, enforcement, and litigation. There are activists in every State, and their numbers, enthusiasm, and determination are growing. They see progress in virtually every tactical area, except the Federal Government's enforcement of laws already on the books. The legal victories, particularly in *Gunther* and *Washington State*, have given people confidence that although pay equity is a moral, social, political, and personal right, it is also a legal right.

The Federal Government's role does not require it to develop a master job evaluation plan for all workplaces. This will take place workplace by workplace as it does now. Of course, it does not require establishing wage boards to determine wages. But the role of the Federal Government does require an executive branch commitment to enforcing laws that Congress has passed and a previous President has signed into law.

CONCLUSION

Pay equity is one of the most fundamentally democratic women's issues to appear in the past 15 years. It will help the many, not the few, and the needy more than the privileged. It is also an issue at the intersection of economic and personal concerns; that is, it promises an end to unnecessarily low wages, but also expresses a new respect for much of the work that women do in this society.

The powerful sentiments that have carried pay equity this far will carry it further. But the elimination of this type of wage discrimination, which runs deep and deprives many, will be easier, faster, and less expensive if the Federal Government can be counted on as an ally in enforcing its own laws.

NO AN ARGUMENT AGAINST COMPARABLE WORTH

June O'Neill

The traditional goal of feminists has been equal opportunity for women—the

U.S. Commission on Civil Rights, *Comparable Worth: Issues for the 80's. A Consultation of the U. S. Commission on Civil Rights,* **June 6–7, 1984 (Washington, D.C.: Commission on Civil Rights, 1984), vol. I, pp. 177–86.**

opportunity for women to gain access to the schools, training, and jobs they choose to enter, on the same basis as men. This goal, however, basically accepts the rules of the game as they operate in a market economy. In fact the thrust has been to improve the way the market functions by removing discriminatory barriers that restrict the free supply of workers to jobs. By contrast, the more recent policy of "comparable worth" would dispense with the rules of the game. In place of the goal of equality of opportunity it would substitute a demand for equality of results, and it would do this essentially through regulation and legislation. It proposes, therefore, a radical departure from the economic system we now have, and should be scrutinized with the greatest care.

The topics I will cover in this paper and the main points I will make are as follows:

1. The concept of comparable worth rests on a misunderstanding of the role of wages and prices in the economy.
2. The premises on which a comparable worth policy is based reflect a misconception about the reasons why women and men are in different occupations and have different earnings. Both the occupational differences and the pay gap to a large extent are the result of differences in the roles of women and men in the family and the effects these role differences have on the accumulation of skills and other job choices that affect pay. Discrimination by employers may account for some of the occupational differences, but it does not, as comparable worth advocates claim, lower wages directly in women's occupations.
3. Comparable worth, if implemented, would lead to capricious wage differentials, resulting in unintended shortages and surpluses of workers in different occupations with accompanying unemployment. Moreover, it would encourage women to remain in traditional occupations.
4. Policies are available that can be better targeted than comparable worth on any existing discriminatory or other barriers. These policies include the equal employment and pay legislation now on the books.

THE CONCEPT OF COMPARABLE WORTH

By comparable worth I mean the view that employers should base compensation on the inherent value of a job rather than on strictly market considerations. It is not a new idea—since the time of St. Thomas Aquinas, the concept of the "just price," or payment for value, has had considerable appeal. Practical considerations, however, have won out over metaphysics. In a free market, wages and prices are not taken as judgments of the inherent value of the worker or the good itself, but reflect a balancing of what people are willing to pay for the services of these goods with how much it costs to supply them. Market prices are the efficient signals that balance supply and demand. Thus, in product markets we do not require that a pound of soybeans be more expensive than a pound of Belgian chocolates because it is more nutritious, or that the price of water be higher than that of diamonds because it is so much more important to our survival. If asked what the proper scale of prices should be for these products, most people—at least those who have taken Economics I—would give the sensible answer that there is no proper scale—it all depends on the tastes and needs of millions of consumers and the various conditions that determine the costs of production and the supplies of these products.

What is true of the product market is equally true of the labor market. There is simply no independent scientific way to determine what pay should be in a particular occupation without recourse to the market. Job skills have "costs of production" such as formal schooling and on-the-job training. Different jobs also have different amenities that may be more or less costly for the employer to provide—for example, part-time work, safe work, flexible hours, or a pleasant ambience. And individuals vary in their talents and tastes for acquiring skills and performing different tasks. The skills required change over time as the demand for products changes and as different techniques of production are introduced. And these changes may vary by geographic region. In a market system, these changing conditions are reflected in changing wage rates, which in turn provide workers with the incentive to acquire new skills or to migrate to different regions.

The wage pattern that is the net outcome of these forces need not conform to anyone's independent judgment based on preconceived notions of comparability or of relative desirability. The clergy, for example, earn about 30 percent less than brickmasons.[1] Yet the clergy are largely college graduates; the brickmasons are not. Both occupations are more than 95 percent male—so one cannot point to sex discrimination. Possibly the reason for the wage disparity lies in unusual union power of construction workers and is an example of market imperfections. But other explanations are possible too. The real compensation to the clergy, for example, may include housing and spiritual satisfaction as fringe benefits. On the other hand, the high risk of unemployment and exposure to hazards of brickmasons may be reflected in additional monetary payments. If enough people require premiums to become brickmasons and are willing to settle for nonmonetary rewards to work as clergy, and if the buyers of homes are willing to pay the higher costs of brickmasons, while churchgoers are satisfied with the number and quality of clergy who apply, the market solution may well be satisfactory.[2]

One can also think of examples of jobs that initially may seem quite comparable but that would not command the same wage, even in nondiscriminatory and competitive markets. The following example is based on a case that has been used before, but it illustrates the point so well it bears repeating.[3] Consider two jobs—one a Spanish-English translator and the other a French-English translator. Most job evaluators would probably conclude that these jobs are highly comparable and should be paid the same. After all, the skills required, the mental demands, the working conditions, and responsibility would seem to be nearly identical. But "nearly" is not equal, and the difference in language may in fact give rise to a legitimate pay differential. The demand for the two languages may differ—for example, if trade with Spanish-speaking countries is greater. But the supply of Spanish-English translators may also be greater. And this would vary by geographic area. It would be difficult to predict which job will require the higher wage and by how much in order to balance supply and demand.

What the market does is to process the scarcity of talents, the talents of heterogeneous individuals and the demands of business and consumers in arriving at a wage. The net outcome would only coincidentally be the same as a comparable worth determination. There are simply too many factors interacting in highly complex ways for a study to find the market clearing wage.

WHY ABANDON THE MARKET?

The argument for abandoning market determination of wages and substituting "comparable worth," where wage decisions would be based on an independent assessment of the "value" of occupations, is based on the following premises: (1) the pay gap between women and men is due to

---

[1] These statistics are based on the median hourly earnings of workers in these occupations in 1981. Rytina, 1982.

[2] If brickmasons' wages are artificially high because of union power, the market would be unstable. More workers would desire to be brickmasons than would be hired at the artificially high wage. Would comparable worth policy help the situation? Not likely. A comparable worth solution would likely require higher pay for clergy than for brickmasons because of the heavy weight placed on readily measured items like education. A wage for clergy that is too high would also be unstable. Only the removal of the union power or restrictions on unions would satisfactorily resolve the issue.

[3] This example was originated by Sharon Smith and described in Killingsworth (1984), who notes it is cited in Gold (1983).

TABLE 1
Female-Male Ratios of Median Usual Weekly Earnings of Full-Time Wage and Salary Workers, by Age, 1971–1983

I. Unadjusted Ratios

Age / Year	May 1971	May 1973	May 1974	May 1975	May 1976	May 1977	May 1978	2nd Quarter 1979	Annual average 1979	1982	1983
Total, 16 years and over	.62	.62	.61	.62	.61	.61	.61	.62	.62	.65	.66
16–19	.89	.82	.82	.86	.86	.88	.86	.85	.87	.88	.94
20–24	.78	.77	.76	.76	.80	.78	.75	.75	.76	.83	.84
25–34	.65	.64	.65	.66	.67	.65	.66	.67	.66	.72	.73
35–44	.59	.54	.55	.57	.55	.56	.53	.58	.58	.60	.60
45–54	.57	.57	.57	.59	.57	.56	.54	.57	.56	.59	.58
55–64	.62	.63	.60	.63	.61	.59	.60	.60	.58	.60	.62

II. Adjusted for Male-Female Differences in Full-Time Hours[1]

Age / Year	May 1971	May 1973	May 1974	May 1975	May 1976	May 1977	May 1978	2nd Quarter 1979	Annual average 1979	1982	1983
Total, 16 years and over	.68	.68	.67	.68	.68	.67	.67	.68	.68	.71	.72
16–19	.94	.86	.87	.90	.90	.92	.91	.90	.92	.91	.96
20–24	.85	.83	.82	.82	.86	.84	.80	.81	.82	.88	.89
25–34	.73	.72	.72	.73	.74	.72	.73	.74	.73	.79	.80
35–44	.66	.61	.61	.63	.61	.62	.59	.64	.64	.66	.66
45–54	.62	.62	.62	.63	.62	.61	.59	.63	.61	.64	.63
55–64	.67	.69	.65	.67	.67	.65	.65	.66	.64	.65	.67

SOURCE: Earnings by age and sex are from unpublished tabulations from the Current Population Survey provided by the Bureau of Labor Statistics, U.S. Department of Labor. Hours data are from U.S. Bureau of Labor Statistics, Employment and Earnings series, January issues, annual averages.

[1]Female-male earnings ratios were adjusted for differences in hours worked by multiplying by age-specific male-female ratios of average hours worked per week (for nonagricultural workers on full-time schedules).

discrimination and has failed to narrow over time; (2) this discrimination takes the form of occupational segregation, where women are relegated to low-paying jobs; and (3) pay in these female-dominated occupations is low simply because women hold them.

The Pay Gap In 1983 the pay gap, viewed as the ratio of women's to men's hourly pay, was about 72 percent overall (Table 1).[4] Among younger groups the ratio is higher (and the pay gap smaller)—a ratio of 89 percent for 20–24-year-olds and 80 percent for the age 25–34 years old. Among groups age 35 and over the ratio is about 65 percent.

What accounts for the pay gap? Clearly, not all differentials reflect discrimination.

[4] The commonly cited pay gap—where women are said to earn 59 cents out of every dollar earned by men—is based on a comparison of the annual earnings of women and men who work year round and are primarily full time. In 1982 this ratio was 62 percent. This figure is lower than the figure of 72 percent cited above because the annual earnings measure is not adjusted for differences in hours worked during the year, and men are more likely than women to work overtime or on second jobs.

Several minorities (Japanese and Jewish Americans, for example) have higher than average wages, and I do not believe anyone would ascribe these differentials to favoritism towards these groups and discrimination against others.

A growing body of research has attempted to account for the pay gap, and the researchers have come to different conclusions. These studies, however, use different data sources, refer to different populations and control for many, but not always the same set of variables. Even the gross wage gap—the hourly earnings differential before adjusting for diverse characteristics—varies from study to study, ranging from 45 to 7 percent depending on the type of population considered. Studies based on national samples covering the full age range tend to show a gross wage gap of 35 to 40 percent. Studies based on more homogeneous groups, such as holders of advanced degrees or those in specific professions, have found considerably smaller gross wage gaps.

After adjusting for various characteristics, the wage gap narrows. Generally, the most important variables contributing to the adjustment are those that measure the total number of years of work experience, the years of tenure on current job, and the pattern or continuity of previous work experience.

Traditional home responsibilities of married women have been an obstacle to their full commitment to a career. Although women are now combining work and marriage to a much greater extent than in the past, older women in the labor force today have typically spent many years out of the labor force raising their families. Data from the National Longitudinal Survey (NLS) indicate that in 1977 employed white women in their forties had worked only 61 percent of the years after leaving school, and employed black women had worked 68 percent of the years.[5] By contrast, men are usually in the labor force or the military on a continuing basis after leaving school.

In a recent study I examined the contribution of lifetime work experience and other variables using the NLS data for men and women aged 25 to 34. White women's hourly wage rate was found to be 66 percent of white men's—a wage gap of 34 percent. This wage gap narrowed to 12 percent after accounting for the effects of male-female differences in work experience, job tenure, and schooling, as well as differences in plant size and certain job characteristics, such as the years of training required to learn a skill, whether the occupation was hazardous, and whether the occupation had a high concentration of women.

The gross wage gap between black men and black women was 18 percent. The gross wage gap was smaller for blacks than for whites because job-related characteristics of black women and black men are closer than those of white women and white men. Black women have somewhat fewer years of work experience in their teens and early twenties than white women, which may be related to earlier childbearing. They are more likely to work continuously and full time later on, however, and thus accumulate more total work experience and longer tenure on their current jobs than white women. The adjustment for differences in the measured characteristics cited above narrowed the wage gap of black men and women to 9 percent.

Are the remaining, unaccounted-for differences a measure of discrimination in the labor market?

If all the productivity differences between women and men are not accurately identified and measured, labor market discrimination would be overestimated by the unexplained residual. Many variables were omitted from this analysis and from other studies because relevant data are not available. These include details on the quality and vocational orientation of education; on the extent of other work-

[5] O'Neill, 1984.

related investments, such as job search; and on less tangible factors, such as motivation and effort. Differences in these factors could arise from the priority placed on earning an income versus fulfilling home responsibilities. If women, by tradition, assume the primary responsibility for homemaking and raising children, they may be reluctant to take jobs that demand an intense work commitment.

On the other hand, the unexplained residual may underestimate discrimination if some of the included variables, such as years of training to learn a job, or the sex typicality of occupations, partially reflect labor market discrimination. Some employers may deny women entry into lengthy training programs or be reluctant to hire them in traditionally male jobs. It is difficult with available data to distinguish this situation from one where women choose not to engage in training because of uncertainty about their long-run career plans or choose female occupations because they are more compatible with competing responsibilities at home.

Occupational Segregation Although occupational segregation clearly exists, it is in large part the result of many of the same factors that determine earnings: years of schooling, on-the-job training, and other human capital investments, as well as tastes for particular job characteristics. In a recently completed study, I found that women's early expectations about their future life's work—that is, whether they planned to be a homemaker or planned to work outside the home—are strongly related to the occupations they ultimately pursue.[6] Many women who initially planned to be homemakers, in fact, became labor force participants, but they were much more likely to pursue stereotyped female occupations than women who had formed their plans to work at younger ages. Early orientation influences

6 O'Neill, 1983.

early training and schooling decisions, and as a result women may be locked into or out of certain careers. Some women, however, by choice, maintain an ongoing dual career—combining work in the home with an outside job—and this leads to an accommodation in terms of the number of hours that women work and other conditions that influence occupational choice.

Women and men were also found to differ sharply in the environmental characteristics of their occupations. Women were less likely to be in jobs with a high incidence of outdoor work, noisy or hazardous work, or jobs requiring heavy lifting. These differences may reflect employer prejudice or the hostile attitudes of male coworkers, but they may also reflect cultural and physical differences.

In sum, a substantial amount of the differences in wages and in occupations by sex has been statistically linked to investments in work skills acquired in school or on the job. Varied interpretations of these results are possible, however. Thus, the precise amount that can be labeled as the result of choices made by women and their families rather than the result of discrimination by employers is not known.

The Trend in the Pay Gap A major source of frustration to feminists and a puzzle to researchers has been the failure of the gap to narrow over the post–World War II period, despite large increases in women's labor force participation. In fact, the gap in 1982 is somewhat larger than it was in 1955.

The wage gap would not, however, narrow significantly over time unless the productivity or skill of women in the labor force increased relative to men's, or discrimination in the workplace diminished. Because the gross wage gap widened somewhat after 1955, either discrimination increased or women's skills decreased relative to men's. Findings from a recent study suggest that changes in skill, as measured by the changes in the education and work experience of men and women in the labor force, strongly contributed to an increase in the wage gap.[7]

In 1952 women in the labor force had completed 1.6 more years of schooling than men. This difference narrowed sharply so that by 1979 it had disappeared. One reason for this is that the educational level of men advanced more rapidly than that of women during the 1950s. Aided by the GI bill educational benefits, more men attended college. Another reason is that the labor force participation of less educated women increased more rapidly than the participation of highly educated women. Thus, the female labor force became increasingly less selective over time in terms of schooling attainment.

The rise in the number of women in the labor force may also have had an effect on the lifetime work experience of the average working women. A large number of less experienced women entering the labor force may have diluted the experience level of the working women. Although the total number of years of work experience of women is not available for periods of time before the late 1960s, data on job tenure—years with current employer—show that in 1951 men's job tenure exceeded women's job tenure by 1.7 years. This difference widened to 2.7 years in 1962 and then slowly declined, reaching 1.9 years in 1978 and 1.5 years in 1981.

The decline in working women's educational level relative to men's alone would have caused the pay gap to widen by 7 percentage points. The initial widening in the job tenure differential contributed another 2 percentage points to the gap. Together the change in education and job tenure would have increased the wage gap by more than it actually increased. Possibly then, discrimination declined during this period even though the wage gap widened. Since the mid-1960s, educational and work experience differences have moved

in different directions. Male educational attainment rose slightly more than that of working women, which alone would have widened the pay gap slightly. Difference in work experience declined overall. Recently (between 1979 and 1983), a narrowing has occurred in the wage gap, from 68 percent to 72 percent overall.

Evidence from the NLS and other sources suggests that the pay gap is likely to narrow perceptibly in the next decade. Not only are young women working more continuously, but they are also getting higher pay for each year of work experience than they were in the late 1960s. This could reflect a reduction in sex discrimination by employers or a greater willingness of women to invest in market skills, or both. Women's career expectations also seem to be rising. In response to an NLS question asked in 1973, 57 percent of women between 25 and 29 indicated their intention to hold jobs rather than be homemakers when they reach age 35. Among women reaching ages 25 to 29 in 1978, 77 percent expressed their intention to work.

Young women have also greatly increased their educational level relative to men. Female college enrollment increased significantly during the 1970s, while male enrollment fell between 1975 and 1980. Moreover, women have made impressive gains in professional degrees during the 1970s. Work roles and work expectations of women and men may well be merging. As these younger women become a larger component of the female labor force, it is anticipated that the overall wage gap will be reduced.

Are Women's Occupations Underpaid? A major contention of comparable worth supporters is that pay in women's occupations is lower because employers systematically downgrade them. The argument differs from the idea that pay in women's occupations is depressed because of an oversupply to these occupations. An

[7] O'Neill, 1984.

oversupply could arise either because large numbers of women entering the labor force choose these occupations (which is compatible with no discrimination) or because women are barred from some causing an oversupply in others (a discriminatory situation). Although comparable worth advocates have taken the view that overcrowding is caused by restrictive measures, they have lately come to believe that this explanation is not the whole cause of "low payment" in women's jobs.[8] The argument is made that employers can pay less to women's jobs regardless of supply considerations, simply reflecting prejudice against such jobs because they are held by women.

The ability of firms to wield such power is highly questionable. If a firm underpaid workers in women's occupations, in the sense that their wages were held below their real contributions to the firm's receipts, other firms would have a strong incentive to hire workers in these occupations away, bidding up the wages in these occupations. Thus, competition would appear to be a force curtailing employer power. This process could only be thwarted by collusion, an unrealistic prospect considering the hundreds of thousands of firms.

Killingsworth (1984) has suggested that the market for nurses may be an example of collusion by a centralized hospital industry that has conspired to hold wages down. Without more careful analysis of the hospital industry, it is difficult to verify whether this is a valid hypothesis. Basic facts about wages and supply in nursing, however, suggest that collusion either does not exist or is ineffective. Despite a perennial "shortage" of nurses that seems to have existed as far back as one can go, the number of nurses has increased dramatically, both absolutely and as a percentage of the population. In 1960 there were 282 registered nurses per 100,000 population.

8 Hartmann, 1984.

In 1980 there were 506 nurses per 100,000. This rate of increase is even more rapid than the increase in doctors over the past decade, and the supply of doctors has been rapidly increasing. Why did the increase occur? Were women forced into nursing because they were barred from other occupations? That does not seem to be the case in recent times. What has happened is that nursing, along with other medical professions, has experienced a large increase in demand since the middle 1960s when medicare and medicaid were introduced, and private health insurance increased. As a result, the pay of nurses increased more rapidly than in other fields. Between 1960 and 1978 the salary of registered nurses increased by 250 percent, while the pay of all men rose by 206 percent and the pay of all women rose by 193 percent. During the 1970s the rate of pay increase for nurses slowed, which is not surprising considering the increase in supply. And entry of women into nursing school has recently slowed, suggesting a self-correcting mechanism is at work.

Another way to attempt to evaluate the contention that lower pay in female-dominated occupations reflects discrimination is through statistical analysis of the determinants of earnings in occupations. In a recent study, I asked the question—after accounting for measurable differences in skill, do these predominantly female occupations still pay less? In an analysis of data on more than 300 occupations, I found that after adjusting for schooling, training, part-time work, and environmental conditions (but not actual years of work experience or job tenure, which were not available), the proportion female in an occupation was associated with lower pay in that occupation for both women and for men. But the effect was not large. For each 10 percentage point increase in the percent female in an occupation, the wage in the occupation went down by 1.5 percent. Again, however, one is left with a question mark. Are there other characteristics of occupations that women, on the average, may value more highly than men because of home responsibilities or differences in tastes and for which women, more so than men, are willing to accept a lower wage in exchange? Characteristics that come to mind might be a long summer vacation, such as teaching provides, or a steady 9 to 5 job close to home that certain office or shop jobs may provide. The true effect of sex on occupational differences or wage rates is, therefore, another unresolved issue. There are many good reasons why women would be in lower paying occupations than men, even in the absence of sex discrimination on the part of employers. That does not rule out the existence of discrimination, but it weakens the case for seeking an alternative to the market determination of occupational wage rates.

COMPARABLE WORTH IN PRACTICE— THE WASHINGTON STATE EXAMPLE

What would happen if wages were set in accordance with comparable worth standards and independently of market forces? Any large-scale implementation of comparable worth would necessarily be based on job evaluations that assign points for various factors believed to be common to disparate jobs. For example, in the State of Washington, where a comparable worth study was commissioned, a job evaluation firm assisted a committee of 13 politically chosen individuals in rating the jobs used as benchmarks in setting pay in State employment. The committee's task was to assign points on the basis of knowledge and skills, mental demands, accountability, and working conditions. In the 1976 evaluation a registered nurse at level IV was assigned 573 points, the highest number of points of any job—280 points for knowledge and skills, 122 for mental demands, 160 for accountability, and 11 for working conditions. A computer systems analyst at the IV level received a total of only 426

points—212 points for knowledge and skills, 92 points for mental demands, 122 points for accountability, and no points for working conditions. In the market, however, computer systems analysts are among the highest paid workers. National data for 1981 show that they earn 56 percent more than registered nurses. The Washington job evaluation similarly differs radically from the market in its assessment of the value of occupations throughout the job schedule. A clerical supervisor is rated equal to a chemist in knowledge and skills and mental demands, but higher than the chemist in accountability, thereby receiving more total points. Yet the market rewards chemists 41 percent higher pay. The evaluation assigns an electrician the same points for knowledge and skills and mental demands as a level I secretary and 5 points less for accountability. Auto mechanics are assigned lower points than the lowest level homemaker or practical nurse for accountability as well as for working conditions. Truckdrivers are ranked at the bottom, assigned lower points on knowledge and skills, mental demands, and accountability than the lowest ranked telephone operator or retail clerk. The market, however, pays truckdrivers 30 percent more than telephone operators, and the differential is wider for retail clerks.

Should the market pay according to the comparable worth scale? Or is the comparable worth scale faulty? In Washington State, AFSCME, the American Federation of State, County, and Municipal Employees, brought suit against the State on the grounds that failure to pay women according to the comparable worth scale constituted discrimination. Judge Jack E. Tanner agreed and ruled in favor of the union. The decision was based largely on the fact that the State had conducted the study. Whether or not the study was a reasonable standard for nondiscriminatory wage patterns was never an issue. The State, in fact, was disallowed from presenting a witness who would have critically evaluated the study.

What would happen if comparable worth were to be adopted as a pay-setting mechanism? Take the example of registered nurses and computer systems analysts. Nurses are 95 percent female; systems analysts are 25 percent female. If a private firm employing both occupations were required to adopt the rankings from the Washington State comparable worth study, it would likely have to make a significant pay adjustment. It could either lower the salary of systems analysts below that of nurses or raise the pay of nurses above systems analysts. If it lowered the pay of systems analysts, it would likely find it impossible to retain or recruit them. The more popular remedy would be to raise the pay of nurses. If the firm did so, it would also be compelled to raise its prices. Most likely, demand for the firm's product would fall, and the firm would of necessity be required to cut back production. It would seek ways of lowering costs—for example, by reducing the number of registered nurses it employed, trying to substitute less skilled practical nurses and orderlies where possible. Some women would benefit—those who keep their jobs at the higher pay. But other women would lose—those nurses who become unemployed, as well as other workers who are affected by the cutback.

Of course, if the employer is a State government, the scenario may be somewhat different. The public sector does not face the rigors of competition to the same extent as a private firm. I suspect this is one reason why public sector employees seem to be in the forefront of the comparable worth movement. The public sector could not force workers to work for them if the remedy was to lower the wage in high-paying male jobs. But that is not usually what employee groups request. It can, however, pay the bill for the higher pay required to upgrade wages in female-dominated occupations by raising taxes.

But in the long run, the State may have financing problems, since taxpayers may not be willing to foot the bill, and the result would be similar to that in the private firm—unemployment of government workers, particularly women in predominantly female occupations, as government services are curtailed.

CONCLUDING REMARKS

Advocates of comparable worth see it as a way of raising women's economic status and, quite expectedly, tend to minimize costs. A typical comment is as follows (Center for Philosophy and Public Policy):

> Certainly, the costs incurred would vary widely depending on the scope of the approach chosen. But the economic costs of remedying overt discrimination should not prove staggering. Employers and business interests have a long history of protesting that fair treatment of workers will result in massive economic disruption. Similar claims were made preceding the abolishment of child labor and the establishment of the minimum wage, and none of the dire predictions came to pass.

Evidently the author is unaware of the numerous economic studies showing the disemployment effects of the minimum wage. However, what this statement fails to see is that comparable worth is in a bigger league than the child labor law or the minimum wage laws that have actually been implemented. It is far more radical. Instituting comparable worth by means of studies such as the one conducted in Washington State could be more like instituting a $15 an hour minimum wage or passing sweeping legislation like Prohibition. Moreover, the costs in terms of economic distortion would be much more profound than the dollars required to pay the bills. Curiously, this is recognized by one comparable worth proponent,[9] who then sug-

9 Barrett, 1984.

gests "that we give very serious consideration to the idea that firms that do raise pay for 'disadvantaged occupations' get special tax incentives for capital equipment that will raise the productivity of these workers. We can't expect firms to swallow these losses; that's crazy." Barrett is willing to go to these lengths because she thinks it might be a way to raise the incomes of poor women heading families on welfare. Long-term welfare recipients, however, are not the women holding the jobs covered by comparable worth schemes. The work participation of women in this situation is very low. Moreover, the lesson of studies of minimum wage effects has been that those who are most vulnerable to disemployment as a result of wage hikes that exceed national market rates are the disadvantaged—those with little education, poor training, and little work experience. Comparable worth would hurt, not help, these women. Subsidies to try to prevent these effects from occurring would be impractical to implement and prohibitively costly.

With all the difficulties that would ensue from implementing comparable worth, it is striking that it would not achieve many of the original goals of the women's movement such as the representation of women as electricians, physicists, managers, or plumbers. In fact, it would likely retard the substantial progress that has been made in the past decade. Younger women have dramatically shifted their school training and occupational choices. They have been undertaking additional training and schooling because the higher pay they can obtain from the investment makes it worthwhile. Raising the pay of clerical jobs, teaching, and nursing above the market rates would make it less rewarding to prepare for other occupations and simply lead to an oversupply to women's fields, making it still harder to find a stable solution to the problem of occupational segregation.

Another byproduct of comparable worth is that it diverts attention away from the real problems of discrimination that may arise. Such problems need not be confined to women in traditional jobs. Pay differences between men and women performing the same job in the same firm at the same level of seniority may no longer be an important source of discrimination. The form discrimination more likely takes is through behavior that denies women entry into on-the-job training or promotions on the same basis as men. The obvious solution is the direct one—namely, allowing or encouraging women whose rights are being denied to bring suit. Existing laws were intended to cover this very type of problem.

The pay-setting procedure in all levels of government employment is another area where remedies other than comparable worth would be more direct and effective. Governments usually do not have the flexibility to meet market demands. The need to adhere to rigid rules under considerable political pressure may result in paying wages that are too high in some occupations and too low in others. (By "too high" I mean that an ample supply of workers could be obtained at a lower wage). This could occur if the private plants covered in a pay survey for a particular occupation are themselves paying above market—for example, as the result of a powerful union. Such a situation could lead to unnecessary pay differentials between certain occupations that are male dominated (which are more likely to be represented by such strong unions) and other male, mixed, and female occupations whose private sector wages are more competitive. Comparable worth is not the solution, however, since it does not address the problem. Pay-setting procedures can be improved by changing the nature of the pay surveys and by introducing market criteria—for example, by considering the length of the queue to enter different government jobs and the length of time vacancies stay open. Such changes may help women and also improve the efficiency of government.

Dramatic changes have occurred in women's college enrollment, in labor force participation, and in entrance into formerly male occupations, particularly in the professions. These changes are taking place because of fundamental changes in women's role in the economy and in the family—changes that themselves reflect a response to rising wage rates as well as changing social attitudes. Pay set according to comparable worth would distort wage signals, inducing inappropriate supply response and unemployment. If women have been discouraged by society or barred by employers from entering certain occupations, the appropriate response is to remove the barriers, not try to repeal supply and demand. Comparable worth is no shortcut to equality.

REFERENCES

Barrett, Nancy. 1984. "Poverty, Welfare and Comparable Worth," in Phyllis Schlafly, ed., *Equal Pay for Unequal Work, A Conference on Comparable Work.*

Gold, Michael Evan. 1983. *A Dialogue on Comparable Worth.*

Hartmann, Heidi I. 1984. "The Case for Comparable Worth," in Phyllis Schlafly, ed., *Equal Pay for Unequal Work, A Conference on Comparable Work.*

Killingsworth, Mark. 1984. *Statement on Comparable Worth.* Testimony before the Joint Economic Committee, U.S. Congress, Apr. 10, 1984.

O'Neill, June. 1983. "The Determinants and Wage Effects of Occupational Segregation." Working Paper, The Urban Institute.

O'Neill, June. 1984. "Earnings Differentials: Empirical Evidence and Causes," in G. Schmid, ed., *Discrimination and Equalization in the Labor Market: Employment Policies for Women in Selected Countries.*

O'Neill, June. 1984. "The Trend in the Male-Female Wage Gap in the United States." *Journal of Labor Economics,* October.

Rytina, Nancy F. 1982. "Earnings of Men and Women: A Look at Specific Occupations." *Monthly Labor Review,* April 1982.

QUESTIONS FOR DISCUSSION

1. How do you measure comparable worth?
2. Do comparable worth laws involve too much government control of private economic conditions?
3. Should (female) teachers be paid as much as (male) truck drivers?
4. Are teachers more important than truck drivers?
5. Is comparable worth an idea whose time has passed?
6. How do you account for the disparity of income between men and women?

RECOMMENDED READINGS

BAIRD, CHARLES W. "Comparable Worth: The Labor Theory of Value and Worse." *Government Union Review* 6 (Winter 1985), pp. 1–29.

HARTMANN, HEIDI I., ed. *Comparable Worth: New Directions for Research.* Washington, D.C.: National Academy Press, 1985.

JOHANSEN, ELAINE. "Comparable Worth: The Character of a Controversy." *Public Administration Review* 45 (Sept.–Oct. 1985), pp. 631–35.

KRAUTHAMMER, CHARLES. "From Bad to Comparable Worth." *Regulation* 8 (July–Aug. 1984), pp. 31–34.

LIVERNASH, E. ROBERT, ed. *Comparable Worth: Issues and Alternatives.* 2nd ed. Washington, D.C.: Equal Employment Advisory Council, 1984.

MAJORS, BRUCE POWELL. "The Comparable Worth Muddle." *Journal of Contemporary Studies* 7 (Summer 1984), pp. 49–57.

ORIENT, JANE M. "Comparable Worth Versus Civil Liberty: Are Feminists Pro-Choice?" *Freeman* 35 (June 1985), pp. 332–40.

U.S. COMMISSION ON CIVIL RIGHTS. *Comparable Worth: Issue for the 80's. A Consultation of the U.S. Commission on Civil Rights.* June 6–7, 1984. Washington, D.C.: Commission on Civil Rights, 1984. 2 vols.

U.S. CONG., SENATE. *Potential Inequities Affecting Women.* Hearings before the Committee on Finance, 98th Cong., 1st Sess., 1983.

YES KEEPING WOMEN OUT: MEN'S CLUBS HAVE CIRCLED THEIR WAGONS

Sydney H. Schanberg

One would have thought that by 1984, after decades of civil rights progress and the lifting of barrier after barrier, the men's clubs in New York City would have done the civilized thing and ended their holy war to keep women out. After all, don't we imagine our city to be the center of civilized thought and discourse, the beacon of liberty for all, the example-setter for the nation?

But the battle against admitting women still rages. A bill will soon be approved by the City Council and signed into law by Mayor Koch that will, by its language, place many of these men's clubs in the category of public accommodations and thereby bring them under the city's laws against bias—and that includes bias on the basis of sex. Yet these institutions plan to dig in their heels and challenge the statute.

The clubs—which have such names as the Century Association, the Union League and the University Club—cite the Constitution for their right to discriminate. It's the part that reads: "Congress shall make no law . . . abridging . . . the right of the people peaceably to assemble. . . ."

And this right of assembly, they say, is

Sidney H. Schanberg, "Keeping Women Out: Men's Clubs Have Circled Their Wagons," *New York Times*, Sept. 18, 1984, p. A27. Copyright © 1983/84 by The New York Times Company. Reprinted by permission.

the source of their privilege to keep women out. It would seem they don't mind appearing foolish in public. It's apparently the price they're willing to pay to bar women from their groaning boards.

Another argument the clubs use to justify their stance is that they are totally private and can therefore be selective about membership without interference from government. That's the same argument that clubs once used to bar Jews and blacks and Irish and Italians and others.

I agree that ideally government should be nowhere in sight on this issue; the clubs should integrate entirely on their own. They should act out of conscience, not out of coercion.

But they have chosen a different course. They want to fight, to stonewall. They have a lawyer, who represents the umbrella New York State Club Association, and he has indicated that they will not voluntarily lower their barriers. "The incursion into private club life would be chilling," he told a City Council committee.

They've spent lots of time and dollars trying to hold off the inevitable outcome. For several years, they've been able to bottle up a similar piece of state legislation in the sympathetic Republican-controlled Senate. They were also successful for a long time in the City Council, until the Mayor threw his full weight behind the city bill. (Now, disingenuously, they plan to argue that the city statute is unconstitutional because it pre-empts the state's anti-bias law.)

When women who would like to join point out that membership in some of these clubs is often a necessity for career advancement in their fields, male members counter by contending virginally that no business is conducted within their august walls. People laugh when they say this, but they don't seem to mind.

These clubs are nothing more than extensions of the workplace, where business negotiations take place and deals are made. The National Club Association has estimated that nearly 40 percent of the income of city clubs comes directly from employer-paid memberships. And most members who pay their own dues and club expenses treat them as deductions on their personal income tax returns.

Moreover, most of these clubs survive financially not from members' payments, but from the extra money earned through the catering and conference-room facilities they provide to *non-members*. So much for the fiction of the "private" club.

Nothing terrible is going to happen when these clubs integrate and accept women. A few all-male clubs here and there around the country have already done so, and there were no cataclysms, no awesome changes in ritual. New York's male clubs would save themselves a great deal of fuss and an equal amount of image if they were to open their doors like gentlemen without being forced to.

One doubts that the courts will have much patience with their arguments. Last week, a state judge in Maryland stopped short of ordering a country club to admit women but ruled that because it does not do so, it must lose its $186,000-a-year real estate tax exemption. And also last week, a Federal judge in New York narrowed the definition of a private club in ruling against a Long Island beach and tennis club whose manager told two members their guests were not welcome because they were Jewish.

Within the key male clubs, there exist minorities who are lobbying for peaceful integration. One wishes them success. Integration after a civil war might be a mess.

NO LA DIFFÉRENCE

Lewis H. Lapham

When I met Grierson for lunch the other day at the Italian Pavilion, he was, as usual, in the throes of a cause. Earlier that morning, he had signed a petition recommending the admission of women to the Century Association, and he was impressed by the loveliness of his hero's pose on the ramparts of justice.

Lewis H. Lapham, *"La Différence," New York Times,* Mar. 4, 1983, p. A31. Copyright © 1983/84 by The New York Times Company. Reprinted by permission.

"This isn't Victorian England," he said. "When will people understand that women cannot be discriminated against?"

Having known Grierson for many years, I was surprised that he didn't also say that some of his best friends were women, that he had grown up in the same neighborhoods with them and that they were amazingly good dancers. During the middle 1960's, Grierson often mentioned the gentleness of the North Vietnamese, whom he regarded as an endangered species as sorely in need of East Hampton lawn parties as the blue whale. Now that he had come to the rescue of women, he wished to invest them with a moral beauty as carefully groomed as his own.

"You might find this hard to believe," he said, "but there are still a lot of people out there who don't know that men and women share the same feelings, think the same thoughts, speak the same language and live the same lives."

Because I counted myself among the dwindling number of such people, I didn't find it at all hard to believe. Since the age of 30, it never has occurred to me to doubt that men and women inhabit reciprocal hemispheres of thought, feeling and language. Except under duress, and then, only with a good deal of shouting, the two genders seldom come close to living the same lives; nor do they look like one another, speak in the same tones of voice, write the same prose, value the same passions or plot the courses of their destinies against the same coordinates of space and time.

Grierson went on with his sermon for the better part of an hour, but rather than argue with him, which would have been as futile as arguing with a Marxist or a twice-born Christian, I passed the time wondering how it came to be that a man of 45 could confuse the drama of human sexuality—sometimes tragic, sometimes comic, always subtle and often beautiful—with a script written for afternoon television. To Grierson, the difference between the genders consisted in styles of dress. Apparently he thought of human nature as a kind of nursery-school clay in which he could model tiny and fantastic images copied from the intellectual fashion magazines.

His naïveté was earnest and well-meant. In other years and other rooms, I had listened to his touching confessions of faith in Consciousness III, the economic theory of zero-growth and the redeeming purity of Jimmy Carter's politics.

But why did he think he could still afford the luxury of ignoring biological fact as well as the lesson, however poorly learned, of his own experience? To my certain knowledge, he had read at least four novels written by women, and his losses in the divorce courts had stripped him not only of his holdings in General Motors but also of his house in Nantucket.

Coming to the crux of his argument, he was saying something about how the admission of women wouldn't change the character of the establishment and how certain women of his acquaintance took offense (properly, he thought) at being excluded from their chance at the big-time literary and financial deals.

Both statements reflected Grierson's considerable talent for denying any reality of which he disapproved or which had failed to receive departmental recognition at Harvard. As late as 1981, he still believed that the world's supply of oil wouldn't last through the summer vacation.

Obviously the admission of women to the Century Association (or to any other club, school, gymnasium, caucus or men's room) would change the character of the place. A women's choir has a different sound than a men's chorus. Join them together, and the harmony of voices makes still a third music. Within the hemispheres of their own sex, men and women speak to one another in ways different from the way in which they speak for publication. This is not to say that one way of speaking is better than the others, merely that they are different. I often have thought that among themselves women communicate in the manner of dolphins, precisely measuring their relative positions in the social sea by means of sonar-like signals inaudible to the ears of men, but this is another subject and not one that I would care to press at a dance sponsored by the American Civil Liberties Union.

Nature divides the whole of its creation into opposing forces (proton and electron, positive and negative, matter and antimatter, masculine and feminine) in order that their dynamic symmetries might decode and organize the unlicked chaos. The clarity of gender makes possible the human dialectic. Let the lines of balanced tension go slack and the structure dissolve into the ooze of androgyny and narcissism.

As for the proposition that the loss of access to the Century Club cheats women of their inalienable right of avarice, this also is a canard. A woman might as well say that she had been denied her constitutional privileges because she wasn't elected governor of New Jersey or made a godperson in the Mafia. Of the property still in the possession of private individuals, roughly 60 percent rests in the safekeeping of women. The daughters of affluence outnumber the sons, and heiresses live longer than their husbands or brothers. The deals done in the nation's secret trysting places (bedroom, kitchen, powder room, dinner table, spa) have a far more direct bearing on the redistribution of the national wealth than all the acts of Congress.

Watching him taste the wine that he pronounced "companionable," it occurred to me that Grierson was either rich enough or frightened enough to imagine that he could substitute words for things. Like so many of his comrades trooping along behind the skirts of the women's movement, he found abstractions so much easier to deal with than facts; so much more refined and so much less likely to make an emotional mess. He could afford to believe that the important differences between the genders were "socially fostered" because he could afford the cost of his opinion.

The nation as a whole paid a much heavier price for its collective fantasy (cherished by a good many of Grierson's friends in Government and the universities) that the happy villagers in North and South Vietnam wished to grow up to look and think like Henry Cabot Lodge.

By denying the reality of women, Grierson granted himself an exemption from the war between the sexes. He didn't have to confront his wife, his mistress or his own feminine impulses; he didn't have to raise his voice or try to impose what little was left of his well-bred will. If things didn't turn out as advertised in the syllabus circulated by the New School for Social Research, certainly it wouldn't be Grierson's fault. He could assign the blame for his inadequacy and fear to the unseen, impersonal and anonymous forces hidden under the blankets of "culturalization."

The pornographers exploit the same lie. They also deny the reality of women; they also think of women as little lumps of modeling clay subject to the shaping tools of commercial or sentimental abstraction. The possibilities implicit in this line of observation struck me as too subversive for Grierson's delicate politics, and I was grateful when he began to speak of oysters. About oysters and Victorian England, Grierson is never wrong.

QUESTIONS FOR DISCUSSION

1. Are private social clubs protected by the right to privacy?
2. Why should women want to join private men's clubs?
3. Is there a constitutional right to associate with whom one pleases that may differ from the constitutional obligation of government to treat all persons equally?
4. Should men be allowed to join private women's clubs?

5. Should all private clubs be treated alike from a constitutional point of view, or are there important distinctions to be made about the particular character of individual private clubs?
6. Groucho Marx once observed that any club that would admit him was not worth joining. Discuss.

RECOMMENDED READINGS

ARCHER, DENNIS W. "Blackballed! The Case against Private Clubs." 10 *Barrister* 22 (Spring 1983).

GOODWIN, CATHARINE M. "Challenging the Private Clubs: Sex Discrimination Plaintiffs Barred at the Door." 13 *Southwestern University Law Review* 237 (1982).

MISHAN, E. J. "Was the Women's Liberation Movement Really Necessary?" *Encounter* (London) 64 (Jan. 1985), pp. 7–20.

NATIONAL CLUB ASSOCIATION. "In Defense of Selective Membership Policies" (Reference Series). Washington, D.C.: National Club Association, 1981.

SCHAFRAN, LYNN HECHT. "Private Clubs: Women Need Not Apply." *Foundation News* 23 (Jan.–Feb. 1982), pp. 3–8.

SCHANBERG, SYDNEY H. "Some of Their Best Friends." *New York Times*, Mar. 26, 1983, p. 23.

IV FREEDOM IN CRIMINAL PROCEEDINGS

With certain exceptions, such as kidnapping and drug trafficking, criminal law is state law, and its provisions will vary from state to state. Similarly the basic tasks of law enforcement and criminal justice have been viewed traditionally as state functions and not those of the national government. Not only did the Supreme Court refuse to apply the procedural safeguards of the Bill of Rights (such as the Fifth Amendment guarantee against self-incrimination) to the states, but for almost 150 years the Court declined to review state trials. Ensuring fairness in state trials was, it was usually believed, the state's responsibility.

But beginning in the 1920s the Supreme Court started to exercise close scrutiny of state criminal trials.[1] Nevertheless a double standard of criminal justice persisted: The few trials conducted in the federal courts were held to the high procedural standards of the Bill of Rights; state trials were subjected to a less rigorous review, although the Supreme Court was prepared to intervene in extreme instances in which fairness had been denied.[2] And most states had their own Bills of Rights.

Over the years increasing federal review of state criminal proceedings revealed glaring discrepancies from state to state. More serious, perhaps, the Supreme Court became concerned that considerable unfairness sometimes resulted because of misbehavior by state law enforcement officers. In *Rochin v. California,* for example, the Court found the use of a stomach pump by police officers to recover evidence that a suspect had swallowed to be contrary to a fundamental sense of justice.[3] The Court also commenced to overturn convictions involving confessions allegedly coerced from defendants, even though the facts confessed to were independently verifiable.[4]

In the 1960s the Supreme Court began to exercise even closer review of state criminal cases. And gradually on a case-by-case basis—as egregious examples of official misconduct presented themselves—the Court incorporated virtually all of the procedural guarantees of the Bill of Rights under the Due Process Clause of the Fourteenth Amendment and made them applicable to the states. (See Chapter I.) This extension of federal constitutional guarantees has been controversial. Many believe that the efforts of the Supreme Court to protect the rights of the defendant in criminal cases have enmeshed law-enforcement officials in excessive technicality and contributed to a rising crime problem. Others agree with Justice Louis B. Brandeis, who observed that "The greatest dangers to liberty lurk in insidious encroachment by men of zeal, well-meaning, but without understanding."[5] Yet another point of view pertains to the nature of the federal union. State judges and state law enforcement officers understandably resent the intrusion of national authority into the realm of criminal procedure. The *nationalization* of the Bill of Rights and the imposition of various interpretations that have evolved from federal cases have been especially galling to the states.

Today criminal justice is a major concern of constitutional law. It now encompasses a single body of national jurisprudence. But it is doubtful whether the establishment of universal standards that are judicially enforceable has had any prolonged deleterious effect on day-to-day law enforcement.

UNREASONABLE SEARCHES AND SEIZURES

The Fourth Amendment to the Constitution states that

> The right of the people to be secure in their persons, houses, papers, and effects, against unreasonable searches and seizures, shall not be violated, and no Warrants shall issue, but upon probable cause, supported by Oath or affirmation, and particularly describing the place to be searched, and the persons or things to be seized.

Thus law enforcement officials have no generalized right to invade a person's home and cannot search someone except under certain conditions. These conditions are highly complex, and the Supreme Court often disagrees on the exact parameters of the Fourth Amendment.

The general rule is that the Constitution protects persons, not places.[6] In addition, it does not forbid all searches and seizures, only *unreasonable* ones. A search is considered reasonable if it is conducted with a person's consent or pursuant to a valid search warrant issued by a magistrate after the police have sworn under oath that they have *probable cause* to justify the search. The proceeding must be at arm's length—that is, the magistrate cannot be merely a rubber stamp for the police.[7] The warrant must describe specifically what places are to be searched and what is to be seized. The *expectation of privacy* prevents warrantless searches of hotel rooms, rental accommodations, and even telephone booths. But once the police have obtained a search warrant, they may enter into places normally considered private, including one's home, and may even break and enter if such entry is the only means by which the search warrant can be executed. In this context it is independent judicial authority—not the police—that has authorized the search, and it is the courts that stand as guardians of Fourth Amendment rights.[8]

THE EXCLUSIONARY RULE

In 1914 in the case of *Weeks v. United States* the Supreme Court held that evidence obtained illegally (that is, in violation of the Fourth Amendment) must be suppressed and excluded from criminal prosecutions. Violation of this *exclusionary rule* would lead to automatic reversal on appeal of any criminal conviction obtained thereby. But the *Weeks* case involved a federal agent, and the exclusionary rule that the Court enunciated at that time applied only to federal court proceedings, not to the states.[9] (See Chapter I.)

In 1949 in *Wolf v. Colorado* the Court held that while the Fourth Amendment guarantee against unreasonable searches and seizures applied to the states, the exclusionary rule did not. The Court was reluctant at that time to establish a national standard of criminal justice and refused to restrain the diversity that then existed among the states. The Court suggested that civil suits against police officers who trespassed and seized evidence illegally provided an adequate remedy by which a defendant's rights could be protected.[10]

By 1961 it had become increasingly clear that the civil remedy was, in many instances, no longer adequate. Police were seldom prosecuted for making illegal searches and were often unable to pay civil damages. This reassessment by the Court traces to the action of Cleveland police, who, without a warrant, broke into the home of Dollree Mapp in search of drugs, ransacked the house, and, finding no drugs, arrested her for possession of obscene pictures that they had discovered. The Supreme Court, in the leading case of *Mapp v. Ohio,* reversed the conviction, holding that the action by the police constituted unreasonable search and seizure because they had not obtained a search warrant, although they had ample time to do so. More important, the Court for the first time held that the evidence obtained illegally could not be introduced at a state trial.[11] This ruling marked not only the application of the federal exclusionary rule to the states but the commencement of a heightened concern by the Supreme Court to the realities of criminal jurisdiction at the state level.

The decision in *Mapp v. Ohio* marked the start of the nationalization of criminal justice. The exclusionary rule was adopted to prevent police misconduct. It had been applied to federal law enforcement officials since 1914, and it was generally perceived to have provided ample protection in federal cases. But its broad application to the states—where the vast bulk of law enforcement problems arise—has been bitterly contested both on the grounds of federalism and in terms of burdening the police unnecessarily. (Local law enforcement, it is sometimes argued, is much more immediate and frequently requires an instantaneous response, whereas federal law enforcement through such agencies as the Federal Bureau of Investigation permits a more careful and deliberate approach that makes the application for search warrants relatively routine.) The most vehement objections to the application of the exclusionary rule to state and local law enforcement comes from those who question why criminals should be set free because of misconduct by the police.

Should the Exclusionary Rule Be Preserved?

The Supreme Court appears to be bitterly divided on the exclusionary rule. A majority of the Court appear to have pulled back from the full rigor of the rule to permit various exceptions to it by police officers acting in good faith. The so-called *good faith exception* does not require the exclusion of evidence obtained by police "in a reasonable belief that they obtained it in a constitutional manner,"[12] but conflicting Court decisions make unclear the circumstances in which the *exception* might apply.

The Congress has also addressed the issue of the exclusionary rule through legislation designed to effect its repeal. But that legislation has not passed. In the debate that follows, Professor Leon Friedman of Hofstra University and Steven R. Schlesinger of the Catholic University of America present alternative viewpoints as to the merits of the exclusionary rule. The statement of each was made to the subcommittee of the Senate Judiciary Committee that was considering legislation to overturn the rule in federal court proceedings. The student should note that Friedman's presentation is directed primarily to the operation of the exclusionary rule in the federal context. Schlesinger's statement is more broadly framed and centers on the rule's application to the states and its overall effect on law enforcement.

CRIME AND PUNISHMENT

The constitutional guarantees pertaining to criminal justice are fundamental freedoms Americans enjoy. In addition to the Fourth Amendment's prohibition against unreasonable searches and seizures, the Fifth Amendment protects the individual from self-incrimination and permits him or her from being tried twice for the same offense (*double jeopardy*). Equally important are the other procedural guarantees of the Bill of Rights: The Sixth Amendment requires "a speedy and public trial, by an impartial jury" and ensures the right "to have the Assistance of Counsel for . . . defense"; the Eighth Amendment forbids excessive bail and fines from being levied and prohibits "cruel and unusual punishments."

The debates that follow examine various aspects of these guarantees and their place in democratic society. For example, the Sixth Amendment right to a speedy trial is often difficult to attain given the backlog of cases that clog most court dockets. A *plea bargain,* by which a defendant pleads guilty to a lesser offense, often permits prosecution and the courts to proceed more efficiently with the remaining cases before them. But does plea bargaining protect the rights of the accused? Similarly the Sixth Amendment's requirement of a "public" trial sometimes raises the question of unfair trial publicity. Does excessive coverage by newspapers and television deny the defendant the right to a fair trial? And what about television in the courtroom itself? Can that be prejudicial? Finally the issue of the death penalty often divides our interpretation of the Eighth Amendment's prohibition of cruel and unusual punishment. The majority of the Supreme Court have held that the Constitution itself is no bar to capital punishment, but their decisions have raised many obstacles to carrying it out.

Should Plea Bargaining Be Abolished?

The essence of the Bill of Rights guarantees involving criminal procedure is to ensure a fair trial for the defendant. Does *plea bargaining* accomplish that? To be sure, the defendant who *cops a plea* is assured a lesser sentence than he or she *might* otherwise be given following a trial if found guilty. But when defendants plead guilty to a lesser offense, they give up their constitutional rights and under most circumstances are forever prevented from raising objections to their conviction. More serious, perhaps, defense attorneys are often under the same caseload pressures as prosecutors. It is worrisome that a harried defense counsel may advise his or her client to plead guilty to a lesser offense rather than fighting a protracted (and expensive) court battle that might prove his or her innocence.

In the debate that follows, Professor Thomas W. Church, Jr., of Oakland University argues that the advantages of permitting plea bargaining far outweigh its disadvantages. But Church insists on four requirements:

1. The defendant must always have the alternative of a fair trial.
2. The defendant must be represented throughout the negotiations by competent counsel.
3. Both defense and prosecution must have equal access to all information likely to bear on the case should it go to trial.
4. Both sides should have sufficient resources to take the case to trial if an acceptable agreement cannot be obtained.

These criteria cannot be guaranteed. The lack of adequate financial resources to take a case to trial is frequently a problem. But more important, as Moise Berger argues, plea bargaining is inherently corrupting. Berger is a county attorney of Maricopa County, Arizona, and it has been his experience that the process of plea bargaining corrupts the prosecutor who can make a deal and avoid time-consuming litigation; it weakens public confidence in the criminal justice system by substituting "bargain justice" for a fair and impartial trial; and it encourages negligence by dispensing justice outside the glare of public scrutiny.

Should Cameras Be Allowed in the Courtroom?

When constitutional values collide, the outcome is never satisfactory. Freedom of the press (which includes television) is one of the most basic democratic values.

But the right of a defendant to a fair trial may be even more precious. Are there circumstances in which media coverage of a trial may have such an impact that the basic business of the courtroom is violated? On the other hand, does the public have a First Amendment right of access that ought not be infringed?

For the most part the Supreme Court has tilted in favor of access, unless the impact of excessive coverage *demonstrably* prejudices the trial. For example, the murder conviction of Dr. Samuel Sheppard was overturned by the Court in 1966 because of "trial by newspaper," although the justices rebuked the trial judge for failing to take positive steps to control the courtroom behavior of the press.[13] But in 1975 in *Nebraska Press Association v. Stuart* a unanimous Supreme Court struck down a so-called Nebraska gag order imposed by the trial court in another sensational murder trial. Justice William J. Brennan, Jr., stated that prior restraints on the press were "constitutionally impermissible" even as a means of ensuring a fair trial.[14]

In the embezzlement trial of Texas wheeler-dealer Billie Sol Estes in 1965, it was television coverage, not the newspapers, that caused the problem. According to Justice Thomas C. Clark (who spoke for the Court's plurality), the precise effect of television could not be gauged, but that it had a prejudicial effect on the jurors could not be doubted.[15] But by 1981 the Supreme Court had apparently changed its mind. In *Chandler v. Florida* a unanimous Court held that television coverage of a trial did not necessarily amount to a violation of Sixth Amendment rights. It was up to the defendant to prove that the cameras had a prejudicial effect—thus shifting the burden of proof to those who opposed television in the courtroom.[16]

In the debate that follows, two Florida attorneys with direct experience with televised trials dispute the effect of cameras in the courtroom. Talbot D'Alemberte argues that not only does television conform with the public's right to know but that the camera was "so unobtrusive that everyone in the court ignored it." By contrast Joel Hirschhorn believes that television threatens to remove the trial from the impartiality of the courtroom to the partisan forum of public opinion.

Is the Death Penalty Justified?

The Eighth Amendment's prohibition of cruel and unusual punishments prevents the use of torture and the holding of prisoners in despicable, unsanitary conditions that involve "the unnecessary and wanton inflection of pain."[17] It also prevents punishments that are grossly disproportionate to the severity of the crime. But it does not, in and of itself, prohibit the death penalty. The Supreme Court has dealt with the relation of capital punishment to the Eighth Amendment in numerous cases,[18] and the clear holding of the Court is that the death penalty does not constitute cruel and unusual punishment if imposed for the crime of murder.[19]

But the Court has been exceedingly reluctant to sanction the death penalty in less than extreme circumstances involving "the death of the victim." It has overturned Georgia's law authorizing the death penalty for rape.[20] It has imposed stringent procedural requirements on prosecutors and judges to ensure careful consideration of the character of the accused and whatever mitigating circumstances might be relevant.[21] It has held that the use of automatic death sentences for certain crimes (killing a policeman, for example) does indeed violate the Eighth Amendment[22] and has indicated that it will also overturn a death sentence in cases where the jury was given no choice but to impose capital punishment or allow the accused to go free. Juries must be able to convict for a lesser offense.[23]

But the Supreme Court's basic holding, delivered in the leading case of *Gregg v. Georgia,* has clearly affirmed that the death penalty is constitutional. That decision was reaffirmed in *McCleskey v. Kemp,* rejecting a challenge that capital punishment was more likely to be inflicted on black defendants than on whites and therefore violated the Equal Protection Clause of the Fourteenth Amendment.[24]

The fact that a majority of the Supreme Court has held that capital punishment was not unconstitutional does not diminish the moral issue involved in taking a life as punishment. Nowhere was that issue posed more sharply, in fact, than in *Gregg v. Georgia.* In the debate that follows, the Court's position, presented by Justice Potter Stewart, traces the history of the death penalty in the United States and explains how, when properly confined and restricted, it is not inconsistent with established views of justice and due process.

The opposite position, resting on moral imperatives as well as constitutional grounds, is ably articulated by Justice Thurgood Marshall. In his view the death penalty neither deters nor furthers any "legitimate notion of retribution." As a result it is "an excessive penalty forbidden by the Eighth and Fourteenth Amendments."

In reading the arguments of Justices Stewart and Marshall, the student should note that Gregg had been convicted of murder and robbery in the death of two persons who had picked him up while he was hitchhiking. The trial judge had adhered closely to the standards previously enunciated by the Supreme Court and had instructed the jury that it "would not be authorized to consider the penalty of death" unless it first found beyond reasonable doubt that the crime of murder had been committed in aggravating circumstances.[25] Accordingly, with all procedural safeguards observed, the only question for the Supreme Court was whether the death sentence per se constituted "cruel and unusual punishment."

NOTES

1. *Moore v. Dempsey,* 261 U.S. 86 (1923).
2. *Powell v. Alabama,* 287 U.S. 45 (1932).
3. 342 U.S. 165 (1952).
4. *Ashcraft v. Tennessee,* 322 U.S. 143 (1944); *Watts v. Indiana,* 338 U.S. 49 (1949).

5. *Olmstead v. United States,* 277 U.S. 438 (1928), dissenting.

6. *Katz v. United States,* 389 U.S. 347 (1967).

7. *Lo-Ji Sales, Inc. v. New York,* 442 U.S. 319 (1979).

8. For a useful summary of Fourth Amendment holdings, see Wayne R. La Fave, *Search and Seizure: A Treatise on the Fourth Amendment* (St. Paul, Minn.: West, 1978 with supplements).

9. 232 U.S. 383 (1914).

10. 338 U.S. 25 (1949).

11. 367 U.S. 643 (1961).

12. *Illinois v. Gates,* 462 U.S. 318 (1983).

13. *Sheppard v. Maxwell,* 348 U.S. 333 (1966).

14. 427 U.S. 539 (1976), Brennan, J., concurring.

15. *Estes v. Texas,* 381 U.S. 532 (1965).

16. *Chandler v. Florida,* 449 U.S. 560 (1981).

17. *Rhodes v. Chapman,* 452 U.S. 337 (1981).

18. See, for example, Raoul Berger, *Death Penalties: The Supreme Court's Obstacle Course* (Cambridge: Harvard University Press, 1982). Compare Charles L. Black, *Capital Punishment: The Inevitability of Caprice and Mistake* (New York: W. W. Norton, 1974).

19. *Gregg v. Georgia,* 428 U.S. 153 (1976).

20. *Coker v. Georgia,* 433 U.S. 584 (1977).

21. *Roberts v. Louisiana,* 431 U.S. 675 (1977).

22. *Woodson v. North Carolina,* 428 U.S. 280 (1976).

23. *Beck v. Alabama,* 447 U.S. 625 (1980).

24. Supreme Court Docket No. 84–6811 (decided Apr. 22, 1987).

25. *Gregg v. Georgia,* 428 U.S. 153 (1976).

16 *Should the exclusionary rule be preserved?*

YES IN DEFENSE OF THE EXCLUSIONARY ROLE

Leon Friedman

My name is Leon Friedman and I welcome the opportunity to testify before this committee on S.101 and S.751 on behalf of the American Civil Liberties Union.

The two bills would limit or eliminate the exclusionary rule in federal criminal proceedings. S.101 would eliminate the exclusionary rule in federal court except where a Fourth Amendment violation was "intentional" or "substantial." We believe that this proposed legislation is unconstitutional. Furthermore it is ambiguous in its reach and uncertain in its application and would create severe problems in the criminal justice process.

S.751 would eliminate the exclusionary rule in federal criminal proceedings entirely and would provide a limited damage remedy against the United States and authorize disciplinary action against those who violate a citizen's Fourth Amendment rights. This bill is, in our view, beyond Congress' power to enact.

Fundamentally we believe that any legislation to eliminate, limit or restrict the exclusionary rule is unconstitutional, unwise and undesirable. The exclusionary rule, though a judicially made remedy, is of constitutional dimension. Furthermore the rule serves the best interests of both law enforcement and the privacy interests of all Americans.

U.S. Cong., Senate, *The Exclusionary Rule Bills,* **Hearings before the Subcommittee on Criminal Law of the Committee on the Judiciary, 97th Cong., 1st Sess., 1981, pp. 163–74.**

It is our position that there is no need for attempting to change the exclusionary rule at this time. The rule is simply not a serious problem for law enforcement at this time, particularly at the federal level. Put another way, the cost of the exclusionary rule to society is quite low. Furthermore the cost can be lowered by better training and instruction. The exclusionary rule is not a bar to effective law enforcement but ineffective law enforcement. Finally the benefit to society and law enforcement by adhering to the exclusionary rule is considerable. It is sound in theory and it works. I will develop each of these points in my testimony today.

COST OF THE EXCLUSIONARY RULE

Whatever studies have been made of the exclusionary rule emphasize the relatively low number of instances in which it produces the evil which has prompted the legislation—setting the criminal free because the constable has blundered. The GAO study, *Impact of the Exclusionary Rule on Federal Criminal Prosecution* (Report by the Comptroller General of the United States, April 19, 1979) shows how rarely suppression motions are made, how rarely they are successful and how seldom they lead to release of the defendant. In the GAO study it was found that in only 16 percent of the 2408 cases analyzed was a suppression motion made. All in all in only 1.3 percent of the 2804 defendant cases (or

36) was evidence excluded. In only 3 percent of the 16 percent was the motion granted in total and in only about 9 percent was the motion granted in part. Typically in the latter situation the defendant will move to suppress some evidence in one place and other evidence in another place. In *United States v. Russell*, 655 F.2d 1261 (D.C. Cir. 1981) the defendant's car was stopped because it lacked license plates. The police saw a glassine envelope containing a white powder in the glove compartment. They arrested the defendants, found a gun in a paper bag under the seat and also seized a grocery bag with heroin in the hatch-back section of the car. The Court of Appeals affirmed the conviction for the weapons offenses but reversed the conviction for possession of the heroin in the grocery bag. Though he won a suppression motion on the heroin, the defendant did go to jail on the weapons charges.

Even if the motion is granted the GAO study concluded that in half of the cases (about 20 cases) the defendant was convicted nevertheless and in about 20 cases the charges were dismissed. That does not mean that the defendant went free altogether. In many situations the government may try to introduce the evidence on some theory other than the one originally urged. Thus in *Mincy v. Arizona*, 437 U.S. 385 (1977) certain evidence was ordered suppressed by the Supreme Court. The State had argued that there should be a "murder scene" exception to the Fourth Amendment and the warrantless search was justified by exigent circumstances. The Supreme Court rejected that argument. The State then retried the defendant, arguing that some evidence was in plain view after Mincy's arrest and other evidence, such as the blood on the floor would have been lost or destroyed if they had to obtain a warrant. The trial court agreed and Mincy was convicted of the homicide charges. Similarly in *Brewer v. Williams*, 430 U.S. 387 (1976) the famous

"*Christian burial* speech" case certain statements made by the defendant were suppressed because they were made after his lawyer had entered the proceedings and had told him not to talk to the police. Chief Justice Burger in his dissent said that the result of the case "ought to be intolerable in any society which purports to call itself an organized society." But Williams was retried and found guilty even after his statements were suppressed. *State v. Williams*, 285 N.W.2d 248 (1979).

In *Franks v. Delaware*, 438 U.S. 154 (1977) the Supreme Court held that a warrant could not be upheld based on material misrepresentation contained in it, but on remand the Delaware Supreme Court upheld the search warrant based on other evidence besides that claimed to be erroneous.

In addition the various studies made of the impact of the exclusionary rule indicate that suppression of evidence does not occur in cases involving murder, assault or rape. It occurs primarily in narcotics or gambling cases. A study prepared by the Institute for Law and Social Research confirmed the low incidence of dismissals for due process violations. In less than 1 percent of the arrests studied was prosecution declined because the police failed to protect the defendant's constitutional rights and thereafter it became a problem at the prosecutor's level in only 2 percent of the cases. INSLAW, "What Happens After Arrest," May, 1978. In a later study, "A Cross-City Comparison of Felony Case Processing," April, 1979, INSLAW concluded that due process reasons had "little impact on the overall flow of criminal cases after arrest." Among the cities studied, Washington, Salt Lake City, Los Angeles, New Orleans, there was only one homicide arrest rejected for due process reasons and no rapes. Drug cases accounted for most of the rejections.

In summary the "cost" to society of the exclusionary rule is quite low: very few defendants walk out of the court-house free of all charges because the constable has blundered. Those few who do may be retried on other charges or theories. And the cases in which successful suppression motions are made rarely involve major index crimes, murder, assault, or rape.

REASONS FOR SUCCESSFUL SUPPRESSION MOTION

More important, the "cost" has to be paid only because a law enforcement officer has not followed the proper procedures. As I said above, the exclusionary rule is a bar to ineffective law enforcement, that is, it operates only when a blunder has occurred by the police. And in virtually every case in which suppression is required, proper operation by the police would allow admission of the evidence.

Let me offer a few examples. In a recent case in the First Circuit, *United States v. Adams*, 621 F.2d 41 (1st Cir. 1981) the FBI had obtained information that an escaped murderer might be hiding out in a house in Revere, Mass., where a former cell-mate lived. On a Wednesday afternoon they heard from a social worker who visited the house that the murderer was there. Did they do anything that afternoon? No. The next morning they checked again to find out whether the murderer was still there. At 8:00 A.M. on Thursday they determined from the social worker that she was. At 9:50 A.M. without obtaining a search warrant or an arrest warrant seven FBI agents and local police converged on the house, came into it and arrested the fugitive.

The government then pressed charges against the former cell-mate for harboring the fugitive. (The fugitive could not assert any rights herself since the exclusionary rule has never operated to suppress the person of the arrestee from later charges. Only evidence can be suppressed, not the person arrested). The government argued that there were exigent circumstances justifying a warrantless entry. The court rejected that argument. "There was no reason why either an arrest or search warrant could not have been obtained during the afternoon or evening of October 16. Like the district court, we are incredulous at the magistrate's finding that the agents might reasonably have assumed that a magistrate or judge would not be available at 8:30 A.M." 621 F.2d at 44–45.

If the agents had acted immediately on Wednesday afternoon—if they had treated the matter themselves as an emergency—the search would probably have been upheld. If they had obtained a warrant in the morning, and it is possible to obtain a warrant by telephone under Rule 41(c)(2) of the Federal Rules of Criminal Procedure, the search would have been proper. But the FBI took their time and then failed to get a warrant. The harboring charges against Miss Adams had to be dismissed.

Similarly in *United States v. Chadwick*, 433 U.S. 1 (1977) DEA agents staked out a railroad station waiting for someone to pick up a footlocker suspected of containing narcotics. Two people picked up the footlocker, carried it to the trunk of the car and then went to the front. They were then arrested, the footlocker was seized, taken to the police station and opened, revealing some marijuana, all without a warrant. The Supreme Court ordered the evidence suppressed.

If the DEA agents had arrested the persons while they were carrying the footlocker and examined it immediately, the search would probably have been upheld as a warrantless search incident to an arrest. If they had sought to obtain a search warrant after seizing the footlocker, they would certainly have obtained one since there was probable cause to believe it contained marijuana. They certainly had the right to seize and hold the footlocker until they went before a magistrate. But the DEA took the one path out of many alternatives that was later found improper. The charges against Chadwick were dismissed.

In case after case decided by federal courts up to the Supreme Court, the courts tell law enforcement officers that they managed to take the one illegal or unconstitutional path where any other procedure would have been proper. Why does this happen?

While I was preparing this testimony I did some research on the number of search warrants and arrest warrants obtained by federal officers from federal magistrates. I discovered what I consider a startling statistic. In the years from 1972 to 1980 there has been a steady decline in the number of warrants issued by federal magistrates. According to the 1980 Annual Report of the Director of the Administrative Office of the U.S. Courts (at p. 140) the warrants issued over the years have gone down:

Warrants Issued by Federal Magistrates

	1972	1976	1977	1978	1979	1980
Search warrants	7,338	6,068	5,203	4,491	4,606	4,756
Arrest warrants	36,833	19,904	17,716	14,721	11,423	9,721

The Fourth Amendment requires that warrants issue for both arrests and searches, signed by an independent magistrate who has determined that there is probable cause for a search or seizure. Even if the grant of a warrant is now quite perfunctory, warrants serve as an important paper record, requiring law enforcement officers to memorialize the evidence they have obtained before a search or seizure is made. This allows a court to test their claims and weigh their evidence in a later adversary proceeding. But federal law enforcement officers are seeking warrants less and less.

The federal rules of criminal procedure were changed in 1974 to allow summons to be issued instead of warrants in some cases but since only 1,552 summons were issued in 1980, that cannot explain the difference. More important the rules were changed in 1977 to make it easier to obtain a search warrant, by telephone, yet the number of search warrants have declined by close to 40 percent since 1972.

Federal officers are simply not seeking or obtaining warrants in cases where the Constitution would require them. And they are doing so in more and more cases while the crime rate has increased. The Constitution has not been amended to eliminate the need for warrants. The Supreme Court held in *United States v. Watson,* 423 U.S. 411 (1976) that arrest warrants were not necessary to effect an arrest in a public place but they held later in *Payton v. New York,* 445 U.S. 573 (1980) that they were necessary to invade a private home. The deep drop in arrest warrants cannot be explained as merely a reaction to the Supreme Court decision in *Watson.*

Thus we still have to ask why federal officers are seeking fewer and fewer warrants. Either they are lazy (it takes time to type up a warrant, seek out a magistrate, etc.) or they are afraid to test out their proof of probable cause before a magistrate or even to write it down so it can be challenged in later court proceedings. Or they are responding to the growing criticism of the exclusionary rule and are assuming that the courts will back them up. This development does not contribute to respect for the law or the courts or to the need to protect the privacy of the American people.

BENEFITS OF THE EXCLUSIONARY RULE

It must be remembered that the purpose of the exclusionary rule is not to protect a handful of drug dealers and allow them to go free. Contrary to what White House counselors may say, the ACLU is not part of a criminal lobby trying to get criminals out on the street as fast as we can. The purpose of the exclusionary rule and the Fourth Amendment is to protect the privacy rights of all Americans, in particular the millions of law abiding Americans who would otherwise be subject to seizure of their persons or invasions of their homes because the police are looking for a criminal. Without the protection of the Fourth Amendment dragnet arrests or seizures and indiscriminate breaking into homes would become a frequent occurrence.

Just to remind the Committee of what could happen, a few years ago there was a search for the so-called Zebra killings in San Francisco. There had been 17 murders of whites in late 1973 and 1974 and two young black males were described as the assailants. The police department issued a directive to stop and pat down all young black males in the city of San Francisco, 20 to 30 years old, 5′ 8″ to 6′ tall. A law suit was immediately filed to stop this indiscriminate frisking of tens of thousands of innocent citizens who merely had some of the same physical characteristics of the suspects. See *Williams v. Alioto,* 549 F.2d 13b (9th Cir. 1977).

In an earlier case in Baltimore *Langford v. Gelston,* F.2d (4th Cir. 1966) the police in Baltimore invaded 300 private homes in the black section of the city looking for suspects in a police killing. They had no warrants to do so and in most cases the searches were based on unverified anonymous tips. They broke into homes at all hours of the day or night without verifying the tips they received. A federal court issued an injunction against any further invasions.

I am afraid that without the full protection of the Fourth Amendment and the exclusionary rule, dragnet arrests or frisks and indiscriminate break-ins of homes could become a far more frequent occurrence.

The importance of the exclusionary rule as the essential remedy to protect the requirements of the Fourth Amendment has been repeated in case after case. See *United States v. Calandra,* 414 U.S. 338, 348 (1974). But at its heart the exclusionary rule is crucial for Fourth Amendment protection for two interrelated reasons: (1) the criminal cases excluding evidence by reason of the exclusionary rule are our chief means of defining the limits and meaning of the Fourth Amendment; (2) the exclusionary rule provides the key incentive for making law enforcement officers obey the law.

Definition: The general words of the Fourth Amendment are not self-defining or self-enforcing. "The right of the people to be secure in their persons, houses, papers, and effects against unreasonable searches and seizures, shall not be violated, and no Warrants shall issue, but upon probable cause, supported by Oath or affirmation, and particularly describing the place to be searched, and persons or things to be seized."

What is probable cause? How is it determined? Are there any exceptions to the warrant requirement? What is the plain view doctrine? How is consent determined? How far may a police officer search incident to arrest? What is a Terry stop? What justifies a pat-down of a suspect?

We have now built up an elaborate body of law answering these and other questions. But it has been done by state and federal courts applying the exclusionary rule in case after case on motions to suppress evidence. Without the exclusionary rule, there would be no occasion to worry about probable cause, plain view, consent, pat-down, Terry stops and so on. It is true that civil suits for damages under 42 U.S. §1983 require the definition of Fourth Amendment protection. But Fourth Amendment violations rarely produce §1983 cases and successful actions are rarer still. Citizens do not bring civil suits for damages under §1983 for bad stops, searches, arrests or seizures. Suits for injunctive orders generally require department-wide or jurisdiction-wide problems before relief can be granted, as in the *Williams* or *Langston* cases. It is only because of the exclusionary rule that we have built up a basic set of rules of what the Fourth Amendment means. That definitional and educational function has been one of the chief benefits of the *Weeks* and *Wolf* rules. In short the law enforcement community have learned what the Fourth Amendment means primarily because of the exclusionary rule.

Enforcement: Once having learned what the rules require, the police must be given an incentive for obeying them. It defies logic to say that the Fourth Amendment means what the courts say it means but the police do not have to pay attention to what the rules are. When we say that the exclusionary rule acts as a deterrent what we mean is that the courts are telling the police that they must obey the law. Otherwise the courts would become accomplices to the violations that occur. For the courts to tell the police that they can disregard the basic tenets of our fundamental charter, that the rules do not mean anything as far as they are concerned, is to ignore the entire meaning of the Bill of Rights. When James Madison introduced the first ten amendments to the Constitution, he relied on the courts as the chief mechanism of enforcement. "If they [the amendments] are incorporated into the Constitution, independent tribunals of justice will consider them in a peculiar manner the guardians of those rights; they will be an impenetrable bulwark against every assumption of power in the legislative or executive; they will be naturally led to resist every encroachment upon rights expressly stipulated for in the constitution by the declaration of rights." Should we

now say that Madison was wrong, the courts should not be a guardian of Fourth Amendment rights, they should not resist encroachment into privacy rights by the police, that they should be a penetrable bulwark when the police invade our homes. To tell the police that they can violate the law is to teach society a terrible lesson, as Justice Brandeis said in his famous dissent in *Olmstead v. United States*, 277 U.S. 438, 483 (1928):

> When the government, having full knowledge, sought, through the Department of Justice, to avail itself of the fruits of the acts in order to accomplish its own ends, it assumed moral responsibility for the officers' crimes . . . and if this Court should permit the Government, by means of its officers' crimes, to effect its purposes of punishing the defendants . . . the government itself would become a lawbreaker.
>
> . . . In a government of laws, existence of the government will be imperilled if it fails to observe the law scrupulously. Our government is the patent, the omnipresent teacher. For good or for ill, it teaches the whole people by its example. Crime is contagious. If the Government becomes a lawbreaker, it breeds contempt for law; it invites every man to become a law unto himself; it invites anarchy.

As Brandeis said, the end does not justify the means since the consequences of sanctioning official lawbreaking would bring "terrible retribution." The police would learn again the advantages of breaking the law, at a terrible cost to the privacy of us all. As Yale Kamisar has written, it was only when the exclusionary rule was applied to the states, that state police officers began to pay attention to the requirements of the Fourth Amendment. Every time a police officer asks his superiors what he is supposed to do, when he can invade a home or stop a car or search a citizen and he is told what the rules are, then the exclusionary rule is working. We cannot retreat into the dark days before *Weeks* and *Wolf*.

[W]e believe it is beyond the Constitutional power of Congress to enact S.101 and S.751. Furthermore the specific language of those bills are ambiguous, vague, unenforceable and inconsistent with the purpose of the Fourth Amendment. The good faith exception would introduce a vague, confusing concept into Fourth Amendment jurisprudence. Instead of one bright line definition of what the Fourth Amendment means, are we to have three or four definitions: (1)what the Fourth Amendment requires; (2) what is a substantial violation requiring application of the exclusionary rule; (3) what is an intentional violation; (4) what violation will give rise to a suit for damages? Such a confusing approach should not be written into law. We have one Fourth Amendment. It has worked and we should not allow it to be eroded away if we are concerned about protecting our right to privacy.

NO IN OPPOSITION TO THE EXCLUSIONARY RULE

Steven R. Schlesinger

My name is Steven R. Schlesinger. I am Associate Professor of Politics at The Catholic University of America and have published a book, a monograph and a number of law review articles dealing with the exclusionary rule. I thank the Subcommittee and its Chairman, Senator Mathias, for this opportunity to contribute to the Subcommittee's deliberations on the exclusionary rule.

INTRODUCTION

The justices of the United States Supreme Court have advanced two primary public policy justifications for the rule. First, it is said to deter improper police behavior because police will have no reason to gather evidence which cannot be used in a court of law. Second, it is said to guarantee that, should the state invade the privacy of

U.S. Cong., Senate, *The Exclusionary Rule Bills,* Hearings before the Subcommittee on Criminal Law of the Committee on the Judiciary, 97th Cong., 1st Sess., 1981, pp. 57–73.

individuals during the course of a search and seizure, the fruits of that invasion will prove useless to the state in its prosecution. In other words, this second justification portrays the rule as a partial protection of the privacy of the victims of illegal searches and seizures, which is said to be guaranteed by the Fourth Amendment search and seizure clause. I will attempt to demonstrate that the rule is not an effective deterrent to police misbehavior and that attempts to justify the rule as an effective protection of privacy are unsatisfactory. In addition, a number of disadvantages of the rule not related to deterrence of privacy will be discussed.

PRIVACY—THE RIGHT TO BE LET ALONE

With respect to the justification for the rule as a protection of privacy, consider the following two situations: First, assume that the person whose privacy is invaded is innocent of the alleged crime (or some other crime); and second, assume that he is guilty. If he is innocent, the rule offers him little help, remedy or protection—and no compensation, for the police will rarely find any excludable evidence and almost never find excludable evidence sufficient to convict a suspect. In a sense, the illegal search or seizure may benefit the victim by indicating his innocence, at least to the police or prosecutor.

If the suspect on whom an illegal search and seizure has been conducted is in fact in possession of incriminating evidence which is used to convict him, then we must ask whether his privacy has been invaded. To frame the question more precisely, we must ask whether evidence or information concerning a crime is of a public or of a private nature. If it is essentially a public concern, then, as I shall shortly argue, it is inappropriate to contend that the state has no right to it.

Why is information and evidence concerning a crime more of public than private concern? A certain portion of the criminal act is private—that part which concerns the perpetrator; his motivations, feelings, and in a certain sense the physical act itself. His perception and understanding of the act, its history, and its consequences to him are clearly his private, singular possession. Publicly admitting that he has committed a criminal act is often painful. But this must be balanced against the pain, harm, and difficulty caused the victim of the crime; this is clearly private to the victim, not the perpetrator. These two considerations seem essentially to cancel each other out. What swings the balance in favor of calling the matter more public than private is society's concern that each criminal act is in violation of the established public order, and if the perpetrator goes unpunished or unrehabilitated, he may repeat his crime. In addition, if he could commit his crime with impunity, that fact might encourage others to criminal activity.

If criminal activity is predominantly a public concern, then when the police, either legally or illegally, find evidence of such activity, it is not an invasion of the individual's privacy to use what the police have found against him in a criminal proceeding. Specifically, since criminal activity is not private, a location is not private if activities of great public interest—crimes—are committed or concealed there; thus, the police cannot be denied access to the location of a crime on the ground of protection of privacy. A policeman who illegally came upon a murder, robbery, assault, or drug factory, cannot realistically be said to have happened upon a private act or a location which should be off limits to the police because it is regarded as private. The legitimate public concern for criminal activity and, in short, the public nature of contraband, renders the search for and the seizure of that contraband (but that only) a necessary and justifiable police activity on behalf of the public. One could put this argument in another way: a person who uses his home to store dead bodies or a drug factory forfeits what would ordinarily be his right to privacy.

This argument for the admissibility of criminal evidence does not, of course, extend to the fruits of police action which are unrelated to search and seizure. But a legislature, by criminalizing a particular activity, indicates that the legislature regards that activity as having a significant public dimension; if this were not the case, why should public money be spent in dealing with persons who commit the designated crime?

This is not to argue that illegal police searches should not be deterred as effectively as possible. It *is* to say that when the deterrent breaks down, when the police illegally uncover a crime, murder, rape, drugs, guns, etc.—the evidence they find should be admissible in a court of law.

Furthermore, this argument justifies only the search for, seizure, and use in court of criminal evidence. It does not legitimate the use of excessive physical force by police officers or unnecessary damage to the personal property of the victim or of another person. Disciplinary action against a misbehaving officer is not limited or discouraged, as his search and seizure would be improper regardless of the guilt or innocence of the person searched. The officer commits an illegal search when he violates the rules governing proper searches and seizures (for example, by failing to obtain a search warrant) and because he cannot know whether the suspect is guilty or innocent. Finally, nothing said here limits financial compensation to the innocent victims of illegal searches and seizures for invasion of privacy. However, the guilty victim, the person with whom incriminating evidence is found, should have no such right of recovery, since, as argued above, his right of privacy has not been invaded by the search and seizure.

DETERRENCE

Professor Bradley Canon describes as a "myth" the claim that empirical studies have shown that the rule is an ineffective deterrent. In fact, the empirical studies, while not conclusive, indicate just that.

In my book, *Exclusionary Injustice: The Problem of Illegally Obtained Evidence,* I reported primarily on the empirical studies of Dallin Oaks, Michael Ban, James Spiotto, and Bradley Canon. Let us review briefly the findings from each of those studies.

Oaks' 1970 study of law enforcement in Cincinnati between 1956 and 1967 convinced him that:

> As a device for directly deterring illegal searches and seizures by the police, the exclusionary rule is a failure. There is no reason to expect the rule to have any effect on the overwhelming majority of police conduct that is not meant to result in prosecutions, and there is hardly any evidence that the rule exerts any deterrent effect on the

small fraction of law enforcement directed at prosecution.

Ban's two studies of the impact of the rule in Boston and Cincinnati, conducted in the mid-1960's, also tend to confirm the ineffectiveness of the rule. Ban concludes that the rule showed spotty effectiveness in Boston and almost none in Cincinnati.

Spiotto's study of motions to suppress in Chicago between 1950 and 1971 convinced him that "the deterrent rationale for the rule does not seem to be justified" and that "given the present status of the law and the workings of the exclusionary rule, change is warranted. . . . "

While Spiotto's research contains real weaknesses, including a faulty research methodology, his study nonetheless tends to show that in Chicago police misbehavior did not decrease over a 21 year period (1950–1971) during which Illinois had a self-imposed exclusionary rule. Likewise, it did not decrease in the 10 years after the rule was imposed on all the states by the United States Supreme Court. Thus, while Spiotto's research decidedly does not answer the question about how much police illegality there would be without the rule, Chicago's experience lends little credence to Canon's thesis that the rule deters over time.

Professor Canon has admitted that it would be fair to treat these studies of Cincinnati, Boston and Chicago, as well as studies of Washington, D.C. and New York, as an indictment of the rule, if not a conviction. But he maintains that two of his studies, published in 1974 and 1977, support the notion that the rule deters.

His 1974 study attempts to update (to 1973) evidence on the rule's deterrent effect. However, it suffers from so many methodological flaws and other difficulties that its findings are not very useful. In fact, Canon admits that "some errors" appear in this article. For example, much of his study was based on questionnaires which he mailed to police, prosecutors, and public defenders in American cities with populations of more than 100,000. But he received returns on only 47.4 percent of the questionnaires sent to the police, 35.2 percent of those sent to prosecutors and 40.2 percent of those sent to public defenders. Thus, the nature and size of his sample simply do not permit valid generalizations; it was neither random nor representative. Those cities whose search and seizure practices were least in conformity with current law—those whose practices would have negated Canon's thesis about the effectiveness of the rule—would have been the ones least likely to respond to a mailed questionnaire; they would hardly have been anxious to acknowledge or to announce their own failure to obey the law.

Professor Canon nowhere stated which officials filled out the questionnaires. And, generally speaking, there is simply no way of knowing whether the questionnaires were answered truthfully. Anyone trying to give the police a favorable image might have been less than candid in reporting about police compliance with proper search and seizure procedures.

In addition to the general methodological difficulties in this study, it is important to examine the research methods that Professor Canon used on three of his major topics: numbers of search warrants issued, changes in police search and seizure policies, and successful motions to suppress evidence.

Canon asked both police and prosecutors to estimate the number of search warrants issued annually in their respective cities. He then compared these estimates for the early 1970s with what he admitted were very thin data concerning the number of search warrants issued in the 1950s and 1960s. He concluded, not surprisingly, that there was an increase in the number issued.

Yet the crucial question is *why* there was such an increase; Canon's own findings on causality seriously undercut his argument

for the rule's deterrent effect. The respondents said that 55 per cent of the increase could be attributed to an upsurge in narcotics crimes, 24 per cent to judicial rulings (all judicial rulings on search and seizure, not just those on the exclusionary rule), 22 per cent to more police and better training, and 4 per cent to other causes. While these findings indicate that the exclusionary rule may have had some impact, they hardly make a case for a substantial deterrent effect.

Professor Canon asked the police in the 1974 questionnaire about the extent to which their search and seizure policies had changed since 1967–68 and, again not surprisingly, they reported that the rule had a substantial impact. Yet the problems with Canon's research strategy here are serious. As he admitted, statements of official "headquarters" policy may not conform to actual police practice in the field. Further, Professor Canon conceded that "such statements were sometimes unduly generalized to conform with sparsely worded questionnaire alternatives."

Professor Canon himself noted that "some policies could be misreported so that they would appear to be in conformity with the law." In fact, for the police to have answered Canon's questions in a manner which conflicted with his thesis would have required them to admit that, as a matter of official policy, they broke the law. To put it mildly, the questions themselves contained strong inducements for the police to answer in a manner which confirmed Canon's thesis. Amazingly, some departments did openly admit to policies which seemed to conflict with rulings of the United States Supreme Court—no splendid testimony to the effectiveness of the exclusionary rule.

Finally, Canon's 1974 study sought to cast doubt on Spiotto's research on successful motions to suppress in Chicago by showing that Chicago was atypical in that it had more successful motions to suppress than the average American city. Though

Canon did demonstrate that in this respect Chicago was atypical, he ignored the fundamental question: what effect did imposition of the exclusionary rule have on successful motions to suppress in Chicago and other American cities? What we really need to know is whether the rule reduced police misbehavior, as we would see from evidence of a decrease over time in successful motions to suppress. Neither Spiotto nor Canon has answered this question.

Professor Canon claims that his more recent study corrects "some errors" in the first, and is more rigorous. In fact, his 1977 study represents one of the most damning pieces of evidence produced so far regarding the rule's ineffectiveness. In his later study, Canon replicated Oaks' 1970 Cincinnati study for 19 other American cities. Summarizing his findings, Canon said the data indicated that the rule "has not always or even *often* worked," "that *Mapp* had seemingly little or no impact on the majority of cases," and that the data "do not come close to supporting a claim that the rule wholly or *largely* works" (emphasis supplied). If these are Canon's own conclusions about the deterrent effect of the rule, he is hardly in a position to criticize those who conclude that, according to the available empirical evidence, the rule is not an effective deterrent against police misbehavior.

Certainly, Professor Canon has not even come close to satisfying the heavy burden of proving the rule's deterrent effectiveness. Such proof is clearly required when deterrence is the primary justification currently used by the Supreme Court for the rule, and when the rule has so many serious costs and disadvantages which I will discuss later in my testimony.

Furthermore, criminal justice literature supplies many reasons for doubting the deterrent effectiveness of the rule. First, the operative scope of the rule is limited— only evidence presented at trial, a narrow stage in the criminal process, is excluded.

Thus, the trial affects only a small proportion of police activity. Given the extraordinary amount of plea bargaining in American courts today, the instances in which the rule can be invoked at trial are dramatically reduced.

Second, the impact of the rule falls only indirectly on police—it does not discipline the errant officer; the brunt of the exclusionary rule's effect is actually borne by the prosecution, which generally has little or no power to punish police misconduct. Third, officers whose illegal actions result in loss of convictions may receive the implicit or explicit approval of their superiors. Fourth, trial judges do not often explain to officers why their evidence is excluded; the impact of the rule is limited if the police are not informed of the nature and effect of their wrongdoing.

Fifth, loss of convictions through exclusion of evidence is not as serious a matter for police as might be thought, since police effectiveness usually is judged by the number of "collars" or arrests, not by the number of convictions. Sixth, in jurisdictions where prosecutors decline to prosecute cases with substantial search and seizure problems, there are relatively few instances in which the rule can be invoked. Seventh, there are some strong indications that the rule even encourages certain forms of police misconduct.

OTHER DISADVANTAGES OF THE RULE

Turning away from the deterrence problem and toward other disadvantages of the rule, another serious difficulty with the rule is that a certain number of guilty persons escape conviction because of its operation. Indeed, Oaks' study of motions to suppress in gambling, narcotics, and weapons cases in Chicago indicates that "in every single one of these cases in which a motion to suppress was granted, the charges were then dismissed." Oaks concludes that these proceedings focus almost entirely on evidentiary questions, rather than on the guilt or innocence of the suspect. It is sometimes possible to retry a suspect on the basis of evidence other than that illegally obtained; often, however, it is not, and persons dangerous to society are released.

Related to this point is another important difficulty with the rule: it undermines public respect for the legal and judicial system. One complaint about the legal system is that too many suspects are released on technicalities. In fact, this complaint most often refers to the operation of the exclusionary rule. Thus, far from increasing public respect for the court system in the public mind, the operation of the rule may cause that system to appear dangerously foolish, not only to the disgruntled police officers directly affected by it, but to large segments of the public. Indeed, the public expects from its courts both adherence to certain standards of due process and conviction of the guilty (and thus acquittal of the innocent); under the operation of the exclusionary rule, it gets the former but in many cases not the latter.

Another difficulty with the rule as it has been applied to the states in accordance with *Mapp v. Ohio* is that it fails to distinguish between more and less serious offenses. Both a gambler and a murderer, having committed crimes of widely differing degrees of gravity, would be given reversals of their convictions because of the illegality of a search and seizure. The operation of the rule frees the criminal without giving any consideration to the danger to which society is exposed by this release. But the law is accustomed to taking into account the seriousness of the alleged crime, even before the trial is completed and sentence is pronounced. Whether a person may be released at all in the pretrial period and the amount of bail, if he is released, are determined in part by the seriousness of the crime allegedly committed (though bail is also determined by the probability of the defendant's appearing for trial). Thus, there is precedent for

applying different standards to crimes of differing degrees of gravity.

Also, as noted earlier, the rule does not distinguish between a willful and flagrant violation by an officer, and an exercise, under strained circumstances, of his best judgment, a judgment which, only after several appeals, may be held by a perhaps divided appellate court to have been improper. The issues which appellate decisions resolve are both controversial and difficult, as evidenced by courts sharply divided on the issue of what is a reasonable search and seizure. After all, if appellate judges are not sure about the legality of an officer's action after long consideration of a written record, it is asking a great deal of the officer that he judge the matter correctly in a few moments. Nor can judges be oblivious to the fact that their opinions sometimes lack that kind of helpful guidance which will aid a law enforcement officer in the actual performance of his duty. Police officers should not be deterred from exercising "reasonable judgment," though that judgment may not represent the final judgment of the appellate courts as to proper behavior in that situation. In the same vein, the rule does not distinguish harmless errors of judgment which work no serious injustice and which do not seriously deprive the suspect of his rights, from the flagrant violations of the Fourth Amendment such as those seen in *Mapp v. Ohio* or *Rochin v. California* which result in serious deprivations of rights. As Chief Justice Burger says in *Bivens v. Six Unknown Named Agents:* ". . . society has a right to expect rationally graded responses to police misconduct— depending on its seriousness—rather than the universal 'capital punishment' we inflict on any and all evidence when police error is shown in its acquisition."

Another problem with the rule is that it often excludes the most credible kinds of evidence. Thus, it is erroneous to link "legal" evidence with the best, most credible kinds of evidence; for evidence that is seized, perhaps illegally, in a "state of nature" has most often not been "prepared" by anyone for presentation as evidence in a court of law and thus, ironically, though it is presently inadmissible because illegally obtained, may be the most credible evidence available to aid in a proper and just disposition of cases. Thus, application of the exclusionary rule on search and seizure grounds is qualitatively different from other types of exclusion such as suppression of unreliable confessions, line-up evidence, or eyewitness identification, for in these other areas suppression takes place because of specific doubts as to the reliability of the evidence. In search and seizure, the probative value of physical evidence, while hardly in doubt, is often ignored.

Finally, application of the rule has two clearly harmful side effects. First, the rule intensifies plea bargaining because prosecutors, who fear suppression of important evidence at trial, may be willing to negotiate regarding the seriousness of the charge or sentencing recommendations rather than risk dismissal. In addition, a number of commentators have pointed out that the necessity of excluding obviously probative evidence under the rule has placed increasing pressure on judges to sanction dubious searches and seizures based on dangerously expanded notions of probable cause. Judges feel they must interpret probable cause expansively in order to admit crucial evidence. Thus, the exclusionary rule may have the perverse and unintended effect of limiting the scope of privacy contemplated by the Fourth Amendment.

ALTERNATIVES TO THE EXCLUSIONARY RULE: A PROPOSAL

Discussion of alternatives to the exclusionary rule must begin with the objectives to be achieved through their use. These are the deterrence of police misbehavior through identification and discipline of offending official(s), a better system than we have at present for compensating the innocent victims of illegal searches and seizures, and conviction of the guilty—a result conspicuously lacking under the rule. These objectives require separate proceedings, a disciplinary proceeding against the offending police officer for deterrence and a civil-action proceeding for damages for compensation. Before discussing these in detail below, a few preliminary points should be made. The guilty victim has no claim to compensation for deprivation of privacy since his privacy, as argued before, has not been invaded. However, while the guilty victim would not be allowed to claim this kind of compensation for the invasion of Fourth Amendment rights, he would still have a civil cause of action if the police do unnecessary violence to his person or damage to his property; for although by his criminal activity he loses his right to privacy, he clearly retains other rights of person and property. Of course, we must discipline the offending officer, be the suspect guilty or innocent, because the officer has no way of knowing before he commits the illegal search and seizure whether the suspect is guilty or innocent, and because he has violated the rules of search and seizure.

What follows is my proposal for an alternative to the exclusionary rule which, I argue, would accomplish the proper objectives of the rule better than does the rule itself. Later in my testimony, a due process argument for the exclusionary rule will be discussed and, finally, some thoughts will be advanced as to how we may move away from the rule as a remedy against police misbehavior.

THE INDEPENDENT REVIEW BOARD

As to discipline of the offending officer, it is clear that prosecutors cannot be relied upon to institute proceedings against offending officers, because they rely heavily on a good relationship with the police in order to carry out their duties. Thus, disciplinary action must be initiated and meted out from some other source. One possible source of such discipline would be the judiciary, aided by an independent review board.

A hearing would be held (separately from the criminal trial of the victim of the search and seizure) before an independent review board which would investigate the nature and severity of the officer's misconduct. It would assess an appropriate punishment ranging from a fine to permanent severance from the police force. The board would take into account the record of the offending official, perhaps being more lenient to first offenders. Furthermore, evidence that the officer acted in good faith (without knowledge of wrongdoing) or evidence that he used reasonable force would be considered. At the review board hearing, there would need to be due process protections for the suspect official, including representation by counsel; a special "prosecutor", entirely separate from the police or prosecutor's office, would have to be appointed in order to prevent any conflict-of-interest problems from arising with the "regular" prosecutor. This hearing would be disciplinary in nature, not criminal, but an officer might, in some instances, face additional criminal liability.

If a trial judge believed that there were evidence of illegal official behavior (regardless of the outcome of the trial), he could order such a hearing to be held. Under such a system, the judge must be particularly alert during testimony to the possibility of illegal behavior by officials, since defense counsel would not have the incentive of a suppression motion to bring forward illegal behavior. The judge must be given discretion to ask questions concerning how evidence was obtained in order to make sure that he has enough information to recommend, where necessary, a hearing on police misconduct. In addition to referral of possible misconduct

by the judiciary, a citizen who is an innocent victim of illegal search and seizure, but who is never brought to trial involving this search, may report his complaint directly to the review board for investigation. Some jurisdictions might even wish to allow suspects, whether convicted or acquitted, to bring their own complaints directly to the board, though (because of anger at the police) this could lead to the filing of substantial numbers of less than meritorious complaints. Such a separate disciplinary hearing would provide an independent forum for investigation of police misconduct, unlike the present system in which police conduct is scrutinized by the judge as one of the numerous issues raised at trial. Such a proceeding, unlike the situation of a judge at trial, can give the misconduct question undivided attention and may well afford more time than a trial to resolve allegations of police misconduct.

Legislative bodies may wish to consider awarding a minimal, but automatic, compensation to the successful complainant as an incentive to bring the complaint; in doing this, however, the problem of encouraging less than meritorious complaints must be considered. Or, as an alternative method of encouraging victims to file complaints, a legislature may wish to allow admission to some degree of the results of the disciplinary hearing in a civil proceeding, though the problem here is that admission of such evidence may be prejudicial.

The functions set out above could be well accomplished by an independent review board made up of citizens, judges, law officers and any other groups whose representation may be desirable. The success of the plan depends on careful composition of the board with a view toward representing differing interests; methods of choosing members of the board could vary from place to place. Board members not on the police force will help to provide public and independent scrutiny of police work and will avoid the pitfalls of governmental self-scrutiny, so well illustrated in the recent Watergate and CIA revelations. In short, the "public members" will help to insure a certain responsiveness on the part of the police to the wishes of the community.

A board would be preferable to an exclusion hearing before a judge for two important reasons. First, as noted above, a board would have more time and resources available for investigating the facts of an alleged misbehavior than would normally be available to a judge while a trial is in progress. Second, a board would have the capacity to investigate the possibility that any of the offending officer's superiors had encouraged or ordered him to act as he did, and to take appropriate punitive action where such a pattern is found.

This proposed system would have the advantage of being paid for by the state and it would not need to depend upon the prosecutor or the possibly indigent victim of alleged misbehavior to initiate or sustain proceedings, but would, in most instances, be initiated by the judiciary. In some cases, the punishments meted out by the board might not be sufficiently severe, but it must be remembered that, under the exclusionary rule, it is extremely rare that direct sanctions are imposed on offending officers at all.

THE CIVIL REMEDY

In addition to police discipline, the innocent victim should have a means by which to collect compensation for an illegal search and seizure, and to point out official misbehavior. The potential for substantial "penalty compensation"—an amount large enough to make the filing of the suit and its attendant responsibilities worthwhile— would go far to correct the problem of insufficient incentive for counsel to point out official misbehavior.

Specifically, I suggest a statutory civil action with provision for the award of monetary compensation, the amount depending on the gravity of the misbehavior (but with a minimum amount to be awarded in the event that any violation is found). Such an action would allow innocent victims to recover a basic compensatory amount plus counsel's fees without any showing of specific damage to the victim or flagrant violation by the officer. The only proof necessary would be a showing that the victim's Fourth Amendment rights had been violated; the greater the invasion of Fourth Amendment rights, the higher the compensation. The seriousness of the invasion, and thus the amount of compensation, would be measured by the amount of mental or physical suffering and inconvenience caused a victim of improper procedure, as well as the degree to which an officer violated clear rules governing proper searches and seizures. There are now in existence state common law causes of action under which victims may recover damages, but civil actions are rarely instituted (and even more rarely won) because it is necessary to show either substantial harm to the victim (for compensatory damages), or outrageous official misconduct (for punitive damages). Winning the proposed civil suit would be easier because no such showing would be necessary. This plan would provide an economic incentive for victims and for lawyers to bring to public attention cases of official misconduct, as well as provide an avenue for compensation. Victims of illegal searches and seizures would be encouraged to bring suit because the regularized procedure suggested here, designed precisely for such victims, would help to overcome reluctance to sue the police. Under existing institutional arrangements, free legal counsel could be provided for indigent persons who wish to bring this type of action.

From where should the money come to

pay the victim if he wins the proposed statutory civil action? I believe it must come from the public treasury of whatever unit of government is involved. If the amounts awarded were considerable enough, superior officers would be discouraged from "making it worthwhile" (through increased pay or promotion) for subordinates to effect illegal searches and seizures. If the public were required to pay for such police escapades in the form of substantial damages taken from general tax revenues, the public would take a dim view of such police activity; predictably, corrective pressure would be brought to bear on the police. Also, law enforcement officers would hardly be overjoyed, were public money to be awarded to criminal suspects. It is worth considering whether the plaintiff should be permitted to collect damages directly from the errant officer, since the threat of such damages would serve, at least in some instances, as a deterrent against official misbehavior. However, individual liability of the officer must not be so imposing that it prevents him from acting where action is necessary. In any event, the errant officer would be subject to discipline imposed by the independent review board.

AN ARGUMENT FOR THE PROPOSAL AS A WHOLE

It is not possible to elaborate all the details of these proposals here, for many of these must be worked out in practice; nor is it possible to answer all possible objections to this kind of proposal. Nevertheless, the preceding proposals are submitted as a method by which we can move away from the difficulties and shortcomings of the exclusionary rule. As the legal literature makes clear, plans like the ones reviewed have been employed only rarely, and even then there was no real incentive to make them work, since most of the states, prior to *Mapp*, had not experienced the great costs of the exclusionary rule—the alter-

native to the kind of plan proposed here. Ironically, there is the other side of the coin, namely, that the *Mapp* decision has largely removed from Congress and from the states the incentive to deal with illegal search and seizure by means other than suppression. As Oaks points out: "By a peculiar form of federal preemption, the *Mapp* decision may sap state officials' energy and determination to control law enforcement officials in alternative ways that might prove just as effective and even more comprehensive than the exclusionary rule. Thus, The President's Crime Commission Task Force Report on the Police observed that the police administrator is ambivalent about the degree of his responsibility for controlling improper law enforcement behavior by his personnel. . . . "

The present system of exclusion does not deter police misbehavior, nor does it provide compensation to the innocent: it simply frees many who, we have argued, have no legitimate claim to that freedom on the basis of invasion of privacy. The recommendations outlined above are intended to move us closer to a system which deters misconduct and compensates those who deserve compensation. There are obvious difficulties with the scheme proposed here which, like any system, will not deal properly with all violations, but at least a substantial number of officers could be disciplined and a substantial number of innocent victims of illegal procedures could be compensated. This is more than one can say for the present system of exclusion.

A DUE PROCESS ARGUMENT CONCERNING THE RULE

Proponents of the exclusionary rule claim that, through enforcement of the rule, our courts gain popular respect because they uniformly refuse to accept illegally obtained, "tainted" evidence; the theory seems to be that, were the courts to accept such evidence, they would be condoning the methods used to obtain it. Through their refusal to admit illegally obtained evidence, the argument goes, the courts demonstrate their unswerving commitment to Fourth Amendment restrictions on search and seizure. This sense of commitment is communicated to police, causing them to respect the judicial system.

Two points must be made concerning this argument. First, does a court not *lose* the respect of citizens when, through its enforcement of the exclusionary rule, it implicates itself in the freeing of a suspect in whose case reliable evidence has been obtained, albeit improperly, indicating that the suspect has committed a serious crime or crimes? Do the courts not *lose* respect when they implicate themselves in a situation so structured that law enforcement officers feel tremendous pressure to commit perjury?

Second, courts surely have a duty to support Fourth Amendment rights, due process, and fair play, but they also have a duty to pursue the truth—to free the innocent and convict the guilty. Under the exclusionary rule, the courts may claim to fulfill only the former duty. Under the system proposed above, the courts to a large extent fulfill both: they clearly express their commitment to Fourth Amendment search and seizure restrictions through their participation in the process of finding and punishing official misbehavior by law enforcement authorities, and they express their commitment to pursuing the truth by judging evidence solely on the basis of its reliability. One hopes it is not asking too much that our courts concern themselves not only with the privacy problems raised by the Fourth Amendment search and seizure clause but also with their general obligation to fairly establish guilt or innocence in criminal cases.

Also, in a real sense, courts would tolerate government wrongdoing (and the "benefits" that government derives from it) less under the proposed system than they do at present since they would participate directly, through the review board and civil damage suits, in a system which would deter wrongdoing more effectively than it is deterred now. At present, judges participate in a system in which misbehavior by law enforcement officials is rampant, apparently not decreasing significantly, and often tolerated or encouraged by superiors. Under the proposed system, the courts would become an integral part of a meaningful deterrent against official misbehavior. This is an improvement, and to the extent that the argument that government should derive no benefit from its wrongdoing is founded on the fear that such benefits would break down any deterrence mechanism (and therefore provide an incentive for wrongdoing), it should be remembered that a system without the rule, such as the one proposed here, would seem to provide a stronger deterrent than the present system of exclusion.

Under the proposed system, the government would obtain some convictions on the basis of improperly obtained evidence (though the stronger deterrent should substantially reduce official misbehavior). The courts would permit these convictions because of their commitment to conviction of the guilty and acquittal of the innocent, just as they would refer errant law enforcement officers to the disciplinary board because of their commitment to fair play, due process, and the deterrence of illegal practices. Such a procedure would strike a better balance between the various objectives of the judiciary than the present, one-sided concern with procedural and evidentiary problems.

THE PATH AWAY FROM THE RULE

The exclusionary rule seems to be so deficient and the alternatives sufficiently promising that we should cease clinging to the rule. Indeed, the rule does not in any substantial way do what the alternatives would—directly punish offending officers and provide compensation to innocent victims of illegal law enforcement activity—and it has at least one serious liability not attached to the alternatives: it releases otherwise convictable and possibly dangerous persons on society.

The practical problem is, of course, how do we move away from the rule as a monolithic remedy for police misconduct? As was pointed out earlier, if the exclusionary rule were simply abandoned without substitute, the police might infer that all constitutional restraints had been removed and that, in effect, open season had been declared on criminal suspects. Chief Justice Burger suggests that Congress should formulate substitutes, as it did in 1946 with the Federal Tort Claims Act, which provides a form of relief for those with claims against the federal government. If such substitutes were successful, the states might then wish to follow the federal model. I strongly endorse the Chief Justice's call on Congress to formulate substitutes for the rule and have suggested in my testimony what form these substitutes should take.

In discussing the path away from the rule, it is important to remember that the United States Supreme Court currently grounds the rule in the policy of deterrance, *not* in the Constitution itself. Therefore, there is no constitutional bar, according to the Supreme Court, to Congress formulating a substitute for the rule. Since the empirical evidence clearly undermines the deterrence argument for the rule, it is high time for Congress to put in place those substitutes for the rule about which Chief Justice Burger spoke ten years ago.

ABOLITION VERSUS MODIFICATION

The Attorney General's Task Force on Violent Crime has recommended that the rule be applied only in those cases in which a judge finds that a law officer acted in bad faith, that is, when he knew that his search or seizure was in violation of the law. In addition to the arguments against the exclusionary rule made previously in this testimony, there are a number of specific reasons for preferring abolition of the rule to the course recommended by the Attorney General's Task Force.

The task force recommendation provides little or no deterrence for violations deemed by the courts to be in good faith; this fact could encourage a careless attitude toward detail on the part of law enforcement officials, and might encourage police to see what can be gotten away with before the courts draw the line on what is an intentional violation.

The task force recommendation virtually guarantees years of trial and appellate litigation focusing on what constitutes good and bad faith violation. The Supreme Court has already made so many fine distinctions in dealing with the question of when police may search and seize that a number of police departments have had to employ attorneys to explain the rules to officers. The task force recommendation would make Fourth Amendment law even more impenetrable to officers, upon whose understanding of the law the privacy of all of us depends. Courts, and especially the Supreme Court, should be given no encouragement to make more fine distinctions.

The task force recommendation puts a substantial premium on the ignorance of law enforcement officers. In order to render legitimate a search or seizure under the task force's proposal, the officer need only convince the judge that he did not know or fully understand the applicable legal requirements. Ignorance may not be bliss, but it surely will have its uses in future search and seizure litigation if the task force recommendation becomes law.

As long as the exclusionary rule exists, even in modified form, it is unlikely that we will try the kinds of alternatives to the rule that I and others have proposed:

police discipline imposed by an independent review board to which cases of official misconduct would be reported by victims, the general public or judges; and a greatly improved civil remedy for innocent victims of illegal searches and seizures.

Such a civil remedy is being considered by a number of members of the Senate Judiciary Committee. These alternatives would deter official misconduct more effectively than does the rule, would involve none of the costs and disadvantages of the rule discussed earlier, and would belatedly bring some serious redress to innocent victims.

As long as the exclusionary rule exists, the rulings of judges in exclusion or suppression hearings may be improperly influenced in some cases by the conclusions reached by independent review boards as to the propriety of officers' actions, not to mention the improper influence on the judiciary which could be exerted by the findings of juries in relevant civil damage suits.

Conversely, the results of suppression or exclusion hearings will in some cases improperly influence the deliberations of jurors in civil damage cases or members of the independent review board. This problem of improper influence can be dealt with most effectively by abolishing the exclusionary rule.

CONCLUSION

The exclusionary rule is fundamentally unsound. The task force's recommended change in the rule would build an unsatisfactory halfway house between retention and abolition of the rule. Only a final end to the rule will produce the necessary incentive to try serious alternatives.

As long as this country, which has adopted a more extensive exclusion policy than that of any other nation, permits the rule to continue, it may well deserve the unhappy consequences of its failure to abolish the rule.

QUESTIONS FOR DISCUSSION

1. Should the guilty go free if the evidence against them has been seized illegally?
2. What is the value of procedural safeguards if the crime rate goes up?
3. Should there be a national standard for criminal justice?
4. Why should the federal courts oversee state law enforcement?
5. What is the *good faith exception?* Do you agree with it?

RECOMMENDED READINGS

BACIGAL, RONALD J. "Some Observations and Proposals on the Nature of the Fourth Amendment." 46 *George Washington Law Review* 529 (1978).

"The Exclusionary Rule Debate." *Judicature* 62 (Nov. 1978), entire issue.

FORKOSCH, MORRIS D. "In Defense of the Exclusionary Rule." *American Journal of Economics and Sociology* 41 (Apr. 1982), pp. 151–56.

GRISWOLD, ERWIN N. *Search and Seizure: A Dilemma of the Supreme Court.* Lincoln: University of Nebraska Press, 1975.

HIRSCHEL, J. DAVID. *Fourth Amendment Rights.* Lexington, Mass.: Heath, 1979.

JENSEN, D. LOWELL. "Does the Exclusionary Rule Exclude Justice?" *USA Today Magazine* 112 (Nov. 1983), pp. 26–29.

KAMISAR, YALE. "Does (Did) (Should) the Exclusionary Rule Rest on a 'Principled Basis' Rather Than an 'Empirical Proposition'?" 16 *Creighton Law Review* 565 (1982–83).

LOEWY, ARNOLD H. "The Fourth Amendment as a Device for Protecting the Innocent." 81 *Michigan Law Review* 1229 (Apr. 1983).

SCHLESINGER, STEPHEN R. *Exclusionary Injustice: The Problem of Illegally Obtained Evidence.* New York: Marcel Dekker, 1975.

SUNDERLAND, LANE Y. "Liberals, Conservatives and the Exclusionary Rule." 71 *Journal of Criminal Law and Criminology* 343 (Winter 1980).

U.S. CONG., HOUSE OF REPRESENTATIVES. *Exclusionary Rules in Criminal Trials: Oversight Hearings.* Hearings before the Subcommittee on Criminal Justice of the Committee on the Judiciary, 98th Cong., 1st Sess., 1983.

U.S. CONG., SENATE. *The Exclusionary Rule Bills.* Hearings before the Subcommittee on Criminal Law of the Committee on the Judiciary, 97th Cong., 1st Sess., 1981.

YES THE CASE AGAINST PLEA BARGAINING

Moise Berger

Had I known that I would have received a mandatory twenty-five-year sentence for bank robbery, without any opportunity to negotiate a plea, there would have been no power on earth strong enough to have forced me to rob the bank I robbed.

I gambled and, really, I won. Please don't get me wrong. Only a fool would consider eight years in prison as a prize. But compared to twenty or possibly thirty (which I faced initially before entering plea bargaining), it is indeed a blessing—however mixed.

I have been in fifty-eight institutions since 1943, including five federal penitentiaries. I know many bank robbers and have learned something quite common about them. They, like myself, are failures. But many of them think along parallel lines with me.

So stated Raymond E. James, a convicted bank robber, on August 28, 1974. With crime increasing at an alarming rate throughout the United States, this statement by a professional in our system of criminal justice is a damning indictment of the practice of plea bargaining.

Plea bargaining has been at the eye of a storm of controversy for many years. Criminal defendants and their attorneys extol the practice and advocate it as a necessary part of the system of criminal justice. Most members of the public abhor it and regard it as bargaining away the interest of society in protection from crime.

Moise Berger, "The Case against Plea Bargaining," *American Bar Association Journal* 62 (May 1976), pp. 621–24. Reprinted with permission from the *ABA Journal*, The Lawyer's Magazine.

Particularly those who are victims of crime hold this view.

Prosecutors and judges have long accepted as an article of faith and belief that plea bargaining is necessary to avoid a congestion of courts that would bring the system to a grinding halt. In recent years a few prosecuting offices have questioned whether a ban on plea bargaining actually would cause the court congestion feared.

Perhaps the most important question is, what does justice require? Our experience in Maricopa County, Arizona, has proved that plea bargaining does not serve any just purpose and that its elimination will not disrupt the system of justice.

To discuss plea bargaining we should first define it. This is necessary because there are different types of plea bargaining. Some offices engage in one type but not in others. The most common practice is "charge bargaining," in which the defense and prosecuting attorneys agree to plead a defendant guilty to a charge in return for the dismissal of other charges. In another form of this practice, the defendant pleads guilty to a lesser charge than the one with which he was originally charged. Many offices that do not allow this practice do engage in "sentence bargaining," which occurs when the defendant pleads guilty to the original charge in return for a recommendation that the defendant receive a sentence of probation or a sentence not to exceed an agreed on term of years.

I use the term to include all of the above

practices of charge bargaining and sentence bargaining. When our office quit plea bargaining, we banned all forms of the practice.

PLEA BARGAINING IS SOMETIMES NECESSARY

It also should be pointed out that although our office prohibits plea bargaining, it recognizes exceptional cases when plea bargaining is still necessary. For example, a case may be so weak that a plea to some other charge may be preferable to going to trial and losing the entire case. This could happen when, for example, a critical witness has died or is unavailable. Another situation justifying a plea bargain is when the defendant has been used by the police as an informer or when he is needed as a witness to convict another defendant who is much more deeply involved in crime.

In these types of cases plea bargaining is recognized by the police and prosecutors as necessary. Any system that eliminates plea bargaining still allows for exceptions when the above facts exist or other conditions of justice require it. In other words, the abolition of plea bargaining is not an inflexible rule that applies in all cases regardless of the requirements of justice. It is, however, the abolition of a system that, on the whole, is unnecessary and corrupts the system of justice.

Those who defend plea bargaining usually have either a vested interest in seeing the practice continue or are seriously mistaken about the value and necessity of plea bargaining. There are a number of serious problems with plea bargaining.

First, it permits a prosecutor to avoid making decisions in the system of justice he is morally and legally obligated to make as a prosecutor. Imagine a case in which a defendant claims he is innocent of murder. If the case is weak or if there is some doubt in the prosecutor's mind, he may offer to plea bargain the case to a lesser charge, such as manslaughter. The defendant is advised by his attorney to plead guilty to the charge because manslaughter carries only a ten-year maximum sentence compared to murder, which could result in a life sentence or even a sentence of death. The defendant pleads guilty to the lesser charge. No one will ever know if he pleaded because he was guilty or because he was afraid of getting the death sentence if he went to trial. The prosecutor is happy because he has been relieved of the extra work and effort required in finding out if the man is innocent or guilty. But was justice done? No one will ever know.

A SIGNAL FOR NONCHALANCE

Second, plea bargaining tends to indicate to a judge that the prosecutor does not feel strongly about a case. This may influence a judge to sentence a defendant more leniently than he would normally. For example, a defendant who is charged with robbery faces a sentence of five years to life. But if the case is plea bargained down to a charge of grand theft in return for a plea of guilty, the man can be sentenced only to one to ten years—even if the judge wanted to sentence more severely, he can no longer give any sentence more than ten years. In other cases the judge has the power, despite the plea bargain, to sentence the defendant to as long a sentence as justice requires. Yet the judge may take the plea bargain as an indication that the prosecutor did not believe that the man should get a severe prison sentence.

Third, when there is a plea bargain there is often also a tacit agreement between the attorneys involved that as part of the deal the prosecution will not press hard for a severe sentence. In the absence of plea bargaining, the prosecutor can ask for any sentence he feels is just without violating an understanding with the defense attorney. But, if the attorneys have agreed to drop a charge in order to get a plea, it is only a short step for the defense attorney also to ask for an additional agreement that they will recommend probation or a light sentence or that the prosecutor will say nothing at the time of sentencing. Although he need not do so, the judge may be willing to accept this recommendation in return for a plea of guilty, since he feels it will help lessen the workload in his courtroom.

Fourth, plea bargaining causes a loss of public confidence in our system of government. At a time when the faith of the public in public servants already has been seriously undermined, we should not contribute further to this lack of faith by trying to plea bargain justice. Justice can never truly be bargained. Yet, in the most sacred part of our system of government we openly talk of "deals" and "bargaining." Even if a ban on plea bargaining caused more trials, which it does not, it would be worth it to avoid this loss of integrity and to see that justice is done.

Fifth, another problem is that plea bargaining makes it easier to have corruption within a prosecutor's office. Under a policy of plea bargaining all types of deals are made. Because of the great variety of facts in each case and because of the great variety of "bargains" that can be negotiated, it is almost impossible to maintain any effective system of checking on these deals to make sure they are proper. Our office is prosecuting more than eight thousand cases a year, which makes it impossible for the county attorney to check every one. It requires a considerable amount of time to check on even one case properly and to learn all the facts that justified a particular deal in a specific case. This makes it quite easy for someone to reduce or dismiss charges against someone deliberately. Corruption, therefore, is much more possible under a system in which plea bargaining is allowed. If the decision to prosecute all felonies must be made by one prosecutor's office, as is often the case, it would be attractive for organized crime to infiltrate that office with personnel in their pay. This situation is much less possible when plea bargaining is not allowed. When a person reduces or dismisses a case, it is easy to turn a spotlight on it. It is easy to detect and to determine what happened since it is allowed only in certain exceptional cases.

INEXPERIENCE CONTRIBUTES TO "DEALS"

Sixth, unjustified "deals" are not only possible through corruption but also through lack of experience or negligence of the prosecuting attorney. A negligent or inexperienced attorney may "deal" a case that never should have been bargained to a lesser charge. As a result, months of work by the police may have been for nothing. It is almost impossible to watch the eight hundred cases filed a month to determine who is making bad "deals." Spot checks help, but are not effective when dealing with seventy-two attorneys handling more than eight thousand felonies a year.

In the January, 1975, *Reader's Digest*, Richard H. Kuh related how an assistant district attorney in New York reduced an armed robbery charge to a misdemeanor despite the fact that the defendant had held a knife to the victim. The assistant somehow had been persuaded to do this. Mr. Kuh, who was then New York district attorney, said, "I boiled when I heard of it." When plea bargaining is not allowed, this type of nightmare simply cannot happen.

Finally, the Arizona legislature recently passed laws providing for mandatory prison terms for certain types of criminals. This action was needed desperately to help curb the rising crime rate in Arizona, which is rapidly becoming a national disgrace. To continue plea bargaining would have defeated the intent of the legislature and rendered its measures useless. The legislature attempted to increase the penalties for crime in order to clear our streets of criminals. Plea bargaining defeats this purpose by allowing the criminal to plead guilty to a charge that carries a lesser penalty.

Approximately five years ago we adopted a policy of not plea bargaining charges of sale of narcotics, sale of drugs, and sale of marijuana. This was an experimental program to see if a ban on plea bargaining would cause an increase in cases taken to trial. We found that this ban did not cause a rise in the number of trials. It resulted in defendants pleading guilty to the charges, and in many cases there were fewer trials. A review of the figures show that this policy has become so successful that the great majority of defendants in narcotic sales cases now plead guilty to the charge without going to trial. This has helped alleviate case backlog rather than cause it.

Because the results of this experiment were so contrary to what we had expected, we decided to move ahead with caution to be sure our results were not misleading. After a few years we were convinced that banning plea bargaining did not slow down the court system but seemed to speed it up. We then tried a new experiment.

THE TOP TEN DEFENDANTS LIST

On March 1, 1972, we created a special prosecution unit of five lawyers to prosecute the top ten worst defendants. Criminal defendants chosen to be prosecuted by this unit were some of the county's most dangerous and antisocial individuals. The charges against them included robbery, kidnaping, child molesting, sale of narcotics, murder, and other serious crimes. The lawyers assigned to this program were instructed not to plea bargain any of the charges against the defendants placed on

this list. As each defendant was convicted and sentenced, his name was replaced by another criminal on the list. This program came to be known as the county attorney's top ten defendants list.

It was assumed that since there was no plea bargaining, these defendants would go to trial in most cases. This was not the case. In a majority of the cases the defendant pleaded guilty to the charges, and a trial was not necessary. Surprisingly, even when a defendant was facing numerous charges, the majority pleaded guilty to all the charges. In fact, one defendant pleaded guilty to all eight counts of armed robbery he was charged with, and he received a sentence of twenty to thirty years in prison. Once again the time-honored assumption that a ban on plea bargaining would cause a backlog of trials in court was proved false. In fact, 70 per cent of these defendants pleaded to the charge in spite of the fact that they had been designated as the county's worst offenders and knew that we intended to ask for severe jail sentences.

After a one-year operation the rate of conviction on these people was 93.3 per cent. We attained average minimum sentences of twenty-six years for those prosecuted under the program and maximum sentences of life imprisonment in 33 per cent of all these cases.

The program was so successful that it was endorsed with approval by the Organized Crime Council, composed of the attorney general of the state of Arizona, the chief of police of Phoenix, and others.

ONLY JUSTIFICATION PROVED GROUNDLESS

Because of the success of these programs, it had become obvious that there were no good reasons for plea bargaining. The one possible justification—an increase of cases taken to trial—had been proved groundless. On May 15, 1973, we decided to expand the top-ten program into a full-scale ban on plea bargaining. We announced that cases of murder, manslaughter, and robbery would no longer be plea bargained by our office.

A comparison of the pleas to robbery charges before and after May 15, 1973, reports that there were more pleas to the charge after we quit plea bargaining. A ban on plea bargaining failed to cause the widely feared increase of trials in court.

The record shows that there were forty-two pleas to the charge for the first four months of 1973 when plea bargaining was allowed. In the four months immediately following the adoption of the no-plea-bargaining ban there were thirty-seven pleas to the charge—almost no change. In the last four months of 1973, when no plea bargaining was allowed, pleas of guilty to the charge rose to eighty-nine. This was an increase of 211 per cent.

A comparison of murder charges before and after May 15, 1973, shows an increase of two cases in the number of cases pleaded to the charge after plea bargaining was banned. The figures show a slight increase in the number of trials (ten) for the last four months of 1973 compared to the first four months. Since murder is an offense bearing the death penalty and the facts on each case vary widely, it would be difficult to interpret the figures with respect to the elimination of the plea bargaining issue.

When we look at the figures for 1974 we find that for the entire year pleas to the charge of robbery had become the established practice. In fact, out of 332 robbery cases closed in 1974, 258 pleaded guilty to the charge rather than go to trial. Three cases were plea bargained due to special circumstances. By pleading guilty, trials were avoided with a savings to the taxpayer on these 258 cases.

Because of the success of the program in getting defendants to plead guilty without causing any backlog in the court sys-tem, we decided in May, 1974, to expand the ban on plea bargaining to burglary cases.

By comparing the first four months of 1974 with plea bargaining to the last four months ending with October, we found 210 per cent more guilty pleas to the charge of burglary than when plea bargaining was allowed.

An increase in trials of burglaries also has been noted beginning in May, 1974. This is due to the general increase in the number of cases being filed. The number of trials also has risen in categories in which plea bargaining is still allowed. Although trials have increased in almost all categories of crime during the last five months, pleas to the charge have increased significantly only in those cases in which plea bargaining is not allowed.

PLEA BARGAINING IS A WEAK LINK

The incidence of crime is at an all time high. So every link in the criminal justice system must be as strong as possible. Plea bargaining is not consistent with strong prosecution. The practice of plea bargaining is not the cause of the lenient treatment of criminals, and the elimination of the practice will not, by itself, do away with leniency. Yet, it is one way of saying to the criminal, "We intend to do everything we can to take you out of society and stop you from preying on law-abiding people."

The system banning plea bargaining has been so successful that this office has expanded its policy against plea bargaining to cover all rape, sodomy, lewd and lascivious acts, and child molestation charges.

In September, 1974, Attorney General William B. Saxbe attacked plea bargaining, which he said was "too often used by prosecutors to allow vast numbers of offenders at the state and local level to receive minimum punishment, if any at all."

On January 23, 1973, the National Advisory Commission on Criminal Justice

Standards and Goals published its *Report on Courts*. The commission condemned plea bargaining in strong and definite language. It stated:

> As one authority has observed, even the observers most critical of today's guilty-plea system usually stop short of total condemnation of plea bargaining as an institution. The commission does not stop short. It totally condemns plea bargaining as an institution and recommends that within five years no such plea bargaining take place. The only concession the commission is willing to make is that total elimination of the practice will take appreciable time. . . .
> . . .Elimination of plea bargaining is likely to create less of an increase in the number of trials than many believe. It is virtually certain, however, that it will increase the fairness and rationality of the processing of criminal defendants. . . .
> By imposing a penalty upon the exercise of procedural rights in those cases in which there is a reasonable likelihood that the rights will be vindicated, the plea negotiation system creates a significant danger to the innocent. Many of the rights it discourages are rights designed to prevent the conviction of innocent defendants. To the extent these rights are rendered nonoperative by the plea negotiation system, innocent defendants are endangered. Plea negotiation not only serves no legitimate function in the processing of criminal defendants, but it also encourages irrationality in the court process, burdens the exercise of individual rights, and endangers the right of innocent defendants to be acquitted.

One argument often given to justify plea bargaining is that it provides flexibility in prosecution. The theory is that the prosecutor should make a judgment as to whether the criminal defendant deserves leniency and then offer him a lesser charge to give the defendant the leniency he deserves. This argument involves a serious misunderstanding of the function of the prosecution in the criminal justice system. The law does provide for the showing of leniency or harshness in a given criminal case. It does so by providing for a range in a term of the sentence or amount of the fine. But this is done by the judge after there has been an investigation of the background of the criminal, of his chance for rehabilitation, and of his propensities for continued criminal activity.

Another reason offered to support the practice of plea bargaining is that it is a necessary evil to prevent a backlog of cases. This argument is, however, based on assumption without any factual proof. Few prosecutors in the United States have bothered to test this assumption. When it has been tested, it is usually discovered, as the National Advisory Commission on Criminal Justice Standards and Goals stated, that elimination of plea bargaining creates less of an increase in the number of trials than many believe. The program followed by the Maricopa County Attorney's Office to eliminate plea bargaining has proved trials are not increased if the prosecutor refuses to plea bargain.

Our experience in eliminating plea bargaining has been surprising. The system has been so successful that this office recently has expanded its policy to cover assault with a deadly weapon and sex crimes. The list of crimes no longer plea bargained now includes murder, manslaughter, robbery, burglary, sale of narcotics, sale of marijuana, sale of dangerous drugs, rape, sodomy, lewd and lascivious acts, child molesting, and assault with a deadly weapon.

NO IN DEFENSE OF "BARGAIN JUSTICE"

Thomas W. Church, Jr.

The strongest critics of plea bargaining argue that the practice should be abolished because it coerces defendants to give up their right to trial and because it results in irrational sentences for criminal defendants. Neither charge is applicable to a system of plea negotiations that meets four basic criteria: (1) the defendant always has the alternative of a jury trial at which both verdict and sentence are determined solely on the merits; (2) the defendant is represented throughout negotiations by competent counsel; (3) both defense and prosecution have equal access to relevant evidence; and (4) both possess sufficient resources to take a case to trial. The most fruitful direction of reform is to seek to achieve these conditions rather than attempt to eliminate plea bargaining.

Although plea bargaining has a venerable history, at least in America (see Alschuler, 1979; Friedman, 1979), its centrality in criminal procedure has come to public prominence only in the past decade. The revelation that the modal criminal conviction in American courts follows a negotiated plea of guilty rather than the jury trial commonly glorified in literature, on television, and in bar association after-dinner speeches has been accompanied by indignant calls for reform, if not eradication, of the practice.

The critics of plea bargaining can be divided into two camps, distinguished primarily by the amount of reform they advocate. The first group, including the American Bar Association (1967) and the President's Commission on Law Enforce-

Thomas W. Church, Jr., "In Defense of 'Bargain Justice,'" *Law and Society Review* **13 (Winter 1979), pp. 509–25. Copyright by Law and Society Review, the official publication of the Law and Society Association.**

ment and the Administration of Justice (1967), urges selected reform. Their concern typically focuses on procedural deficiencies of particular bargaining systems: the possibility of broken or misunderstood promises, for example, or of prosecutorial caprice in determining which defendants are to be offered a plea bargain. The seriousness of these concerns has been substantiated by scholars and practitioners alike, but the faults can be redressed through changes that fall short of a fundamental alteration in dispositional procedures. A remedy often advanced for broken promises is the formalization of plea bargains: agreements are placed on the record in open court (see, e.g., U.S. National Advisory Commission, 1973:50). Abuse of prosecutorial discretion can be lessened considerably if prosecutors promulgate and enforce office standards to guide the plea bargaining decisions of their deputies (see, e.g., Davis, 1971: ch. 7; American Law Institute, 1972: §350.3(2)).

Many of the proposals for adding procedural safeguards to present plea bargaining practices have considerable merit; there is little question that bargain justice is subject to abuse. My concern in this paper is with a second group of commentators who assert the inherent impropriety of *any* system of negotiated guilty pleas. These critics conclude that the defects of bargain justice are irremediable and that a defensible system of criminal justice can only be achieved by eliminating bargaining. The prestigious U.S. National Advisory Commission on Criminal Justice Standards and Goals made such a far-reaching recommendation (1973:46) as have a growing number of scholars (see, e.g., Alschuler, 1968, 1975, 1976; *Harvard Law Review,* 1970; Kipnis, 1976).

Two separate arguments support the recommended abolition of plea bargaining. The first focuses on procedural fairness for individual defendants: any system of plea bargaining is held to be improper because it places a price—forfeiture of those concessions available after a guilty plea—on the exercise of important constitutional rights. In particular, plea bargaining allegedly operates to encourage, if not coerce, even innocent defendants to waive their right to trial by jury. The second argument is quite different. Rather than solicitude for individual defendants, the concern is for the societal interest in rational (and appropriately stringent) criminal sentences. Plea bargaining, particularly in pressured urban jurisdictions, is said to encourage harried prosecutors and judges to make dispositional concessions to defendants on the sole ground of administrative expediency. The resulting sentences therefore cannot be justified by any rationale for the penal sanction, whether it be deterrence, societal protection, rehabilitation, or (even) retribution. When this argument is combined with the preceding due process critique, the current system of plea negotiation is placed in the unenviable position of being assaulted by civil libertarians and law-and-order advocates at the same time.

This "abolitionist" literature coexists with a growing body of behavioral research on criminal courts whose common theme is the extraordinary resistance of court systems to change, particularly in the negotiation process by which most criminal and civil cases are resolved (see Church, 1976; Heumann, 1975; Heumann and Loftin, 1979; Nimmer, 1976; *Iowa Law Review*, 1975). This paper grew out of my reflection on the demonstrated difficulty of eliminating plea bargaining, together with an observation from my own research that is confirmed by a number of current empirical studies of plea negotiation: in many court systems across the country,

bargain justice does not appear to suffer from the systematic irrationality and unfairness attributed to it by many critics. Indeed, a number of studies have found that the flexibility of plea bargaining as a dispositional device has substantial advantages over the formal rigidities of the jury trial (see, e.g., Heumann, 1978; Rosett and Cressey, 1976; Utz, 1978; Enker, 1967).

If plea bargaining cannot readily be eliminated and operates in a tolerable, or even desirable, manner in many jurisdictions, a careful examination of abolitionist arguments is surely in order. Although plea bargaining is not without its supporters, particularly among those prosecutors, defense attorneys, and judges involved in the daily administration of criminal justice, most of these defenders fail to address the arguments charging the inherent impropriety of the process. Rather, they claim that we must live with plea bargaining because of the enormous financial burden that would accompany any increase in already crowded trial dockets. It is in this context that Chief Justice Burger repeated a familiar refrain in *Santobello v. New York* (404 U.S. 257, 260, 1971), a case that gave bargain justice the constitutional stamp of approval:

> "[P]lea bargaining" . . . is an essential component of the administration of justice. Properly administered, it is to be encouraged. If every criminal charge were subjected to a full-scale trial, the States and the Federal Government would need to multiply by many times the number of judges and court facilities.

But a defense grounded upon economics or administrative convenience is somewhat beside the point against the kind of fundamental charges leveled against plea bargaining by its strong critics. It is surely beneficial to reduce the costs of running a criminal justice system, but not by utilizing procedures that are irrational and unfair, if not unconstitutional. The frequent assertion that plea bargaining introduces much needed dispositional flexibility into an overly rigid trial system is similarly incomplete: flexibility may be a virtue, but it surely should not be obtained through methods that conflict with substantive goals of the penal law or with constitutional requirements of due process.

The conception of plea bargaining applied in this analysis is very broad, and consists of two elements: (1) the defendant's decision not to assert his innocence, and (2) a systemwide expectation that such cooperative defendants will ultimately receive less severe sentences than those who demand a formal adversarial determination of guilt. A plea bargain may be an explicit *quid pro quo* or merely a tacit understanding. So long as defendants routinely expect to receive some form of sentencing consideration in exchange for an admission of guilt, the essence of a system of bargain justice is present. This inclusive definition is adopted here because it reduces the practice to its lowest common denominator. Focus on a sentence discount both emphasizes the key element that critics most decry and avoids the artificial distinctions of a more limited perspective based upon the nature of the bargaining (explicit versus implicit; "higgling" versus exchange of nonnegotiable offers) or the currency in which it is conducted (charge or sentence).[1]

Most critics of plea bargaining accept the theoretical framework of the Anglo-American adversary system. Within this context, it is my contention that the case for the inherent impropriety of plea bargaining is groundless. A system that confers sentence discounts on those defendants who waive an adversarial determination of guilt need violate neither the tenets of rationality in the penal law nor the Constitution. Negotiated dispositions in a properly constructed system will approximate the probable results of trial, and any remaining distance between a bargained disposition and what "would have been" the result of trial involves no inherent illegitimacy. The following two sections discuss, in turn, the allegations that plea bargaining is unfair to defendants and that it subverts rational sentencing goals. I will reply that neither charge is applicable to a plea bargaining system that meets four basic requirements:[2] (1) The defendant must always have the alternative of a jury trial at which both verdict and sentence are determined and can be justified solely on the merits of the case. (2) The defendant must be represented throughout negotiations by competent counsel. (3) Both defense and prosecution must have equal access to all available information likely to bear on the outcome of the case should it go to trial. (4) Both should possess sufficient resources to take the case to trial if an acceptable agreement does not result from the negotiations.

I am aware that these conditions are not always met in American jurisdictions. And it is not my contention that operationalization of these conditions will produce a flawless criminal justice system. *I am simply arguing that such a system of plea bargaining is*

---

[1] The focus of this analysis is on sentencing because plea bargaining is conceptualized primarily as a sentencing process. The "currency" of the negotiation may be the number or seriousness of charges, but charge is of importance primarily because of its direct effect on sentence.

Bargains are also diverse in the degree of certainty they provide: some assure a specific sentence lower than what would be expected upon conviction at trial; some involve only the guarantee of a sentence lower than the maximum that *could* be imposed after trial. Because plea bargaining is typically discussed by both practitioners and critics *as though* defendants received a sentence discount for pleading guilty, this form of bargaining will serve as the focus of the analysis that follows. If so clear and unambiguous a differential in disposition is justifiable, lesser distinctions should readily pass muster.

[2] These requirements are discussed at greater length in the final section of this paper.

no less rational or constitutional than the trial process upon which the negotiation is based. I will argue in a final section that the most fruitful direction of reform in the operation of our system of criminal courts is to seek to achieve these conditions rather than attempt to eliminate plea bargaining. The discussion that follows is of necessity very general: I make no distinctions between different plea bargaining mechanisms and practices. My thesis is that plea bargaining in its broadest sense—the implicit or explicit exchange of sentencing consideration for a defendant's admission of guilt—need not be unfair to either the defendant or the public.

I. PROCEDURAL FAIRNESS AND THE DEFENDANT

The basis of the due process critique of plea bargaining is summed up in the following passage from the report of the U.S. National Advisory Commission on Criminal Justice Standards and Goals (1973:48).

> [A] major cost involved in plea negotiation is the burden it inevitably places upon the exercise of the rights involved in trial—the rights to jury trial, to confront and cross-examine witnesses, to have the judge or jury convinced of guilt beyond a reasonable doubt, and similar matters. . . . It is inevitable that exercising these rights often will involve financial costs to defendants, time commitments, and the emotionally unpleasant experience of litigation. But it is wholly unacceptable to add to this the necessity of forfeiting a discount that could otherwise be obtained.

Since this argument speaks to the plight of the individual criminal defendant, an evaluation of its validity can best begin by examining the concrete situation of a person indicted. Any criminal defendant faces unpleasant alternatives: he can either plead guilty or defend himself at trial. The overriding motivation of most defendants confronting this choice is to minimize postconviction sanction. In a plea bargaining situation the defendant must weigh the sentence he expects will follow a trial conviction, discounted by the possibility of acquittal, against the sentence expected after a guilty plea. The greater the guilty plea sentence discount, the more attractive that alternative becomes—at least for those defendants with some significant chance of being convicted. In practical terms, when a defendant elects to plead guilty he trades his chance of acquittal for a reduction in the expected posttrial sentence. Viewed in this way, much of the talk about the burden that plea bargaining places on the right to a jury trial is irrelevant. It can hardly be contended, at least from the perspective of the individual defendant, that a jury trial is somehow intrinsically beneficial independent of its result. Trials are costly and psychologically unpleasant. Our adversary process was hardly designed to be otherwise. Criminal trials produce one "winner" and one "loser." As the uncertainty of that result increases, so does the incentive for both sides to find some mutually satisfactory accommodation in which the benefits of success at trial are discounted by the possibility of failure.

Although there are obvious differences, plea bargaining operates in a manner roughly analogous to pretrial negotiations in a civil suit. A plaintiff may offer the defendant a chance to "settle" the suit by paying less than the amount sought at trial. Like the criminal defendant, the civil defendant faces a mandatory trial with an uncertain outcome and judgment should he decline the settlement offered. The attractiveness of a particular offer will depend on the strength of the plaintiff's case. Yet surely it would be nonsensical to argue that the civil defendant's constitutional right to a jury trial is "burdened" by these negotiations, even though they are supported, indeed encouraged, by the legal system. The criminal defendant, like the civil defendant, possesses the right to a jury trial up to the time he decides it would be preferable to accept a nontrial disposition. It is precisely his possession of that right—with the uncertainty for both sides that its exercise necessarily entails—that allows bargaining to occur. If the sole benefit a defendant expects from a jury trial is the chance for acquittal, it is difficult to argue that the state somehow burdens the right to trial merely by posing an alternative that may be more attractive.

Other procedural rights of criminal defendants are formally protected only at trial: the right to have illegally obtained evidence excluded from consideration by the trier of fact, for example, or the right to cross-examine witnesses. This fact has led some critics to maintain that plea bargaining is an essentially lawless process in which important evidentiary protections are irrelevant. An extension of this argument is the frequently expressed concern that innocent defendants are encouraged to plead guilty through bargaining. Again, in the words of the U.S. National Advisory Commission:

> By imposing a penalty upon the exercise of procedural rights in those cases in which there is a reasonable likelihood that the rights will be vindicated, the plea negotiation system creates a significant danger to the innocent. Many of the rights it discourages are rights designed to prevent the conviction of innocent defendants. To the extent these rights are rendered nonoperative by the plea negotiation system, innocent defendants are endangered. [1973:48]

This assertion that "there are no rules of evidence in plea negotiation" (Alschuler, 1968:78) ignores the fact, documented by almost every published study of plea bargaining, that the primary determinant of any plea agreement is the assessment by counsel of the probable outcome of a trial. Thus if a confession or other crucial item of evidence is likely to be ruled inadmissible, any bargain struck will almost certainly

reflect the altered probabilities of conviction, at least if both attorneys are informed and diligent.

A major problem in evaluating the alleged danger of plea bargaining to an innocent defendant is the singular ambiguity of the key term. "Innocent defendant" can refer either to a person objectively innocent of the crime charged (but who still presumably has some risk of conviction at trial) or to a person who would be acquitted were a trial held (whether objectively innocent or not). With apologies to the late Herbert Packer[3] I will term the former defendant "factually innocent," the latter "legally innocent." Albert Alschuler, a leading academic critic of bargain justice, cites examples of the effect of plea bargaining on both types of defendants. The factually innocent defendant:

> San Francisco defense attorney Benjamin Davis recently represented a man charged with kidnapping and forcible rape. The defendant was innocent, Davis says, and after investigating the case Davis was confident of an acquittal. The prosecutor, who seems to have shared the defense attorney's opinion on this point, offered to permit a guilty plea to simple battery. Conviction on this charge would not have led to a greater sentence than thirty days' imprisonment, and there was every likelihood that the defendant would be granted probation. When Davis informed his client of this offer, he emphasized that conviction at trial seemed highly improbable. The defendant's reply was simple: "I can't take the chance." [1968:61]

The legally innocent defendant:

> Before his appointment to the bench, Judge Harold Leventhal of the United States Court of Appeals for the District of Columbia Circuit once represented an indigent

[3] See his discussion of "legal guilt" and "factual guilt" (1968: ch. 8).

sailor charged with the unauthorized use of a motor vehicle. The only evidence against the defendant was his confession, and Judge Leventhal estimated that the odds against the admission of this confession in evidence were approximately three to one. Even this slight [?] chance of a felony conviction was sufficient, however, to induce the defendant to plead guilty to a misdemeanor. [*Ibid.*]

In both circumstances, plea bargaining operated to make a guilty plea seem more attractive than a trial, even though it appears that the former defendant had not committed the act charged, and the latter defendant, although factually guilty, had a decent chance of acquittal.

The problem with the case against plea bargaining from the perspective of the factually innocent defendant is that the critics seem to assume that such blameless defendants are necessarily exonerated at trial. It is a sobering fact that this is not always the case. Trials do involve a risk that the factually innocent defendant may be found legally guilty. Legal innocence is merely an attorney's prediction prior to a trial. And the most competent attorney can err in predicting success on the basis of procedural defenses such as exclusion of incriminating evidence, or entrapment, alibi witnesses, and the like. If most defendants did not face a very real chance of conviction at trial, all incentive to bargain would be eliminated, and with it this criticism of plea bargaining. It is therefore somewhat disingenuous to argue that the innocent defendant suffers from being offered an alternative to the high stakes of a trial. So long as the choice of trial or plea rests with the defendant, competently advised by informed counsel, the alternative posed by the state of a certain but less severe sentence need not improperly encourage or coerce a guilty plea from "innocent" defendants any more than it does from "guilty" ones. Benjamin Davis, counsel for the defendant in the rape case

cited above, puts the problem into perspective. According to Alschuler:

> Davis reports that he is uncomfortable when he permits innocent clients to plead guilty; but in this case it would have been playing God to stand in the defendant's way. The attorney's assessment of the outcome at trial can always be wrong, and it is hard to tell a defendant that "professional ethics" require a course that may ruin his life. [1968:61]

Indeed. It is equally difficult to argue that concern for the individual defendant dictates a system in which there can be no alternative to that potentially ruinous course of action. Whether the substantive goals of the penal law require an end to the practice of offering sentences discounted for the uncertainty of the trial result will be examined in the following section. It cannot be maintained that posing such an alternative is inherently unfair to the defendant.

II. PLEA BARGAINING AND THE PUBLIC WELFARE

Most academic "abolitionists" adopt the civil libertarian stance discussed in the preceding section. In the more intensely political environment of the local criminal justice system, however, the case against bargain justice is typically based upon the widespread view that plea bargaining results in excessive and undeserved leniency in the sentencing of admitted criminals. This concern was echoed in the report of the U.S. National Advisory Commission (1973:44): "Since the prosecutor must give up something in return for the defendant's agreement to plead guilty, the frequent result of plea bargaining is that defendants are not dealt with as severely as might otherwise be the case. Thus plea bargaining results in leniency that reduces the deterrent impact of the law." Again it is argued that this alleged problem can only be solved by eliminating the sentencing differential between plea and trial convictions.

This argument clearly has a kind of crude plausibility. If the sentences regularly meted out by judges after trial are defined as those that best serve the goals of the penal system, then any lesser sentence following a guilty plea appears irrationally lenient almost by definition. Like the due process critique of plea bargaining, however, this argument ignores the uncertainty and risk of trial—in this case, the prosecutor's concern that a factually guilty defendant may be acquitted.

To defend plea bargaining in this context, one must come to grips with the pervasive prosecutorial assumption that the vast majority of criminal defendants—at least by the time they reach the plea bargaining stage—are factually guilty. Such a perspective appears to contradict a justly cherished, but often misunderstood, principle of our criminal justice system: the presumption of innocence. The mandate that all defendants must be presumed innocent until proven guilty applies to a presumption of *legal,* not factual, innocence. The rights to bail, to the writ of habeas corpus, to a speedy trial are all grounded in the principle that criminal defendants are to be treated *as if* they were innocent until they are adjudged guilty through due process of law. The presumption of innocence is thus a normative directive to criminal justice personnel; it does not require legal officials to assume that all criminal defendants are *factually* innocent. Indeed, we surely would not want a prosecutor, for example, to hale into court people whom he believed to be innocent of wrongdoing.[4]

In our adversarial system, the prosecutor's role is ambiguous. He is an advocate, to be sure, facing the defense and putting forth the "people's" case as strongly as he can. But he has a quasi-judicial role as well. Studies of prosecuting attorneys across the country regularly reveal their almost universal concern for making sure that dispositions are appropriate and, particularly, for ensuring that no factually innocent defendant is convicted (see Carter, 1974; Rosett and Cressey, 1976; Utz, 1978). As a society we obviously are not prepared to accept the prosecutor's judgment as final in such matters; hence, the right to trial by jury. The point is, however, that at the time of plea negotiations a criminal case has progressed through a police investigation, a prosecutorial (and at least a formal judicial) determination of "probable cause," and the final review of the evidence by a prosecutor prior to plea discussions with defense counsel. At this point most prosecutors assume that those defendants remaining in the system are very probably factually guilty of the offense charged, or of one closely related to it. Whether a particular defendant will be found guilty at trial, however, is subject to the uncertainties of judicial rulings on admissibility of evidence, the availability and persuasiveness of witnesses, the rhetorical ability of opposing counsel, and the unpredictable vagaries of the jury. A conscientious prosecutor, mindful of his responsibility to protect the public welfare, might rationally conclude that the certainty of a lower sentence might better serve the public than the risk of acquittal at trial. In this sense, the prosecutor does not make the defendant a concession for his plea any more than the civil defendant receives a concession from the plaintiff who agrees to an out-of-court settlement. Both defendants exchange their chance of complete exoneration for the security of a judgment less onerous than that which might be imposed after trial. Each party thus trades the pos-

[4] I am indebted to Herbert Packer's discussion of the "presumption of innocence" in the preceding analysis (1968: ch. 8).

sibility of total victory for the certainty of avoiding total defeat.

Our judicial system contains significant protections against the conviction of factually innocent defendants: the fundamental rights to trial by jury, to counsel, to hear and cross-examine witnesses; the constitutional, statutory, and common law rules of evidence; the requirement that guilt be proved beyond a reasonable doubt. The system reflects Blackstone's dictum that "it is better that ten guilty men go free than that one innocent man be convicted." Although no empirical evidence on this point is available, it would be extraordinary if a system guided by so single a purpose did not have the expected effect: factually guilty defendants undoubtedly are freed by the courts more often than factually innocent defendants are convicted. If we assume that the trial system will acquit a predictable number of factually guilty defendants, as it is designed to do, the public policy question is not whether defendants who plead guilty receive sentences lighter than optimum for deterrence purposes. Rather, we must ask whether it is necessarily irrational or otherwise detrimental to the deterrent function of the criminal law to allow procedures in which (1) proportionately more criminal defendants are convicted than would be if all cases went to trial, but (2) the sentences imposed are less severe. Given the recent discussion of the importance of sure (although not necessarily harsh) punishment for effective deterrence of criminal behavior (see, e.g., Twentieth Century Fund, 1976; Wilson, 1975: ch. 8), a choice for more convictions is, at the very least, not inherently irrational.

III. REFORM

As I indicated at the outset, no attempt is made here to defend any existing plea bargaining system, much less the totality of varied practices found in American jurisdictions. Plea bargaining, particularly when judge or prosecutor manipulates posttrial sentences to "punish" those who refuse to plead guilty, can operate to coerce or unfairly encourage guilty pleas. And bargain justice in a court whose resources are inadequate to its caseload may very well result in excessively lenient sentences. These are serious problems, and warrant immediate remedial action. Contrary to what is coming to be conventional wisdom, however, I have argued that these pathologies are not inherent in plea bargaining, that it is quite possible to construct a system of plea negotiation that is at least as defensible as the trial process upon which it is based. In this section I will outline the requirements for such a system. I should indicate that these requirements, like the original definition of plea bargaining, are phrased in very broad terms. I have made no attempt to indicate the specific currency in which plea bargaining should operate (charge reduction or sentence assurance) or who the primary official participant should be (judge or prosecutor). These complex issues are important but not central to my present argument.

The negotiation processes discussed here are centered entirely upon predictions by counsel of the likely trial outcome. This view of plea bargaining is substantiated by a number of recent studies of both prosecutors and defense attorneys: although practitioners admit that considerations such as docket backlog, the economic costs of trial, or pretrial publicity may affect plea negotiations, they are virtually unanimous in asserting that the primary influence in most nontrial dispositions is predicted trial outcome (see Mather, 1974, 1979; Vera Institute of Justice, 1977; Lachman and McLauchlan, 1977). The conceptualization of plea bargaining discussed in this essay thus has considerable basis in the reality of American criminal procedure.

Four theoretical assumptions concerning the operation of bargaining processes underlie the defense set forth above. These requirements, their rationale, and some suggestions for implementing them must now be discussed. First, those cases that go to trial must be decided on the merits, without penalizing the defendant for not pleading guilty. In other words, trial sentences must be objectively *deserved* according to whatever sentencing philosophy is embodied in the penal code. Plea bargaining should therefore result in sentences *less than* this theoretically correct sentence. Posttrial sentences that include a surcharge for refusal to plead guilty would very probably constitute the unconstitutional burden on the right to trial that, critics charge, inheres in all plea bargaining.

In the real world of criminal court operation most trial judges are virtually unfettered in their sentencing decisions, with few statutory guidelines aside from maximum (and occasional minimum) sentences. It is thus virtually impossible to determine whether any individual sentence includes a penalty for demanding a trial. Changes in the sentencing system designed to confine and structure judicial discretion, such as current proposals for "flat time" sentences, would significantly limit opportunities to subvert this standard.[5] In addition, the motivation for imposing a sentence surcharge on those defendants convicted after trial could be reduced substantially if the judges presiding over criminal trials had no professional stake in the success or failure of prior plea negotiations. Creation of two separate benches—one for supervising plea negotiations and one for conducting trials—might be a step toward such a goal, particularly if the trial bench possessed staff adequate to handle all trials in timely fashion. Eliminating prosecutorial sentence

recommendations to trial judges would also further the goal of insulating the trial process from recriminations by official participants in the previous plea negotiations.

Second, every defendant should be represented by counsel throughout the negotiations. If these focus on the likely outcome at trial, it is obviously crucial that a defendant be represented by an attorney with the competence to assess the factual and legal elements of the prosecution's case and to advise him on the relative merits of trial and negotiated settlement. I am not unaware of the growing body of literature that posits an inherent conflict of interest between defendant and defense attorney, which may limit the effectiveness of this requirement (see Blumberg, 1967; Casper, 1972; Skolnick, 1967). A court system in which prosecutor, judge, and defense counsel interact on a continuing basis motivates all participants to cooperate rather than maintain strictly adversarial roles. And this cooperation—of which plea bargaining is the most visible symbol—may result in injustice to the interests of individual defendants and of society at large. Obviously no system of "enlightened plea bargaining" can address this problem. But the institution of plea bargaining is not the cause, nor would its abolition be a cure, for this possible disharmony between the interests of defendants and their attorneys. The incentive to reduce conflict among regular system participants exists equally at trial—as "slow pleas of guilty" and the like well illustrate (see Mather, 1974).

Third, if plea negotiations are to focus on predicted trial outcome, all information and evidence bearing on that outcome should be available equally to prosecution and defense. Procedures for pretrial discovery of relevant evidence held by an adversary are not as fully developed in criminal cases as they are in civil cases, and need improvement. The accuracy and rationality of negotiated pleas could also

[5] I am aware that these proposals are not without their difficulties. For a review of the relevant literature, emphasizing the expected impact of plea bargaining on sentencing reform, see Alschuler (1978).

be enhanced if more complete personal information about the defendant were available at the time of plea negotiations. Information of this sort is generally compiled only after conviction, in a presentence report by the probation department.

The final requirement for a defensible plea bargaining system may be the most difficult to achieve. Participation in a trial is always costly. The problem for plea bargaining is not that the alternative of a trial may cost the parties something but that one party may be unable to absorb these costs. Such circumstances can give the adversary an unfair advantage and any settlement reached may not reflect predicted trial outcome. The fourth requirement, then, is that each side possess sufficient resources to take the case to trial if it believes that the settlement offered does not adequately reflect the likely trial result.

It is important to emphasize that the prosecutor and the defendant may both be plagued by inadequate resources. Large urban jurisdictions often provide the prosecution with insufficient staff to take more than a handful of cases to trial. If the defense can pose a credible trial threat, a defendant very likely to be convicted at trial on a serious charge may be able to bargain for an inappropriately lenient sentence because the prosecution cannot afford an additional trial. To solve this problem it is not necessary to increase staff and courtrooms to provide every defendant with a trial but only to expand the resources of the prosecutor so that his bargaining position reflects the evidentiary strength of his cases and not the size of his backlog.

The problem for the defense is more complex. Theoretically, at least, all defendants have a right to trial. Unfortunately, this view is simplistic. An indigent can demand a trial and be assured that the state will provide the necessary resources to see it through, but a lengthy trial may virtually bankrupt a defendant of moderate means. Flexibility is clearly needed in the concept of indigence to allow some financial assistance to defendants who may be able to absorb limited legal costs but not the expense of a full jury trial.

Public defenders or private attorneys assigned to represent indigent defendants are similarly under economic constraints that may lead them to prefer a guilty plea to a trial, regardless of the facts of the case or the bargaining power of the prosecutor. Public defenders often labor under the same intense caseload pressures experienced by their counterparts in the prosecutor's office. As a result they may urge their clients to settle for a less advantageous bargain than the facts warrant because a trial would constitute an unacceptable drain on scarce resources. When indigent defendants are represented by private court-appointed counsel, a similar situation may arise. Assigned counsel typically are woefully underpaid in comparison to the fees they charge private clients. Compensation for trials is particularly low and defense attorneys therefore maximize their earnings by disposing of an assigned case as quickly as possible through a plea bargain. Trial disincentives could be lessened by increasing public defender staffs and raising the fees paid to appointed counsel. These reforms may not entirely equalize the costs of trial to prosecution and defense but they would help to prevent resources from dictating the level of criminal sentences.

IV. CONCLUSION

In the preceding pages I have tried to show that negotiated settlements of criminal cases need not involve either violations of due process or unjustifiable leniency.

The underlying requirement for such a system is that pretrial negotiations be influenced solely by informed predictions of counsel as to the likely result of a fair trial on the merits of the case. The bargaining positions of the parties should thus be based upon strengths or weaknesses in the case itself and not on unequal access to information or unequal ability to hold out for a trial in the event that a mutually satisfactory settlement cannot be reached. I do not believe these conditions are utopian. As with any reform of the courts, the attempt to implement them must contend with the "local discretionary system" (Nimmer, 1976) of existing relationships and practices among attorneys, prosecutors, and judges. But the basic model of plea bargaining put forward is consistent with nearly every prior study of the practice I have seen. And unlike the call of the "abolitionists," the conditions for a defensible system of plea negotiation need not run counter to the existing structure of incentives and interrelationships in a court.

As indicated at the beginning, this paper is premised on two observations drawn from the growing body of behavioral research on the operation of criminal court systems: the difficulty of eliminating plea bargaining and the positive aspects of less formal adjudication procedures reported in many jurisdictions. These factors mandate a careful rethinking of the case against plea bargaining. It clearly makes considerable difference whether reform efforts over the next decade are directed at the substantial task of abolishing the predominant mode of disposition of criminal cases throughout the country or at achieving less fundamental changes.

My major thesis is that a system of negotiated justice can be as defensible as the trial system upon which the negotiations are based. Our judicial system, for better or worse, is based on the proposition that just resolution of disputes will flow from the clash of interests of litigants whose legal fates are committed almost entirely to the hands of professional counsel. Much of the criticism of plea bargaining is more aptly directed at this laissez-faire model of adjudication than at the informal dispositional procedures that may very well be its logical outgrowth. A necessary accompaniment to arguments for the abolition of plea bargaining is distrust of the capacity of both prosecutor and defense attorney adequately to advance the interests they formally represent. If such distrust is justified, it is unclear how the trappings of formal trial will protect those interests any more effectively than informal negotiation, at least as long as the conduct of the case remains primarily in the hands of lawyers.

If an unavoidable and pernicious disharmony exists between the goals of attorney and client, the only conceivable solution is not abolition of plea bargaining but rather a significant reallocation of responsibility for the conduct of the case from counsel to judge, possibly along the lines of the continental "inquisitorial" system. A certain longing for the judicial oversight and administrative rationality of the civil law countries can be detected in many criticisms of plea bargaining.[6] I do not believe the evidence warrants so drastic a step, however, and I suspect that most of the critics would agree. If such a massive change is not contemplated, this essay argues that an attempt to purify the existing system of bargain justice constitutes a more rational public policy than an expensive—and very possibly futile—effort to abolish plea bargaining.

[6] See, for example, the suggestions for reform of plea bargaining suggested by Alschuler (1976). If accomplished, the resulting system would closely resemble the continental model.

REFERENCES

Alschuler, Albert W. (1968) "The Prosecutor's Role in Plea Bargaining," 36 *University of Chicago Law Review* 50.

———(1975) "The Supreme Court, the Defense Attorney, and the Guilty Plea," 47 *University of Colorado Law Review* 1.

———(1976) "The Trial Judge's Role in Plea Bargaining, Part I," 76 *Columbia Law Review* 1059.

———(1978) "Sentencing Reform and Prosecutorial Power: A Critique of Recent Proposals for 'Fixed' and 'Presumptive' Sentencing," 126 *University of Pennsylvania Law Review* 550.

———(1979) "Plea Bargaining and Its History," 13 *Law and Society Review* 211.

American Bar Association. Project on Minimum Standards for Criminal Justice (1967) *Standards Relating to Pleas of Guilty*. New York: Institute for Judicial Administration.

American Law Institute (1972) *A Model Code of Pre-Arraignment Procedure, Tentative Draft No. 5*. Philadelphia: American Law Institute.

Blumberg, Abraham S. (1967) "The Practice of Law as a Confidence Game: Organizational Cooptation of a Profession," 1 *Law & Society Review* 15.

Carter, Lief H. (1974) *The Limits of Order*. Lexington, Mass.: Lexington Books.

Casper, Jonathan D. (1972) *American Criminal Justice: The Defendant's Perspective*. Englewood Cliffs, N.J.: Prentice-Hall.

Church, Thomas W., Jr. (1976) "Plea Bargains, Concessions, and the Courts: Analysis of a Quasi-Experiment," 10 *Law & Society Review* 377.

Davis, Kenneth Culp (1971) *Discretionary Justice: A Preliminary Examination*. Urbana, Ill.: University of Illinois Press.

Enker, Arnold (1967) "Perspectives on Plea Bargaining," in President's Commission on Law Enforcement and the Administration of Justice.

Friedman, Lawrence M. (1979) "Plea Bargaining in Historical Perspective," 13 *Law and Society Review* 247.

Harvard Law Review (1970) "The Unconstitutionality of Plea Bargaining," 83 *Harvard Law Review* 1387.

Heumann, Milton (1975) "A Note on Plea Bargaining and Case Pressure," 9 *Law & Society Review* 515.

———(1978) *Plea Bargaining: The Experiences of Prosecutors, Judges, and Defense Attorneys*. Chicago: University of Chicago Press.

——— and Colin Loftin (1979) "Mandatory Sentencing and the Abolition of Plea Bargaining: The Michigan Felony Firearm Statute," 13 *Law and Society Review* 393.

Iowa Law Review (1975) "The Elimination of Plea Bargaining in Black Hawk County: A Case Study," 61 *Iowa Law Review* 1053.

Kipnis, Kenneth (1976) "Criminal Justice and the Negotiated Plea," 86 *Ethics* 93.

Lachman, Judith and William McLauchlan (1977) "Models of Plea Bargaining," in Stuart Nagel (ed.) *Modeling the Criminal Justice System*. Beverly Hills, Calif.: Sage Publications.

Mather, Lynn (1974) "Some Determinants of the Method of Case Disposition: Decision-Making by Public Defenders in Los Angeles," 8 *Law & Society Review* 187.

———(1979) *Plea Bargaining or Trial? The Process of Criminal Case Disposition*, Lexington, Mass.: Lexington Books.

Nimmer, Raymond (1976) "A Slightly Moveable Object: A Case Study in Judicial Reform in the Criminal Justice System," 48 *Denver Law Journal* 206.

Packer, Herbert (1968) *The Limits of the Criminal Sanction*. Stanford, Calif.: Stanford University Press.

President's Commission on Law Enforcement and the Administration of Justice (1967) *Task Force Report: The Courts*. Washington, D.C.: Government Printing Office.

Rosett, Arthur I. and Donald R. Cressey (1976) *Justice by Consent: Plea Bargains in the American Courthouse*. Philadelphia: Lippincott.

Skolnick, Jerome (1967) "Social Control in the Adversary System," 11 *Journal of Conflict Resolution* 52.

Twentieth Century Fund Task Force on Criminal Sentencing (1976) *Fair and Certain Punishment*. New York: Twentieth Century Fund.

U.S. National Advisory Commission on Criminal Justice Standards and Goals (1973) *Courts*. Washington, D.C.: Government Printing Office.

Utz, Pamela (1978) *Settling the Facts: Discretion and Negotiation in Criminal Court*. Lexington, Mass.: Lexington Books.

Vera Institute of Justice (1977) *Felony Arrests: Their Prosecution and Disposition in New York City's Courts*. New York: Vera Institute of Justice.

Wilson, James Q. (1975) *Thinking about Crime*. New York: Vintage Books.

QUESTIONS FOR DISCUSSION

1. Is justice served when a defendant "cops a plea"?
2. Should a defendant always seek an open trial?
3. Does the plea bargaining process create a system of backroom punishment?
4. Can plea bargaining corrupt the evenhanded administration of justice?
5. Are plea bargains constitutional?

RECOMMENDED READINGS

ALSCHULER, ALBERT W. "The Supreme Court, the Defense Attorney and the Guilty Plea." 47 *University of Colorado Law Review* 1 (1975).

BOND, JAMES E. *Plea Bargaining and Guilty Pleas*. 2nd ed. New York: Clark Boardman, 1982.

HALBERSTAM, MALVINA. "Towards Neutral Principles in the Administration of Criminal Justice: A Critique of Supreme Court Decisions Sanctioning the Plea Bargaining Process." 73 *Journal of Criminal Law and Criminology* 1 (Spring 1982).

HARRIS, RONALD A., and J. FRED SPRINGER. "Plea Bargaining as a Game: An Empirical Analysis of Negotiated Sentencing Decisions." *Policy Studies Review* 4 (Nov. 1984), pp. 245–58.

HUGHES, GRAHAM. "Pleas without Bargains." 33 *Rutgers Law Review* 753 (Spring 1981).

KAMISAR, YALE, WAYNE R. LA FAVE, and JEROLD N. ISRAEL. *Basic Criminal Procedure*. 5th ed. St. Paul: West, 1980.

LEVY, LEONARD. *Origins of the Fifth Amendment: The Right against Self-Incrimination*. New York: Oxford University Press, 1968.

MAYNARD, DOUGLAS W. *Inside Plea Bargaining: The Language of Negotiation*. New York: Plenum Press, 1984.

MCDONALD, WILLIAM F. *Plea Bargaining: Critical Issues and Common Practices*. Washington, D.C.: U.S. National Institute of Justice, 1985.

PUGH, GEORGE W., and DALLIS W. RADAMAKER. "A Plea for Greater Judicial Control over Sentencing and Abolition of the Present Plea Bargaining System." 42 *Louisiana Law Review* 79 (Fall 1981).

SCHULHOFER, STEPHEN J. "Is Plea Bargaining Inevitable?" 97 *Harvard Law Review* 1037 (Mar. 1984).

18 *Should cameras be allowed in the courtroom?*

YES CAMERAS SHOULD BE ALLOWED IN THE COURTROOM

Talbot D'Alemberte

When Theodore Bundy was tried for murder in Miami, Florida, the trial was a major media event. Bundy's background as a former law student from the Northwest, his handsome appearance and self-assured demeanor, the sorority house victims, his alleged participation in other crimes, his prison escapes and even the novel forensic evidence (teeth-bite marks) combined to attract attention from national news organizations and from a vast number of local news operations not only in Florida but also in places as distant as Salt Lake City, Utah, and Seattle, Washington.

With this intense news interest, the normal rituals of highly publicized trials naturally were expected—mobs of photographers assembled on the courthouse steps to snap pictures of jurors getting off buses, cameramen walking backwards down courthouse corridors taking pictures of other cameramen walking backwards, newspaper reporters gathered together outside the courtroom swapping gossip or packed inside scribbling notes, sketch artists lined up in the front row with their pencils and chalk.

This trial wasn't like that. There were no cameramen on the front steps or in the corridors, few reporters in or about the

Talbot D'Alemberte, "Cameras in the Courtroom? Yes," *Barrister* 7 (Spring 1980), pp. 6, 8, 38–39.

courtroom and no sketch artists. Instead, the court contained a single modern television camera that operated from a fixed position, established by the court. No movement of the compact camera was allowed; no bright lights were permitted. Courtroom access also was provided for a press-pool photographer, and the sound system of the courtroom was made available to the media.

The dozens of news organizations covering the Bundy trial with hundreds of reporters, cameramen and technicians were located in a large room several floors from the courtroom. A cable carried the signal from the television camera to that area. Television and radio production people worked there, and many of the print media also made the remote facility their headquarters because, from there, the trial could be seen and heard, typewriters could be pounded, cigarettes smoked, coffee brewed and drank, phones talked into.

As a result, the highly publicized trial of Theodore Bundy was quite different from some of the other trials in the news spotlight in recent history. Because the camera provided access, the press was not nearly as obtrusive in the trial environment and the courtroom was not even crowded much of the time. Indeed, there were times when a citizen entering the courtroom could not be certain if any news personnel were present.

CAMERAS COOL RIGHTS CONFLICT

The contrast is startling to those who have viewed other highly publicized trials because it now is clear that courtroom access for cameras and electronic reporting devices carries not only the potential argued for it—entirely accurate reporting of trials by the electronic media and the public education that should result—but also the potential for resolution of one of the most troublesome problems in legal theory, the result of conflict between the right to a fair trial and the right to a free press.

Television cameras in the courtroom have reduced the confusion and disruption normally associated with major trials, for without access to the real story of a trial, the courtroom events, cameramen are forced to get their pictures elsewhere—on the sidewalks, steps and corridors of the courthouse. Without the mobs of photographers and reporters, the environment of a major trial becomes much calmer.

Simply stated, camera access to the courts has tended to reduce rather than enlarge the problems of press attention at a highly publicized trial.

There is less disruption in the entire trial environment and no disruption in the courtroom. Indeed, the arguments of disruption made over the years are not made now by the candid advocates who have experienced television in the courtroom. Those arguments are not tenable with modern low-light-level and compact television equipment.

The debate now has turned to other factors mentioned in the landmark case *Estes v. Texas* [381 U.S. 532, 595 (1965)]. That case becomes very important because opponents of television access must base their arguments against the growing trend toward camera access on some of the more esoteric passages from *Estes*. Estes held that, under the disruptive environment that was factually present in the proceedings, there was interference with Estes' right to a fair trial.

But, as Mr. Justice Harlan stated in his concurring opinion, "the day may come when television will have become so commonplace an affair in the daily life of the average person as to dissipate all reasonable likelihood that its use in courtrooms may disparage the judicial process." The plurality opinion of Mr. Justice Clark also is filled with references to future developments: "When the advances in these arts permit reporting by . . . the television without their present hazards to a fair trial, we will have another case. . . . We are not dealing here with future developments in the field of electronics. . . ."

TV: THE NO. 1 NEWS SOURCE

Thirteen years later, television is an accepted part of modern life, the dominant medium of communications in contemporary American society. According to studies by A. C. Nielsen, *Broadcasting Magazine, Television Digest,* McCann Erickson and the Federal Communications Commission, television households in 1975 numbered 70,100,000, or 97.5 percent of the total homes in the country. At least 74 percent of all homes contain color televisions and 43 percent have more than one television. Americans spent more than $4.8 billion on television sets in 1974 alone, and now devote an average of six hours, 19 minutes per day to viewing them.

A 1977 report by a leading public opinion researcher, the Roper Organization Inc., indicates that the American public regards television as the number one source of news, and by a wide margin. The survey asked people where they get most of their news, and the response indicated that television by far is the most popular medium for news.

Not only is television the most relied-upon medium for news, it also has led for over 15 years as the most believable news medium. According to the Roper report, by 1968 television had reached a two-to-one advantage and this margin remained in 1976.

A person simply cannot participate in modern life without exposure to camera coverage. Book stores use closed circuit television cameras, banks use them at remote banking locations and cameras are found in hotel lobbies, apartments and condominiums, convenience stores and countless other places.

A HISTORY OF ACCEPTANCE

Television routinely is used to provide detailed coverage of the deliberations of government. Citizens expect to find cameras at meetings of administrative agencies, school boards and county commissions, city councils, legislative deliberations and other events of public debate. For example, Florida administrative agencies generally are covered by television news organizations through televised hearings. Many of the agencies are considering matters of great consequence, including, for instance, environmental cases and utility rate cases.

Detailed broadcasts of Florida legislative hearings by public and educational television have drawn particular attention. Since June 12, 1978, the U.S. House of Representatives has allowed radio coverage of the day-to-day procedings in that chamber, and regular access to television cameras is under study by both houses of Congress.

Moreover, Florida, the state that recently led the way in reviewing restrictions against camera access, has a national reputation for openness in government due largely to the decisions of the Florida Supreme Court in "Sunshine Law" cases (such as *Canney v. Board of Public Instruction of Alachua County* [278 So. 2d (Fla. 1973)], but also attributable to the pioneering of television coverage of public meetings.

Florida citizens are exposed to television cameras when they testify at zoning hearings, appear before school boards, petition for changes in county ordinances and seek some relief from the state cabinet. There is no evidence that this coverage, operated under proper guidelines, has caused any loss of rights to any citizen. Don Mac-Cullough, director of educational media programs for Dade County, has observed board meetings and states:

> Since 1972, approximately thirty meetings, lasting from two to eight hours, have been broadcast each year. . . . Those citizens who attend the public hearings, often as many as twenty to thirty speakers at a single meeting, present their views with little apparent concern for the fact that they are on television. We believe, in fact, that participation at meetings is better and public understanding of education improved since Board meetings have been televised. I do not know of an instance in which an individual who wanted to present ideas to the School Board hesitated to do so because of the television cameras.

DECORUM PRESERVED

Moreover, the photographic and electronic media have proven that they can cover events without detracting from the solemnity. The televising of religious services provides a particularly enlightening parallel. In modifying its canon barring camera access, the Alabama Supreme Court cited with approval these statements:

> It is now universally recognized that the dignity of a church service is not affected in any degree by photographing or broadcasting by television or radio of a church service when sophisticated and advanced equipment and technology is used. Photographing or broadcasting by television or radio of a church service will not distract any church participant or degrade the solemnity of the service if sophisticated and advanced tech-

nology is employed. [Commentary, Canon 3A (7), Alabama Canons of Judicial Ethics.]

Nor are television and radio equipment strangers to the courts. The equipment necessary for radio broadcast—microphones and tape recorders—is used routinely by courts and courts reporters. For example, a circuit court in Michigan for many years used closed circuit television cameras to transmit actual trials to the University of Michigan School of Law.

In 1971, the Supreme Court of Michigan authorized an experiment to determine the feasibility of using videotapes for the record on appeal. Justice Brennan of that court reported:

> The net result was singularly successful. The trial judge and participating counsel agreed that the often mentioned fears of distraction, showboating and witness hesitation simply did not materialize. The videotapes themselves were near-masterful. They were clear and understandable and could be transcribed easily into a typewritten record. The innuendoes and emphasis of questions and answers were captured. Despite the fact that there had been no prior selection of cases to be taped, the combination of subtleties which comprise the total impact of courtroom drama was clearly evident.

EXPERIMENTING OKAYED

The growth of videotape use for depositions also is remarkable, and cases decided by judges should dispel the thought that cameras are incompatible with due process. In *Colonial Times Inc. v. Gasch* [509 F.2d 517 (D.C. Cir. 1975)], the United States Court of Appeals for the District of Columbia granted a writ of mandamus to compel the district judge to allow the taking of a deposition by videotape under the rule. Writing for the unanimous panel, Chief Judge Bazelon noted that the government's objection to videotaping was an insufficient ground to deny the discovery. After discussing the procedural standards

imposed by courts to insure accuracy and trustworthiness of nonstenographic recording, the chief judge concluded, "experimentation with [Rule 30 (b) (4)'s] newly authorized procedure should be encouraged rather than blocked."

Similarly, in the *Matter of Daniels* [68 F.R.D. 579 (N.D. Ga. 1975)], the court denied a witness' motion for a protective order to prevent his deposition being taken by videotape. The witness contended that the presence of a videotape camera at his deposition would affect his concentration and the accuracy of his testimony to the extent of presenting a demeanor to the jury that was false and unnatural. Rejecting his argument, District Judge O'Kelley commented that the videotaping of a witness not available for trial should be allowed to give the fact finders greater insight by observing demeanor and manner of testifying. With respect to the relative novelty of the rule permitting videotaping, the judge opined, "The court should not be like an ostrich sticking its head in the sand and being oblivious to advances in technology which can aid in the judicial process."

In an article in the October 1971 issue of *Judicature*, U.S. District Court Judge Jack B. Weinstein recounted his experience with cameras in a New York courtroom in the following words: "In our court we have had occasion to use video equipment, and there was no evidence of disruptive effect. No one was guilty of 'playing' to the camera, or of altering his or her behavior in any way. The camera ought to be so unobtrusive that everyone in the court ignored it."

Many state rules are modeled after the federal rule and allow recording of depositions by other than stenographic means, including videotaping.

Even the ABA canon, on which opponents of access rely, implicitly concedes that cameras are not disruptive of the trial. Canon 3A (7) of the Code of Judicial Conduct prohibits "broadcasting, televising, recording, or taking photographs in the courtroom. . . ." The canon enumerates, however, certain exceptions: A judge has the power to authorize use of electronic or photographic means for a variety of judicial and administrative functions, including the presentation of evidence, the perpetuation of a record, as well as for broadcasting investiture or naturalization proceedings.

If cameras are neither disruptive when used for purposes of court administration nor distracting when used for videotaped depositions, prohibition of the use of the same equipment by the media is not based on the merits. Newsworthy trials will be covered by the media and there is no justification for denying electronic media and photojournalists the tools of their trade in providing such coverage. Our system of justice will be aided by the availability of more accurate information, and newsworthy trials will become more orderly. Television access is a benefit to the public and to the administration of justice.

NO CAMERAS SHOULD NOT BE ALLOWED IN THE COURTROOM

Joel Hirschhorn

Cameras do not contribute one whit to a defendant's right to receive a fair and impartial trial, which is guaranteed by the Sixth Amendment to the United States Constitution. Media proponents proudly proclaim their right to televise and broadcast criminal trial proceedings in progress, while at the same time, the accused's right to a trial free from the possibility of prejudice is ignored.

The First Amendment guarantees the right of a free and unfettered press. It does not permit or authorize unlimited media access. *Gannett Co. v. DePasquale,* — U.S. —, 99 S.Ct., 2898 (1979). The Sixth Amendment, on the other hand, makes it clear that the *accused* is entitled to a public trial. These two important constitutional rights are on a direct collision course, mainly because of commercial television's need to satisfy the American public's virtually insatiable appetite for the salacious, regardless of the cost to the individual, the criminal justice system or society.

Joel Hirschhorn, "Cameras in the Courtroom? No," *Barrister* **7 (Spring 1980), pp. 7, 9, 56.**

The American Bar Association adopted Canon 35, prohibiting radio and media broadcasting after the (in)famous Lindbergh kidnapping trial of Bruno Hauptmann. [*New Jersey v. Hauptmann,* 180 A. 809 (NJ, 1935).] Similar ethical proscriptions were adopted by all the states (except Texas and Colorado). In the only televised criminal trial case ever decided by the United States Supreme Court [*Estes v. Texas,* 381 U.S. 532, 85 S.Ct. 1628 (1965)], a coalition of five members of the Court agreed that the presence of television cameras over a defendant's objection violated his Sixth Amendment rights. Mr. Justice Harlan, while concurring in the judgment reversing Billie Sol Estes' conviction, was not able to agree to the flat, *per se* prohibition against televised criminal trials.

Since 1965, therefore, it was assumed that televising a criminal trial over a defendant's objection invited the possibilities of reversal (assuming a conviction). Undaunted, Post-Newsweek Stations of Florida Inc. successfully petitioned the Florida Supreme Court for a one-year experimental period during which all criminal trials were open to live broadcasting regardless of a defendant's objections, or those of counsel, jurors or witnesses.

The constitutionality of that experiment (which has since become a permanent rule of court in Florida and numerous other states) is now pending before the United States Supreme Court in the case of *Chandler and Granger v. Florida*. The Court agreed on April 21, 1980, to hear the appeal in the case [United States Supreme Court, Case No. 79–1260].

The rule appears to have caught fire as state after state has rushed to judgment in an effort to appease media proponents within their own respective jurisdictions. Little, if any, concern has been given to the rights of the accused, witnesses, jurors and attorneys. Instead, we have conducted an experiment in living judicature, and then, without properly and objectively evaluating the program, have made the rule permanent, which to those of us who still adhere to notions of precedent and *stare decisis* is a mighty peculiar way indeed to "reform" the system.

A PEDANTIC PICTURE

When the Florida Supreme Court first authorized the experiment, media proclaimed it a great "educational" tool. Yet, rather than televise criminal trials involving matters which would "educate" the public (e.g., mail, land, security or insurance frauds), the citizens of Florida (and the nation) were treated to the Zamora, Hermann and Bundy murder trials.

There was nothing particularly educational about the Zamora murder trial (except for the unique and unsuccessful "television intoxication" defense); nor was the Hermann murder trial especially enlightening except to certain members of the Palm Beach County, Fla., society set. Similarly, Theodore Bundy's trial accomplished little by way of public education except to make a national television star out of the accused (and now twice-convicted) murderer.

At the same time, dozens, if not hundreds, of truly "educational" trials were being conducted in Florida courts—criminal trials which, if televised, might have shown the public the true meaning of *caveat emptor* with respect to the purchase of land, securities, notes, mortgages and insurance. Those trials, however, failed to excite news editors and their commercial sponsors; hence, the public was denied television access to those particular courtrooms.

Another reason for the experiment advanced by media is that the presence of television cameras "improves" the quality of justice. Judges stay awake, lawyers are better prepared and witness testimony "improves." If our system needs television cameras to keep judges awake, then we are in sad shape indeed. Any trial attorney worthy of his law degree will prepare his case thoroughly whether television cameras are present or not.

Whether the criminal justice system is served better as a result of "improved" witness testimony is yet to be seen. It is certain, however, that efforts by honest, ethical members of the criminal defense bar to assist a witness in preparing his or her testimony is rarely, if ever, looked on by the prosecution as an effort to "improve" that witness's testimony.

TV'S ADVERSE IMPACT

Florida's (now permanent) televised criminal trial rule is troublesome for other, more specific reasons. The concerns voiced by the *Estes* court remain proper objects of apprehension today. The spectre of undesirable psychological effects on jurors and witnesses has increased as a result of the persuasiveness of the electronic media.

Mr. Justice Clark's concern in *Estes*, with the additional political pressures on the trial judge, is even more frightening today in view of the examples of extreme media abuses demonstrated in this country and around the world, where televised tribunals affect justice aimed at inflaming the masses, politicizing an issue or otherwise abusing the very purpose of a "trial" in the traditional sense. Nor have the problems of media abuse or the need for lucrative sponsorship been resolved to assure that televised trials will not be another electronic narcotic serving the public's addiction to the sensational.

Clearly, the televising of a criminal trial fails to aid the achievement of the primary purpose of our judicial system, to ascertain the truth. The presence of television cameras in the courtroom ". . . amounts to the injection of an irrelevant factor into court proceedings." [*Estes, supra,* 381 U.S. 544.]

The constant concern over the dangers of a publicity-polluted trial to a defendant's Sixth and Fourteenth Amendment rights led to the U.S. Supreme Court's ruling in *Gannett Co. v. DePasquale.* The interests protected by the closure order in *Gannett* are the sort threatened by televised trials, and the potential for injury of constitutional magnitude is multiplied many times by the pervasive presence of electronic media coverage.

In Florida, under the new rule, even after *Gannett,* pretrial publicity has not been minimized; rather, it has been expanded, frequently in "living color." The concerns for protective measures so central to the Gannett decision are especially pressing when even a pretrial motion to suppress (heard a few scant weeks before trial) is *subject* to televised coverage over the defendant's objection.

PRESSURE BY THE MEDIA

Another aspect of the new rule is even more troublesome—namely, the manner in which the change was effected. Virtually every respectable and respected bar and professional group opposed the initial request for the new rule, which was instituted at the behest of the media itself. This belies any claim of broad legal support for the alteration of the experimental

canon and raises the spectre of both commercial self-interest and the utilization of, at least, undue and subtle pressure by media on the elected Florida Supreme Court justices.

By its own account, the Florida Supreme Court from the very outset was forced to enlarge continuously the scope of the experiment in an effort to obtain "volunteer" participation by wary litigants and participants during the early stages of the experiment. [*Post-Newsweek Stations, Florida Inc.,* 370 So. 2d 764, 766 (Fla. 1979).] The court's original order authorizing televised trials was amended no fewer than five times in an effort to solicit "voluntary" participation, which ultimately was conscripted for a one-year period when it became painfully apparent that trial judges, lawyers, jurors, witnesses and litigants wanted nothing to do with Post-Newsweek's intimidating experiment in jurisprudence. Even the Florida Supreme Court noted that the overwhelming majority of trial judges was generally unsympathetic to the experiment.

After the one-year period ended, in an effort to lift the experiment up by its own bootstraps, the Florida Supreme Court for the first time attempted to evaluate the effect of cameras in the courtroom on witnesses, jurors, attorneys, judges and litigants. Those attempts at a controlled, empirical study of the results went totally astray. Ultimately, the sole "objective" study conducted by the court, through the Judicial Planning Coordination Unit of the Office of the State Courts Administration (OSCA), was a subjective questionnaire distributed to some of the participants in televised trials.

MYOPIC METHODOLOGY

Though outwardly cautious about the significance of such unscientific a study, the court used its interpretation of the results as the hub for its conclusion that television coverage should be permitted because it did not infect the trial proceedings. [*Id.,* at 766–69, 781.] In fact, even this survey, when read objectively, reveals that the court used general terms to gloss over the fact that a constitutionally significant number of persons who responded to the questionnaire were in some way affected, influenced by or aware of the camera's presence during trial.

Worse still, an independent analysis of the method used and details of the questionnaire revealed serious defects that rendered the entire questionnaire meaningless. And extensive proffers of previous empirical studies tending to confirm the dangers foreseen by the United States Supreme Court in *Estes* were ignored by the Florida Supreme Court in its final opinion that made the rule permanent.

Thus, the sum of the Florida Supreme Court's efforts is characterized fairly as having foisted an experimental program on an unremitting and unyielding legal community at the behest of a commercial entity, without having properly "tested the water" to ascertain the implications and effect on Sixth and Fourteenth Amendment rights. Despite this lack of safeguards, as documented by surveys of questionable value and, themselves contradicted by empirical evidence, the Florida Supreme Court made the experimental canon permanent, ostensibly to assure the continued desirability of open judicial proceedings. [*Post-Newsweek, supra,* 370 So. 2d 781.]

There is no doubt that except for the clicking of the still camera shutter and the changing of the TV camera lens, the physical presence of photographic equipment is not distracting to the participants. The psychological impact on jurors, judges, witnesses (both for and against the accused), attorneys and courtroom personnel is quite another issue that can be predicted fairly on the basis of empirical studies: Human nature, being what it is, clearly will react to the existence of the camera's lens, frequently producing an unnatural, affected, or distorted presence and presentation.

A LOOK AT THE RISKS

Some interesting questions are raised. For example, is the witness "squirming" because of the defense attorney's piercing question on cross-examination, or because of the presence of the television camera? Will juror anonymity be destroyed by the presence of television cameras? What will an insecure trial judge do, in an election year with a well-financed opponent, when the defendant's motion to suppress his confession should be granted because of a clear violation of *Miranda?*

Should media be permitted to film and edit a "one-eyed" view of the courtroom for the 6 and 11 p.m. news? And, if so, won't future jurors be subjected to rather myopic images of the courtroom, thus tarnishing their abilities to serve? Who should bear the cost of witness and juror sequestration in lengthy, highly publicized trials that television stations decide to cover—the media or the taxpayer? And, finally, who knows how many innocent people will be convicted, how many guilty people acquitted by virtue of Cyclops' presence?

Social scientists measure the intelligence of monkeys more effectively than courts have attempted to ascertain the effects of television in the courtroom. Even the distinguished George Gerbner, professor of communications and dean of the Annenberg School of Communications at the University of Pennsylvania, in the April 1980 edition of *Judicature,* has concluded that before we allow television into one more courtroom, we must know more about its effects at trials and on our image of the judicial system.

Television does have its place in our society as an entertainment and news medium, but it contributes nothing to the search for truth in the hallowed halls of justice.

QUESTIONS FOR DISCUSSION

1. Do courtroom television cameras transform trials into media events?
2. Does the public have a First Amendment right to witness trial proceedings on television?
3. Can judicial decorum be maintained with television cameras present?
4. Are the rights of the defendant to a fair and speedy public trial served or infringed by the presence of television cameras?
5. Is the presence of television cameras in the courtroom a federal problem? Does it present a constitutional issue?

RECOMMENDED READINGS

ALTHEIDE, DAVID. *Creating Reality: How TV Distorts Events.* Beverly Hills: Sage, 1976.

BARBER, SUSANNA. "The Problem of Prejudice: A New Approach to Assessing the Impact of Courtroom Cameras." 66 *Judicature* 248 (Dec. 1983–Jan. 1984).

DAVIS, NORMAN. "Television in Our Courts: The Proven Advantages, the Unproven Dangers." 64 *Judicature* 85 (Aug. 1980).

GERBNER, GEORGE. "Trial by Television: Are We at the Point of No Return?" 63 *Judicature* 416 (Apr. 1980).

KIELBOWICZ, RICHARD B. "The Story behind the Adoption of the Ban on Courtroom Cameras." 63 *Judicature* 14 (June–July 1979).

KRONENWETTER, MICHAEL. *Free Press v. Fair Trial: Television and Other Media in the Courtroom.* New York: Franklin Watts, 1986.

KURIYAMA, DAVID N. "The 'Right of Information Triangle': A First Amendment Basis for Televising Judicial Proceedings." 4 *University of Hawaii Law Review* 85 (1982).

MARCUS, PAUL. "The Media in the Courtroom: Attending, Reporting, Televising Criminal Cases." 57 *Indiana Law Journal* 235 (Spring 1982).

U.S. CONG., SENATE. *Impact of Media Coverage of Rape Trials.* Hearing before the Subcommittee on Criminal Law of the Committee on the Judiciary, 98th Cong., 2nd Sess., 1984.

YES DECISION: *GREGG V. GEORGIA*

Justice Potter Stewart

[1a] The issue in this case is whether the imposition of the sentence of death for the crime of murder under the law of Georgia violates the Eighth and Fourteenth Amendments.

I

The petitioner, Troy Gregg, was charged with committing armed robbery and murder. In accordance with Georgia procedure in capital cases, the trial was in two stages, a guilt stage and a sentencing stage. The evidence at the guilt trial established that on November 21, 1973, the petitioner and a traveling companion, Floyd Allen, while hitchhiking north in Florida were picked up by Fred Simmons and Bob Moore. Their car broke down, but they continued north after Simmons purchased another vehicle with some of the cash he was carrying. While still in Florida, they picked up another hitchhiker, Dennis Weaver, who rode with them to Atlanta, where he was let out about 11 p.m. A short time later the four men interrupted their journey for a rest stop along the highway. The next morning the bodies of Simmons and Moore were discovered in a ditch nearby.

On November 23, after reading about the shootings in an Atlanta newspaper, Weaver communicated with the Gwinnett County police and related information concerning the journey with the victims,

including a description of the car. The next afternoon, the petitioner and Allen, while in Simmons' car, were arrested in Asheville, N. C. In the search incident to the arrest a .25-caliber pistol, later shown to be that used to kill Simmons and Moore, was found in the petitioner's pocket. After receiving the warnings required by Miranda v Arizona, 384 US 436, 16 L Ed 2d 694, 86 S Ct 1602, 10 Ohio Misc 9, 36 Ohio Ops 2d 237, 10 ALR3d 974 (1966), and signing a written waiver of his rights, the petitioner signed a statement in which he admitted shooting, then robbing Simmons and Moore. He justified the slayings on grounds of self-defense. The next day, while being transferred to Lawrenceville, Ga., the petitioner and Allen were taken to the scene of the shootings. Upon arriving there, Allen recounted the events leading to the slayings. His version of these events was as follows: After Simmons and Moore left the car, the petitioner stated that he intended to rob them. The petitioner then took his pistol in hand and positioned himself on the car to improve his aim. As Simmons and Moore came up an embankment toward the car, the petitioner fired three shots and the two men fell near a ditch. The petitioner, at close range, then fired a shot into the head of each. He robbed them of valuables and drove away with Allen.

A medical examiner testified that Simmons died from a bullet wound in the eye and that Moore died from bullet wounds in the cheek and in the back of the head. He further testified that both men had sev-

Excerpted from *Gregg v. Georgia*, 428 U.S. 153 (1976).

eral bruises and abrasions about the face and head which probably were sustained either from the fall into the ditch or from being dragged or pushed along the embankment. Although Allen did not testify, a police detective recounted the substance of Allen's statements about the slayings and indicated that directly after Allen had made these statements the petitioner had admitted that Allen's account was accurate. The petitioner testified in his own defense. He confirmed that Allen had made the statements described by the detective, but denied their truth or ever having admitted to their accuracy. He indicated that he had shot Simmons and Moore because of fear and in self-defense, testifying they had attacked Allen and him, one wielding a pipe and the other a knife.[1]

The trial judge submitted the murder charges to the jury on both felony-murder and nonfelony-murder theories. He also instructed on the issue of self-defense but declined to instruct on manslaughter. He submitted the robbery case to the jury on both an armed-robbery theory and on the lesser included offense of robbery by intimidation. The jury found the petitioner guilty of two counts of armed robbery and two counts of murder.

At the penalty stage, which took place before the same jury, neither the prosecutor nor the petitioner's lawyer offered any additional evidence. Both counsel, however, made lengthy arguments dealing generally with the propriety of capital punishment under the circumstances and with the weight of the evidence of guilt. The trial judge instructed the jury that it could recommend either a death sentence or a life prison sentence on each count. The judge further charged the jury that in determining what sentence was appropri-

ate the jury was free to consider the facts and circumstances, if any, presented by the parties in mitigation or aggravation.

Finally, the judge instructed the jury that it "would not be authorized to consider [imposing] the penalty of death" unless it first found beyond a reasonable doubt one of these aggravating circumstances:

One—That the offense of murder was committed while the offender was engaged in the commission of two other capital felonies, to-wit the armed robbery of [Simmons and Moore].
Two—That the offender committed the offense of murder for the purpose of receiving money and the automobile described in the indictment.
Three—The offense of murder was outrageously and wantonly vile, horrible and inhuman, in that they [sic] involved the depravity of [the] mind of the defendant. Tr 476–477.

Finding the first and second of these circumstances, the jury returned verdicts of death on each count. . . .

We granted the petitioner's application for a writ of certiorari limited to his challenge to the imposition of the death sentences in this case as "cruel and unusual" punishment in violation of the Eighth and the Fourteenth Amendments. 423 US 1082, 47 L Ed 2d 93, 96 S Ct 1090 (1976). . . .

In the assessment of the appropriate sentence to be imposed the judge is also required to consider or to include in his instructions to the jury "any mitigating circumstances or aggravating circumstances otherwise authorized by law and any of [10] statutory aggravating circumstances which may be supported by the evidence. . . ." §27–2534.1(b) (Supp 1975). The scope of the nonstatutory aggravating or mitigating circumstances is not delineated in the statute. Before a convicted defendant may be sentenced to death,

[1] On cross-examination the State introduced a letter written by the petitioner to Allen entitled, "[a] statement for you," with the instructions that Allen memorize and then burn it. The statement was consistent with the petitioner's testimony at trial.

however, except in cases of treason or aircraft hijacking, the jury, or the trial judge in cases tried without a jury, must find beyond a reasonable doubt one of the 10 aggravating circumstances specified in the statute.[9] The sentence of death may be imposed only if the jury (or judge) finds one of the statutory aggravating circumstances and then elects to impose that sentence. §26-3102 (Supp 1975). If the verdict is death the jury or judge must specify the aggravating circumstance(s) found. §27–2534.1(c) (Supp 1975). In jury cases, the trial judge is bound by the jury's recommended sentence. §§26–3102, 27–2514 (Supp 1975). . . .

[9] The statute provides in part:
"(a) The death penalty may be imposed for the offenses of aircraft hijacking or treason, in any case.
"(b) In all cases of other offenses for which the death penalty may be authorized, the judge shall consider, or he shall include in his instructions to the jury for it to consider, any mitigating circumstances or aggravating circumstances otherwise authorized by law and any of the following statutory aggravating circumstances which may be supported by the evidence:
"(1) The offense of murder, rape, armed robbery, or kidnapping was committed by a person with a prior record of conviction for a capital felony, or the offense of murder was committed by a person who has a substantial history of serious assaultive criminal convictions.
"(2) The offense of murder, rape, armed robbery, or kidnapping was committed while the offender was engaged in the commission of another capital felony, or aggravated battery, or the offense of murder was committed while the offender was engaged in the commission of burglary or arson in the first degree.
"(3) The offender by his act of murder, armed robbery, or kidnapping knowingly created a great risk of death to more than one person in a public place by means of a weapon or device which would normally be hazardous to the lives of more than one person.
"(4) The offender committed the offense of murder for himself or another, for the purpose of receiving money or any other thing of monetary value.
"(5) The murder of a judicial officer, former judicial officer, district attorney or solicitor or former district attorney or solicitor during or because of the exercise of his official duty.
"(6) The offender caused or directed another to commit murder or committed murder as an agent or employee of another person.

III

We address initially the basic contention that the punishment of death for the crime of murder is, under all circumstances, "cruel and unusual" in violation of the Eighth and Fourteenth Amendments of the Constitution. In Part IV of this opinion, we will consider the sentence of death imposed under the Georgia statutes at issue in this case.

[2a] The Court on a number of occasions has both assumed and asserted the constitutionality of capital punishment. In several cases that assumption provided a necessary foundation for the decision, as the Court was asked to decide whether a particular method of carrying out a capital sentence would be allowed to stand under

"(7) The offense of murder, rape, armed robbery, or kidnapping was outrageously or wantonly vile, horrible or inhuman in that it involved torture, depravity of mind, or an aggravated battery to the victim.
"(8) The offense of murder was committed against any peace officer, corrections employee or fireman while engaged in the performance of his official duties.
"(9) The offense of murder was committed by a person in, or who has escaped from, the lawful custody of a peace officer or place of lawful confinement.
"(10) The murder was committed for the purpose of avoiding, interfering with, or preventing a lawful arrest or custody in a place of lawful confinement, of himself or another.
"(c) The statutory instructions as determined by the trial judge to be warranted by the evidence shall be given in charge and in writing to the jury for its deliberation. The jury, if its verdict be a recommendation of death, shall designate in writing, signed by the foreman of the jury, the aggravating circumstance or circumstances which it found beyond a reasonable doubt. In non-jury cases the judge shall make such designation. Except in cases of treason or aircraft hijacking, unless at least one of the statutory aggravating circumstances enumerated in section 27–2534.1(b) is so found, the death penalty shall not be imposed." ᵗ 27–2534.1 (Supp 1975).
The Supreme Court of Georgia, in Arnold v State, 236 Ga 534, 540, 224 SE2d 386, 391 (1976), recently held unconstitutional the portion of the first circumstance encompassing persons who have a "substantial history of serious assaultive criminal convictions" because it did not set "sufficiently 'clear and objective standards.'"

the Eighth Amendment.[12] But until Furman v. Georgia, 408 US 238, 33 L Ed 2d 346, 92 S Ct 2726 (1972), the Court never confronted squarely the fundamental claim that the punishment of death always, regardless of the enormity of the offense or the procedure followed in imposing the sentence, is cruel and unusual punishment in violation of the Constitution. Although this issue was presented and addressed in Furman, it was not resolved by the Court. Four Justices would have held that capital punishment is not unconstitutional per se;[13] two Justices would have reached the opposite conclusion;[14] and three Justices, while agreeing that the statutes then before the Court were invalid as applied, left open the question whether such punishment may ever be imposed.[15] We now hold that the punishment of death does not invariably violate the Constitution.

[12] Louisiana ex rel. Francis v Resweber, 329 US 459, 464, 91 L Ed 422, 67 S Ct 374 (1947); In re Kemmler, 136 US 436, 447, 34 L Ed 519, 10 S Ct 930 (1890); Wilkerson v Utah, 99 US 130, 134–135, 25 L Ed 345 (1879). See also McGautha v California, 402 US 183, 28 L Ed 2d 711, 91 S Ct 1454 (1971); Witherspoon v Illinois, 391 US 510, 20 L Ed 2d 776, 88 S Ct 1770, 46 Ohio Ops 2d 368 (1968); Trop v Dulles, 356 US 86, 100, 2 L Ed 2d 630, 78 S Ct 590 (1958) (plurality opinion).

[13] 408 US, at 375, 33 L Ed 2d 346, 92 S Ct 2726 (Burger, C. J., dissenting); id., at 405, 33 L Ed 2d 346, 92 S Ct 2726 (Blackmun, J., dissenting); id., at 414, 33 L Ed 2d 346, 92 S Ct 2726 (Powell, J., dissenting); id., at 465, 33 L Ed 2d 346, 92 S Ct 2726 (Rehnquist, J., dissenting).

[14] Id., at 257, 33 L Ed 2d 346, 92 S Ct 2726 (Brennan, J., concurring); id., at 314, 33 L Ed 2d 346, 92 S Ct 2726 (Marshall, J., concurring).

[15] Id., at 240, 33 L Ed 2d 346, 92 S Ct 2726 (Douglas, J., concurring); id., at 306, 33 L Ed 2d 346, 92 S Ct 2726 (Stewart, J., concurring); id., at 310, 33 L Ed 2d 346, 92 S Ct 2726 (White, J., concurring). Since five Justices wrote separately in support of the judgments in Furman, the holding of the Court may be viewed as that position taken by those Members who concurred in the judgments on the narrowest grounds—Mr. Justice Stewart and Mr. Justice White. . . .

A

The history of the prohibition of "cruel and unusual" punishment already has been reviewed at length.[16] The phrase first appeared in the English Bill of Rights of 1689, which was drafted by Parliament at the accession of William and Mary. See Granucci, "Nor Cruel and Unusual Punishments Inflicted:" The Original Meaning, 57 Calif L Rev 839, 852–853 (1969). The English version appears to have been directed against punishments unauthorized by statute and beyond the jurisdiction of the sentencing court, as well as those disproportionate to the offense involved. Id., at 860. The American draftsmen, who adopted the English phrasing in drafting the Eighth Amendment, were primarily concerned, however, with proscribing "tortures" and other "barbarous" methods of punishment. Id., at 842.[17]

In the earliest cases raising Eighth Amendment claims, the Court focused on particular methods of execution to determine whether they were too cruel to pass constitutional muster. The constitutionality of the sentence of death itself was

[16] 408 US, at 316–328, 33 L Ed 2d 346, 92 S Ct 2726 (Marshall, J., concurring).

[17] This conclusion derives primarily from statements made during the debates in the various state conventions called to ratify the Federal Constitution. For example, Virginia delegate Patrick Henry objected vehemently to the lack of a provision banning "cruel and unusual punishments":
"What has distinguished our ancestors?—That they would not admit of tortures, or cruel and barbarous punishment. But Congress may introduce the practice of the civil law, in preference to that of the common law. They may introduce the practice of France, Spain, and Germany—of torturing, to extort a confession of the crime." 3 J. Elliot, Debates 447–448 (1863).
A similar objection was made in the Massachusetts convention:
"They are nowhere restrained from inventing the most cruel and unheard-of punishments and annexing them to crimes; and there is no constitutional check on them, but that *racks* and *gibbets* may be amongst the most mild instruments of their discipline." 2 Elliot, supra, at 111.

not at issue, and the criterion used to evaluate the mode of execution was its similarity to "torture" and other "barbarous" methods. . . .

But the Court has not confined the prohibition embodied in the Eighth Amendment to "barbarous" methods that were generally outlawed in the 18th century. Instead, the Amendment has been interpreted in a flexible and dynamic manner. The Court early recognized that "a principle to be vital must be capable of wider application than the mischief which gave it birth." . . . Thus the Clause forbidding "cruel and unusual" punishments "is not fastened to the obsolete but may acquire meaning as public opinion becomes enlightened by a humane justice." . . .

In Weems the Court addressed the constitutionality of the Philippine punishment of cadena temporal for the crime of falsifying an official document. That punishment included imprisonment for at least 12 years and one day, in chains, at hard and painful labor; the loss of many basic civil rights; and subjection to lifetime surveillance. Although the Court acknowledged the possibility that "the cruelty of pain" may be present in the challenged punishment, 217 US, at 366, 54 L Ed 793, 30 S Ct 544, it did not rely on that factor, for it rejected the proposition that the Eighth Amendment reaches only punishments that are "inhuman and barbarous, torture and the like." Id., at 368, 54 L Ed 793, 30 S Ct 544. Rather, the Court focused on the lack of proportion between the crime and the offense:

> Such penalties for such offenses amaze those who have formed their conception of the relation of a state to even its offending citizens from the practice of the American commonwealths, and believe that it is a precept of justice that punishment for crime should be graduated and proportioned to offense. Id., at 366–367, 54 L Ed 793, 30 S Ct 544.[18]

[18] The Court remarked on the fact that the law under review "has come to us from a government of a

Later, in Trop v Dulles, supra, 2 L Ed 2d 630, 78 S Ct 590, the Court reviewed the constitutionality of the punishment of denationalization imposed upon a soldier who escaped from an Army stockade and became a deserter for one day. Although the concept of proportionality was not the basis of the holding, the plurality observed in dicta that "[f]ines, imprisonment and even execution may be imposed depending upon the enormity of the crime." 356 US, at 100, 2 L Ed 2d 630, 78 S Ct 590.

The substantive limits imposed by the Eighth Amendment on what can be made criminal and punished were discussed in Robinson v California, 370 US 660. . . . It held, in effect, that it is "cruel and unusual" to impose any punishment at all for the mere status of addiction. The cruelty in the abstract of the actual sentence imposed was irrelevant: "Even one day in prison would be a cruel and unusual punishment for the 'crime' of having a common cold." Id., at 667, 8 L Ed 2d 758, 82 S Ct 1417. Most recently, in Furman v Georgia, supra, 33 L Ed 2d 346, 92 S Ct 2726, three Justices in separate concurring opinions found the Eighth Amendment applicable to procedures employed to select convicted defendants for the sentence of death.

It is clear from the foregoing precedents that the Eighth Amendment has not been regarded as a static concept. As Mr. Chief Justice Warren said, in an oft-quoted phrase, "[t]he Amendment must draw its meaning from the evolving standards of decency that mark the progress of a maturing society." . . . Thus, an assessment of contemporary values concerning the infliction of a challenged sanction is relevant to the application of the Eighth Amendment. . . . [T]his assessment does not call for a subjective judgment. It requires, rather, that we look to objective

different form and genius from ours," but it also noted that the punishments it inflicted "would have those bad attributes even if they were found in a Federal enactment and not taken from an alien source." 217 US, at 377, 54 L Ed 793, 30 S Ct 544.

indicia that reflect the public attitude toward a given sanction.

But our cases also make clear that public perceptions of standards of decency with respect to criminal sanctions are not conclusive. A penalty also must accord with "the dignity of man," which is the "basic concept underlying the Eighth Amendment." . . . This means, at least, that the punishment not be "excessive." When a form of punishment in the abstract (in this case, whether capital punishment may ever be imposed as a sanction for murder) rather than in the particular (the propriety of death as a penalty to be applied to a specific defendant for a specific crime) is under consideration, the inquiry into "excessiveness" has two aspects. First, the punishment must not involve the unnecessary and wanton infliction of pain. Furman v. Georgia, supra. . . . Second, the punishment must not be grossly out of proportion to the severity of the crime. . . . [I]n assessing a punishment selected by a democratically elected legislature against the constitutional measure, we presume its validity. We may not require the legislature to select the least severe penalty possible so long as the penalty selected is not cruelly inhumane or disproportionate to the crime involved. And a heavy burden rests on those who would attack the judgment of the representatives of the people.

This is true in part because the constitutional test is intertwined with an assessment of contemporary standards and the legislative judgment weighs heavily in ascertaining such standards. "[I]n a democratic society legislatures, not courts, are constituted to respond to the will and consequently the moral values of the people." . . .

C

In the discussion to this point we have sought to identify the principles and considerations that guide a court in addressing an Eighth Amendment claim. We now consider specifically whether the sentence of death for the crime of murder is a per se violation of the Eighth and Fourteenth Amendments to the Constitution. We note first that history and precedent strongly support a negative answer to this question.

The imposition of the death penalty for the crime of murder has a long history of acceptance both in the United States and in England: The common-law rule imposed a mandatory death sentence on all convicted murders. . . . And the penalty continued to be used into the 20th century by most American States, although the breadth of the common-law rule was diminished, initially by narrowing the class of murders to be punished by death and subsequently by widespread adoption of laws expressly granting juries the discretion to recommend mercy. . . .

It is apparent from the text of the Constitution itself that the existence of capital punishment was accepted by the Framers. At the time the Eighth Amendment was ratified, capital punishment was a common sanction in every State. Indeed, the First Congress of the United States enacted legislation providing death as the penalty for specified crimes. C 9, 1 Stat 112 (1790). The Fifth Amendment, adopted at the same time as the Eighth, contemplated the continued existence of the capital sanction by imposing certain limits on the prosecution of capital cases:

> No person shall be held to answer for a capital, or otherwise infamous crime, unless on a presentment or indictment of a Grand Jury . . .; nor shall any person be subject for the same offense to be twice put in jeopardy of life or limb; . . . nor be deprived of life, liberty, or property, without due process of law. . . .

And the Fourteenth Amendment, adopted over three-quarters of a century later, similarly contemplates the existence of the capital sanction in providing that no State shall deprive any person of "life, liberty, or property" without due process of law.

For nearly two centuries, this Court, repeatedly and often expressly, has recognized that capital punishment is not invalid per se. . . .

The most marked indication of society's endorsement of the death penalty for murder is the legislative response to Furman. The legislatures of at least 35 States[23] have enacted new statutes that provide for the death penalty for at least some crimes that result in the death of another person. And the Congress of the United States, in 1974, enacted a statute providing the death penalty for aircraft piracy that results in death.[24] These recently adopted statutes have attempted to address the concerns expressed by the Court in Furman primarily (i) by specifying the factors to be

weighed and the procedures to be followed in deciding when to impose a capital sentence, or (ii) by making the death penalty mandatory for specified crimes. But all of the post-Furman statutes make clear that capital punishment itself has not been rejected by the elected representatives of the people. . . .

The jury also is a significant and reliable objective index of contemporary values because it is so directly involved. . . . The Court has said that "one of the most important functions any jury can perform in making . . . a selection [between life imprisonment and death for a defendant convicted in a capital case] is to maintain a link between contemporary community values and the penal system." . . . It may be true that evolving standards have influenced juries in recent decades to be more discriminating in imposing the sentence of death.[26] But the relative infrequency of jury verdicts imposing the death sentence does not indicate rejection of capital punishment per se. Rather, the reluctance of juries in many cases to impose the sentence may well reflect the humane feeling that this most irrevocable of sanctions should be reserved for a small number of extreme cases. . . .

As we have seen, however, the Eighth Amendment demands more than that a challenged punishment be acceptable to contemporary society. The Court also must ask whether it comports with the basic concept of human dignity at the core of the Amendment. . . . [T]he sanction

---

[23] Ala HB 212, §§2–4, 6–7 (1975); Ariz Rev Stat Ann §§13–452 to 13–454 (Supp 1973); Ark Stat Ann §41–4706 (Supp 1975); Cal Penal Code §§190.1, 209, 219 (Supp 1976); Colo Laws 1974, c 52, §4; Conn Gen Stat Rev §§53a–25, 53a–35(b), 53a–46a, 53a–54b (1975); Del Code Ann tit 11, §4209 (Supp 1975); Fla Stat Ann §§782.04, 921.141 (Supp 1975–1976); Ga Code Ann §§26–3102, 27–2528, 27–2534.1, 27–2537 (Supp 1975); Idaho Code §18–4004 (Supp 1975); Ill Ann Stat c 38, §§9-1, 1005–5–3, 1005–8–1A (Supp 1976–1977); Ind Stat Ann §35–13–4–1 (1975); Ky Rev Stat Ann §507.020 (1975); La Rev Stat Ann §14:30 (Supp 1976); Md Ann Code, art 27, §413 (Supp 1975); Miss Code Ann §§97–3–19, 97–3–21, 97–25–55, 99–17–20 (Supp 1975); Mo Ann Stat §559.009, 559.005 (Supp 1976); Mont Rev Codes Ann §94–5–105 (Spec Crim Code Supp 1976); Neb Rev Stat §§28–401, 29–2521 to 29–2523 (1975); Nev Rev Stat §200.030 (1973); NH Rev Stat Ann §630:1 (1974); NM Stat Ann §40A–29–2 (Supp 1975); NY Penal Law §60.06 (1975); NC Gen Stat §14–17 (Supp 1975); Ohio Rev Code Ann §§2929.02–2929.04 (1975); Okla Stat Ann tit 21, §701.1–701.3 (Supp 1975–1976); Pa Laws 1974, Act No. 46; RI Gen Laws Ann §11–23–2 (Supp 1975); SC Code Ann §16–52 (Supp 1975); Tenn Code Ann §§39–2402, 39–2406 (1975); Tex Penal Code Ann § 19.03(a) (1974); Utah Code Ann §§76–3–206, 76–3–207, 76–5–202 (Supp 1975); Va Code Ann §18.2–10, 18.2–31 (1976); Wash Rev Code §§9A.32.045, 9A.32.046 (Supp 1975); Wyo Stat Ann §6–54 (Supp 1975).

[24] Antihijacking Act of 1974, 49 USC §§1472(i), (n) (1970 ed Supp IV) [49 USCS §§1472(i), (n).]

[26] The number of prisoners who received death sentences in the years from 1961 to 1972 varied from a high of 140 in 1961 to a low of 75 in 1972, with wide fluctuations in the intervening years: 103 in 1962; 93 in 1963; 106 in 1964; 86 in 1965; 118 in 1966; 85 in 1967; 102 in 1968; 97 in 1969; 127 in 1970; and 104 in 1971. Department of Justice, National Prisoner Statistics Bulletin, Capital Punishment 1971–1972, p 20 (Dec. 1974). It has been estimated that before Furman less than 20% of those convicted of murder were sentenced to death in those States that authorized capital punishment. See Woodson v North Carolina, post, at 295–296, n 31, 49 L Ed 2d 944, 96 S Ct 2978.

imposed cannot be so totally without penological justification that it results in the gratuitous infliction of suffering. . . .

The death penalty is said to serve two principal social purposes: retribution and deterrence of capital crimes by prospective offenders.[28]

In part, capital punishment is an expression of society's moral outrage at particularly offensive conduct.[29] This function may be unappealing to many, but it is essential in an ordered society that asks its citizens to rely on legal processes rather than self-help to vindicate their wrongs. . . .

"Retribution is no longer the dominant objective of the criminal law," . . . but neither is it a forbidden objective nor one inconsistent with our respect for the dignity of men. . . . Indeed, the decision that capital punishment may be the appropriate sanction in extreme cases is an expression of the community's belief that certain crimes are themselves so grievous an affront to humanity that the only adequate response may be the penalty of death . . .[30]

28 Another purpose that has been discussed is the incapacitation of dangerous criminals and the consequent prevention of crimes that they may otherwise commit in the future. See People v Anderson, 6 Cal 3d 628, 651, 493 P2d 880, 896, cert denied, 406 US 958, 32 L Ed 2d 344, 92 S Ct 2060 (1972); Commonwealth v O'Neal, supra, at —, 339 NE2d, at 685–686.

29 See H. Packer, Limits of the Criminal Sanction 43–44 (1968).

30 Lord Justice Denning, Master of the Rolls of the Court of Appeal in England, spoke to this effect before the British Royal Commission on Capital Punishment:
"Punishment is the way in which society expresses its denunciation of wrong doing: and, in order to maintain respect for law, it is essential that the punishment inflicted for grave crimes should adequately reflect the revulsion felt by the great majority of citizens for them. It is a mistake to consider the objects of punishment as being deterrent or reformative or preventive and nothing else. . . . The truth is that some crimes are so outrageous that society insists on adequate punishment, because the wrong-doer deserves it, irrespective of whether it is a deterrent or not." Royal Commission on Capital Punishment, Minutes of Evidence, Dec. 1, 1949, p 207 (1950).

Although some of the studies suggest that the death penalty may not function as a significantly greater deterrent than lesser penalties,[32] there is no convincing empirical evidence either supporting or refuting this view. We may nevertheless assume safely that there are murderers, such as those who act in passion, for whom the threat of death has little or no deterrent effect. But for many others, the death penalty undoubtedly is a significant deterrent. There are carefully contemplated murders, such as murder for hire, where the possible penalty of death may well enter into the cold calculus that precedes the decision to act.[33] And there are some categories of murder, such as murder by a life prisoner, where other sanctions may not be adequate.[34]

A contemporary writer has noted more recently that opposition to capital punishment "has much more appeal when the discussion is merely academic than when the community is confronted with a crime, or a series of crimes, so gross, so heinous, so cold-blooded that anything short of death seems an inadequate response." Raspberry, Death Sentence, The Washington Post, Mar. 12, 1976, p A27, cols 5–6.

32 See, e.g., The Death Penalty in America, [H. Bedau ed. 1967], at 258–332; Report of the Royal Commission on Capital Punishment, 1949–53, Cmd. 8932.

33 Other types of calculated murders, apparently occurring with increasing frequency, include the use of bombs or other means of indiscriminate killings, the extortion murder of hostages or kidnap victims, and the execution-style killing of witnesses to a crime.

34 We have been shown no statistics breaking down the total number of murders into the categories described above. The overall trend in the number of murders committed in the nation, however, has been upward for some time. In 1964, reported murders totaled an estimated 9,250. During the ensuing decade, the number reported increased 123 percent, until it totaled approximately 20,600 in 1974. In 1972, the year Furman was announced, the total estimated was 18,520. Despite a fractional decrease in 1975 as compared with 1974, the number of murders increased in the three years immediately following Furman to approximately 20,400, an increase of almost 10 percent. See FBI, Uniform Crime Reports, for 1964, 1972, 1974 and 1975 Preliminary Annual Release.

The value of capital punishment as a deterrent of crime is a complex factual issue the resolution of which properly rests with the legislatures, which can evaluate the results of statistical studies in terms of their own local conditions and with a flexibility of approach that is not available to the courts. Furman v Georgia, supra, at 403-405, 33 L Ed 2d 346, 92 S Ct 2726 (Burger, C. J., dissenting). Indeed, many of the post-Furman statutes reflect just such a responsible effort to define those crimes and those criminals for which capital punishment is most probably an effective deterrent.

In sum, we cannot say that the judgment of the Georgia legislature that capital punishment may be necessary in some cases is clearly wrong. Considerations of federalism, as well as respect for the ability of a legislature to evaluate, in terms of its particular state the moral consensus concerning the death penalty and its social utility as a sanction, require us to conclude, in the absence of more convincing evidence, that the infliction of death as a punishment for murder is not without justification and thus is not unconstitutionally severe.

Finally, we must consider whether the punishment of death is disproportionate in relation to the crime for which it is imposed. There is no question that death as a punishment is unique in its severity and irrevocability. . . . When a defendant's life is at stake, the Court has been particularly sensitive to insure that every safeguard is observed. . . . But we are concerned here only with the imposition of capital punishment for the crime of murder, and when a life has been taken deliberately by the offender,[35] we cannot say that the punishment is invariably dis-

proportionate to the crime. It is an extreme sanction, suitable to the most extreme of crimes.

We hold that the death penalty is not a form of punishment that may never be imposed, regardless of the circumstances of the offense, regardless of the character of the offender, and regardless of the procedure followed in reaching the decision to impose it. . . .

In summary, the concerns expressed in Furman that the penalty of death not be imposed in an arbitrary or capricious manner can be met by a carefully drafted statute that ensures that the sentencing authority is given adequate information and guidance. . . .

V

The basic concern of Furman centered on those defendants who were being condemned to death capriciously and arbitrarily. Under the procedures before the Court in that case, sentencing authorities were not directed to give attention to the nature or circumstances of the crime committed or to the character or record of the defendant. Left unguided, juries imposed the death sentence in a way that could only be called freakish. The new Georgia sentencing procedures, by contrast, focus the jury's attention on the particularized nature of the crime and the particularized characteristics of the individual defendant. While the jury is permitted to consider any aggravating or mitigating circumstances, it must find and identify at least one statutory aggravating factor before it may impose a penalty of death. In this way the jury's discretion is channeled. No longer can a jury wantonly and freakishly impose the death sentence; it is always circumscribed by the legislative guidelines. In addition, the review function of the Supreme Court of Georgia affords additional assurance that the concerns that prompted our decision in Fur-

---

[35] We do not address here the question whether the taking of the criminal's life is a proportionate sanction where no victim has been deprived of life—for example, when capital punishment is imposed for rape, kidnapping, or armed robbery that does not result in the death of any human being.

man are not present to any significant degree in the Georgia procedure applied here.

For the reasons expressed in this opinion, we hold that the statutory system under which Gregg was sentenced to death does not violate the Constitution. Accordingly, the judgment of the Georgia Supreme Court is affirmed.

It is so ordered.

NO DISSENTING OPINION: *GREGG V. GEORGIA*

Justice Thurgood Marshall

In Furman v Georgia, 408 US 238, 314, 33 L Ed 2d 346, 92 S Ct 2726 (1972) (concurring), I set forth at some length my views on the basic issue presented to the Court in these cases. The death penalty, I concluded, is a cruel and unusual punishment prohibited by the Eighth and Fourteenth Amendments. That continues to be my view.

I have no intention of retracing the "long and tedious journey," id, at 370, 33 L Ed 2d 346, 92 S Ct 2726, that led to my conclusion in Furman. My sole purposes here are to consider the suggestion that my conclusion in Furman has been undercut by developments since then, and briefly to evaluate the basis for my Brethren's holding that the extinction of life is a permissible form of punishment under the Cruel and Unusual Punishments Clause.

In Furman I concluded that the death penalty is constitutionally invalid for two reasons. First, the death penalty is excessive. Id., at 331–332, 342–359, 33 L Ed 2d 346, 92 S Ct 2726. And second, the American people, fully informed as to the purposes of the death penalty and its liabilities, would in my view reject it as

Excerpted from *Gregg v. Georgia*, 428 U.S. 153 (1976).

morally unacceptable. Id., at 360–369, 33 L Ed 2d 346, 92 S Ct 2726.

Since the decision in Furman, the legislatures of 35 States have enacted new statutes authorizing the imposition of the death sentence for certain crimes, and Congress has enacted a law providing the death penalty for air piracy resulting in death. 49 USC §§1472(i), (n)(1970 ed, Supp IV) [49 USCS §§1472(i), (n)]. I would be less than candid if I did not acknowledge that these developments have a significant bearing on a realistic assessment of the moral acceptability of the death penalty to the American people. But if the constitutionality of the death penalty turns, as I have urged, on the opinion of an *informed* citizenry, then even the enactment of new death statutes cannot be viewed as conclusive. In Furman, I observed that the American people are largely unaware of the information critical to a judgment on the morality of the death penalty, and concluded that if they were better informed they would consider it shocking, unjust, and unacceptable. 408 US, at 360–369, 33 L Ed 2d 346, 92 S Ct 2726. A recent study, conducted after the enactment of the post-Furman statutes, has confirmed that the American people know little about the death penalty, and that the opinions of an informed public would differ significantly from those of a public unaware of the consequences and effects of the death penalty.[1]

Even assuming, however, that the post-Furman enactment of statutes authorizing the death penalty renders the prediction of the views of an informed citizenry an uncertain basis for a constitutional decision, the enactment of those statutes has no bearing whatsoever on the conclusion that the death penalty is unconstitutional because it is excessive. An excessive penalty is invalid under the Cruel and Unusual Punishments Clause "even though popular sentiment may favor" it. Id., at 331, 33 L Ed 2d 346, 92 S Ct 2726; ante, at 173, 182–183, 49 L Ed 2d 874–875. (opinion of Stewart, Powell, and Stevens, JJ.); Roberts v Louisiana, post, at 353–354, 49 L Ed 2d 974, 96 S Ct 3001 (White, J., dissenting). The inquiry here, then, is simply whether the death penalty is necessary to accomplish the legitimate legislative purposes in punishment, or whether a less severe penalty—life imprisonment—would do as well. Furman, supra, at 342, 33 L Ed 2d 346, 92 S Ct 2726 (Marshall, J., concurring).

The two purposes that sustain the death penalty as nonexcessive in the Court's view are general deterrence and retribution. In Furman, I canvassed the relevant data on the deterrent effect of capital punishment. 408 US, at 347–354, 33 L Ed 2d 346, 92 S Ct 2726.[2] The state of knowledge at that point, after literally centuries of debate, was summarized as follows by a United Nations Committee:

It is generally agreed between the retentionists and abolitionists, whatever their opinions about the validity of comparative studies of deterrence, that the data which now exist show no correlation between the existence of capital punishment and lower rates of capital crime.[3]

The available evidence, I concluded in Furman, was convincing that "capital punishment is not necessary as a deterrent to crime in our society." Id., at 353, 33 L Ed 2d 346, 92 S Ct 2726. . . .

. . . The evidence I reviewed in Furman[13] remains convincing, in my view, that "capital punishment is not necessary as a deterrent to crime in our society." 408 US, at 353, 33 L Ed 2d 346, 92 S Ct 2726. The justification for the death penalty must be found elsewhere.

The other principal purpose said to be served by the death penalty is retribution.[14] The notion that retribution can serve as a moral justification for the sanction of death finds credence in the opinion of my Brothers Stewart, Powell, and Stevens and that of my Brother White. . . . It is this notion that I find to be the most disturbing aspect of today's unfortunate decisions.

The concept of retribution is a multifaceted one, and any discussion of its role in the criminal law must be undertaken

[1] Sarat & Vidmar, Public Opinion, The Death Penalty, and the Eighth Amendment: Testing the Marshall Hypothesis, 1976 Wis L Rev 171.

[2] See e.g., T. Sellin, The Death Penalty, A Report for the Model Penal Code Project of the American Law Institute (1959).

[3] United Nations, Department of Economic and Social Affairs, Capital Punishment, pt II, ;pg 159, p 123 (1968).

[13] See also Bailey, Murder and Capital Punishment: Some Further Evidence, 45 Am J Orthopsychiatry 669 (1975); W. Bowers, Executions in America 121–163 (1974).

[14] In Furman, I considered several additional purposes arguably served by the death penalty. 408 US, at 314, 342, 355–358, 33 L Ed 2d 346, 92 S Ct 2726. The only additional purpose mentioned in the opinions in these cases is specific deterrence–preventing the murderer from committing another crime. Surely life imprisonment and, if necessary, solitary confinement would fully accomplish this purpose. Accord, Commonwealth v O'Neal, — Mass —, — 339 NE2d 676, 685 (1975); People v Anderson, 6 Cal 3d 628, 651, 493 P2d 880, 896, cert. denied, 406 US 958, 32 L Ed 2d 344, 92 S Ct 2060 (1972).

with caution. On one level, it can be said that the notion of retribution or reprobation is the basis of our insistence that only those who have broken the law be punished, and in this sense the notion is quite obviously central to a just system of criminal sanctions. But our recognition that retribution plays a crucial role in determining who may be punished by no means requires approval of retribution as a general justification for punishment.[15] It is the question whether retribution can provide a moral justification for punishment—in particular, capital punishment—that we must consider.

My Brothers Stewart, Powell, and Stevens offer the following explanation of the retributive justification for capital punishment:

> The instinct for retribution is part of the nature of man, and channeling that instinct in the administration of criminal justice serves an important purpose in promoting the stability of a society governed by law. When people begin to believe that organized society is unwilling or unable to impose upon criminal offenders the punishment they "deserve," then there are sown the seeds of anarchy—of self-help, vigilante justice, and lynch law. Ante, at 183, 49 L Ed 2d 880, quoting from Furman v Georgia, supra, at 308, 33 L Ed 2d 346, 92 S Ct 2726 (Stewart, J., concurring).

This statement is wholly inadequate to justify the death penalty. As my Brother Brennan stated in Furman, "[t]here is no evidence whatever that utilization of imprisonment rather than death encourages private blood feuds and other disorders." 408 US, at 303, 33 L Ed 2d 346, 92 S Ct 2726 (concurring).[16] It simply defies

belief to suggest that the death penalty is necessary to prevent the American people from taking the law into their own hands.

In a related vein, it may be suggested that the expression of moral outrage through the imposition of the death penalty serves to reinforce basic moral values—that it marks some crimes as particularly offensive and therefore to be avoided. The argument is akin to a deterrence argument, but differs in that it contemplates the individual's shrinking from antisocial conduct, not because he fears punishment, but because he has been told in the strongest possible way that the conduct is wrong. This contention, like the previous one, provides no support for the death penalty. It is inconceivable that any individual concerned about conforming his conduct to what society says is "right" would fail to realize that murder is "wrong" if the penalty were simply life imprisonment.

The foregoing contentions—that society's expression of moral outrage through the imposition of the death penalty pre-empts the citizenry from taking the law into its own hands and reinforces moral values—are not retributive in the purest sense. They are essentially utilitarian in that they portray the death penalty as valuable because of its beneficial results. These justifications for the death penalty are inadequate because the penalty is, quite clearly I think, not necessary to the accomplishment of those results.

There remains for consideration, however, what might be termed the purely retributive justification for the death penalty—that the death penalty is appropriate, not because of its beneficial effect on society, but because the taking of the murderer's life is itself morally good.[17] Some of the language of the opinion of my Brothers Stewart, Powell, and Stevens in

---

[15] See, e.g., H. Hart, Punishment and Responsibility 8–10, 71–83 (1968); H. Packer, Limits of the Criminal Sanction 38–39, 66 (1968).

[16] See Commonwealth v O'Neal, supra, at 236, 339 NE2d, at 687; Bowers, supra, n 13, at 335; Sellin, supra, n 2, at 79.

[17] See Hart, supra, n 15, at 72, 74–75, 234–235; Packer, supra, n 15, at 37–39.

No. 74—6257 appears positively to embrace this notion of retribution for its own sake as a justification for capital punishment.[18] They state:

> [T]he decision that capital punishment may be the appropriate sanction in extreme cases is an expression of the community's belief that certain crimes are themselves so grievous an affront to humanity that the only adequate response may be the penalty of death. Ante, at 184, 49 L Ed 2d 880–881 (footnote omitted).

The plurality then quotes with approval from Lord Justice Denning's remarks before the British Royal Commission on Capital Punishment:

> The truth is that some crimes are so outrageous that society insists on adequate punishment, because the wrong-doer deserves it, irrespective of whether it is a deterrent or not. Ante, at 184, n 30, 49 L Ed 2d 881.

Of course, it may be that these statements are intended as no more than observations as to the popular demands that it is thought must be responded to in order to prevent anarchy. But the implication of the statements appears to me to be quite different—namely, that society's judgment that the murderer "deserves" death must be respected not simply because the preservation of order requires it, but because it is appropriate that society make the judgment and carry it out. It is this latter notion, in particular, that I consider to be fundamentally at odds with the Eighth Amendment. See Furman v. Georgia, 408 U.S., at 343–345 (Marshall, J., concurring). The mere fact that the community demands the murderer's life in return for the evil he has done cannot sustain the death penalty, for as Justices Stewart, Powell, and Stevens remind us, "the Eighth Amendment demands more than that a challenged punishment be acceptable to contemporary society." Ante, at 182. To be sustained under the Eighth Amendment, the death penalty must "compor[t] with the basic concept of human dignity at the core of the Amendment," ibid.; the objective in imposing it must be "[consistent] with our respect for the dignity of [other] men." Ante, at 183. See Trop v. Dulles, 356 U. S. 86, 100 (1958) (plurality opinion). Under these standards, the taking of life "because the wrongdoer deserves it" surely must fall, for such a punishment has as its very basis the total denial of the wrongdoer's dignity and worth.[19]

The death penalty, unnecessary to promote the goal of deterrence or to further any legitimate notion of retribution, is an excessive penalty forbidden by the Eighth and Fourteenth Amendments. I respectfully dissent from the Court's judgment upholding the sentences of death imposed upon the petitioners in these cases.

[18] Mr. Justice White's view of retribution as a justification for the death penalty is not altogether clear. "The widespread reenactment of the death penalty," he states at one point, "answers any claims that life imprisonment is adequate punishment to satisfy the need for reprobation or retribution." Roberts v Louisiana, post, at 354, 49 L Ed 2d 974, 96 S Ct 3001 (White, J., dissenting). But Mr. Justice White later states: "It will not do to denigrate these legislative judgments as some form of vestigial savagery or as purely retributive in motivation; for they are solemn judgments, reasonably based, that imposition of the death penalty will save the lives of innocent persons." Post, at 355, 49 L Ed 2d 974.

[19] See Commonwealth v O'Neal, supra, at —, 339 N. E. 2d, at 687; People v Anderson, 6 Cal. 3d, at 651, 493 P. 2d, at 896. 8

QUESTIONS FOR DISCUSSION

1. Is capital punishment a deterrent to murder?
2. Is it morally just to inflict capital punishment?
3. What purposes does capital punishment serve?
4. Is the death penalty a violation of the Eighth Amendment's prohibition against cruel and unusual punishment?
5. Who should be able to affix the death sentence? For what crimes?

RECOMMENDED READINGS

BEDAU, HUGO ADAM, ed. *The Death Penalty in America.* 3rd ed. New York: Oxford University Press, 1982.

BERGER, RAOUL. *Death Penalties: The Supreme Court's Obstacle Course.* Cambridge: Harvard University Press, 1982.

BERNS, WALTER. *For Capital Punishment: Crime and the Morality of the Death Penalty.* New York: Basic Books, 1979.

BLACK, CHARLES L. *Capital Punishment: The Inevitability of Caprice and Mistake.* New York: W. W. Norton, 1974.

BOWERS, WILLIAM J., with GLENN L. PIERCE and JOHN F. MCDEVITT. *Legal Homicide: Death as Punishment in America, 1864–1982.* Boston: Northeastern University Press, 1984.

DRAPER, THOMAS, ed. *Capital Punishment.* New York: H. W. Wilson, 1985.

GORECKI, JAN. *Capital Punishment: Criminal Law and Social Evolution.* New York: Columbia University Press, 1983.

GRANELLI, JAMES S. "Justice Delayed." 70 *American Bar Association Journal* 51 (Jan. 1984).

KAPLAN, STANLEY M. "Death, So Say We All." *Psychology Today* 19 (July 1985), pp. 48, 50–53.

KOCH, EDWARD I. "Death and Justice." *New Republic* 192 (Apr. 15, 1985), pp. 12–15.

SELLIN, JOHAN T. *The Penalty of Death.* Beverly Hills: Sage, 1980.